To Louise & Pete

12-25-77

From Dad & Mother

BORN GROWN

FIRST APPROVED PROJECT
OKLAHOMA BICENTENNIAL COMMISSION

APPROVED PROJECT
OKLAHOMA CITY BICENTENNIAL COMMISSION

BORN GROWN

AN OKLAHOMA CITY HISTORY
BY ROY P. STEWART

RESEARCH AND EDITING ASSOCIATE
PENDLETON WOODS

PUBLISHED BY

FIDELITY BANK

NATIONAL ASSOCIATION
OKLAHOMA CITY 1974

Books by Roy P. Stewart

Oklahoma: A Guide to the Sooner State (with others)
    Norman, University of Oklahoma Press, 1957
The Turner Ranch: Master Breeder of the Hereford Line
    Oklahoma City, Homestead House, 1961
Country Boy Hornbook
    Oklahoma City, Colorgraphics, 1968
Born Grown: An Oklahoma City History
    Oklahoma City, Metro Press, Inc., 1974

Books by Pendleton Woods

You and Your Company Publication
    Oklahoma City, Semco Color Press, Inc., 1950
Church of Tomorrow (with L. C. Mersfelder)
    Oklahoma City, Semco Color Press, Inc., 1964
Myriad of Sports—Profile of Oklahoma City (with Frank Boggs)
    Oklahoma City, Times-Journal Publishing Co., 1971

Library of Congress Catalog Card Number: 74-78648
Copyright   1974 by FIDELITY BANK, National Association, Oklahoma City, Oklahoma

Produced by METRO PRESS, Inc., Oklahoma City, Oklahoma
MANUFACTURED IN THE UNITED STATES OF AMERICA

Dedication

This book is dedicated to those people who built Oklahoma City and who will continue to make it move, whether they came early, eighty-five years ago, or later, and found here a home and kinship with those whose spirit is epitomized in our historical progress.

. . . and this was said

"Cities, like persons, are born and they die. People die before they are buried but it is possible to bury a city before it is quite dead. Not everyone who received advantages from the birth and growth of this city and state had a hand in encouraging that growth; not everyone who will share our future is lending a hand in shaping it. It ill behooves the laggards to toss sand into the gears of progress."
— *Country Boy* column, *The Daily Oklahoman,* January 10, 1956.

Photo Credits

OKLAHOMA HISTORICAL SOCEITY: 3—Payne, Couch, Colcord, Overholser; 9—Grand & Broadway 1889; 10—Postoffice 1889; 14—Oklahoma Station 1889; 16—Clarke, Richardson, Guthrie; 18—Grand Avenue 1891; 20—Postoffice prior to Run; 21—Main Street 1889; Samuel Crocker; 22—C.G. Jones, Train arrival 1889; 24—Third Postoffice; 26—DeBolt Lumber Co.; 27—Scott, Peery, Trosper, Lee; 28—Parade of 1893; 29—Street scene 1906, parade of 1910; 30—Colcord home; 31—St. Anthony Hospital; 32—First Methodist; 33—St. Luke's Methodist, First Methodist; 46—City Market 1913; 49—Early City Hall; 51—Lady bootblacks 1898, Tornado 1896, MK&T Depot 1904; 54—Johnsons, Overholser, cotton compress; 57—Tilghman, Madsen; 58—Main Street 1912; 60—McNabb, Owen; 66—State Capital Billboard; 67—State Capital postcard; 81—Embry, Dunjee, 90—Delmar Gardens; 93—Country Club 1906; 96—Play Cast 1890; 100—First orchestra; 113—First baseball stadium; 152—Shartel, Ames, Heyman, Brock; 171—Haskell; 173—Street fair; 176—State Fair, Street fair; 200—Canton; 220—Franklin; 237—Downtown construction; 287—Huckins Hotel; 307—Farmers State Bank.

OKLAHOMA HERITAGE ASSOCIATION: 78—Long, Hutchinson, Lain, Blatt; 81—Casady, Sheets; 127—Hefner, Shirk; 136—Browne, Brown, Anthony, Dulaney; 142—Gaylord, Kennedy, Draper; 143—Everest, Kirkpatrick, McGee; 171—J.F. Owens; 200—Hoffman, Barrett, McLain; 220—Gould, Buttram, Kerr; 240—Peters, Jones, Key, Harrison; 250—Turner, Murrah, Abernathy, Vaught.

OKLAHOMA COUNTY LIBRARIES: 76—Carnegie Library; 74—Belle Isle Boardwalk; 161-Street car terminal; 163—University Station; 165—Epworth University; 285—Downtown in 1937.

OKLAHOMA CITY CHAMBER OF COMMERCE: 85—Main Library; 119—National Finals Rodeo; 139—Stockyards; 149—Civic Center; 157—Floodway Project; 190—FAA; 193—FAA Center, FAA Aeromedical Research Institute; 194—Aero-Commander; 219—Lighted Oil Well; 256—Tinker Field; 257—Tinker Field; 277—Turner Turnpike.

UNIVERSITY OF OKLAHOMA WESTERN ARCHIVES: 6—Wagons lined up for Run; 57—Henry A. Thomas.

OKLAHOMA CITY URBAN RENEWAL AUTHORITY: 169—Medical Center Heating Plant; 287—Baum Bldg. demolition; 290—Scale model of renewal plan; Looking northwest over Myriad; 293—Myriad; 299—Kerr-McGee Center; 300—COTPA Building.

OKLAHOMA HIGHWAY DEPARTMENT: 302—State Capitol complex.

JOHN KNUPPEL: 64—First motorized fire fighting vehicle; 71—State Capitol; 72—Historical Society; 73—Capitol cornerstone laying; 104—Downtown parade; 148—Last Rock Island at old station; 149—Civic Center at night; 150—45th Division Monument; 214—City oilfield, night oilfield scene; Looking south from Capitol; 287—Huckins Hotel.

JOAN KEYS: 5—Carson camp; 47—Captain Sommers home; 52—Home in 1887, Zulite Water Company; 56—Fifth Street in 1907; 106—Double wedding in Wheeler Park 1903.

WALTER NASHERT: 56—Early generating plant; 301—County Office Building; 180—State Fair.

GEORGE H. SHIRK: 42—Oklahoma City High School; 62—Oklahoma City drawing 1890.

Acknowledgements

It is difficult to express thanks adequately to all sources who were of assistance in compiling this work. Listed below are some who provided special help in important areas of research.

Bagby, Jack — Director of public relations, Urban Renewal Authority.
Bennett, Paul L. — Metro Press, Inc.
Dahlgren, E. G. "Ty" — Professional writer in the field of petroleum.
Hurst, Irvin — Former newspaperman and historian.
Keys, Mrs. Mott and Joan — Members of a pioneer city family.
Northe, James Neill — Book dealer.
Oklahoma Christian College, Living Legends Library.
Oklahoma Heritage Association.
Oklahoma Historical Society.
Oklahoma Publishing Company.
Park, Joe — Public relations director for city schools.
Saulsberry, Charles — Former sportswriter and a preserver of sports history.
Schweikhard, Earl R. — President of Oklahoma National Stockyards Company.
Shirk, George H. — President of Oklahoma Historical Society and former mayor.
Smith, Nina — Public relations director for Oklahoma City University.
Stewart, Ronald L. — For his thesis on the city power structure.
Thompson, Horace (the late) — Former assistant to the city manager.
Tuohy, Neil — Longtime observer of city's development.

Frieze of the Run of 1889 from a model by Laura Fraser at the National Cowboy Hall of Fame and Western Heritage Center.

TABLE OF CONTENTS

Preface

IT IS DIFFICULT TO VIEW the people and events of another epoch in history without distortion of a lens ground in one's own time, as he attempts to adjust to the life style and mores of other eras.

Yet, as Francis Haines wrote in "The Western Historical Quarterly" of April 1973: "Historians say that history needs to be rewritten for each succeeding generation, not because history has changed, but because the new generation is asking new questions that can best be answered by an examination of records of the past from a new viewpoint."

In one sense it is unfortunate that much of the earliest Oklahoma City history was recorded later in life by those who made a part of that history. Their recollections were dimmed by the passing of time and clouded by their own prejudices. Naturally their recall of incidents and events was highly selective. Newspapers contemporary to the early period are an information source, except in matters political, where they were vehemently partisan. Periodic special editions contain flashbacks that are noticeably variable.

Tales told by a grandfather too often are more for effect and personal satisfaction than to be ground in the crucible of time and weighed on the neutral scales of fact. A researcher must heed the admonition of Rabbi Seymour Essrog to "beware of the half-truth — you may have gotten hold of the wrong half."

The continuing saga of Oklahoma City is indeed unique, as its story has been from the beginning. It was different then. It has had just enough differences since to set it slightly apart from cities with which in other ways it shares a commonality. From 1889 onward the essential ingredient of this variance has been civic leadership, with all the cooperation and contribution that implies, to make a reality of what at times appeared to be visionary ideas.

Historical events, for good or ill, are but the lengthened shadows of those who make them. In its historical heritage and in its spirit Oklahoma City is larger than its statistical area, which is second in the nation only to Jacksonville, Florida.

Certainly people who ventured their capital and gave of their time to build the city expected ultimately to benefit. The main impetus for progress here came from people willing to risk their money, their energy and their ambition, to achieve that progress. They held the belief that if the community prospered they would, too.

Oklahoma Station had little advantage over its neighbors so far as natural environment was concerned. It began with one primary asset, shared to an extent, in a single north-south railroad. It had the North Canadian River. City builders did have to be aggressive. They had to make this a regional hub, a distribution and financial center drawing upon an agricultural base, and assistance in the development of industry and natural resources.

In answer to a question about what makes a city, posed by Gilbert Stetler in "The City and Westward Expansion: A Western Case Study," our response would be that Oklahoma City grew, not because of strategic location or natural advantage, but because of enterprise of its people. To that assumption the text of this book bears witness.

We hope this book will serve you in two ways: To be informative, as factually correct as research from dated accounts can make it; to be entertaining, for history is but an account of real people and genuine events. When possible it should regain for a moment the color and zest of times it portrays.

We have avoided making this work a glamorized city directory. We have attempted to keep statistical material to a minimum. There had to be a high degree of selectivity to confine this material to one standard sized book. There are countless persons who, in some degree, were a part of our history.

We have tried to use those events, and to talk about those persons, who helped make the continuing story, or who were significant to an understanding of what really happened — for good or ill — since Oklahoma City is not, nor has it ever been, only primroses and platitudes.

Those are the only obligations with which this work was undertaken by the writers, researchers, consultants and our sponsors, Jack T. Conn and the folks at Fidelity Bank. It has been quite a task for, as Gene Allen remarked to us: "No one who has tried it seriously really wants to write a book — they merely want to have written one."

Roy P. Stewart,
Pendleton Woods

Prologue

I N ITS INCREDIBLY SHORT PERIOD, measured in historic time, Oklahoma has moved with a never-ending restlessness from arrows to astronauts. The first were made from the native bois d'arc tree, the second came from indigenous family trees of the state's four space men.

Oklahoma's name came from Choctaw words attributed to Reverend Allen Wright, of that tribe, at a post Civil War treaty session in Washington. It means, loosely, "Home of the Red Man."

There were six land openings. Five were "Runs," while the sixth was a lottery, giving lucky registrants a specified quarter-section for homesteading. All land except platted city lots had to be proved up to obtain a patent. This normally meant paying a small registration fee, making improvements on the land, with residence six months out of a year for five years, or to live on it fourteen months and pay it off at $1.25 per acre. Union army veterans got a two year credit off the five years. In 1900 the Free Homes Act dropped the acreage charge which amounted to $200 for a quarter-section.

These openings were the Unassigned Lands of Central Oklahoma in 1889; land just east of it previously assigned to the Iowa, Sac & Fox, Pottawatomie and Absentee Shawnee, in 1891; the Cheyenne-Arapaho Country of Western Oklahoma, generally north of present Interstate 40 to the southern boundary of the Cherokee Outlet, and west of present U.S. 81, in 1892; the Cherokee Outlet across the northern tier below Kansas, west of the Osage Nation to the 100th meridian, with the south border roughly east and west through Perry, in 1893; the Kickapoo land just east of central Oklahoma Country in 1895. The Wichita, Caddo, Kiowa, Comanche and Apache lands in Southwest Oklahoma opened with a drawing at El Reno in 1901. About one-fourth of the latter was reserved as the "Big Pasture" for grazing land of those tribes, but this was sold on bids for quarter-sections in 1906, exclusive of 25,000 acres more for Fort Sill.

We are concerned here primarily with the "Unassigned Lands of Oklahoma Country," as they came to be known before those lands were opened, due to pressure of homeseekers. But those who made the celebrated "Run of '89" were not even the first after nomadic Plains Tribes passed this way in their wide ranging.

Across these rolling prairies traveled to some extent Clovis and Folsom Man of pre-history. Pre-pottery area cave dwellers lived on high mesas in the extreme northwest, while in eastern river valleys dwelled the Spiro mound builders. These are authenticated by artifacts and carbon dating.

The "dawn horse," Eohippus, left his tiny skeletal remains near those of the mastodon in shale beds, many thousands of years old. A reconstruction can be seen in the Stovall Museum at the University of Oklahoma. Geological, paleontological and ethnological ages have a long history here in shades of our pre-Christian past, from fossil remains gathered by talented amateur enthusiasts such as "Uncle Bill" Baker in

Cimarron county, and Moore Hess, of the Concho firm. Hess stopped excavation in Permian beds under Persimmon Hill, at the National Cowboy Hall of Fame building site, until a mastodon jaw and thigh bone could be removed.

The Adams-Onis Spanish Treaty of 1819 set the American boundary at the 100th meridian, east-to-west, which later became the western boundary of Oklahoma prior to the 1890 inclusion of the Panhandle. Red river, by the same treaty, was declared the southern American boundary for this region, before conflict and colonization led to formation of the Republic of Texas in 1836.

That young nation, later a state, claimed an area east of the 100th meridian, called "Old Greer County." A United States Supreme Court decision of 1896, after years of litigation, awarded the disputed area to Oklahoma Territory. This was based on the treaty of 1819 and upon a mapping mistake made in 1852 by Captain Randolph B. Marcy, United States Army. He had used erroneously the North Fork of Red river instead of the main stream for his map boundary. The court decision caused reversion of 1,372,666 acres with 8,500 people, of whom some 2,000 held preference right to 640,000 acres of the territory, and left some for homesteading in 1901.

With exception of the Panhandle — which was west of the 100th meridian and for some reason was not claimed by earlier nineteenth century governmental entities — all of present Oklahoma originally was set aside as Indian Territory, along with vast expanses of other lands in the trans-Mississippi west. That space was diminished, in part, by change in 1854 of the 1820 Missouri Compromise, which held that no state created after Missouri would be a slave state. The amendment to Henry Clay's oratorical victory, known as the Kansas-Nebraska bill, left slavery optional to those respective territories, but also shoved official Indian Territory south of the thirty-seventh parallel.

Deeper in its historic past our land was first claimed by Spain, because of exploration by Coronado in the northwestern portion in 1541 — the first poor farm boy to seek his fortune on these plains — by Andreas de Camp, Juan de Onate, and De Soto. The latter, after exploring the Mississippi, accentuated a grandoise claim to all lands in the drainage area of the Father of Waters.

French claims were made after explorations of La Salle, De La Harpe, and Du Rivage. From 1763 this was Spanish land, with trading and trapping permits issued by Spanish governors. It reverted to French ownership in 1800 under the "secret" treaty of San Ildefonso. Napoleon, who was badly in need of money, let it be known that the land was for sale. This led to President Jefferson's purchase of Louisiana Territory in 1803, through a federal bond issue of $15 million, which meant a value of less than four cents an acre.

Acquisition of that vast area led to administrative changes in 1804. Instead of New Orleans, administration was placed under Indiana Territory, this being the closest United States governing unit. In 1812 Missouri Territory took over administration of our region and in 1819 Arkansas Territory was formed and took charge. The area already had been explored, after a fashion. Manuel Lisa, who held his trapping and trading franchises from Spain, had competition from Pierre and August Chouteau who held French authority, and in 1817 founded a post on Grand river, near Salina of the future, in Eastern Oklahoma.

The Lewis and Clark expedition of 1806, although proceeding up the Missouri seeking a route to the western ocean, had an effect on our future. It helped open up country to the north. Resultant waves of immigrants' and settlers' pressure contributed to Indian upheavals that fanned fires of the Plains Wars, led to creation of a chain of military forts, and eventually to concentration of many Plains Tribes in future Western Oklahoma. Their counterparts, after 1832, settled Eastern Oklahoma with the Five Civilized Tribes removed in a tragic migration from the Southeast. Splinter groups of tribesmen came from as far away as the lake country of Western New York.

The expedition of Captain Zebulon M. Pike in 1806 increased knowledge of future Oklahoma. His second in command, Lieutenant James Wilkinson, son of the first United States Louisiana Territory governor, made the first recorded and definitive trip down the Arkansas river from the Rocky mountains (leaving a peak named in Pike's honor) to Red River.

Fort Smith was activated in 1817; Forts Gibson and Towson in 1824; Fort Coffee and Fort Holmes in 1834; Fort Washita in 1842; Camp Supply (later Fort) in 1868; Fort Sill in 1869 and Fort Reno in 1874.

Jesse Chisholm and Robert Bean laid out the first military road from Gibson to Towson more than thirty years before the part-Indian trader marked a trail through Central Oklahoma for his freighter wagons. After the Civil War this became a guide for a famed cattle trail, as Texans pointed their herds north to railheads in Kansas.

There were others whose writing and art helped the slow buildup of information on all western lands and, in particular, to that which later became Oklahoma. Washington Irving toured our area and told of it in "A Tour on the Prairies." Charles Latrobe, the British naturalist, and John James Audubon, found much book material; George Catlin, the artist, accompanied General Henry Leavenworth and the First Dragoons under Colonel Henry Dodge in 1834 from Fort Gibson to the confluence of the Red and Washita rivers, thence upstream and westward to the Wichita mountains. Catlin's drawings from that excursion and elsewhere in the newly explored lands added to Eastern interest.

As time unrolled its historic pages with cumulative national concern following the Medicine Lodge Treaty of 1867, the eastern half of future Oklahoma held the transplanted, more sedentary Indians, and the Osage. The western half held tenuously resettled nomadic Plains Tribes except for the "No Man's Land" Panhandle corridor. We were to be represented soon with sixty-seven tribes of eleven distinct lingual groupings, for more than a third of the nation's Indians in the forty-eight contiguous states.

In the center of all this domain were 1,877,640 acres that had been ceded to the Creeks and Seminoles but not assigned formally. That land was the magnet that drew those thousands here on April 22, 1889, for the most spectacular land opening in international history.

1

The Land Lure Buildup

I N ALL RECORDED HISTORY THERE was never anything like the "Run of '89" that opened Oklahoma Country. There never will be another — anywhere — because those conditions that brought about this unusual event cannot be duplicated.

"Manifest Destiny" still was a shibboleth used by proponents of westward expansion. The lure of free land attracted those who had none, or whose spirit of adventure was tantalized by tales in many accounts. For two decades after the Civil War this was the most publicized region of the growing nation.

People believed what they read, or what was read to them, for this "proved" something they wanted to believe. Their attitude had been summed up centuries before by Paul, in his *Letter to the Hebrews*: "Now faith is the substance of things hoped for, the evidence of things not seen."

The War Between the States left an aftermath of economic depression or, at best, creeping recovery. This was not confined entirely to the South, nor were conditions in Europe much better. Effects of the panics of 1873 and 1884, although felt primarily in Eastern financial centers, trickled down through each successive economic stratum.

One plan discussed in Congress after the war was to move freedmen into Indian Territory and resettle them. The treaty of 1866 already had shrunk that territory to the eastern half of the future state with western areas not all assigned. From 1866 to 1879 there were dozens of bills introduced in Congress to create a state out of all Indian Territory. The Five Civilized Tribes in the east later were to attempt creating their own State of Sequoyah. Names such as Neosho and Lincoln were suggested for a proposed state.

On March 17, 1870, Senator Benjamin F. Rice of Arkansas introduced a bill to organize Indian Territory of the eastern half into the Territory of Oklahoma, twenty years before the western half was so named. T. C. Sears, an attorney for the Missouri, Kansas and Texas Railroad (Katy) in Eastern Oklahoma, and Elias Boudinot, the Cherokee leader and writer, lobbied for such a bill. They proposed also that some land to the west be opened.

A story by Boudinot in the *Chicago Times* in 1879 had some affect in publicizing the possibility of a land opening. He claimed there were 14,000,000 acres available for settlement in the portion reserved for the Kiowas, Comanches, Cheyennes and Arapahoes. Not, naturally, in his area.

This, with increasing publicity generated by David L. Payne,

1

the "Boomer" leader, had a cumulative effect on drawing more national attention to our region. While contributory, these efforts were but portions of the total buildup that began with stories told by trappers and traders; by military explorers such as Pike, Wilkinson and Marcy; by authors Irving, Latrobe and Audubon.

This was continued by widely distributed stories from such writers as Milton Reynolds of the *New York World* and *Chicago Times*. He covered the Fort Smith Treaty meeting and its followup at Medicine Lodge in 1867, agitated for land opening later and made the Run of '89 himself, to found the *Edmond Sun*. Reynolds used the pseudonym "Kicking Bird" on some of his articles, perpetuated today by a golf course at Edmond, on land which Reynolds gave to the city.

Folks back east read about this country, too, from Henry M. Stanley, then of the *Cincinnatti Commercial*, later of the *New York Herald* before James Gordon Bennett sent Stanley to Africa with the cryptic instruction: "Find Doctor Livingston."

All these widely circulated accounts fanned the tiny flames of hope for many persons. They saw in the unknown but enticing land a place that might give them, as Thomas Wolfe put it in *"You Can't Go Home Again,"* "... to every man his chance — to every man, regardless of his birth, his shining, golden opportunity — to every man the right to live, to work, to be himself, and to become whatever thing his manhood and his vision can combine to make him...."

The dreamers were not alone. Practical men also thought this land was "wasted" on Indians. Cattlemen pointing their herds north from Texas to railheads in Kansas after the Civil War, found that much of the country was suitable for winter grazing. Some found it quite profitable to lease land, especially from Cherokees in the Outlet, but desired permanent ownership more. They would take land wherever they could get it.

Certainly railroads wanted more land opened up because that meant people and people meant passenger and freight traffic. In 1884 the later Atchison, Topeka and Santa Fe, then a subsidiary of the Southern Kansas Railway, laid track from Arkansas City to Purcell, at the northern boundary of the Chickasaw Nation. This included depots at Guthrie, and Oklahoma Station (later Oklahoma City), in the Unassigned Lands. In 1887, the Gulf, Colorado and Santa Fe built up from the south to Purcell, making it a division point. In 1887, also, the Choctaw Coal and Railway Company got a permit to build a railroad west-to-east.

By accident or intent — the reasons are in a rather vague bureaucratic limbo — there were 1,877,640 acres in the central area left unassigned after the last Indian reservation was defined in 1881. This was the central portion west of the ninety-sixth, or Indian Meridian. It included approximately 2,949 square miles, or 11,796 quarter-sections of primeval land which could be homesteaded, or platted for town sites. It was no wonder that many persons, certainly the ambitious Payne and his Boomer followers, considered this public domain.

Yet the Creeks and the Seminoles had to be considered. By treaty they had a "residual interest" in the Unassigned Lands, which had been intended to resettle some tribes, but had not been so used. In January,

DAVID L. PAYNE
Original Head of Boomer movement

WILLIAM L. COUCH
Boomer head following Payne death

CHARLES F. COLCORD
Pioneer city lawman and builder

HENRY OVERHOLSER
Territorial financier and builder

1889, negotiations were held to recover interests of those two tribes, represented basically by Governors Pleasant Porter of the Creeks and John G. Brown for the Seminoles. Relinquishment gave those tribes $2,280,000 and $1,912,000, respectively. Thus the two tribes received a bit more than $2 per acre for land for which the United States paid France four cents an acre. (In 1972 land sixteen miles from the original Oklahoma Station sold for $8,500 per acre.)

Perhaps no one had more influence on opening of the Unassigned Lands than did David L. Payne, whose attempts to colonize Oklahoma Country spanned five years, with a tremendous national publicity campaign either by Payne and his chief followers, or the national media as it existed in those days. Payne generated good copy. He put the word "Boomer" into the language and eventually into the dictionary.

Born in Indiana, son of a farmer, and a mother who was a first cousin of Davy Crockett, (who was killed at the Alamo two years before Payne was born) he was highly intelligent but largely self-educated. Payne homesteaded in Doniphan County, Kansas Territory, and for three years in the Civil War was a private in the Fourth Kansas Infantry Regiment. In 1866 Payne was sergeant-at-arms of the Kansas house of representatives. He was postmaster at Leavenworth in 1867; in 1868 a captain in the Nineteenth Kansas Volunteer Cavalry, serving part of the time under Custer's general command in Southern Kansas and Western Oklahoma. The latter gave him the first inspection of a portion of the land that eventually he would try to settle.

Payne in 1879 became an assistant doorkeeper in the United States House of Representatives. That is where he heard of the Unassigned Lands in Oklahoma Country, read everything he could find about attempts to settle that domain, started the Boomer movement, and for five years did everything that he could to publicize it. He tried eight times to settle a colony in the disputed land. Usually Payne and his people were just escorted to the border. Twice he landed in federal court at Fort Smith.

Payne was something of an idealist. Although he was head of but one of three colonization movements his was best known, and has obscured the others, historically. His favorite cry, in oratorical style, was: "And the Lord commanded unto Moses, 'Go forth and possess the Promised Land.'"

By February 1, 1883, there were some 250 members with more

than eighty wagons for transport in Payne's Oklahoma Colony movement. The $2.50 membership included fifty cents to the secretary for a certificate, and $2 to Payne, for which he "guaranteed" them a quarter-section of land or a $25 town lot — on land that he did not own.

Much of the publicity Payne's activities received came from the colony's own publication, widely circulated, called *"The Oklahoma War Chief."* It was edited by Samuel Crocker who, in July 1885, was arrested and charged with sedition, conspiracy and inciting insurrection. Put in the Cowley County jail in Kansas he languished there for several months without the case coming to trial. Charges then were dismissed.

Payne seemed to dote on being arrested since that provided him a forum. His only court victory was after an August 9, 1884, arrest at Rock Falls, in the Cherokee Outlet, four miles south of Hunnewell, Kansas, with seven others. They were charged with conspiracy against the United States by intruding on Indian lands. United States District Judge C. G. Foster decreed that title to all Oklahoma lands was vested in the United States, and that settlement by its citizens was not a criminal offense.

Someone forgot to tell the troopers, especially the Ninth and Tenth Cavalry (the black "Buffalo Soldiers") because they kept on booting Payne and his people out.

Payne died November 28, 1884, from an apparent heart attack, while at breakfast in the Barnard House, at Wellington, Kansas, in company of his prospective wife, Mrs. K. A. Haines, and John S. Koller. Like Moses, Payne was destined to die without a home in his "promised" land.

A trusted lieutenant of Payne's, William L. Couch, then took over. Prior to this his principal job had been to keep supplies coming to members of the colony and otherwise handle logistics of their travels. This was more difficult than it might appear. Two weeks after Payne's death, Couch took a large body of people about sixty miles south of Arkansas City to the valley of Stillwater Creek — in what later became a county named for Payne — laid out a townsite, staked claims and started erection of cabins from timber against rigors of an early winter.

There were some 200 men with women and children, the largest of the colonization groups, and this time the men were armed and determined to stay put. This was evident to Lieutenant M. W. Day, who came there from Camp Russell with forty men and two six-mule teams of Troop I of the Ninth Cavalry. It was a standoff. Day just drew back a bit and pitched his own camp, sending a courier dashing off to Fort Reno for reinforcements.

This lasted about a month before Colonel Edward Hatch and Major Thomas B. Dewees arrived with some 600 cavalrymen from the Ninth and Tenth Regiments, an infantry company and two small cannons, that ringed the Couch camp to prevent supplies from going in. This was effective. No shots were fired by either side and rations were provided only if the colonists headed back north. Under escort, naturally.

This late January 1885 reverse movement was more official than previous ones since Chester A. Arthur, in his last days as president, had ordered all persons in Oklahoma Country illegally to depart or be forced out. On November 10, 1885, the last attempt to create a colony in Okla-

Lieutenant Carson's camp on the North Canadian River about the time of the Run of 1889.

homa Country was made by the group under Couch. They penetrated as deeply into the Unassigned Lands as Council Grove, near the present Oklahoma-Canadian county line, where there was wood and water. There also was a spur from the Chisholm Trail a bit farther west, since Jesse Chisholm for a time had a trading post in Council Grove.

The would-be colonists were moved out again for the final time by troops from Fort Reno, under command of Lieutenant Colonel E. V. Sumner of the Fifth Cavalry. Couch and others believed that some land opening surely would occur soon. In little more than three years they were to find that assumption true. Couch himself was in the area with a railroad crew at the time of the Run and was one of raw Oklahoma Station's first leaders. Couch's claim of a homestead created trouble later.

Just what was this country — to be so highly prized? Early in the Boomer movement a delegation was sent to view possibilities and scout the land along what became Santa Fe trackage. A trio consisting of C. P. Walker and James McCartney of Colony, Kansas, and John W. Beard of Burlington, took a train to Arkansas City, then rented a buckboard to finish the journey overland to Oklahoma Station. According to John Holzapfel, this is the report they brought back:

"Oklahoma Station, on the North Canadian River, is the ideal spot. (There is) a beautiful stream of swift, running water, and in the valley a very rich, sandy loam soil, covered with bluestem grass as high as a man's head."

For all the glowing reports made by scouts into the promising land, Oklahoma Country was no Garden of Eden, agriculturally — and it was agriculture that attracted a numerical majority. This land lay in the red beds extending north and south through the center of the state, with a preponderance of Renfrow clay soil. The surface sloped west to east while underlying rock, sandstone and shale, sloped east to west.

This was in a zone of geological change. Across it was a wide belt of small trees of the Cross Timbers formation, at times almost impenetrable, while the wood itself was of little use in other than a temporary struc-

Four hundred wagons cross the Salt Fork railroad bridge in preparation for the 1889 Run.

ture. Except for river and creek bottoms there was little alluvial soil that retained fertility. Upland crust was thin and highly subject to wind and water erosion when broken.

The soil was formed by seas late in the Cambrian period, that remained through the Ordovician era, which produced sands that outcrop to the south in the Arbuckle area and are more than 6,000 feet deep in Central Oklahoma. The Permian Age left many a puzzle for grangers whose knowledge of soils and agronomy was gained in Appalachian hill country.

The hopeful across our older states and even in Europe where the exciting stories had gone knew none of these things. Neither did losers in existing territories not yet designated states, who got there too late or who lost struggles to uncompromising natural vicissitudes. They added to a clamor for opening the country.

As Howard R. Lamar said in the *Western Historical Quarterly* in our times: "Of these ideological drives (to settle and develop the farming west) the one which has affected the West most has been the homestead concept . . . the homestead principle was at war with the Republican theory of industrial development as embodied in land grants to railroads, but even those railroad lands were awarded in the hope that they would eventually go to individual farms."

The Unassigned Lands could not be opened without congressional authority. For a decade there had been excessive lobbying both for and against that action in Washington. Pressure came from the physical presence and action of proponents and opponents, and by the slow buildup of a discernable public opinion from citizens not otherwise represented in Congressional halls.

A land opening bill passed the House of Representatives in February 1889 but failed in the Senate, where leaders of the western expansion movement were more concerned with lands drained by the Missouri. In March Representative William M. Springer of Illinois, long a champion of the land opening, succeeded in getting his measure through the House as a rider on an Indian appropriation bill, which got it through the Senate at last. The years of argument were over.

On March 3, 1889, in the fading hours of his administration (as presidential tenure was then in effect) President Grover Cleveland signed the bill. On March 23, 1889, President Benjamin Harrison, in his third week in office, signed a proclamation calling for opening the land at high noon on April 22. As originally prepared in the Department of the Interior — which had supervision of Oklahoma Country — the proclamation called for opening on April 20, a Saturday, but President Harrison's religious scruples led him to believe folks would ignore the significance of Sunday if that date was fixed. So Monday it was.

The legal aspects were interesting. Boundaries of the district were set at the southern line of the Cherokee Outlet on the north; the Indian Meridian (ninety-sixth meridian) on the east; the South Canadian River on the south; the Cheyenne-Arapaho country on the west, roughly where US 81 is now.

There were no future county lines or townsites designated then. The land was to be surveyed into 160 acre homesteads for single entry, although a number of persons could join in taking two quarter-sections and platting them for a townsite, making it exempt from farms by conversion to homestead lots. This was to cause quite a hassle in what became Oklahoma City, for a person could claim and defend his rights to more than one lot. In addition there were conflicts between rival townsite companies that created wounds long in healing.

The proclamation declared that persons eligible to file claims were those who observed the restraining lines; were male citizens twenty-one years old or more; unmarried, legally divorced or widowed females twenty-one or more; and aliens who formally declared their intent to become naturalized citizens — a provision that opened land to the world.

There were other permitted actions. For three days prior to the opening, people could travel across restricted Indian lands to get in position on boundaries in either of the four compass directions. This naturally made possible a golden opportunity for "Sooners" to enter Oklahoma Country and hide out until April 22. Freight could be shipped in and left in sealed cars on sidings at depots, primarily at future Guthrie and Oklahoma City, although Oklahoma Station would draw the most. (Town names would come later, even be changed, as Lisbon became Kingfisher, but if you were buying a ticket to the only known place, Oklahoma Station appealed as a destination.)

For restraint on "Sooners" there were four infantry companies spread among the four main prospective townsite areas of Guthrie, Kingfisher, Oklahoma Station, and along the South Canadian below Norman, with cavalry units riding the more distant lines. Most of these troops came from Fort Reno. Captain David F. Stiles, who had been provost marshal at Waco, Texas, in reconstruction days, had a company of the Tenth Infantry here and was provost marshal for the Station. The Tenth Cavalry had some elements available.

As Doctor Angelo C. Scott said of the land opening: "It was just a land. It was not a (formal) territory. It had no organization, no government and no laws except those applicable to the opening." For one year and eleven days laws or ordinances were what the citizen's groups said that they were in assembled consensus. Enforcement was only that which a majority was willing to accept. Troops were only to keep the peace.

At no other time and in no other place did such conditions exist. George Shirk underlined this in writing an introduction to an article by Berlin B. Chapman in *Chronicles of Oklahoma.* "The circumstances that there existed no formal law nor civil code for a period of almost thirteen months is in itself incredible. The remedies that today we accept as commonplace such as probate, suits for debt, actions because of accidents, and so on, simply did not exist. . . . Yet, remarkably enough . . . the fact that (citizens) were able to live side by side, jostling for their claims and their ground with relative harmony and concord, is probably the greatest tribute of all."

So the vast, scenic panoramic stage was set for entry of the players. Some were to see dreams become reality, others to see reality become a nightmare of broken hope and wasted effort. But, poised for the entry, it was chance and change that occupied their thoughts. Even if they had heard about it, no one here that late April of 1889 was thinking about opening of the Exposition Universelle in Paris fourteen days later, featuring something called the Eiffel Tower.

2

A City Born Grown

THAT MONDAY ON APRIL 22, 1889, was a bright, sunny day, a bit warm even for the time of year. Perhaps to some eager folk waiting impatiently along the four restraining lines, it was an omen that nature favored the land opening, as it had favored man by putting the soil and trees and water there in the first place.

At last high noon came. Accounts vary slightly on signals for the Run of '89. We believe that among cavalrymen posted on each restraining line was a bugler, and a trooper with a triangular yellow guidon, so that they could be seen at a distance. As the first note of the bugle sounded, the guidon, raised on high, was dropped sharply as though in salute. From this sound and sight, down the line, infantrymen and cavalrymen fired their weapons which, far in distance, made a few seconds handicap.

Mounted men were in the vanguard while behind them came light buggies and buckboards, or wagons drawn by horses, mules and oxen, some of which contained women. Around and between them were men on foot, weighted down by little except a wood stake and something with which to pound it into the seasonally softened ground, and a slim bedroll.

The race was to the swift, so far as lots in the rumored town loca-

Grand and Broadway in Oklahoma City, photographed April 30, 1889, a week after Run.

tions were concerned, but the fabled terrapins in many cases won over the hares in securing a better claim. It is factual that from many a gully sprang a Sooner who might later have to prove what time he crossed the line. A man who laid the lash to a team pulling a mouldboard plow from the entry line was no dumbjohn. He was claiming land and "improving" it at the same time.

Doctor Scott said that William J. McClure, later a prominent rancher, was conceded to be the first legal settler in the future Oklahoma City area, riding in from the east boundary. He used a relay of "five blooded horses," Doctor Scott recalled, and his entry later received legal blessing. It was in what now is called the Maywood area.

Distance to Oklahoma Station was shortest from the south although the South Canadian River — which was the restraining line — first had to be crossed. Depending upon where one forded it was dry, or wet sand, and mud. Low banks at favored crossings, scouted in advance, were jammed. Worn equipment breaking down added to the confusion and disappointment.

Passenger trains on the Santa Fe began their movement at noon. The short length, wood fired steam engines, normally could make a maximum speed of thirty miles per hour. Freights could make that speed with twenty loaded cars or twenty-nine empties. Such speed did not apply on the exciting day of the Run. The first train from Purcell had twenty-five cars and made the trip in two hours and five minutes. The first train from the northern line, below later Perry, reached the station after a pause at Guthrie at three o'clock. It had about twenty cars.

People were in, on and all over the cars, with or without tickets.

G. A. Beidler, first postmaster following the Run, at his post office at 8 West Main.

They jumped from slowly moving trains, off the steps, and some were said to have dived out of windows. Some hopefuls from the south with good horses beat the train to Oklahoma Station in their approximately fifteen mile dash.

There were some women and children, but the people, regardless of the method they used in their hopeful dashes, were predominantly male. And they were of all types. There were the business folk who had made a competence somewhere else and had freight cars of various types of goods waiting on sidings at Oklahoma Station or to lesser extent at Guthrie. There were quite a few lawyers and other professional men. There were land owners and successful farmers. There were also the unskilled, who had nothing to lose and everything to gain. Some folk were well educated. Some were illiterate. Their signature was an "X" while some of the tribesmen whose land the whites long coveted, such as Hooley Bell, the Cherokee lobbyist for territorial status, could quote poetry in three languages.

Just how many made the Run no one will ever know. Brigadier General Wesley Merritt of Fort Reno put the first day crowd around Oklahoma Station at "from 10,000 to 12,000." Captain D. F. Stiles, the provost marshal and commander of the Tenth Infantry unit tented a short distance east of the Santa Fe tracks, said there were about 12,000 in the Station area by nightfall. The one-star commander from Fort Reno, who had courier reports from all over the Unassigned Lands, put the total first day entrants at around 20,000, from all points.

Most recorded accounts, many of them made years later, simply shrugged off any statistics by saying "thousands of people." There apparently were few photographers around, either, at least to take pictures that are still extant. Equipment in those days was heavy and cumbersome. W. S. Prettyman, a most notable photographer, who for years worked through the Nations and who left an invaluable collection of glass plates — some of which in our era were discovered and rescued by Robert Cunningham of Stillwater — stopped at Guthrie and did not reach Oklahoma Station until May.

An ironic and slightly amusing fact is that Prettyman made the Run into the Cherokee Outlet in 1893 and took many pre-dash photos, leaving it to an assistant atop an especially built tower to photograph actual start of that Run. This photograph of horsemen and wagons, has been used many times and identified as a "scene of the Run of '89," and even was so labeled in Doctor Scott's memoirs of the Run set down fifty years later. Many of the Prettyman plates now are in western history archives of the University of Oklahoma Library.

It is understandable that so few on-the-spot accounts of the Run were made, for in the excitement of that historical happening itself, even those present who had the ability to record events were busily engaged in claiming lots or farms, or starting whatever business enterprises they intended to follow.

Less than three years later, using the talent and experience that made him the most noted reporter of his time, Richard Harding Davis visited Oklahoma City. From persons whom he interviewed he gathered information that, in his own colorful style, may well be a descriptive overlay of the opening scene, as he wrote it for *Harpers* in 1892.

"These modern Pilgrims stand in rows twenty deep, separated from the Promised Land not by an ocean, but by a line scratched in the earth with the point of a soldier's bayonet. The long row toeing this line are bending forward, panting with excitement, and looking with greedy eyes toward the New Canaan, the women with their dresses tucked up to their knees, the men stripped of coats and waistcoats for the coming race.

"And then, a trumpet call, answered by a thousand angry yells from all along the line, and hundreds of men and women on foot and on horseback break away across the prairie, the stronger pushing down the weak, and those on horseback riding over and in some cases killing those on foot, in a mad, unseeming race for something which they are getting for nothing.

"These Pilgrims do not drop on one knee to give thanks decorously . . . but fall on both knees, and hammer stakes into the ground and pull them up again and drive them down somewhere else, at a place which they hope will eventually become a corner lot facing the post office, and drag up the next man's stake, and threaten him with a Winchester because he is on *their* land which they have owned for at least three minutes.

"There are no Indians in this scene. They have been paid one dollar and twenty-five cents an acre for this land, which is worth five dollars as it lies, before a spade has been driven into it or a bit of timber cut, and they are safely out of the way.

". . . to appreciate Oklahoma City of this day it is necessary to go back three years ago. At that time it consisted of a home for the railroad agent, and four other small buildings. The rest was prairie land with low curving hills covered with high grass and thick timber. This as far as the eye could see, and nothing else."

Davis compared the then three-year-old city to "a portrait finished by a lightning crayon artist . . . a city that grew up overnight and did in three years or less what other towns have accomplished after only half a century."

In another aspect he was less complimentary, with the appraisal that: "I think any man who can afford a hall bedroom and a gas stove in New York City is better off than he would be as the owner of 160 acres on the prairie."

Among those who made advance preparations for activity in the new district were developers of two townsite companies from Kansas. One was the Oklahoma Town Company, also called the Oklahoma Colony Company in some accounts, which came in from the south in livery hacks brought for that purpose, and made the fifteen mile trip in one hour and fifteen minutes. Doctor Delos Walker was president of this group. They started surveying for their platted townsite east of the tracks, on the military reservation, and were advised to move elsewhere.

The Seminole Land and Improvement Company had men, it was alleged later, who were dragging surveying chains and lugging transits up what they declared would be Main Street within a few minutes after twelve o'clock. Former Congressman Sidney Clarke was the Seminole leading light, assisted vocally in hastily called street meetings by General

James B. Weaver of Iowa, the 1880 Greenback candidate for president of the United States — but rather unsuccessful in securing and keeping a town lot here.

The Oklahoma Colony Company set up a huge headquarters tent where the American National Bank stood later, and proclaimed its town to be South Oklahoma, below later Grand Avenue. Members of the Colony assembled a crowd to hold a town election and managed to get some 400 persons to vote on a hastily scribbled ballot. James Murray was "elected" mayor and C. P. Walker city clerk. They never did get to assume office.

The Seminoles, meanwhile, were trying to plat lots from Clarke Street northward. (Later that was Grand Avenue and still later Sheridan). The government had not made any provision for city lots or for streets and alleys. This resulted in a great amount of turbulence with fights, lot jumping, hasty sales of lots for $25 by the "owner" and general confusion. The street jogs that for years featured north-south streets at Grand Avenue, and one on West Main, were a natural result of disputes between the two townsite firms. The Seminole townsite was called simply Oklahoma. (The "City" part was to come later on formation of territorial government that forcibly merged the two areas. It was used locally but not recognized by the Post Office Department until July 1, 1923).

There were so many arguments and complaints by advocates of the Colony company, against the Seminoles, that they were called "Kickers" at first, then given the name of Kickapoos. This title remained through the early days and was expanded to a political coalition between the Colony group, and citizens outside either organization, as a recognized faction as people took politics quite seriously.

One can only imagine the bedlam. No one really knew who owned anything. Claimants were trying to hold their space against trespassers, to erect a tent or some form of shanty to prove occupancy or, after being bumped off one location, trying to find another soul more timid whom they could bounce in turn. There was one water well in the vicinity of later Main and Broadway and the owner briefly did a brisk business selling water for five cents a pint cup. And everyone was thirsty. Captain Stiles put a stop to that as a humanitarian gesture.

Stiles and his men tried also to confiscate any visible weapon if the man carrying it would surrender it peacefully. He found some unsavory whiskey peddlers and broke their stock in trade. Not only did "Satan Come Also," as Albert McRill used that as a title for his book later, with the verb in past tense, but he came early. Stiles, a white haired, quiet man, had a good record in the Union Army in the Civil War. He was dropped in rank afterward, as were most officers of the diminished army, and only after being provost marshal at Waco during reconstruction did he get his "railroad tracks" back.

He faced armed lot jumpers or defenders without a qualm but refused to engage in any ownership arguments. "I'm here to see that you keep the peace," his routine comment was, "not to decide who owns a lot." Captain and Mrs. Stiles lived in a tent on the reserved military camp location and she may have had the envy of what few women were around. She had a wood floor in her tent.

Here is a view of Oklahoma Station, taken about two weeks following the Run of 1889.

In all the excitement, noise and strange happenings, people that first night also could laugh at something. This was a cry: "Oh, Joe, here's your mule!" Every so often someone would start that and it would roll across the area, being picked up by scores of voices. The same yell, probably meant seriously at first, then said in jest, actually began on the restraining line north of Guthrie the night before the opening.

Water and food were most important. A small creek existed then between Broadway and the tracks. Another ran toward the North Canadian, also, in the vicinity of later Hudson Avenue. Food was harder to come by since early merchants had to construct a safe haven for their wares, which required a few days. It took L. L. Land, Z. T. and D. P. Wright from Coldwater, Kansas, three days to put up a shelter for their grocery stock, for example, shipped into Purcell to await the opening. W. J. Pettee also was much in evidence. His hardware stock, basically ordinary household utensils and tools, was shipped in advance to Oklahoma Station. By evening of the opening day he had a bit of it in a shack on West Main, on a lot he was able to hold from then on. As soon as possible he put up a prefabricated store building that also was shipped down in advance from Kansas.

In the absence of any formal law, citizens on Tuesday after the Monday opening, sought to make some order out of the near chaos regarding lot ownership. A group of persons not connected with either town company walked about, asking people to attend a mass meeting at three o'clock near where the Lee-Huckins Hotel stood later. The purpose was to form a committee to adjudicate claims and make a spot decision which a majority of citizens at the meeting agreed to accept and support.

Doctor Scott was named chairman of the meeting and M. H. Woods of Kansas selected as secretary. Speakers yelled at the assembled crowd from the rear of a wagon bed. Every time someone was proposed for membership on the lot committee there would be yells of, "Let's see what he looks like," or similar requests. Then the less controlled would yell such taunts at the would-be candidate as, "What was your name where you came from?" and "Why did you leave?" A committee of fourteen finally was selected to hear arguments, and to define the streets, alleys and blocks. So many persons would surround the committee whenever it paused that a large triangle made of cottonwood logs was put together and carried on volunteer shoulders. From inside that the committee made its deliberations.

It was obvious that the people must have some sort of government. On April 26 another mass meeting was called and temporary officers for a provisional government elected. They were Captain W. L. Couch, of Boomer fame and a leader of the Seminole faction, as mayor, and the Reverend W. P. Shaw, a Methodist minister, as recorder. Articles of Confederation were adopted. April 29, Mayor Couch called for an election two days later, on May 1, which gave citizens two days to campaign.

Were it not so serious this could have been a most unusual election. The ballots were hand written on small pieces of paper and dropped into a large coffee pot. The Seminoles had a clean sweep of offices. Couch was named permanent mayor; John A. Blackburn, recorder; O. H. Violet, police judge; Ledru Guthrie, city attorney; M. C. Quinton, city treasurer; Charles Chamberlain, city engineer; councilmen Sidney Clarke, E. G. Hudson, John Wallace, C. T. Scott, W. C. Wells and J. E. Jones. There were only two wards.

There was somewhat of an anomaly in that South Oklahoma, that region below Grand Avenue, was organized on April 27, with but one ticket of candidates. Elected were G. W. Patrick, mayor; W. D. Bodine, recorder; L. P. Ross, attorney; N. C. Helburn, marshal and John Cochran, treasurer. This "city" lasted slightly more than a year before being incorporated into the larger entity.

The Town of Oklahoma government started action immediately. The first ordinance passed was one against lot jumping, providing a fine of $100 for anyone who caused any action against a person already residing on a lot, which in essence was a protective measure for the Seminole faction. It was an ineffective action, at best, for when a legal tribunal was established about a year later many lot "ownerships" then held were protested successfully. A supplemental ordinance provided for issuance of lot certificates, and for those issued previously by the Seminole Company to be filed on equality by the city recorder, with those filed with him originally. More to the point for a penniless city government, an ordinance assessed an occupation tax upon everyone doing business of any sort. Enough money was collected to pay councilmen two dollars per meeting and to provide $300 for a city jail, promptly dubbed "Bastille de Cottonwood," because of its construction. The small police force survived on fines as did other officials.

The crude city was being stabilized in some respects but its people had too much of local interest to be concerned about, to realize enormity of a disaster at Johnstown, Pennsylvania, on May 31, where 2,200 lives were lost in a flood. The news trickled in here slowly over the clicking telegraph key at the depot and, in larger volume, through outside newspapers that came by train.

DENNIS T. FLYNN
*Territorial Delegate
to Congress*

SIDNEY CLARKE
*'89er and second
provisional mayor*

T. M. RICHARDSON
*Early banker,
lumberman, builder*

LEDRU GUTHRIE
*Provisional city
attorney following Run*

On June 5 another citizens' meeting was called. Its purpose was to secure an election of delegates to a convention which would prepare a charter defining powers of the city government. This was requested of the city council, which said it had a charter of its own prepared, although the council did name a charter committee friendly to its group. When presented, this document ratified all previous actions of the city government, but the issue never was put to a public vote.

The dissident Kickapoos then submitted their own idea of a charter, defining personnel and duties of city government, and calling upon the mayor and council to set an election on their proposal. Mayor Couch refused to call an election. The Kickapoos then declared they would hold an election, anyway, on September 21. Tension was building up but cooled somewhat September 17 when a congressional investigating committee came to town. A truce was called and both major factions joined in hosting the committee at a barbecue seven miles west of the city.

The feud resumed a few days later. An abortive move by the Kickapoos to get their charter voted failed when Mayor Couch and Chief of Police Charles F. Colcord, simply picked up ballot boxes at the two wards by direction of the council. That made proponents even more determined. They insisted upon elective action on their charter. Mayor Couch not only refused to call for a vote; he forbade any such action, and was upheld by military authorities passing word down to Captain Stiles that the elected government was to be upheld in its actions. Soldiers were marched to the proposed polling places and ordered crowds to disband. They were aided by two Kickapoo leaders, Captain A. B. Hammer and Judge J. H. Woods, who also pleaded for peace. Some Kickapoos were arrested but released. A few angry charter adherents demanded that Captain Stiles be court-martialed. His superiors at Fort Reno investigated and refused to bring charges.

Failure of the charter election marked the beginning of the end of provisional government. On November 11, Mayor Couch resigned and moved upon his claim west of town, in the vicinity of present May Avenue and Main streets, where he had a personal problem of his own regarding contested ownership. On April 14, 1890, Couch was shot by John C. Adams in an argument over the claim and died a week later. Colcord, who then also was a Deputy United States Marshal, arrested Adams and took him to Wichita for trial in federal court.

Sidney Clarke became acting mayor upon Couch's resignation and proclaimed an election to fill the office on November 27. The Kickapoos put up Doctor A. J. Beale, while by petition the Seminoles nominated Henry Overholser, one of their wheel horses and one of the great civic leaders of his time. Beale beat Overholser by fourteen votes. The two men were quite different in many aspects. Each in his own way made a bit of history.

Mayor Beale wasted no time issuing manifestoes. Immediately after his election a fresh wave of lot jumping took place. On December 14 the mayor gave a letter to the city council, telling it that the only title to lots was that of occupancy and that the right to ownership through certificates, denoted in an early ordinance, should be repealed and along with it the fee system for recording. Although the Kickapoos earlier had been able to put two men on the Seminole dominated council in J. E. Love and J. B. George, the council stood four to two against the mayor on the certificate question. He declared two of the Seminole seats vacant, those held by J. E. Jones and W. C. Wells, because they moved from their wards. Both men joined in a flaming letter saying if an election were held to replace them they would ignore it.

There also was a hot issue in filing town site plats, the six months interval from opening having transpired. Mayor Beale espoused the so-called Murray Plat, brought here by James Murray, Walter Holzaphel and others of the Oklahoma Colony Company. He opposed a compromise plat agreed to by the Seminoles and a major Citizens Group — as it was called — and to which many persons offered allegiance in matters political. The Murray Plat varied from the compromise. It had never been in effect. To apply it now would invalidate claims held during the half-year interval. It also would alter streets and blocks which most people considered variable enough. One of the most tempetuous times in the lusty young town was shaping up.

Upon appeals by some of the leaders, United States Marshal R. A. Walker of Kansas, who had jurisdiction over the Oklahoma District under authority of the United States Attorney General, forbade the election. Walker and his appointed deputies, Ransom Payne, a second cousin of Boomer David L. Payne, and Charles F. Colcord, were to take over the city and hold everything in status quo until the Congress could act on organizing a territorial government. This the marshals did for five months. That was the end of self-government in the pioneer town.

Some extravagant claims on population and kindred statistics made by persons who wrote chronicles of early day Oklahoma Station must be minimized, although it is quite certain that many of the people who found neither land, lots nor livelihood here, drifted away.

A survey made on June 14, 1889, by volunteers, was unearthed by Horace Thompson in 1959 when he was compiling a history of city government for Sheldon Stirling, then city manager. In the 1889 survey a door-to-door canvass was made. The town at that time was bounded by

A view of Grand Avenue, now Sheridan Avenue, as it was seen two years after the Run.

the Santa Fe railway on the east, Seventh Street on the north, Walker Street on the west, and Seventh Street on the south. It disclosed:

Men 2,681; women, 721; children, 736, for a total population of 4,138. There were 1,603 occupied dwellings, three water wells, no street surfacing, no sewers, no permanent sidewalks, certainly no parks.

As for businesses, this was the tally: groceries, thirty-four; drug stores, twenty-one; dry goods stores, twenty-eight; bakeries, ten; meat markets, fifteen; furniture stores, five; restaurants, thirty-seven; hotels, ten; boarding houses, twenty; barber shops, fourteen; banks, four, with deposits of $120,000; real estate firms, twenty-nine; physicians, fifty-three; dentists, two; newspapers, five; ice cream parlors, seven; laundries, eleven; livery stables, six; flour and feed stores, eleven; confectioners, twenty-one; lumber yards, twenty-seven; churches, eight; schools, one. (We must remember that some of these establishments were only what the proprietor said they were — that the census takers were volunteers — that some of the "business establishments" were almost of the handcart variety).

The Barber's Union got into action early, organizing on August 27, 1889, and declaring their prices so there would be no arguments about the finished job. They decreed that shaves would be fifteen cents, haircuts twenty-five cents, shampoos an equal amount, as was mustache dyeing.

Less than a month after the opening a Board of Trade was formed with Henry Overholser as president and James Geary as his first assistant. This was the predecessor of one of the nation's most unusual Chambers of Commerce, which will be described later. It marked an influence on the business community which was to dominate the city from its inception. That first Board of Trade sponsored the first convention in the unorganized territory in November 1889 when a Retail Lumber Dealers Association was organized.

There were other events also which cast long shadows over the future. One was location of a capital for the territory — and hopefully the state — which would come in time. Horace Speed proposed the idea of a capital for a provisional government, rather than local administrative arms. Guthrie was all for this because at that time it was four times as large as Oklahoma City, which immediately opposed such an idea. El Reno and Kingfisher were discussed but did not work very hard to secure the location, although Kingfisher did have its plans and boosters.

A long fight began which was to reach its climax years later in one of the frequently misinterpreted historical happenings. Guthrie citizens called for a "territorial" convention at Guthrie on July 17, 1889. A mass meeting at Oklahoma Station naturally opposed this and a committee was appointed to visit El Reno, Kingfisher and other towns to secure help in opposition to the Guthrie maneuver. They were successful. A meeting was called at Frisco, on July 15, to consolidate opposition to a joint provisional government. Even the Seminoles and Kickapoos got together on this. Frisco, now vanished, was about halfway between El Reno and Oklahoma Station, on the north bank of the North Canadian river. People from southern and western portions of the Unassigned Lands met at Frisco and effectively killed the movement — at that time. It would recur later.

To the ordinary citizen there were some consolations. Claims were not taxed, even by a temporary government, before they were proved up or sold. The autumn and winter of 1889 were mild, which helped those with inadequate shelter. Water supply was a nagging problem. There were many cases of malaria, through the summer, due to use of ditch and creek water and primitive sewage disposal. There were feeder creeks to the North Canadian in the principal inhabited area. The North Canadian was not in its present banks. It ran near Main Street where the Ford plant was later, along the south side of Main Street, then crossed northward near present Hudson Street, went east and crossed again southward near Robinson, and thence back southeast.

The interminable winds, quite a surprise to most of the newcomers that first year, brought sandstorms that filtered minute pellets into every form of living quarters and made outdoor cooking a problem. People didn't know it but this presaged a dry crop year coming up. Women who followed their men after the Run were perhaps not quite as enthusiastic about the new land as their husbands. This was, in many aspects, a primitive land, with primitive conditions. Mud frequently followed dust that first summer.

Former City Manager McRill partially summed up the early day city scene with a very apt title for his book: *And Satan Came Also*. Certainly along with the home and opportunity seekers, the religious minded, decent people, there were those who came to prey on their fellowmen. Homer Croy said it another way in his book on Deputy Marshal Chris Madsen, *Trigger Marshal*, when he wrote: "It was the old sheep and wolves story. If there were a few sheep there were only a few wolves. But if there were many sheep, then the wolves came on the run."

Vice conditions of the early days were just as much a factor of life in the town as any of its better attributes. To ignore that fact is poking one's head into sand of the Canadian. This was a wide open town. It had no formal law, no courts, no organized enforcement code or people to apply a substitute, except that which came from voluntary compliance; the

This building served as a hotel for Oklahoma Station and as a postoffice, beginning in 1887 — two years before the Run. Samuel A. Radebaugh was postmaster prior to Run.

efforts of a pair of Deputy United States Marshals, and presence of an infantry company whose mission simply was to keep the peace.

In addition to violence emanating from the saloons, gambling halls and bawdy houses, the very nature of disputes over lot and land claims led to assault and at times to homicide. The claim arguments by December, after the opening, created such a tense situation that Brigadier General Wesley Merritt at Fort Reno sent two troops of the Fifth Cavalry here for a time to back up Captain D. F. Stiles' infantrymen.

Broadway, from Main south to Grand Avenue, was called "Battle Row." On the west side of the street there were six buildings, five of which were saloons with gambling above, or in the basement. The City Hall later was on the second floor above Black and Rogers Liquor Dealers, at 13 North Broadway, about where urban renewal demolishing crews struck the later Wells-Roberts Hotel. After city offices shifted to the corner southward the Turf Club, striving for the title of "most infamous," moved in. On the east side, following the town's first saloon just below where the Lee Hotel, later Huckins, was built, there was the Vendome, the plushiest bawdy house in that area, and four saloons. From Broadway east to Front Street, later Santa Fe, and from Grand Avenue to California Street, was the quite properly named Hell's Half-Acre. The block on California had the additional enlightening name of Alabaster Row.

There were some notorious characters although through the transitional period many purveyors of assorted offerings left town. Some had the assistance of federal court at Wichita. Some went to the graveyard. A few were to linger around for years, such as John Burgess, operator of Two Johns Saloon by City Hall, when it moved to the northwest corner of Broadway and Grand. Most notorious of all was Mrs. Anne "Big Anne" Wynn, who came here from the wild mining towns of Colorado.

Here is Oklahoma City's Main Street, looking
west from Santa Fe, on June 18, 1889.

SAMUEL CROCKER
Boomer and Oklahoma
War Chief Editor

Born in Illinois in 1863 as one of a family of eighteen children, she went to Leadville at age seventeen and learned many things in seven years experience in the mining camps. She was intelligent, shrewd, a political strategist of the worst sort. She pitched her "Madame's" tent on Front Street the day of the opening and stocked it with females willing to provide companionship for the predominantly masculine population. Later she moved to an area on Northwest Second Street, near Walker, and for twenty years was a power in city politics. There was nothing in her dress or mannerisms to indicate the type of life from which she gained financial success. Stores were glad to get her patronage.

As it has been written, ". . . There is an immutable hunger in men. They want the love of a good woman. They want land to offer her as assurance of their earnesty, and, at last, when they have tried for those things — and particularly when they have no specific person in mind to whom to offer these gifts, they turn for relief of tension to women of the crib houses." In the main this early was a womanless society. Most of the rules of "decent society" were made by people who themselves were detached from that other society, in the sense that they were not alone, nor lacked for the amenities of standard and accepted familial living.

At year's end of 1889, collapse of the provisional government over a charter fight, factional division within the town and restraint provided only by an absentee federal government, represented primarily by the United States Marshal of Kansas, led to a major wave of assorted crimes. Deputy Marshal Charles Colcord had his hands full. Sometimes that was literal in the sense of a gun which he used seldom as a shooting tool, yet often found to be a good persuader. Mostly he made his point verbally and apparently without fear. Except for major street scenes requiring some of Captain Stiles' troops, Colcord was the law, until joined by Ransom Payne as another deputy. The two arrested thirty saloon keepers once in a ten-day period for lack of license.

Lot jumpers, held in some restraint by the citizens' groups before, took advantage of the muddled situation to get into action, illustrated by the case of one Eddie B. Townsend, who jumped a lot on Grand Avenue and was bounced off by friends of the other claimant. He sued and the case wound through Federal District Court at Wichita to the United States

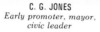

C. G. JONES
Early promoter, mayor, civic leader

The arrival of the morning train at the city's Santa Fe station on July 4, 1889.

Supreme Court, which made a decisive ruling that affected many other cases, leading eventually to the basic rule by which in 1891 a great many lot arguments were settled. That was to adhere — in lay language — to the dictum that "anyone who was in Oklahoma Country (the Unassigned Lands) at twelve noon on April 22, 1889, illegally, and claimed land, had no legal status." Townsend later used the same ruling by which he was dispossessed to challenge a claim filing of Alexander F. Smith, an employee of the Santa Fe Railroad, who filed on a claim near Edmond.

3

People and Public Affairs

WITH ALL ITS TURBULENT FOLLOWUP, the opening came too late in 1889 for crops to be planted by those intending to farm in the Unassigned Lands. In months following the end of April there were many seeds germinated of a business, civic and cultural nature that in time would be harvested. Not all of it would be beneficial.

Folk in the new town had to draw upon local newspapers and a few from outside to learn what was going on in their own locality and the broader world. The only way stories from other places could get here was by train mail or off the clicking telegraph key — with a Prince Albert tobacco can for a resonator — at the depot. (Radio did not come into limited usage until about 1921).

There were four dailies in Oklahoma (City) the first year following the opening. One was *The Oklahoma City Times* which had been published at Wichita, Kansas, by Hamlin W. Sawyer, beginning December 29, 1888 — bearing the name of a city that did not exist. The first paper actually published here was on May 9, 1889, when *The Oklahoma Times,* was printed in a tent by the brothers Angelo C. and Winfield W. Scott. For their second issue they changed its name to *The Oklahoma Journal,* a name picked up years later by W.P. "Bill" Atkinson at Midwest City.

The Scotts in September leased their paper to Elmer E. Brown and J.J. Burke, who later bought the *Journal,* then added the *Oklahoma City Times,* combining the masthead into the *Times-Journal.* Through a varied progression of ownership this paper continues to the present as the *Oklahoma City Times.* It is the oldest surviving paper, having been acquired at a sheriff's sale in 1916 by *The Daily Oklahoman.* The Browns retained the Times-Journal Publishing Company as a commercial plant.

Early in 1889 Reverend Sam Small, an itinerant evangelist and reformed drinker, started *The Daily Oklahoman.* Later it was sold to Roy Stafford, who in 1903 sold interests in the paper to Edward K. Gaylord, R.M. McClintock and Ray Dickinson. By 1917 the surviving partners were Gaylord and Dickinson. The latter in 1912 left the city for California but retained an interest for himself and his family. *The Oklahoman's* first location was on South Broadway, below Grand Avenue, then at California and Robinson, where its plant was destroyed by fire. In 1909 it moved to the corner of Broadway and Northwest Fourth Street.

In contrast to the earlier opinion of Richard Harding Davis, Gaylord, who first visited here late in 1902, found, as he recalled much

24

Oklahoma City's third post office, dedicated July 4, 1890, had financial assistance from the Oklahoma City Masonic bodies, which used the third floor for their functions.

later: "The hastily built town of Oklahoma City was crude and uninspiring, but its possibilities as the metropolis of a future state intrigued the imagination." So he bought into *The Oklahoman* with funds from sale of an interest in a Colorado Springs paper and from savings. Seventy-two years later he remained actively at its helm and was head of one of the state's major diversified companies, of which the continuously surviving early day newspaper remains the parent.

Early that first year Frank McMasters started *The Evening Gazette*. McMasters was a staunch believer in "personal journalism." He used livid, at times florid language, in his front page editorials, but so did "Ham" Sawyer of the *Times*, which in town matters usually supported the Kickapoo faction. For that matter, personalized journalism, as it had been since the *Cherokee Advocate* of 1844, transplanted from the *Cherokee Phoenix* of Georgia over the Trail of Tears, was a characteristic of the American West.

There were other papers, too, such as *The Oklahoma Chief* of R.W. McAdams. Charles F. Barrett, later long time adjutant general of the state, edited *The Oklahoma City Press*. There were minor, struggling papers from time to time, espousing the Populist and Socialist causes, with Oscar Ameringer later earning more of a national reputation for brilliantly supporting Socialist philosophy than he ever gained at home, until the wave of Socialism reached its crest and receded in 1916 as a political movement. It almost put Ameringer into the mayor's chair at one point.

The first marriage took place May 16, 1889, between Mary Moore, of Peru, Indiana, and a W. Wilkenson of Bell Plaine, Kansas, with the

Reverend James Murray officiating. The first club of which we have record was the Ladies Relief Club, organized July 17 in the home of Mrs. D.W. Gibbs, for the laudable purpose of supplying organized help to those people in need. The first public social event is said to have been a dance, sponsored by the Ladies Relief Club as a money raising venture. It was held in August at the home of a Captain Sommers, a sutler providing quartermaster supplies to the post at Fort Sill and to the army's Indian Department.

On May 19, just twenty-seven days after the opening, the first child was born here. She was named Oklahoma Belle and was the daughter of Mr. and Mrs. Jefferson W. Cunningham, of Taylor, Texas. They lived at 324 Northwest Third Street. Cunningham later built a three-story brick building on the future post office site. Oklahoma Belle married L.L. Cheever on May 15, 1912, and in 1973 was still active here in the floral business.

There were some independent souls among women attracted here who found a way to make a little income. One was a "button woman," who made a precarious living sewing buttons on clothes of the nominally masculine dominated society. She had a large purse slung by a shoulder strap — far ahead of the Women's Army Corps of War II or the western leather workers of our time — in which she carried all manner of buttons. She would stop any male with an obviously missing button and offer to sew one on immediately for five cents.

Another woman, G. E. "Jack" Massey once said, antedated Annie Oakley's early exploits by shooting wild game and selling it to the meat markets. There were more than thirty at the time that displayed game outside their shops, complete with hide or feathers, with gutting the only processing provided.

There was work for males in the "have not" category, meaning neither a profession nor means of subsistence while trying to prove a claim — or who had none — in the early months.

Arthur W. Dunham of the Santa Fe said that at times there were up to 150 cars a day on sidings or backed up along the line. Freighters went both west and east as this became a growing distribution point.

Without doubt one of the busiest men of all was Henry Overholser, in his own commercial activities and in all civic efforts, for he combined a business sense with a pride in the city's future. He came in on the first train from the north. At that time he had a grown son in Wisconsin (Ed, who later was to make his mark indelibly on the town, too) and a married daughter near El Dorado, Kansas, where his divorced wife lived. Overholser was nearly fifty years old at the time he came here. Thirty of those years had been spent in diversified businesses with financial success. A few days after the opening the Santa Fe brought in several cars of building material in prefabricated condition, with which he was to erect eight, two-story buildings with commercial establishments below and offices or living quarters above. He acquired eight lots from others on Grand Avenue, just west of Robinson, on part of which later the Colcord Building, the city's first "skyscraper" of twelve stories, would stand.

Henry Overholser, as Doctor Scott said, "kept building in the early years when others stopped. He built a dwelling far away from the nearest habitation, too extravagant for his own needs, but he wanted to set an example of city dwellings, not those of a small, crude town. He was involved also in the cultural side of life. He built the Overholser Opera House, where under his son's management such actresses as Sarah Bernhardt, Maude Adams and Olga Nethersole came, with celebrities from the symphony world. He ushered in the 'age of brick' to the city, 'saved' the Oklahoma State Fair, and piloted Oklahoma City later through its darkest hours."

Another dominant figure in early years was C. G. "Gristmill" Jones, a person of enthusiasm for any sort of promotion. The nickname came from his milling. Jones conceived the first grandiose community project undertaken in the winter of 1889-1890. A canal was dug connecting a stream with the North Canadian river, which was intended to move barge traffic and to provide power for Jones' flour mill and for the town. Hundreds of men needing jobs found them that mild winter. The canal was slightly more than six miles long, taking advantage of a minimum fall of thirty-two feet. Unfortunately the sandy soil would not hold water. Citizens who had subscribed funds for the venture tried for six months to solidify banks and bottom of the channel to no avail. McRill later called "the Grand Canal a Grand Illusion." (In our times contractors on the downtown Mummer's Theater, and an apartment building at Northwest Fifth and Hudson, learned something of tricky sands in sub-strata along old creek beds).

Charles F. Colcord drove in for the opening, after an adventurous early life on the regional plains, and traded his team and wagon for Lot 1, Block 1, on Reno street near the tracks, to George Patrick, another native Kentuckian. Colcord later sold the lot, on which he was living in a shanty, to A. M. DeBolt for $450. With that he bought two lots just north of Fourth

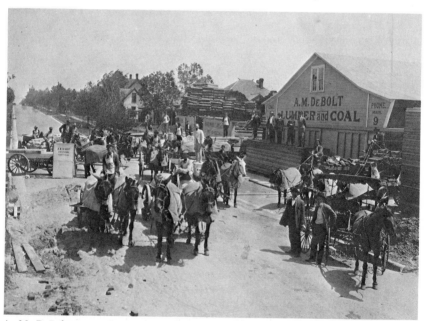

A. M. DeBolt operated this lumber and coal company around the turn of the century.

ANGELO C. SCOTT
*First newspaper
publisher; educator*

DAN W. PEERY
*Territorial legislator
and historian*

H. G. TROSPER
*Original
Territorial legislator*

OSCAR G. LEE
*Hotel builder and
land developer*

Street on Broadway. He built a frame house there and lived in it for four years. He was the first chief of police under provisional government, the first sheriff after organization of the county under the Organic Act of May 1890, and was a fearless United States Deputy Marshal most of the early years. He made the Run into the Cherokee Outlet in 1893 and was one of the early "laws" in Perry, where he homesteaded. He made a fortune later when the vast Glenn Pool was opened in East Central Oklahoma.

Sidney Clarke, after a distinguished political record in Kansas and in the Congress, was one of the most able peacemakers during the townsite arguments. He worked closely with Henry Overholser and C. G. Jones in securing railroad connections, east and west. Clarke was a prime mover in the statehood fight, served in the Territorial Council (Senate) and was twice its president.

A "first bank" was opened May 30, 1889, at the southeast corner of Main and Broadway, with James Geary, a former associate of Buffalo Bill Cody, as president, and L. A. Gilbert as cashier. "Kid" Bannister always claimed that he had the first "bank" in Oklahoma City, but that was a faro bank, on Santa Fe south of Grand Avenue. He was to be a disreputable character around here for fourteen years before being shot fatally at the Turf Club. This was at 12-plus-1 North Broadway, after superstitious gamblers took over 13 North Broadway, which was the second City Hall. Geary sold his bank interest in July 1892 to Captain Stiles, and others, and went into real estate.

But there was another claimant for "first bank" recognition. This was T. M. Richardson, who said he opened a "bank" from the rear of a covered wagon, within hours after the opening April 22. Richardson sent several freight cars of lumber to sidings ahead of the Run. His lumber yard shifted from the wagon position, after the first flurry of sales, to the corner of Grand and Harvey. With George T. Reynolds and J. P. Boyle, Richardson did start the second bank, The First National, a few days after the Citizens Bank opened. The men paid $300 for a lot on Main Street, the south side, just west of Broadway. The bank failed a year or so later, then James Wilkins and Ed Cooke bought it from the United States receiver, reorganized it as the State National. That name was used for thirty years before it again became The First National Bank.

J. B. Wheeler and his son, James, with Eugene Wallace, organized

Looking north from Broadway and Grand, we watch an Oklahoma City parade of 1893.

The Wheeler Bank, which failed in 1905. Robert Kincaid, a railroad man and banker, with John Wallace, organized The Bank of Oklahoma City at the southwest corner of Grand and Robinson, which later became the Farmer's National Bank. This was in a two-story frame house, lower floor, with living quarters upstairs. (Another account called this The Bank of Commerce). Wheeler later gave the city forty-four acres of land for Wheeler Park. This was home of the first zoo.

Doctor J. B. Rolater, from Georgia, and with a medical degree earned in 1884, made the Run from the South Canadian. He continued riding a horse in his general practice. In fact, in a downtown parade on a Run anniversary in 1926, he rode horseback wearing the same coat, using the same saddle and carrying the same saddlebags that he used in those early days. Later he was chief surgeon for the Rock Island Lines and for the telephone company. He founded Rolater Hospital at 324 Northeast Fourth Street, which for a time later was used as a teaching hospital for the infant University of Oklahoma Medical School.

C. W. McQuown, a telegraph operator for the Santa Fe, acquired lots at the southwest corner of Northwest Third and Harvey, where the Oklahoma Gas & Electric Company is now. He had a basement room in the house he built there, where he indulged his hobby of taxidermy, mounting then plentiful specimens of native animals and birds.

M. L. Nix bought two lots at the Northeast corner of Second and Harvey Streets, later claiming the honor of building the first two-story house in the city. He was a contractor and builder and did several Main Street jobs, including the Pettee Hardware Store building. His son, Oscar V. Nix, managed the Overholser Opera House for a time. A daughter, later Mrs. E. G. Remmers, taught in the first public school.

James L. Wyatt, a Kentuckian who made the Run from the Kansas side, started what later was the Crescent Market. He sold many provisions to Indians who visited the town from the east, and bought wild game from them to sell to meat hungry whites, including deer, turkey,

Fruit companies in Oklahoma City depended upon wagon delivery to customers in 1906.

quail, rabbit and prairie chicken. Wyatt's store, built from material purchased from Richardson on a lot for which he paid $300, was on the south side of Main Sreet, between Robinson and Harvey, in an eighteen by twenty-four foot building. An oddity was that Wyatt traded a carpenter a horse to erect the building, then hired himself to the contractor for $1.50 a day as a carpenter's helper. He had $65 left to start his grocery when he moved in. He lived in rear of the store. Later Wyatt built the first unit of what became the sprawling John A. Brown Dry Goods Company.

Wichita had a short lived real estate boom in 1887, with town lots changing hands so rapidly with increasing prices and with so many small homes being built, that Marcellus Murdock, editor of the *Wichita Eagle,*

A parade in Oklahoma City in 1910 moves north on No. Broadway from Grand.

The home of Charles Colcord when it was a country estate on N.W. 13th

predicted in large print that the boom would not last. It didn't, as Charles Colcord and his father learned, but Boston Wilson took advantage of depressed house prices at Wichita and moved some two-story houses here, dismantled, on railroad flat cars.

Will and George Hale also were serving needs of the day with a wagon yard, and horse and mule market on Main Street, east of Broadway.

Isaac Lowenstein came here on May 1, 1889, and bought a lot and three-room frame house for $225 from a woman whose "rights" were protected by two brawny males. The house was between the Coney Island Saloon and the Star Meat Market, which used its back yard for sausage and lard making, providing an aroma that was noticeable. This was offset, partially, by strains of harp music coming from the saloon where Pedro Lapitino, an itinerant Italian harpist, was a featured attraction. But Pedro couldn't stay away from the gaming tables and one day Wally Long, a barber, turned up as owner of the harp. The Lowenstein family acquired the Majestic Theater on Grand Avenue in 1914, which was built in 1909 as the first "twenty-four hour construction job" in the city. Morris Lowenstein started school in a one-room affair in the 100 block of West California and finished Irving High School in 1905.

Meanwhile, not everyone was interested in the downtown area. Dan W. Peery, later a long time official and historian, made the Run from the Pottawatomie Indian reservation, to the east, and homesteaded about fifteen miles southeast of the city on Crutcho Creek.

There were folk such as David M. Carlton, of Indiana, then forty-six, who served four years in the Union Army and had a damaged left arm. He was living at Wichita before the Run. He settled on high ground about two and one-half miles northeast of Oklahoma Station, north of the present capitol building, built a twelve by fourteen foot shack and started cultivating. Within a year he had sixty acres under plow and 300 fruit trees planted. Because he was a Union veteran he could prove up his claim in three years instead of five. So he sold out and went homesteading again in North Dakota. Part of his homestead here later became site of the rather appropriately named "89'er Inn." It was sold in 1973 to Rodeway Inns.

Many people lived in half-dugouts those early days, particularly on farms surrounding the town, but some were even inside the indistinct city limits. If there was some slope digging was not difficult. Lumber was hard to come by for many families. Turf cut in blocks, or thatch, made the roof covering.

This could be a fire hazard as the Swateks learned. Frank Swatek Senior, and his son, Mike A., came from Nebraska to make the Run. They paused briefly near Kingfisher, then near where Wheatland is now, southwest of the city. They first built a ten by twelve foot shack for each, then in 1890 Frank had a half-dugout on a creek bank, covered with grass and thatch. He got burned out about a month later because of a faulty stovepipe. The family lived in a brush arbor during that summer then built a two-room frame house to hold the parents and five children. Game provided the table meat.

A big social event of the year was a visit by Representative William M. Springer of Illinois, author of the rider by which the Unassigned Lands were opened to settlement, who wanted to see what he had caused. He was reported to be quite pleased with the result.

A tragedy for the community happened on the first July Fourth. Bleachers were erected on the military reservation for spectators to view horse and foot races, a baseball game and Indian dances. The stands collapsed and killed a young girl of the Ryan family.

After the opening, G. A. Beidler was postmaster. He used for his office a shack made of logs, with labor provided by the military, since this was government property. Long before the days of home delivery — or even rented boxes — people would gather at the post office after trains came in to seek mail. Beidler would sort the mail by surnames, listed alphabetically, and call out in such fashion as: "All you K's line up."

First building of St. Anthony's Hospital, built in 1903 at N.W. Ninth and Lee.

A gathering at First Methodist Church at present site — N.W. Fourth and Robinson.

The first Sunday after the opening six days before, Private Joseph Perringer, an infantry bugler, walked about the downtown area tooting "Church Call." This meant little to most of the hearers but, as in the case of the Pied Piper, they followed him to see what this was all about. Under sponsorship of the Methodist Episcopal Church and the Methodist Episcopal Church, South, a union service was held in the 100 block of Northwest Third Street. Reverend James Murray, in other activities a leader of the Kickapoo faction, preached a sermon on lots staked out by W. P. Shaw of Missouri. Shaw was a lay preacher and a giant of a man, who intended his lots to be for religious use. Reverend Charles Hembree of the Presbyterian faith had a street service at Main and Broadway.

Murray was a former superintendent of missions in Indian Territory, and in parlance of the times, a Yankee. This soon caused the two versions of the Methodist denomination to go separate ways, for Shaw represented the South branch. The Southerners organized about June 1 with Reverend I. L. Burrow in charge, and Reverend A. J. Worley took over as pastor September 1. They built an arbor type meeting place at Northwest Third and Robinson, "The Tabernacle," and later had a brick building there. The name was changed to St. Luke's Methodist Episcopal Church, South. In 1908 this church moved to Northwest Eighth and Robinson where it remained for forty-four years, before as the world's third largest United Methodist Church, it located at Northwest Fifteenth and Harvey in 1950. This initially $500,000 edifice was a far distance, as indicated by the times, from "The Tabernacle," which was boarded up on the street side, had a dirt floor, while pew seats were board laid atop beer kegs.

On May 5, 1889, a Methodist Sunday School was organized by Doctor D. W. Scott, a local minister from Hutchinson, Kansas, assisted by Postmaster Beidler, and others. They first used an unfinished building being erected for a post office on Main Street, near Santa Fe. Scott was superintendent and Ed C. Rixse was secretary.

June 23, the First Methodist Episcopal Church Society was organized by Reverend Murray with seventeen charter members. They pur-

St. Luke's Methodist Church was on the corner of N.W. Eighth and Robinson 44 years. *A view of First Methodist Church when N.W. Fourth and Robinson was a residence area.*

chased two lots at Northwest Fourth and Robinson for $500. A shack on the rear was used for a parsonage. The first building was completed in October. There were 500 people at the dedication, the *Oklahoma City Gazette* of October 28 said, in a building intended for a congregation of 300 persons. Those in attendance represented many creeds since so few churches existed.

The first Catholic service was on May 19 at Indiana House, on Main Street between Robinson and Harvey. A temporary organization was formed of fifty-five heads of families and forty-two single men. The group was headed by J. P. Martin, as chairman; Joseph Chrisney, secretary; Colonel J. T. Hickey as treasurer, and Father N. F. Scallan as director and principal architect. The chosen name: St. Joseph's. The first church at the corner of Northwest Fourth and Harvey was built largely by members. Many non-Catholics aided for that was the spirit of the times. The cross was raised on the spire on July 31, the bell hung in the tower on August 2, with the first Angelus that afternoon at six o'clock.

First endeavor of the Baptists was a call by W. H. Tompkins and L. H. North, through newspapers, for people interested in forming a church of that persuasion. They met July 21 in a hall above Winningham Brothers Hardware Store, at 123 West Grand. Formal organization did not come until November 2, with eleven charter members, including eight women and three men, all married except one woman. Officers were elected November 16. The deacons were North and Kendall Elder; trustees were I. N. Phillips, F. V. Brandom and T. M. Richardson; Tompkins was treasurer and North the clerk. They met in various buildings until their first frame structure was built early in 1890 at 115 Northwest Second Street. It was destroyed by fire in 1906. For seven months prayer meetings were held in the First Presbyterian Church, and Sunday services in the Overholser Opera House, with a few at the First Methodist Church. September 23, 1906, the Baptists moved to the northeast corner of Northwest Third and Broadway, and in 1912 to Northwest Eleventh and North Robinson.

After his initial street service the first Sunday after the Run, Reverend C. C. Hembree set about organizing the Presbyterians. He was the first minister, preaching until September, when he moved to Norman and was succeeded by Reverend W. L. Miller from the Home Missions Board. The congregation met in various places until April of 1890, when it went to a former store building at Grand and Harvey. Formal organization was

This First Presbyterian Church building at N.W. 25 and Western, completed in late 1950s.

in December, 1889, however, with election of Will Young, J. D. Brough and J. Downie as elders. Trustees were Doctor A. C. Scott (Ph.D.); Doctor H. Davis (M.D.), Henry Overholser, J. C. Anderson, a Mister Banks and a Captain Givens.

The First Christian Church (Disciples of Christ) grew from a street meeting, with the location given by one source as the corner of Main and Broadway and by another as Northwest First and Harvey, with Reverend T. J. Head officiating. There were ten persons signed up as charter members. They included Mr. and Mrs. G. H. Newey, Mr. and Mrs. C. A. Galbreath, Mrs. J. T. Newell, C. O. Sewell, J. H. Everest, Z. T. Wright and Mrs. C. H. Keller.

They met first in a small frame building on the northwest corner of Northwest First and Harvey. Later they paid $150 for a building there on what became part of the Frisco passenger station grounds. At various times they met in the YMCA building, at 225 West Reno Avenue, even in a former tavern at 301 Northwest First Street, then at Cuppey's Hall at 208 North Broadway. The first "permanent" home was where the Federal Reserve Bank stands now, in a brick building with stained glass and a bell tower, dedicated in December 1894. Then there was shift in 1903 to the southeast corner of Northwest Third and Robinson, later occupied by the Braniff building, in a fine structure used until December of 1911. Next came the building at Northwest Tenth and Robinson where they remained until the mid-1950's, before going to the "Church of Tomorrow" at North-west Thirty-sixth and Walker. The edifice at Northwest Tenth and Robinson became home of the Central Christian Church. Now it is Central City Baptist Church.

Two other religious bodies which had their roots in the Alexander Campbell movement have played a strong role in Oklahoma City's religious community, and both have established colleges in Oklahoma City.

There are thirty-seven Churches of Christ in the Oklahoma City area. Affiliated with the churches is Oklahoma Christian College on the north side of Memorial Road, about one-fourth mile east of Eastern. It organized as Central Christian College in Bartlesville in 1950, and was moved to Oklahoma City in 1958. It opened in Oklahoma City with 200 students, and enrollment has grown to approximately 1,200. The college has been a pioneer in the development of the use of electronic media in teaching and in 1966, when its library-learning center was completed, it rated a full page picture story in *Time Magazine.* Several thousand educators have visited the center, coming from all states and many countries. Externally Oklahoma Christian College is well known for its Citizenship Center, keyed to high school students, operating in Oklahoma, Texas and Kansas, and for its oral history program, now affiliated with the Oklahoma Historical Society. Oklahoma Christian College is also the hub of religious activity for Churches of Christ in Oklahoma.

Also rooted in the Alexander Campbell movement are the In-dependent Christian churches. In Oklahoma City these churches had their beginning with a mission group which organized in 1909 at 500 West Chick-asaw. It met in borrowed and rented locations and without a church name until 1929, when it moved to California and Shartel and became the Central Christian Church. It is now at 2627 Southwest Thirty-first. There are now nine Independent Christian Churches in Oklahoma City.

Affiliated with the church is Midwest Christian College on the northeast corner of Northeast Sixty-third and Kelley. The college was

The First Christian Church at N.W. 10 and Robinson cost $140,000 when built in 1910.

Rolater Hospital, first in the city, on the northwest corner of Fourth and Walnut.

A campus scene at Oklahoma Christian College on N.E. Memorial Road east of N. Eastern.

A drawing of South Oklahoma City Junior College, largely underground, at 77 and South May.

A view of the Student Center of the Oklahoma City Southwestern College at 4700 N.W. 10.

The administration-classroom building of Midwest Christian College at N.E. 63 and Kelley.

organized in 1947 at Northwest Twenty-sixth and McKinley. In 1952 it purchased the former W. T. Hales estate, and has since added classrooms and other facilities. The college is scheduled to begin construction of a learning center and gymnasium in the summer of 1974. Midwest Christian College has 200 students and grants a bachelor's degree in the ministry and fields related to the church.

Pilgrim Congregational Church, of the early denominations organized here, was formed in November after the Run, in the parlor of Mrs. Brown's Boarding House at the northwest corner of Hudson and California. Later the group met at Fulsom Hall, over a building on West Main. Official recognition from the national order came on March 2, 1890. While the first frame building was under construction at Noble and Harvey, meetings were held in A. H. Denny's Feed Store, at Washington and Harvey. In 1905 the frame structure was torn down and a brick building replaced it, after using the original since April 30, 1890. In 1924 this building became the property of St. Mark's Methodist Church.

There had been changes at work since 1914. Members of the Pilgrim Congregational Church merged with the Harrison Avenue Church, started in 1900, and continued as Pilgrim Congregational at Northwest Thirteenth and Classen Drive. Founders included Mr. an Mrs. James M. McCornack, Mr. and Mrs. William Lewis, Mrs. Martha C. North, Mr. and Mrs. C. A. McNabb, and Mr. and Mrs. P. G. Burns. McCornak and Lewis previously had been Presbyterians.

Oklahoma Country's first Jewish settlers came in the Run of '89. Most of them first settled in Guthrie but a number came here. By 1890 there were several families in the new town but it was 1902 before they held regular religious services. These were in the old Huckins Estate Building, in a second floor room. Soon membership increased to twenty-two persons. A move was made then to 119 West Grand Avenue, where people of Jewish faith met for two years. Children were taught Hebrew there, also. On a donated bit of land at West Reno and Dewey Streets the first synagogue was built and dedicated in 1904 as Congregation Emmanuel. Another synagogue was built in 1917 and a community center in 1931.

Early in 1903 the Temple B'Nai Israel was formed. Its first meetings were in the First Christian Church in May. Rabbi Joseph Blatt came here from Columbus, Georgia, in 1906 to head the Temple. A building was begun in mid-1907 and dedicated the next year.

The first real social life of this new city centered in its churches, even if a popular thing that first summer was gathering in D. W. Gibbs' ice cream parlor, where one could hear his daughter, Frances, play the first piano brought to the town.

Not all was sunbonnets and gingham gowns for the ladies. The early period saw social life emerge, especially among those who could afford the time and had the means, and there were many. Women wore new styles in good materials — as late as the mails and catalogues could bring them — with black velvet a popular cloth for dress-up affairs. Dust ruffles were of taffeta, three to eight inches wide, sewed to hems of dresses. Skirts were about three inches off the ground for street wear and touched the floor, or had a train, for more formal attire.

The ladies of society wore high busted corsets tightened to give them a small waist. Often they had bustles on the rear to add a stylish conformation, over many petticoats. They effected long sleeves and high collars for more sedate wear, usually had large buttons for trim, and wore all sizes of hats although large ones predominated. Often hats were decorated with feathers. Women wore high topped shoes, laced or buttoned, with sharply pointed toes. The outer wear, in season, usually was a swirling cape, dark trimmed. The others might even have gossipped about Mrs. Henry Overholser's party costume at one large function. It was an original creation by Worth of Paris.

The modernistic First Christian Church at N.W. 36 and Walker, was completed in 1956.

4

School Bells Ring — And Ring

SCHOOLS FOR CHILDREN WERE A CONCERN of parents. No provision for publicly supported schools was made in the authorization for opening Oklahoma Country, any more than it provided for organization and means of support for a provisional government. But the people were not without schools. There were subscription schools from soon after the opening until May of 1890. Mrs. L. H. North started one in a tent about a month after the opening, with a number of pupils, variously estimated from twenty to seventy by different accounts. There were no desks. Boards on nail kegs formed the seats. Fees ranged from $1.50 per month upward, depending upon ability to pay and the grade level students were said, or presumed, to hold.

Miss Jenny McKeever, later Mrs. Fred Sutton, started a subscription school in the rear of a building on First street, between Broadway and Robinson. The front room was used to store machinery. There were twenty-five dollars worth of chairs, benches and a stove, for autumn was coming on. She took the lower grades. Professor Frederick H. Umholtz had the higher grades. Between them they laid a foundation for the elementary system to follow with publicly supported schools. During the summer Mrs. Lucy E. Twyford gathered her neighbors' children and instructed them in the shade of blackjack trees. Also in September, Miss Alice Biteman, later Mrs. A. S. Haney, opened a young ladies seminary.

It was February 1891 before public schools were opened. Doctor Delos Walker was president of the first board and Major D. D. Leach was secretary. Professor R. A. Sullins was superintendent, with eighteen teachers, who were paid in scrip worth from eighty to eight-five cents to the dollar face value. It was not until 1894 that Congress gave the town "Military Hill" east of the Santa Fe tracks for aid of the school fund. Sale of those lots helped build the first two schools, Washington and Emerson.

It was only after the Organic Act of 1890 that general support for elementary and secondary schools in the territory was assured, by reservation of sections sixteen and thirty-six of each township for school support. This was the foundation of the continuing State School Land Commission. For Oklahoma Territory Congress appropriated initially $50,000 for schools, with teachers' salaries set at twenty-five, thirty, or thirty-five dollars per month, according to the grade taught.

A school code was compiled by President T. H. Thacker of the State Normal School at Edmond, and adopted by the territorial legislature.

The first elementary public schools here were in rented buildings.

Most of the children in Ward One were in a building at Northwest Fourth and Broadway; Ward Two students were in a former dry goods store in the Wolfe Building at Main and Broadway; Ward Three pupils were in Robby's Hall on California, near Broadway; Ward Four's younger students were in a building on California between Broadway and Santa Fe. The school superintendent taught older pupils in a storeroom on Northwest First street.

Public schools opened on March 1, 1890. There was so much enthusiasm at this indication of culture that, although there was a fairly heavy snowfall that day, almost 1,000 children marched around town when school was dismissed. The first school bond issue for building purposes was voted June 15, 1893, but bonds were not issued because of doubt over legality of the issue. In February the next year the district court ruled that only $45,000 of the $70,000 voted could be used. That amount of bonds was issued and preparations made to construct a school building in each ward. The first two constructed and furnished cost $44,000. A high school was completed in time for opening of school in September 1896. Later this building, known as Irving, served as a temporary capitol for the state. It burned in 1937.

During the first year of public schools, grades at the secondary level were taught in a former military barracks, where Mrs. Selwyn Douglas was principal. Athletics were whatever youths wanted to do voluntarily but each of them had to belong to a literary society and take part in its programs.

The first high school graduating class had six members and graduation exercises were held in the Overholser Opera House. After 1900 grade school construction was almost an annual project for a decade, at least. In 1910 grade school children were moved to different sections of town and the Oklahoma City High School, later Central, had its first unit built. It was then, and is today, an outstanding example of ornate stone trim in somewhat classical design.

From its beginning, and under state law typical of southern oriented states, Oklahoma had segregated schools for whites and blacks until the landmark 1954 United States Supreme Court decision. (Brown vs. Board of Education). The principle of "separate but equal" facilities applied. Oklahoma City had done a better job than some cities in making that "equal" bit more than a catch word, although the extent was debatable. The most controversial experience in school history was not far away.

In October, 1961, Doctor Alfonso L. Dowell, an Oklahoma City optometrist living in a suburban, dependent school district whose pupils attended Oklahoma City high-schools after their eighth year, contested the assignment of his son, Robert, to Douglass High School. White students from that suburban district were then being assigned to Northeast High School. No blacks attended Northeast at that time. No whites attended Douglass. A school policy existed permitting transfer from a school already assigned if a needed course was not offered at the assigned school. Robert Dowell sought the transfer because of an electronics course not offered at Douglass but available at Northeast.

Before the issue was settled, Doctor Dowell filed a federal suit for

Oklahoma City High School was complete in 1910 at N.W. Eighth and Robinson Ave.

desegregation against the Oklahoma City Public Schools, alleging racial discrimination and a quota system in making pupil assignments. That case continued and is the basic litigation on which all desegregation court orders for Oklahoma City Public Schools has been issued. Young Dowell enrolled at Bishop McGuiness Catholic High School and completed his education long before the case was completed.

In 1963 Luther Bohanon, United States District Judge, ordered full desegregation by the fall term. Oklahoma City's Board of Education outlined a long-range desegregation policy in 1964 which Judge Bohanon declined to approve, or disapprove, asking instead that the board appoint a panel of experts to come up with a long range plan of implementation. The board declined to delegate such authority. Consequently a three-member team, nominated by Dowell and his attorney, was appointed by the court. The team was to submit a plan for school desegregation in Oklahoma City. It was submitted, approved by the District Court, contested by the Board of Education at the Tenth Circuit Court of Appeals in Denver, and then before the United States Supreme Court.

In June 1967, with appeals exhausted, Doctor Bill Lillard, superintendent, was ordered to present to the court a plan for implementing the desegregation plan prepared by the three-man panel nominated by Dowell and his attorney.

Their plan called for pairing of four seventh to twelfth grade, junior-senior high schools (Harding, Northeast, Classen and Central) making two schools into three-year high schools, and two into three-year junior high schools, with the junior high schools feeding into the high schools. Their plan called also for faculty desegregation in all schools to provide a black-white ratio in each school, approximately the same as the black-white ratio, district wide. Their plan called also for a majority — to — minority transfer policy, permitting any student who attended school in a building where his race was in the majority, to transfer to one where his race would be in the minority.

School Board Officials determined that Northeast would become the high school and Harding the junior high for that one attendance area pairing those schools. Because of shifting population Northeast by then had become about ninety percent black enrollment. Classen was to become the high school, Central the junior high for that paired attendance area. Central had become predominantly black in enrollment. Controversy erupted over whether the pairing should be accomplished in one year or over two years. The board suggested a two year phasing, not affecting seniors the first year. The court agreed.

In later court hearings, white parents in the affected schools prevailed upon the court to widen the attendance area of Northeast-Harding to include other white pupils from other schools to more nearly approach the seventy-to-thirty percent ratio. Residents in newly affected areas created opposition to inclusion in the pairing. Pupils from Northwest, Taft, John Marshall, Hoover and Eisenhower, suddenly found themselves assigned to Harding and Northeast. They appealed to the Circuit Court in Denver. On a Wednesday, the week before school was to begin the following Tuesday, the appellate court ruled in their favor, nullifying assignment to Harding and Northeast, after some pupils had begun working out with the Northeast football team, or gone through school elections. Three days later, on Friday before school opening on Tuesday, a United States Supreme Court justice overruled the appellate court. A year later that ruling, too, was reversed, though students then were given the option to continue at their newly assigned school or to return to their previous attendance area.

One family affected by the shifting order was that of Mr. and Mrs. Ray York whose oldest son was assigned from Taft to Harding. The younger Ray continued attending Taft, listing an address other than that of the family home. The address was determined to be illegal and the family became involved in a federal court case which eventually resulted in a fine against the Yorks. The case gained considerable notoriety when federal marshals eventually were forced to remove Ray York from Taft to force compliance with the court's order.

Thus began Oklahoma City's efforts to fully desegregate the Oklahoma City schools additionally through voluntary measures. The so-called "cluster-plan" was an effort to desegregate high schools. Four northside city schools formed a north cluster. Four southside schools formed a south cluster. Each cluster contained a school with predominantly black enrollment. The black schools were designated a science center for all advanced science subjects taught in the cluster. All advanced math subjects were removed from the "black" high schools. Students from those schools wishing to take advanced math had to enroll at one of the other three schools in their cluster. This was designed to encourage racial mixing in all high schools. Special time blocks were designated so students could attend classes away from their home school twice weekly, for approximately two and one-half hours each time. No student would be required to take such advanced classes in order to graduate. It was hoped an incentive for taking advanced math or science would be great enough to entice participation. Some language classes and other special offerings also were added as cluster courses. But any student could complete basic graduation requirements without leaving his home school.

Junior high school desegregation was to be accomplished by offering special "exchange" programs, in which black students from schools predominantly black, would visit and participate with those in schools predominantly white, and vice versa.

The "Opening Doors" program was designed to desegregate elementary schools. Again, clusters of elementary schools were selected so that within a cluster the student body of all schools would contain about twenty percent black and eighty percent white pupil enrollment — though there was some variation among these clusters. Special programs were planned to give youngsters from these schools special educational benefits involving cultural resources within the community.

Plaintiffs in the case, Doctor Dowell as a matter of record but the NAACP as a matter of fact, argued that this was not enough. They sought further desegregation. The court appointed a two-member panel of expert consultants to plan it. They recommended modifications to make the cluster plan mandatory by adding required subjects as cluster courses, extending the cluster concept to junior high schools, and expanding the "opening doors" to a once-a-week special "interaction" centers approach for elementary pupils.

Then the plaintiffs (the NAACP) asked to bring in their own expert consultant to present a plan and the court agreed. The NAACP employed Doctor John Finger, a Rhode Island professor who had been consultant for the NAACP in the Charlotte-Mecklenburg (North Carolina) public school case which had been approved by the United States Supreme Court. He evolved what has become known as the "Finger Plan." Utilizing essentially the same schools that had formed the elementary clusters for the "opening doors" program —with its eighty-to-twenty, white-to-black enrollment ratio, Doctor Finger formed his elementary plan. Within these sixteen clusters he designated the predominantly black school as a "fifth-year center" housing the fifth year program for all students in that cluster. Black students in first, second, third and fourth year programs were to be apportioned to those schools that were predominantly white within the cluster. Intent supposedly was to provide an approximate eighty-to-twenty, white-to-black ratio in all these schools.

All junior high schools were to become Middle Schools to house sixth, seventh and eighth grades. Students who already lived far enough from their assigned schools to necessitate riding a bus would simply be reassigned to another school in order to change racial balance at all schools. High school students were to be similarly affected. However, students who were to be shifted during the junior high or middle school years, were not to be shifted during their high school time, and vice versa.

Oklahoma City schools opened their doors in August 1972, with sixteen fifth-year centers, eleven elementary schools housing kindergarten through fifth year pupils, fifty-six elementary schools housing kindergarten through fourth year pupils, eleven middle schools and nine high schools.

Kennedy Junior High had become a part of the Douglass High School campus. Dunjee Junior-Senior High School was closed. Moon Junior High was closed. All had been predominantly black schools.

Nearly two-thirds of the city students were in buildings they had not previously attended. This included seventh and tenth graders who normally moved up to junior or senior high schools. It also included the sixth and ninth graders who moved up. It included white fifth graders moving to fifth year centers. Also black pupils in four grades who were assigned kindergarten to fourth year schools.

Implementation of the Finger Plan with its crosstown busing, which during the season may see four yellow carriers crossing each others' path as they head toward four compass points, has not been without its material price in higher costs and its cost in human terms. Racial mores and family patterns change slowly. There have been a number of incidents that disrupted schools because of personal clashes. An opinion survey of parents and pupils of both races, made by Kay Dyer of the *Oklahoma City Times* in late May 1973, did project an overall hopeful prospect for the ensuing year.

The city has come a long way since those early day subscription schools. Population shifts have made some buildings obsolete and new ones necessary. The 200 square mile Oklahoma City school district serves 60,674 regular students in 112 physical plants, with an evaluation of $136 million. The system has 5,000 employes including 2,400 teachers. That $780 annual salary paid the first superintendent, Sullins, could be multiplied forty-five times to approximate the salary of Doctor Bill Lillard in 1973. A product of the system itself, he has rejected opportunities elsewhere for a greater personal financial return. A seven member board, nominated by wards and elected at large, sets policies for the system. Salaries of instructional staff are in the thousands where hundreds marked those of early day teachers. Adult and special education classes undreamed of years ago are offered.

Through the years the city system has made accomplishments to which it can point with pride. Edgar S. Vaught, superintendent in 1905 and later a distinguished federal district judge, put the first vocational course into Oklahoma City High School when there were 388 students. Increased attention to vocational education did not begin really until the early 1950's, when there were some ten programs divided among but a few schools. Now there are eighty-nine in addition to an Area Vocational-Technical Education Center, with a full-time vocational director for the system in Doctor Sizemore Bowlan. He initiated the first vocational agriculture program in John Marshall High School, now one of the Nation's largest of such programs in an urban center. The wide range of vocational-technical programs at the area center is an indication of a national movement since passage of 1968 amendments to the 1963 Vocational Education Act. Programs are coordinated with the local and regional skill market. Through exposure to "world of work" and "world of manufacturing" programs below the secondary level, young students are better able to make choices of their own career.

The Oklahoma City school system has received wide recognition for its Special Education programs, which first began at Bryan Elementary

School. This was the first integrated school since, without pressure of federal law, it accepted all physically handicapped children regardless of race. Later Carver Center was opened for high school age handicapped children. The system has been a leader also in a cooperative education program, where handicapped students combine work and study to the extent of their capabilities. This was first in the state and first in the nation in developing a secondary curriculum and instructional guide for such persons. Students with learning disabilities and perceptual handicaps have been aided greatly. There is a total communication program for deaf, blind, emotionally disturbed and otherwise handicapped children, who are trainable to a certain extent.

The school system also ranks among the first — if not the first — to use open channel television as an instructional tool. This was a follow to closed circuit instruction. Facilities of the state owned Educational Television Authority, (KETA-TV, Channel 13) and, since 1958, the system's own KOKH-TV, Channel 25, are used. For a time the school system had KOKH-FM radio in its broadcasting center but that license was permitted to lapse. Schools within a ninety mile radius of Oklahoma City also use the televised instruction. It provides many subjects that are not available in small schools. Assistance has been received from the Frontiers of Science and from the Ford Fund for the Advancement of Education. The school system provides studio facilities in the Classen school building. This has been a cooperative community-state project. In the beginning, although the Educational Television Authority was created by legislation, there was a delay in funding. A $50,000 contribution by E. K. Gaylord, which remained anonymous for several years, helped get it off the ground. Channel 9, KWTV, has donated tower space and ground for a transmitter. WKY-TV provided some equipment. Engineers of all local television stations have been helpful in the efforts.

In a statistical summary of the Oklahoma City school system area,

City market on California Street during a principal marketing day about 1913.

This was the 1888 home of Captain C. F. Somers, quartermaster agent here for the Army.

the ethnic division (to nearest rounded percentage figures) is: white, eighty-four percent; black, fourteen percent; Indian, two percent; others, less than one percent. The median educational level of adults is 12.4 years. Twenty-nine percent of persons in the sixteen to sixty-four year bracket have had some vocational training. Forty percent of the households have less than $6,000 annual income; twenty-nine percent of the households have less than $4,000 annual income while six percent of them are on some type of public assistance program. This comes from a population, within the city district limits, classed as ninety percent urban, nine percent suburban, one percent rural.

Of 60,674 pupils there are 9,600 who come from families on some welfare type support and there are 10,435 in families with less than $2,000 annual income. There are 3,336 who are physically or emotionally handicapped. There are eighty-nine vocational or occupational training courses offered with twenty-five industrial arts programs for below secondary level students. Home economics and business courses are offered from the sixth grade through the twelfth. The adult training section has thirty-eight academic courses and forty-one vocational training courses. There are some transfers from the sixteen adjacent bedroom communities although since desegregation the movement has been greater the other direction. With the area vocational center, there are nine high schools, eleven middle schools, sixteen fifth grade centers, eleven schools from kindergarten through fifth grade and fifty-seven schools in grades K-4, with the Adult Institute and special programs such as those at Carver, for the handicapped.

Mount St. Mary's Catholic Academy, standing all by itself at 2801 S. Shartel.

5

City Has Growing Pains

ITH TERRITORIAL STATUS A FACT, Oklahoma City could boast three hotels in addition to numerous boarding and rooming houses, with Pickwick and Grand Hotels on Grand Avenue, and the Weaver Hotel on Main Street where the Criterion Theater stood later with its ornate, gingerbread front, before urban renewal demolition in 1973. For their day hotels were lavish, too.

As in most operations not directly concerned with an individual business in those days, the Weaver Hotel illustrates the "family syndicate" type of operation. It was built by John J. Wetzel, his brother-in-law, Joseph C. Chrisney, and a cousin, Louis F. Kramer. They acquired two lots in that first block of Main west of Broadway. Wetzel was a baker by trade and used one of the lower floors of the two comprising the hotel for a bakery and confectionary. During construction of the building Wetzel cooked in the street, on an open fire, to feed nine carpenters and their helpers. His culinary reputation was enhanced.

The election in November 1890 provided one highlight for the entertainment starved populace and it was all free, too, with public meetings and speeches made from the back of wagons, some of which had a bit of humor. One "Judge" G. W. Adams, who had been a leader in the Kickapoo town site faction, stood as a candidate for the territorial legislature. Campaign rumors were spread around that Adams had been a principal in a "woman" case prior to coming here. He ignored this until the last speech of his campaign, when he asked himself a question, loudly, and answered it quickly by borrowing an idea from Abraham Lincoln: "Do you think there is a woman on earth who would have anything to do with a mug like mine?" He won by a good majority.

An elected city government with enforcement beyond that of the voluntary, provisional government, found people in the main ready to turn to legal means of adjudicating land and lot claims around and in the new city by 1891. A surprising number of "deeds" were honored, considering the often questionable transfer of titles, but others were questioned. In light of the United States Supreme Court decision in Townsend vs. Smith, that "anyone who was within the territorial limits illegally at twelve noon on April 22, 1889, was disqualified to take a homestead therein," there was a method of settling some lingering disputes.

William Fremont Harn of Ohio was sent here as a special agent for the General Land Office to assist the United States Attorney in prosecuting cases of perjury arising from land jumping, and "Sooners." One almost essential requirement for a protestor, or plaintiff, was that he

This building on the northwest corner of Grand and Broadway served as City Hall for Oklahoma City until railroads were removed and Civic Center constructed in the 1930s.

needed two witnesses to back up his claim, whom the court might believe more easily than witnesses for the defendant. Harn brought some 150 indictments in a relatively brief time and secured convictions on about two-thirds of them.

Harn himself liked the country. He bought a relinquishment in northeastern Oklahoma City, although it was out in the country then. Later he gave forty acres, as did J. J. Culbertson, to the state for capitol grounds and other purposes. His court duties over, Harn turned in 1902 to development of the street railway system with such people as John Shartel and Anton Classen, and to real estate. He was a developer of Harndale, in the later Heritage Hills section, and Harn Park on Classen Drive. He died in 1944. A niece, Miss Florence Wilson, lived for years in the old home near Stiles and Northeast Seventeenth Streets. In 1967 she donated it to the city, and under supervision of the Historical Society and City Park Department, it is being preserved and prepared as an '89'er type museum.

In contrast to Sooners who attempted to keep their claims when questioned by the land courts, Emil Bracht was quite different, and the most publicised "honest Sooner" of them all. A native of Kentucky, he was in Denver when talk of the imminent opening of Oklahoma Country came up. He joined one of the Boomer groups and was in the area on March 1, 1889, being included in a group photo taken at Oklahoma Station on the railway. The later court decision removed any claim of legality by the group. Bracht had staked a claim on a quarter section just north of the present state capitol. When asked in court where he was at noon on April 22, 1889, Bracht replied, with the utmost candor:

"I was lying in a little clump of brush about 100 yards east of the Santa Fe tracks." He lost his claim but saved his personal honor. His hideout was approximately where Dolores Restaurant now stands. Afterward Bracht bought a relinquishment straddling future North Lottie Avenue and Northeast Twenty-third Street. He was quite an orchard man and also imported purebred Jersey dairy cattle to the area. He was president of the Oklahoma Improved Stock Breeders Association, helped promote the first state fair prior to statehood, and later served as its president. His honesty may have had a reward in oil leases on the property later, as history buff Irvin Hurst points out.

The summer of 1892 saw political heat added to the natural variety. One Colonel Leslie T. Ross, a personal friend of President Grover Cleveland, was the loudest drum thumper for the national ticket. The state capital location fight was quite an issue, with an assist from Congress that year, and for three successive bienniums, that no bills should be passed to remove the seat of government. In a repetitive action this language was attached to appropriation bills for the territory. At the capitol in Guthrie, Governor C. M. Barnes gave a boost by vetoing a Council (Senate) bill providing $100,000 for a state library building at Guthrie, which proponents intended to be first building of a capitol complex. Barnes did not like either the size of the appropriation or the suspected sheenanigans by which it was amended and passed. Congress in 1900 reinforced that action by declaring that the territory could not appropriate money for construction of public buildings. That is why the territory literally had no offices of its own until statehood in 1907 — even after the capital was removed to Oklahoma City in 1910.

A feature of the 1892 political campaign was a contest between Dennis Flynn, Guthrie postmaster, and David A. Harvey, the incumbent territorial delegate to Congress, who won over Flynn the first time in 1890. Flynn was the dominant figure of Republican forces. Retention of the capital at Guthrie entered the picture. Uppermost in Flynn's pledges, and one that eventually would affect not only Oklahoma Territory but all the homesteaded West, was the matter of "free homes." Here, in addition to the five years residence requirement on homesteads, was a tax varying from $1 to $2.50 per acre. Payments were due and few people had any cash money. Monetary charges on homesteads were intended to offset the small payment per acre given Indians for land. Again, using the appropriation bill rider method, Flynn finally got his measure through Congress — even though as a mere territorial delegate he could not vote for it himself. The fees were dropped. From former Indian lands the provision spread to all Western homesteads. When even a dollar per acre tax was levied this meant $160 to the claimant of a quarter section. It would have been quite a blow to the city trying to grow through becoming a wholesale and distribution center, as well as territorial economy in general, in addition to personal hardship for families still looking for a decent crop year.

Oklahoma's military history — aside from establishment of posts by the regular establishment in the first half of the nineteenth century and later — began with organization of the Oklahoma Territorial Volunteer Infantry in 1892. Headquartered at Guthrie, a company of the regiment was located in Oklahoma City. The regiment saw its first action in the Spanish-American War of 1898, although by then most of its members had shifted over to the First Volunteer Cavalry, recruited by Major General Leonard Wood, and commanded by Colonel Theodore Roosevelt. There were twenty-three men killed and 105 wounded of the Oklahomans, about

Oklahoma City's lady bootblacks in 1898.   *This tornado hit the City May 12, 1896.*

one-fifth of the territory's military personnel. Roy Cashion of Hennessey was the first casualty.

In 1899 the First Oklahoma Infantry regiment was organized with twelve companies and a band. It saw action on the Mexican border in the punitive expedition against Pancho Villa, preceding the war in Europe in 1914. The unit had a month's release from active duty before being called out for World War I. Oklahoma men were mostly in the 90th Infantry Division, called the T-O Division because it was largely Texans and Oklahomans. Here began one of the most illustrious careers of a citizen soldier in America's military annals.

Raymond S. McLain of Oklahoma City commanded a machine gun company in the T-O Division. He was a staff officer of the 45th Infantry Division, formed among four states (Oklahoma, New Mexico, Arizona and Colorado) in 1924, subsequent to passage of the National Defense Act of 1920. Oklahoma had the largest numerical strength in the division. McLain later commanded 45th Division artillery in early World War II. With Major General Troy Middleton, then Thunderbird commander, McLain formed tactical dispositions at Salerno that kept the 45th and 36th Infantry Divisions from being thrown back into the sea. At Anzio, in command of combined artillery of the invasion force, he provided more concentrated fire than the world had ever seen to that time. Taken to Britain for the invasion of France, he commanded 30th Division artillery, then the battered 90th Infantry Division, which he led to major victories at Metz, Julich and other strongholds.

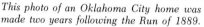

This photo of an Oklahoma City home was made two years following the Run of 1889.   The Zulite Water Company was located at 1419 N.W. 16th early in the century.

As commander of the XIX Corps of the Ninth Army, McLain was first across the Elbe, in command of more troops than any other citizen soldier in our history, except for the corps that Dan Sickles raised in Pennsylvania and fought at Gettysburg. Integrated into the regular establishment, McLain was the first guardsman to be a lieutenant general of the United States Army. He was later director of army information and first statutory comptroller general of the Department of Defense.

The national financial panic of 1893 had its effect on Oklahoma City economy. Two of its three banks closed and there was a run on the other, the First National, at Main and Broadway. Although he was interested in a competitive bank on Grand Avenue himself, Henry Overholser went into typical action that made him such a leader, and averted potential closure of the First National, of which T. M. Richardson was president. Overholser was married (for the second time) to Anna Murphy in 1890. Her father, Samuel Murphy, was the territorial treasurer at Guthrie. Overholser asked Murphy to deposit territorial funds to the amount possible in the threatened bank. He got $5,000 in silver and currency, putting some of the paper money around similarly cut bundles of paper, and carried several sacks of dollar sized washers to enhance the idea of more coinage.

With quite a bit of publicity, such as telegraphing to Oklahoma City for guards to transfer money from a train to the bank, Overholser took the loot to the city. Before closed doors of the bank he displayed genuine bills and dollars from bags, and asked people milling around to have patience until tellers could count the money and deposit it properly. Planted rumor was that $25,000 was available for those who wanted it. This averted the run and let the bank proceed with business without mammoth withdrawals until the situation stabilized. The Oklahoma National, successor to the original Citizens Bank, did not reopen. Richardson, president of First National, had some effect on calming depositors, too. Overnight he had help from Guthrie bankers M. L. Turner and Joe McNeil. Oklahoma City then had about 5,000 residents.

The severe economic situation also brought to prominence in his own right Ed Overholser, son of Henry, who had been somewhat overshadowed by his popular father. Ed Overholser's first official position here was that of town assessor in 1891. In the 1893 near disastrous situation he was named receiver for the Bank of Oklahoma City, at the Southwest corner of Grand and Robinson. He called for a mass meeting of all depositors, explained that if everyone wanted his money at the same time the bank would fail, even though it had assets above the deposit total. He asked them to request only such funds as they needed for actual living expenses, as individuals, or for the most acute bills payable for stock, if they were in business. He guaranteed personally that interest would be paid on the remainder of their deposits until such times as normal business could be resumed. He received enough acceptance that all demands were paid out within one year. Cost of the receivership was but $1,200, which was Overholser's salary.

Later Ed Overholser was a county commissioner for four years from 1895. Creation of the first municipal reservoir was one of his major accomplishments and Lake Overholser was named for him. At this time the county could not pay its warrants, as aftermath of the 1893 panic. Overholser got the territorial legislature to authorize issuance of bonds to take up the warrants outstanding, as a county investment, since it could receive interest on them until conditions got to the point where they could be redeemed. (This rather patterned a later situation in the depression beginning in 1929 on state, county and school district warrants). Ed Overholser, with his father and others, also was a prime mover for a state fair. He bought enough lots on Northeast Seventh Street leading to the selected

The MK&T railway depot, about 1904, was on E. Reno to the east of the Santa Fe tracks.

HUGH M. JOHNSON
*City banker and
community leader*

FRANK JOHNSON
*Early Oklahoma City
banking leader*

ED OVERHOLSER
*Mayor and Chamber
president-manager*

SAMUEL HAYES
*Chief Justice
Supreme Court*

fairgrounds on North Eastern, to assure that fifty percent of property owners could sign petitions to improve the street surface and secure extension of the street railway to the grounds in 1907.

In 1893 the Oklahoma Territorial Press Association, then based at Kingfisher, formed the Oklahoma Historical Society, fourteen years before statehood, which was to become a major feature of the state capitol area complex after 1929 and a cultural asset to the state. A companion organization at the University of Oklahoma was created in 1894 before the two were consolidated because of unity of purpose. Identified prominently with historical preservation then were Jasper Sipes. Oklahoma City; W. T. Little, Perry; W. P. Campbell, Kingfisher; Joseph B. Thoburn and Roy Hoffman, especially after 1900. Collections were housed at the university until 1901, then moved to an upper floor of the original Carnegie Library in Oklahoma City until 1917, when objects were taken to basement quarters in the new state capitol building. The present building construction began in July 1929. The Society now is a recognized agency of state government. It depends upon memberships and contributions to carry out activities in historic preservation above the basic state appropriation.

When cotton was King Oklahoma City's cotton compress was located at Reno and Eastern.

There were other activities to cast long shadows in this period. The Womens Christian Temperance Union was organized here in 1890, four months before saloons were officially licensed, but the temperance organization failed to prevent that happening. It did carry on a continual crusade for seventeen years when constitutional prohibition came to the state. The ladies thought they had a helper in one Reverend Sam Small, an evangelist, politician and editor from Atlanta, Georgia, who was also a reformed drunkard.

Late in 1893 when Small announced he was beginning a newspaper, *The Daily Oklahoman*, he said it would have two purposes; single statehood and constitutional prohibition. His first issue appeared on January 14, 1894, which happened to be a Sunday. This made many of his hoped for supporters critical about doing business on the Lord's Day. His moral crusades did not bring much support from the business community since a majority favored an open town. Small lasted about six months and left town. Roy Stafford picked up the pieces. The open town hassle would continue for a decade before reaching its first periodic crest.

On June 30, 1895, Chief of Police Milton Jones was killed after a jail break by three outlaws, Jim Casey, and brothers Bob and Bill Christian. All were being held after conviction of murder and had reputations with which children could be threatened to secure good behavior. The county jail was in a two-story wooden structure with steel cages on the first floor, at the intersection of Wall Street and Maiden Lane, alley type passageways to center of the block. Maiden Lane ran from Broadway west to Robinson. Wall Street ran north of Grand to the other alley. The outlaws overpowered a guard, got his keys and weapon, then ran north, evidently heading for a livery stable on East Main to get horses. At the intersection stood Chief Jones on one side of the street and two officers opposite him on the other side. None of them knew of the jail break. Bill

Here is a view looking north from about N.W. Fourth and Broadway in 1906 or 1907.

Making electricity at OG&E's first generating plant at S.W. Third and Broadway in 1902.

Paving of Oklahoma City's N.W. Fifth Street gets underway in 1907. Note the bricks.

Famed U.S. deputy marshals, known popularly as "The Three Guardsmen," are (left to right) Henry A. "Heck" Thomas, Chris Madsen and William Tilghman.

Christian shot the chief in the throat. The other officers killed Casey and Bob Christian was captured. There was a near lynching.

By 1896 Oklahoma City was growing but without pains. The original townsite and South Oklahoma, incorporated into it after territorial government came, were filled up. A 160 acre military reservation east of the tracks was added by Congress, through efforts of Dennis Flynn, and sale of lots aided the school fund. George W. Massey opened a quarter section east and north of the existing town and named it Maywood, in honor of his daughter, May. The "Gault Eighty," owned by W. J. Gault, the first mayor, just north of Northwest Seventh Street, was platted and filled in early 1898.

Frank Dale owned forty acres north of the Gault addition. In laying out his street, Dale kept about the same distance west of the Santa Fe tracks as existed farther south — but the tracks do not run in a straight compass line. Dale's projection of Broadway bent a little west, just north of Northwest Tenth Street and up to Northwest Thirteenth, which accounts for that jog. Also for addition of another short street east of Broadway and between it and the tracks. This was a planning error, not a townsite argument such as accounted for jogs to the south off Grand Avenue. Those who owned land north of Dale's addition expected that Broadway would continue north from the south, although it still expires at Northwest Twenty-fourth Street. Many other jogs in city streets resulted from correction lines due to original surveying errors, and to inept control — or complete lack of it — over approval of platted additions to existing areas as the city grew.

In April of 1901 Owen and Welch bought and platted the Higgins quarter section laying just west of the early city. The original Couch claim was nearby. A native stone county courthouse stood there later for many years. The Downtown Holiday Inn is there now.

Republicans returned to city hall in 1896 with C. G. Jones as mayor. Recurrent pleas of reform and cleanup of vice — which in Oklahoma City have been more easy to plot than cycles in the economy — were made editorially by the party's newspaper backer, the *Times-Journal*, by resolution at civic clubs and by leaders of opposition to an open town. The red light districts, licensed saloons and illegal gambling houses were primary targets, with the "Red Onion" at that time the most notorious. It was first

A principal shopping area in downtown Oklahoma City, looking west on Main, in 1912.

Automobiles, but more wagons were seen, looking west on Grand from Broadway in 1915.

to be raided before a sweep was made and all places shut down — temporarily — with exception of "Big Anne" Wynn's house. *The Daily Oklahoman* blasted at this discrimination, declaring that she was protected because of her influence at the top in city politics, not without a large measure of truth in the assertion.

Early banks in the territory were in the nature of private banks, not at the time subject to examination or supervision by either national or state authorities, but operated to suit the owners and directors. Eugene P. Gum, for many years head of the later Oklahoma Bankers Association, once recalled looking at some musty old records. He found a report which he considered typical of the era but did not disclose which bank made the report. It said, in effect:

"The Directors met on December 20, 1898, examined the books and found the bank solvent. Crops have been better than usual. We have nineteen notes on hand and they are good. Deposits have climbed back to $11,000 but will run down again when the spring demand for loans comes around. Salary of the cashier, who runs the bank, has been increased to $25 a month. He has been granted part time to keep books for the livery stable which the president owns. All accounts are in good shape and the books balance."

A highlight of social events in 1898 was an "Emigrant Party," given by Mr. and Mrs. M. C. Milner, Mr. and Mrs. A. L. Welsh and Mr. and Mrs. George W. Spencer. All persons living here were emigrants, in the sense of leaving their former locality to settle elsewhere, although many persons came from a foreign country. At least 200 persons showed up for the party, many of them in colorful costumes of foreign origin, according to Kerr's history.

One of the city's oldest institutions came into being in 1899 with organization of the Oklahoma City Building and Loan Association. It opened its books with $4,000 of its original capital subscribed. By 1901 it had loans out on thirty-seven homes and had assets of $20,000. Dividends were good, in today's terms, although one must remember that interest rates were about comparable. Investors in the concern received semi-annual dividends of nine percent in those days for an annual rate of eighteen percent. Anton H. Classen was president of the original firm and J. M. Owen was vice-president. Later Owen was to head the firm and attain the status of senior ranking head of such an association in the city before his death in 1952. He was also treasurer of the Oklahoma State Fair for some two-score years.

Born in Illinois, Owen made the Run in the opening of Oklahoma Country as a twenty-four year old. His first real estate venture was a partnership with Major L. L. Bell. In 1890 he formed the Owen and Vance Real Estate and Abstract Company. Upon the death of Vance, Owen teamed up with A. L. Welsh. Owen sold his abstract business in 1906. He had been elected registrar of deeds in 1898, before organizing the building and loan company, which later became Oklahoma City Federal Savings and Loan.

The first permanent hospital in Oklahoma City, and one that was to grow to prominence among the state's largest, was St. Anthony

This was the first business building in Okla-
homa City. G. A. McNabb was proprietor.

J. M. OWEN
Loan company
president, civic leader

Hospital, founded in 1898 by the Sisters of Saint Francis, of Marysville, Missouri. They began activities in two small wooden buildings with a total of twelve beds for patients, at 219 Northwest Fourth Street. About a year later the city fathers wanted to assist the worthy effort and provided $800 to purchase lots covering a block, between later Northwest Ninth and Tenth Streets; Dewey and Lee, then a carriage drive from the principal residential area. With subsequent and periodic drives for public support the hospital now covers more than one block of area, including auxiliary facilities such as a nurses' home and parking. It now has more than 800 beds. The hospital's innovations are many.

One of the names important to Oklahoma City in this period is that of a man who did not live here. Neither was he a holder of major political office. He was an investor, a developer, and a contributor to the city's cultural, educational and public life. This was J. J. Culbertson of Paris, Texas, who from 1884 had a chain of cottonseed oil mills. Culbertson purchased three farms on the edge of the young city which for several years were used as garden tracts to provide fresh produce for the town. He made other investments and in 1899 started the first "skyscraper," a five story building on Grand Avenue, facing up Broadway. It possessed proudly the first elevator in town, even if when it was in use lights dimmed down, because of weak power production. This became a hotel the next year.

When the state capital location fight was at its peak, before the elections, Culbertson joined with W. F. Harn in providing land for the capitol complex. His forty was on the east, Harn's on the west. The free land was an obvious inducement. The Governor's Mansion stands upon former Culbertson land. The elder Culbertson and his son, J. J. Culbertson Junior, contributed land for the grade school that bears the family name and for a park similarly named, in addition to that for Nichols· Court.

6

Politics, People Warm Up

![O]N MARCH 11, 1890, THE Democratic Party held its first state convention here with some 200 delegates. There were attempts to form a coalition with the Populists, for it was known that impending territorial organization would be dominated by Republicans under that form of national administration. Then Democrats were about equal in some aspects to the Populists or pure Agrarians in political philosophy.

Land titles, except for Union Army veterans, would have to await about four years, making taxes collectable only on personal property, or lots. Even then, some eyes looked eastward.

Democrats demanded that the federal government provide financial aid for school and governmental purposes; that it remonetize silver; exempt homesteads from future taxation; protect labor; provide more railroad building grants and inhibit private corporations from issuing bonds that would increase the debt. (Much of that platform was incorporated later into the state constitution). Populists, in their first convention in 1890, went a bit farther in calling for a graduated income tax, free silver, secret ballots, government owned railways, boards of arbitration and no bond issues.

Passage of the Organic Act for Oklahoma Territory on May 2, 1890, altered many things and put a more effective means of control over unsavory elements. The laws of Nebraska were to apply until a territorial assembly enacted its own. A good idea in principle, this did not work very well, for situations in the two areas were different. The Act created seven counties, first identified by number, including Oklahoma, Logan, Payne, Cleveland, Canadian and Kingfisher. To them was added Beaver, then including all three later counties of the Panhandle, up until then commonly called "No Man's Land." All boundaries were defined.

On appointment by President Benjamin Harrison, Major George W. Steele of Indiana became territorial governor. He in turn appointed commissioners in each county who had authority to call municipal elections. A petition for incorporation of Oklahoma Station as Oklahoma City was signed in 647 places. W. D. Gault and H. T. Betts signed more than once. Some of the signatures, although apparently the same surnames, were spelled differently by a typist on one of those new fangled machines when names were copied. Some obviously were only guessed at — but there were enough clear ones to validate the petition.

The commissioners ordered that Oklahoma, as the townsite

Artist's drawing of Oklahoma City in 1890.

north of Grand Avenue was called commonly, and South Oklahoma, below that site, were to be consolidated into Oklahoma City on July 15, 1890. Created was a city of the second class, population being the deciding factor, at 5,086 persons. Guthrie then had 5,884, Kingfisher 1,234, Norman 764; Stillwater 625 and El Reno, 519. An election August 9 saw lumberman W. J. Gault elected mayor and an aldermanic system installed. Except for two aldermen, or councilmen, it was a victory for the Democrats. Mayor Gault appointed H. B. Mitchell as city attorney and Charles F. Colcord as chief of police. Named to the police force were big John Hubatka (who, like Colcord, also carried a Deputy United States Marshal badge), William Gill, F. M. "Bud" Reynolds and Abner J. Day. In February 1891 the first county elections were held and Colcord was elected sheriff. After leaving his native Kentucky in the late teens, Colcord rode the ranges of Texas and Kansas as a ranch hand. He knew the booming cow towns and exuberance of cowboys at end of a trail drive from first hand experience, as he said later in his diary.

The early provisional government council had its chamber at Main and Santa Fe. The organized government leased quarters above the liquor dealers at 13 North Broadway, using the basement for a jail, for $25 per month. In 1893 city hall was moved to the northwest corner of Broadway and Grand. The Hill Brothers had a meat market there, at first, then sold out to a saloon and gambling house. The Hills were said to be Sooners and their sale of a two story building on that lot illegal. The purchasers refused to go along with that idea. Under the "Squatter Law" of 1892, the decision returned in the Townsend case, Mayor O. A. Mitscher (father of Admiral Marc Mitscher) ordered the police force to raid the former Hill property and destroy equipment. The city, which had offices dispersed, moved in and remained nine years in the building as it stood. Then, and until statehood in 1907, liquor was legal, provided dealers paid a license fee of $250 annually, a principal source of revenue for the young city.

One of the more unusual early events happened in 1893 at the Black and Robert saloon, while the city offices were above it and before the Turf Club moved in. Ada Curnett, the only woman United States Deputy Marshal, arrested nineteen men one midnight for false swearing in land contests. She handcuffed them, took them on a train to Guthrie for territorial court trial, then on to federal prison at Leavenworth.

In 1890, after the Organic Act was passed, President Harrison asked William Grimes of Kingfisher to be United States Marshal for Oklahoma Territory. He was to be allowed twenty men. This included Colcord and Hubatka of Oklahoma City in a dual role. Among the others, three were to emerge as legendary figures: Chris Madsen, Henry Andrew "Heck" Thomas, and William Tilghman — the "Three Guardsmen." Their duties were more in the rest of the territory than in Oklahoma City, although for a number of years their exploits, and the people with whom they dealt made good reading for folk in the city.

Colcord and Tilghman also were to be "the law" at Perry in 1893 on opening of the Cherokee Outlet. Later that year, when E. D. Nix became territorial United States Marshal, both were made deputies. Included in the Nix force were others from Oklahoma City: J. M. Jones, John Quimby, Sam Bartell and Hubatka.

During early territorial days outlaw names became common words, even if they were but nicknames and the bearers came from places unknown. Such as Blackface Charley Bryant, Red Buck, Bitter Creek Newcomb, Tulsa Jack, Dynamite Dick, Arkansas Tom, Red Horse Hays, Zip Wyatt and Bee Dunn, brother of Rose Dunn, "The Rose of Cimarron." Then there were the Daltons — Bill, Bob and Grat — with Dick Broadwell, Jim Casey, Bill Doolin, Charley Pierce, Ol' Yantis and even later, a self confessed train and bank robber named Al Jennings, who got far more on the lecture circuit as a reformed bandit than he ever did using a gun to make collections. In a race for governor he ran third.

Admitted to be the best horse thief in the territory, although operating in the more widely spaced areas, was "Tom King," who in reality was Flora Quick Mundis, who came out of Missouri wearing man's apparel. She was a reckless, hard riding daredevil who raised horse stealing to a fine art. There were times when she was caught by deputy marshals and put in jail. Turned over to the county involved, she never remained in durance very long. Her usual method of escape was to seduce the jail guard, obtaining keys and gun in the distraction, and flee, leaving a soon jobless guardian behind.

Meanwhile, Oklahoma City was having growing pains complete with a grand jury investigation that the *Oklahoma City Gazette* called "a Republican grand jury." In January, 1892, the jury criticized city officials for assessment of fines to make the monthly payroll of $548. Mayor Gault was reelected with little opposition. A Citizens ticket, dubbed "the Mule Ticket," by the outspoken *Gazette* and led by C. G. Jones was proposed, but all nominees withdrew before the election.

Then came a lesson in city financing peculiar to almost any time — certainly to that one — as McRill told the story: "Outstanding among events of the Gault administration was granting of a franchise to the Choc-

Here is the first motorized fire fighting equipment used by the city fire department.

taw Coal and Railway Company to build an east-west railroad through the city. Because of a grant made by the United States in 1888, granting a 200-foot right-of-way through Indian Territory (later Oklahoma Territory, in part) conflicting claims arose between the Choctaw Company and Oklahoma City lot claimants, who staked lots on right-of-way the day of the opening.

"A compromise was effected, the Choctaw firm reducing the right-of-way to 100 feet by taking the alley between First and Second Streets and forty feet off lots on either side. Value of all lots was fixed at $16,000 and citizens were asked to subscribe that amount to pay claimants for their land. A committee was unable to raise that much money.

"Then came some high financing unique in the history of city goverment. Mayor Gault and Henry Overholser, two resourceful citizens who believed in getting things done and talking later, proposed that if citizens increased their subscriptions sufficiently to raise the required sum, the city would issue them Choctaw scrip in the amount of their respective subscriptions, then pass an ordinance accepting the scrip at face value in payment of saloon licenses. The scrip would be sold to saloon keepers at a discount of twenty-five percent.

"On the face of the scheme, the citizens paid one-fourth and the city three-fourths of this bonus. But a part of the plan was to raise the saloon licenses from $250 to $300, so that everybody became civic minded except the saloon keepers."

In 1890, the first year that ad valorem taxes were levied, Oklahoma County took in $66,000. By 1894 this total grew to $107,000 and by 1906 to $500,000, all in even figures. This sort of growth surprised George Tucker, who came in on the opening with the T. M. Richardson party and helped start a bank. Tucker staked a lot on Main Street. He sold it a year later for $200, saying "I caught a sucker," and departed. Twenty-five years later, on a visit, he learned the lot was worth in excess of $25,000. By 1973 county evaluation passed the billion dollar mark.

Uppermost in the minds of many persons in 1890, after passage of the Organic Act, was location of the territorial capital. By projection that location would, some day, be capital of a resultant state. If there was anything in the new territory that could be said to cast long shadows, location of a capital was the projection that would cast the longest. The Act itself designated Guthrie as a temporary capital, saying that "the legislative assembly of the Territory of Oklahoma shall hold its first session at Guthrie in said Territory, at such time as the governor thereof shall appoint and direct." It said also that as soon thereafter as expedient, the governor and legislature should seek to establish the seat of government at such a place as deemed desirable.

The competition caused more excitement here in 1890 than did the Ghost Dance movement of Indians of the Plains, built around the idea that an Indian Messiah would drive out the whites. Although this kept troopers busy, Oklahomans took even little note than an intelligent Oklahoma Kiowa, Apiatan, had a large part in dispelling the fantasy.

Governor Steele had to see that a census was conducted in the seven counties to determine a basis for representation in the first territorial

This billboard promoted the vote for Oklahoma City as the State Capital for Oklahoma.

legislature. He had volunteers from other Republicans to help make a count. This led later to Democratic charges of politicking while enumerating, with Guthrie and Oklahoma City the principal capital seekers. Kingfisher was a third but weaker contestant and more amenable to siding with Oklahoma City than with Guthrie. The census revealed that Oklahoma county had 12,794 inhabitants while Logan county boasted 14,254. An election was set for July 8, 1890, for members of the legislature.

Twice the preceding year Guthrie called for conventions there to boost its capital chances. Both failed. Both Democrats and Republicans, and the third but visible Populist Party, held conventions in Oklahoma City. There was at stake also a seat as territorial delegate to the fifty-first Congress, then underway, and a full term for the fifty-second Congress. In the summer of 1890 a convention was held at Guthrie. Dennis T. Flynn, then Guthrie postmaster and a homesteader, sought the delegate's post against his fellow Republican, David Harvey of Oklahoma City, a native of Nova Scotia. There were reports that Governor Steele believed that since Guthrie had the capital, to start with, Oklahoma City should have the delegate to Congress. Someone forgot to tell the Oklahoma City folk for, after Harvey was nominated, and elected, they continued seeking the capital location. Harvey's Democratic opponents were James L. Mathews of Payne county for the short term and J. G. McCoy of El Reno for the long term. The Democrats met at Norman. Samuel Crocker, Oklahoma City, was the losing Populist candidate.

The location fight took precedence over almost everything else at the first legislature. It was said that 100 days were spent on that problem and ten days on other matters. Organization of the legislature came first. There were twenty-six house members, of whom fourteen were Republicans, nine were Democrats, and three were Populists. The Council — or Senate — had seven Republicans, five Democrats and one Populist. The Republicans, with a numerical majority, naturally expected to organize both houses but had a shock. C. G. Jones and H. B. Trosper of Oklahoma County deserted the Grand Old Party and threw in with Democrats to elect A. N. Daniels of El Reno as speaker of the House. J. L. Brown, the

Republican senator from Oklahoma County, joined Democrats to put the lone Populist, George W. Gardenhire, of Stillwater, in as president pro tempore. In other means of courting support in the capital location matter, Oklahoma County members supported Cleveland county in securing the state university for Norman, the Payne County delegation in getting an agricultural and mechanical college, and Edmond folk in securing a state normal school.

Senator J. L. Brown got a bill through establishing Oklahoma City as the capital. Governor Steele vetoed it, saying he was more unhappy with its provisions than the location selected. There were threats of a lynching bee and even a crowd scene around the temporary capital but people dispersed at request of the governor. The least uncomplimentary remark made about Governor Steele in Oklahoma City was that he was a "Republican carpetbagger." Railroads were in the middle of most arguments. Each wanted the capital and the Santa Fe was the only line with two possibilities.

Guthrie house member William H. Merten was a leader of his town's forces. Merten believed there was collusion between Oklahoma City and Kingfisher, so when a new bill came up placing the capital at Kingfisher, he had a substitute bill ready for presentation by a Logan county member, Charles Brown. There was so much heat generated that fist fights took place, including one in which Brown was floored. When order was restored by the sergeant-at-arms, skilled parliamentarian Merten pointed out where his own man was in violation of the rules. It didn't make much difference. Governor Steele was again ready to veto the location bill, when passed. First it had to be rescued from Dan Peery, who just grabbed the bill and tried to make off with it.

In the Kerr-Gainer history of Oklahoma City, there is a story that

This postcard promoted the move of the State Capitol from Guthrie to Oklahoma City.

an agreement was made between Oklahoma City and Kingfisher, for the eager "city" capital seekers to pay Kingfisher $5,000 for help in securing enough votes to override the governor's veto. It was stipulated additionally, the tale goes, that if Oklahoma City lost, it would help Kingfisher secure the location and that city would return the money. When Oklahoma City lost it demanded the funds. By now a near legend, and one that cannot be authenticated by personal witnesses, the story is that Kingfisher folk put the money into a keg in a certain room and told the Oklahoma City people to come get it. Their representatives made the trip. The keg was found — empty — but principals were not held liable. Bugging was not yet a refinement of the American scene but this was not the first time, nor would it be the last in our history of civic affairs, when a keyhole fit someone's ear.

Dennis Flynn did not give up easily. Elected as the second territorial delegate to Congress, he was able to get into a legislative appropriation bill on June 28, 1892, a provision not to move the capital away from Guthrie. The question came up again in 1894, 1896 and 1898. In 1906 Bird McGuire, of Pawnee, then the delegate to Congress, got a proviso in the Enabling Act for statehood, to permit the capital to remain at Guthrie until 1913.

Neither did Oklahoma City give up. At the constitutional convention of 1906 the Oklahoma City Chamber of Commerce attempted to throw a big barbecue for members of the legislature but Speaker William H. Murray cooled that idea. Murray, the "Sage of Tishomingo," did not want the capital in the city but in a completely new area. He accepted, for the most part, an idea from Campbell Russell of Warner, to create "A New Jerusalem," with enough space to sell lots and gain funds to erect a capitol building, although Murray's idea was not quite so grandiose as Russell's.

Russell wanted from nine sections up to sixteen sections of land, or 6,660 to 10,240 acres, respectively. E. K. Gaylord and C. B. Ames had three alternative proposals. One would be a constitutional amendment altering the location from Guthrie; another that the capital should be within three miles of Guthrie, Oklahoma City or Shawnee; the third was a location proposed by Representative I. M. Putnam. Putnam had an exact area in mind. Putnam City, it was called later, on the west interurban.

Gaylord actually preferred a petition route and was chairman of an Oklahoma City committee to develop such a plan of action. With assistance of Attorney W. A. Ledbetter of Ardmore, two initiative petitions then were proposed: First, the constitutional amendment, and, second, a straight petition on two phases of a relocation bill that would permanently fix the location, create a three-man commission to be appointed by the governor; appropriate $600,000 for not to exceed 2,000 acres, the state to be reimbursed by sale of lots to create a building fund for a capitol building. Another phase would offer citizens a choice between Oklahoma City, Guthrie and Shawnee. The petition for amendment received 39,764 signatures and the location bill 27,944. Petitions were passed around largely by circulation men of *The Daily Oklahoman*. When signed they were presented July 21, 1909, to Leo Meyer, assistant secretary of state at Guthrie, in the absence of Bill Cross, secretary of state, who was ill. According to

Meyer's sworn testimony later, Governor Charles Haskell was present when the petitions were filed.

What caused contention later was that for six days — one more than the normal five day protest period — there was not a line about the petitions being turned in published in any newspaper. Least of all at Guthrie. The story broke actually on July 27 in the *Kansas City Journal*. Judge Frank Dale was among those protesting loudly at the "secrecy" with which the petitions were filed. A mandamus action was sought against the secretary of state and issued by Judge A. H. Huston. Attorney Ledbetter sought a writ of prohibition against Judge Dale — as a person and not in his official capacity — to keep him from interfering, declaring the petitions to have been filed legally. Meyer said simply that there was no attempt at concealment, that no one even asked about it until the *Journal* reporter, O. D. Hall, made a query. Secretary of State Cross held the signatures sufficient on the petition for capital location. The amendment petition was dropped.

On January 10, 1910, Attorney General West transmitted a ballot title to Secretary of State Cross. A. G. C. Bierer of Guthrie filed the main argument against the petition. On March 28, 1910, Governor Haskell by proclamation set a special election for June 11, a Saturday, which itself was a bit unusual but quite legal. With seventy-five days to work Oklahoma City went all out. By train, primarily, trade tour type groups went from place to place in the state; papers told of a population increase that nearly doubled that of Oklahoma City from 32,452 in 1907 to 64,205. (Comparable year figures for other larger cities were: Guthrie, 11,652 and 11,654; Shawnee, 10,955 and 12,474; Tulsa, 7,298 and 18,182; Enid, 10,087 and 13,799; Lawton 5,562 and 7,788 and Muskogee, 14,418 and 25,278).

Other promotions included a tag day on May 28 when funds raised from sale of tags to be worn provided $3,303 for campaign expenses; the baseball club donated ninety-percent of its gate for three days; theaters put in from twenty-five percent to fifty percent of their admissions for the same time. There were no party lines. George H. Dodson, the Republican county chairman, and Sam A. Calhoun, the Democratic chairman, pooled forces. O. B. Kee recruited citizens who had moved here from other state locations to return and tell friends what a good selection Oklahoma City would be. Charles F. Colcord headed the campaign organization; W. L. Alexander was in charge of the speakers' bureau; Dennis T. Flynn, now living in Oklahoma City and as gung-ho for its location as he had been previously for Guthrie, got in the act with C. G. Jones and a host of other civic leaders.

The election was held on June 11, with 135,944 persons voting. They all were men since the XIX Amendment, granting women suffrage, was ten years away. The official vote was: Oklahoma City, 96,261; Guthrie, 31,301 and Shawnee, 8,382. Governor Haskell, by his own story later told to Irvin Hurst, who has done more research on this tangled facet of our history than anyone else — said he was attending a banquet at the Commercial Club in Tulsa that evening. Haskell went on to say that afterward he went to Tate Brady's hotel, had Brady secure unofficial returns from Guthrie by telephone, and learned that Oklahoma City had a clear majority of all votes cast.

The midnight train from Tulsa to Oklahoma City already had

departed. Haskell called the division office at Sapulpa and got a special, an engine and tender with sleeping car attached, and prepared to go to Oklahoma City. He telephoned W. B. Anthony, his private secretary, who had gone that day to his home in Marlow to vote, and located him at political headquarters in the Huckins Hotel. Anthony was told by the governor to get in touch with Bill Cross at Guthrie, get the state seal, and return with it to Oklahoma City and meet Haskell at the Huckins the next morning. Haskell walked into the Huckins about six o'clock Sunday morning, wrote a proclamation on hotel stationery declaring Oklahoma City to be the capital, posted it on the wall, and went into the coffee shop for breakfast.

Meanwhile, Anthony picked up Luther Harrison, later a long time editorial writer for *The Daily Oklahoman*, then publicity man for the state Democratic organization, to accompany him to Guthrie. Harrison said later that nothing was said about the mission. He was actually in on what would be a big and often confused story later yet knew nothing about it. Someone in Oklahoma City must have known what was happening. Hurst says that Anthony, Harrison and S. F. Price went to Guthrie in a Cadillac driven by Bill Light and provided by the Chamber of Commerce. Earl Keys, in the secretary of state's office, said later in refutation of some other claims, that he had a note from Secretary of State Cross to deliver the state seal to Anthony and did so, wrapped in a piece of brown paper. It was as simple as that, evidently. Keys refuted a tale of someone going in a window. Another tale told seventeen years later, said that the seal was put in a bundle of laundry and carried out by Paul Nesbitt, a clerk in the governor's office, then to Keys.

Fred P. Branson of Muskogee, later chief justice of the state supreme court, but then state Democratic chairman, said that Haskell dictated his location proclamation that Sunday morning in the presence of Colcord, Flynn, Ledbetter, Jones and Edgar S. Vaught as other witnesses. *The Oklahoman*, not surprisingly, had an extra on the street by noon. The odd thing was that, after all its efforts, Oklahoma City had no place for a capitol. The Huckins was a natural pausing place, being almost Democratic headquarters, so much so that even in modern times State Senator W. C. Fidler was called "The Senator from Huckins County."

Sidney Brock said that Oklahoma City had no advance notice of Haskell's prompt action, that removal really was not anticipated until the 1913 date fixed by Congress. Editorially, even *The Oklahoman* on May 12, and again on June 14, said that Oklahoma City would have been satisfied for the capital to remain at Guthrie until the later date. However, the paper did not advocate giving it back. To loud charges of seal theft, Haskell declared that "Oklahoma City did not steal anything." There was a big victory celebration at the fairgrounds on June 15, but the argument was not quite over. The fight was taken to the state supreme court which would require months to hand down a decision.

Meanwhile, after his proclamation, Governor Haskell appointed a capital commission consisting of Tate Brady, Tulsa, as chairman; J. B. A. Robertson, Chandler, and Doctor Leo Bennett, Muskogee, (whose wife was the Indian Territory "bride" at the symbolic wedding of the two territories in 1907) as the Republican member. Developer I. M. Putnam and

A night view of the Capitol before other state buildings were constructed there.

John W. Shartel, general manager of the Oklahoma Railway Company (street cars and interurbans) offered the state 1,600 acres of land and $1,700,000 cash to go to the northwestern section of the city area on the El Reno interurban route. (Putnam City). Of this amount $1,500,000 was to be for a building, $150,000 for furnishings, $40,000 for salaries and expenses of the commission, and $10,000 for moving expenses from Guthrie. They expected to recoup from sales of surrounding land.

Both the governor and commission agreed to this. Then the roof fell in. The State Supreme court on November 15 knocked out the petition that was responsible for it all, because the ballot title did not pose the legal question: "Shall it be adopted?" (Coyle vs. Smith). This came right after the general election. Lee Cruce of Ardmore had been elected second statehood governor, defeating William H. Murray in the process. The third legislature would convene in January but terms of old members of the house and one-half of the senate would expire fifteen days after the election. On November 19, Governor Haskell ostensibly went to Guthrie to see his first grandchild — daughter of the Leslie Niblacks. He went also to the courthouse and called a special session of the legislature to convene November 28, with the specific issue of locating the state capital. Under law the legislature could convene legally anywhere "proper for the peace and safety," although that body must ratify the place by a two-thirds vote. So the legislature met at the Huckins Hotel with W. B. Anthony, who meanwhile was elected to the house, as speaker, and Elmer Thomas of Lawton as president pro tempore of the senate. The ratification vote was: House, eighty to twenty-six; Senate, thirty-three to nine.

Being legally placed and constituted, the legislature then adopted House Bill Number Seven — with the same language as that in the disputed senate bill away back in 1890 — with Representatives J. H. Wright, Oklahoma City; Dan Peery, Carnegie; and W. A. Durant of Durant, as authors. The house was willing to accept the offer of Putnam and Shartel, it appeared, but the senate objected. A local committee of Colcord, Jones,

The Oklahoma Historical Society to the south and east of the Capitol on Lincoln Blvd.

Vaught and Gaylord, with others, saw a better site at Northeast Twenty-third and Lincoln Boulevard, on the half-section line. William Fremont Harn had land west of Lincoln that was staked in the Run although he acquired it around 1891. J. J. Culbertson had land on the east side of Lincoln. All of them joined forces to make some decision. Harn offered forty acres to the state for free. Culbertson offered a land gift. The senate appointed a location committee headed by J. B. Thompson of Pauls Valley to make a recommendation.

At an Oklahoma City mass meeting in the Levy Building, later the Mercantile Building at Main and Hudson, December 11, Edgar S. Vaught presided as twenty-five businessmen signed bonds for $5,000 each to guarantee that Oklahoma City would give the state a "free" $1 million capitol. The Thompson committee had squashed the Putnam-Shartel project for these stated reasons: It was seven to ten miles from the City Center; rapid transit (street cars) would require twenty minutes each way compared to seven minutes to the Northeast Twenty-third Street site. The recommendation was adopted by a vote of thirty-five to four.

Colcord, Vaught, Sidney Brock, S. C. Heyman and twenty-seven others posted a $100,000 performance bond to back Oklahoma City's offer (a pattern begun in 1889 for civic endeavors and continued to the present) and offered free quarters for state offices during construction of the capitol, in a school building. But the citizens were to get still another jolt. Governor Haskell said, before signing the bill to accept the Oklahoma City proposition, that the city had to raise $71,200 for the Putnam-Shartel syndicate's expenses, of which $9,200 was for Putnam himself, $30,000 for architectural fees expended, $14,000 for attorneys, $18,000 for expenses of the original commission, and interest on $70,000 advanced by the state to pay for temporary office quarters. By December 29, Oklahoma City citizens had secured $66,000 and guaranteed the rest. With W. A. Ledbetter, the governor then went to Guthrie on the train and signed the final capital removal bill in the Harvey House at the Santa Fe depot, then returned immediately to Oklahoma City.

The following January, incoming Governor Lee Cruce took no chances at his inauguration. He was sworn into office at Oklahoma City, then went to Guthrie and took the oath all over again. He had lost to Haskell in the first gubernatorial election by 3,000 votes and was dubious about the railroad promoter's "legal" knowledge as to just where the capital was located. In anti-climax, the United States Supreme Court later ruled that the legislature had a right to put the capital wherever it chose, regardless of the 1913 detainer, so long as the citizens had a right to express their views at the polls.

The cornerstone is laid for the Oklahoma State Capitol on November 16, 1915. Wielding the trowel is Almer E. Monroney. The lad in the stocking cap is his son, Mike.

7

Social Life Blooms

OCIAL LIFE IN OKLAHOMA CITY began with the spirit of neighborliness usually found among pioneer people. It has grown into a maze of social, civic, professional and charitable organizations. It is impossible to discuss, even in briefest detail, the thousands of groups to which residents belong or the tens of thousands of social events which have attracted their participation. However, there are some highlights for "civilization followed the frontier."

The best remembered early social was a ball given July 2, 1900, in honor of New York Governor (soon to be a vice-presidential candidate) Theodore Roosevelt, who was attending a reunion here of Rough Riders from the Spanish-American War. The ball was held in the unfinished Street and Reed Furniture Store. The building was owned by J. G. Street, father of later Mayor Allen Street, and Fred H. Reed. The national colors and bunting covered walls and ceiling of the unfinished building and gave the room a military appearance. The formal ball began at 10 o'clock. It was shortly after midnight when Governor Roosevelt arrived. Today the building which hosted this famous party houses Lerner Shops, a clothing store, at 214 West Main.

The Philomathea Club claims distinction of being the oldest of all women's clubs in Oklahoma City. It was founded in 1891, and grew out of a literary society organized in 1889. Over the years it has combined study with community activity. In its early days, with few sidewalks and no pavements, weather often was responsible for small attendance. Philomathea joined the Kansas State Federation of Women's Clubs, since there was no Oklahoma Federation at that time. Philomathea later organized the Sans Souci Club for young unmarried women.

Because Oklahoma City had no public library, the Philomathea Club began in 1897 to develop a public collection of books. In January 1898, it held a sale of miscellaneous articles to raise funds for books and magazines. Packages were sold at ten cents each. All sorts of unexpected things, from postage stamps and perfume to fruitcake, tinware and Sapolio, were disclosed in packages. By May, the club had formed a Public Library Association and stock was being sold. Five hundred dollars were raised and additional books purchased. The collection was installed over what later became the Farmers' National Bank at the corner of Grand and Robinson. Club members acted not only as librarians, but as janitors. Those books later became a part of the Carnegie Library collection.

Early in 1895 the first card club was organized. This club met in the evening and played bid euchre. Whit M. Grant was its first president. In 1897 it was changed to a whist club, and at that time took in women. By 1899, the women had taken over and men were dropped from membership. It became an afternoon club called the Duplicate Whist Club, and continued holding meetings into the 1920s.

The Chafing Dish Club was organized in 1899 by Mrs. M. L. Turner. Members of this group continued for many years to meet each week for luncheon. Bid euchre, played when the group first organized, gave way to bridge. Mrs. Turner was president of the club throughout her lifetime, then Mrs. Henry Overholser, a charter member, became president.

In the summer of 1898, during the war with Spain, a group of women met under leadership of Mrs. Selwyn Douglas, to form a study club called the Twentieth Century Club. Afternoon programs were held in homes of members to study literature.

A civic project arose early for this club. With a population of 10,000 Oklahoma City needed a public library. The Twentieth Century Club worked with the Philomathea Club, and wrote Andrew Carnegie of the need. After two years of effort and correspondence, spearheaded by Mrs. Douglas, a building was begun at the northeast corner of Northwest Third and Robinson. It was replaced by the four story Central City-County Library on the same site in the mid-1950s.

Another major project of the Twentieth Century Club was organization of the Young Women's Christian Association in 1907. Members of the club assisted in a fund drive to finance the YWCA here.

The Twentieth Century Club continues to be active, mixing study of literature with civic activity. The women rolled Red Cross bandages and served the national defense in both World Wars.

Two years after founding of the Twentieth Century Club, Mrs. Douglas — often called the mother of adult study clubs — organized the New Century Club. This club met, first in homes, and later in a meeting room of the new Carnegie Library, which the club supported in its effort to obtain new books and other materials. This club, too, is extant and continues its functions.

Mrs. Douglas also was founder of the "Do All You Can" (DAYC) club, founded in 1901, which later became known as the Cosmopolitan Study Club. Its purpose was to promote intellectual development and improvement of social conditions.

The Bridge Club was organized by Mrs. James H. Wheeler in 1902. It was originally a Bowling and Bridge Club, but soon gave way only to bridge. Another early club was the Lotus Club, organized in 1905, which was high in social standing in early Oklahoma City. Each year it gave a series of dinner-dances except during World War I.

In May 1898, twenty-four delegates from eleven clubs, met in the Presbyterian Church to form a Federation of Women's Clubs for Oklahoma and Indian Territories. Mrs. Douglas was elected first president, and continued in that capacity until her death in 1902.

After Mrs. Douglas' death ten clubs withdrew to form a new Federation for Indian Territory. Membership of these clubs was composed largely of women with Indian blood. The two groups re-joined in 1908 to

This Carnegie Library was built in 1903 and served Oklahoma City until razed in 1953.

form the Oklahoma State Federation of Women's Clubs. Mrs. John Threadgill of Oklahoma City was first president of the re-united group.

During its growth and development, the federation has been responsible for building of libraries, establishing city parks, planting memorial lanes of trees, bringing about hot lunch programs for schools and promoting fine arts in the communities. State club members also have led in the fight against venereal diseases; education for early detection of cancer; establishing scholarships; developing legislation pertaining to child welfare and living conditions. It has also aided fine arts and youth organizations.

Although she died three months before its founding Mrs. Douglas was largely responsible for the formation, in November 1902, of the Oklahoma City Federation of Women's Clubs. This federation, which started with four member clubs, concentrated in its early years on promoting and obtaining books for the Oklahoma City Carnegie Library, founded one year earlier. Another project was opening of the Good Will Center on Exchange Avenue, now supported by Baptist Churches of Oklahoma City. Another was the Community House of the Episcopal Church, which later evolved into the Variety Health Center, now a United Appeal Agency located at Southwest Fourteenth and Walker, which serves health needs of underprivileged children.

The only women's organization which literally "grew up" with Oklahoma City is the Ready to Help Club, organized in 1902 by four young girls not yet in their teens. Mrs. Douglas helped the girls to organize the club. At first it limited itself to twelve members but enlarged later. Projects have been varied. Typical activities have been providing clothing for needy families, supplying braces for crippled children, and helping with relief campaigns. The club furnished a room at the Sunbeam Home at 620 Northwest Twenty-first Street.

Daughters of the American Revolution founded a chapter in Oklahoma City in December 1904, for educational and patriotic purposes. In

1905 a chapter of the United Daughters of the Confederacy was organized in the Threadgill Hotel.

Linking present day Oklahoma City with its beginning is the 89ers organization, founded in Wheeler Park in 1905. It was originally limited to persons who arrived in Oklahoma Country in 1889. This organization now also includes direct descendents of 89ers. The organization was involved in civic and social activity during its earlier years, but more recently has concentrated its efforts on historical work.

One of the most exclusive early clubs here was the 5 O'Clock Tea Club, organized in the spring of 1906 in the home of Mrs. Oscar G. Lee. With charitable work as a goal, its first important project was establishment of a day nursery for children of mothers who worked. Later it built and furnished the children's ward at St. Anthony Hospital.

It was in 1907 that the Joy de Vie dancing club was organized. This became one of the most important social clubs in the city for more than twenty years. It was composed of prominent people in social and business circles. The first dance held by this club annually marked opening of the social season. Prior to World War I, these opening dances were described as "never equalled in beauty and brilliance by any other event of the season." During the war they were characterized by simplicity, which remained after the war.

Many clubs are formed for different reasons, but perhaps the most interesting beginning was that of the Coterie Club. This organization began when a promotional group called the Delphians came to Oklahoma City during the 1920s selling books. Promotion included organizing a study group, using the Delphian books as basis of the course. After the promoters left, the ladies who had purchased books started trying to use them in study meetings. They found them unindexed and of unacceptable quality. The texts were thrown out, but the ladies, who shared the dubious honor of "being taken," liked the idea of a study club. As a result the Delphians became the Coterie Club, which meets monthly in members' homes during fall, winter and spring. Programs are presented on current events, art, history, literature or music. Mrs. Jack T. Conn is current president.

By the time of statehood, Oklahoma City had nine women's clubs. They were the Philomathea, Bible, Twentieth Century, New Century, Cosmopolitan (later Cosmopolitan Study), Renaissance, Cosmos, Ready to Help, and Sans Souci clubs. There were also patriotic and fraternal organizations. Among fraternal groups were the Masons, Odd Fellows, Knights of Pythias, Woodmen of the World, Modern Woodmen, Elks and Eagles. These, too, were part of social life.

The '89ers had hardly landed at Oklahoma Station when members of the Masonic body began to get together. September 7 following the Run, the first official meeting of the North Canadian Lodge was held in a temporary lodge room on the corner of California and Broadway — an area now covered by the Myriad. F. L. Cramer was elected the first Worshipful Master. In 1892 the group became Oklahoma Lodge Number Three of Oklahoma Territory, with Selwyn Douglas as Worshipful Master. With statehood it became Oklahoma Lodge Number Thirty-six.

DR. LEROY LONG
*Medical School
Builder*

DR. FORNEY HUTCHINSON
*Longtime St. Luke's
pastor*

EVERETT S. LAIN, MD
*City surgeon of the
early 1900s.*

RABBI JOSEPH BLATT
*Early city
Jewish leader*

The Masons met in various locations in their earlier years, and in 1902 secured quarters above the old Western National Bank on the northwest corner of Main and Broadway. In 1903 they moved to the new India Temple at Northwest Second and Broadway. In 1910 the thirteen Masonic and affiliated bodies then operating in Oklahoma City purchased the Baptist Church at Northwest Third and Broadway. This building became known as the White Temple. In 1921 a Masonic Temple Building Association was organized, which began construction of a large Masonic Temple on the Southwest corner of Northwest Sixth and Robinson. This building, completed in 1923, included a large auditorium. For the next fourteen years this would be the principal auditorium of Oklahoma City and would host some of the most illustrious entertainers and events.

But the depression struck the Masons and the temple was lost in 1930. The organization met in several temporary locations until 1933, when it obtained its own building at Northwest Thirteenth and Broadway. This served as the home of Oklahoma Lodge Number Thirty-six until 1963, when it moved to 2935 West Britton Road. However, as Oklahoma City grew, the number of Masons and Masonic bodies grew, and today there are nine lodges and about 12,000 Masons here.

India Temple Shrine received its charter in 1894, with thirty-eight charter members. The first ceremonial session was held at the Knights of Pythias Hall at Main and Robinson. A delegation from Missouri conducted the ceremonies, coming to the city with tuxedos for the occasion. Since cowboy hats and riding boots were more the lifestyle of Oklahoma City at that time, the ceremony was a mixture of the most formal and informal dress. H. T. Smith of El Reno was elected first Potentate. The Shrine met in various locations in its early years, finally securing quarters, along with the Masonic Lodge, over the Western National Bank at Main and Broadway. Its next building was on the northwest corner of Northwest Second and Broadway. This building, dedicated in 1903, cost $50,000. It had a fine auditorium. The Shrine took over the top story and rented space below for business. The Shrine remained there until about 1910 when the Shriners moved, along with other Masonic bodies, to the White Temple. The previous building was sold and became the Wright Building. For a time this former Shrine Building was a meeting place of the Oklahoma

Legislature. The building exists today, in completely remodeled form, as the southeast corner of the Kerr-McGee complex.

The Shriners remained in the temple until 1923, then moved with other Masonic groups to Northwest Sixth and Robinson. After that temple was lost in the depression, Shriners purchased from the Elks a building at Northwest Fourth and Harvey, which the Elks had purchased from the Knights of Columbus just a year earlier. This building, which had been a depression casualty of two lodges, remained home of the Shrine until 1973. Then the Shriners started a new home north of Will Rogers Park at Northwest Thirty-sixth and Portland.

The Shrine has concentrated its service efforts to working with crippled children. The Shrine Circus, which benefits such children, is an annual event.

The Benevolent and Protective Order of Elks started in Oklahoma City in February, 1898. In its earliest years it operated in rented space in a building, now gone, on West Main. It moved in 1898 to a building immediately east of the former Huckins Hotel. It moved again in 1916, and occupied various rental spaces until 1926, when it constructed a three story Lodge building on the northwest corner of Third and Harvey. That building has been enlarged upward and is now the Oklahoma Natural Gas Company Building. In 1930 the lodge took over the building at Northwest Fourth and Harvey, formerly owned by the Knights of Columbus. Two years later the Shrine took over this building from the Elks. The Elks then moved into quarters at the University Club, which had merged into the Oklahoma Club, on Grand at Robinson. The next move was to Couch Drive west of Robinson, then to 4711 North Tulsa, where the Elks constructed a new building and a Junior Olympic size swimming pool.

The Elks always have been heavily involved in youth activities. It is the only organization in Oklahoma which sponsors units of all three age groups in both Boy Scouts and Girl Scouts. One early major charitable project of the lodge was sponsoring activities for the Pauls Valley Boys Home. This program was particularly active from 1925 to 1935. During the 1930's the Elks sponsored the Oklahoma City Golden Gloves Tournament.

Earl E. James, an Oklahoma City lawyer, served as Grand Exalted Ruler (or national president) of the organization in 1953-1954.

The Knights of Columbus organized in Oklahoma City in 1905, electing Mont F. Highley its first Grand Knight. Its first meeting hall was in the Maney Building, built by contractor and railroad builder J. W. Maney, who was one of its leaders. In 1912 Maney built the first K. C. Hall at 503 North Broadway. Six years later it moved to 225 Northwest Fourth Street, where it occupied a two story former residence which it later tore down to construct a new hall. This beautiful building was lost in the depression, but for many years later, until 1973, it served as the Masonic Temple. After several depression period moves, the Knights took the upper chamber of the Security National Bank Building at Main and Broadway, then in 1940 moved to 16½ West Main, where they remained for sixteen years. Its present building, completed in 1958, is at 5501 North Classen.

The Knights of Columbus have stressed patriotism in their program, and during World War I, the Oklahoma group sent a service unit to

France in uniform to provide gifts and comfort items to soldiers. The men were known as "Caseys" (phonetic pronunciation of K. C.). During World War II the K.C.'s worked as volunteers with U.S.O., which had its headquarters in the K.C. Hall. The organization also works with orphanages and with sports programs. Much of its budget is used in publicizing an understanding of the Catholic faith.

The Business and Professional Women's Club of Oklahoma City was founded in 1915, with Helen Ferris as its first president. It was originally an Oklahoma City Business Women's Club, but became a part of the national BPW organization in 1919. The club served in the war effort of World War I, and established day care centers for working mothers during World War II. Its major effort has been elevating standards of women in business and professional fields. It obtained the right of women to serve on juries. It lobbies on various bills for women's rights. There are now six Business and Professional Women's Clubs in the Greater Oklahoma City area. Their public service work is valuable.

The first three of the men's international civic clubs were Rotary, Kiwanis and Lions Clubs. The Oklahoma City clubs were among the first organized nationally, and have played important roles in each of these organizations.

First was Rotary International, formed in 1910. The Downtown Oklahoma City club was organized in November 1910, and is Number Twenty-nine among the 15,750 clubs worldwide. It was the first formed in Oklahoma. Colin Campbell was its charter president. Everett Hill, now retired and still living in Oklahoma City, rose from local to district to international leadership following World War I, and was international president during 1924-1925. The Downtown Club constructed Rotary Park near banks of the North Canadian River. Its principal service project is its annual Christmas gift, ranging from $10,000 to $30,000. This gift goes to a selected charity or service project, with a different project being selected almost every year. Another special activity of the Downtown Rotary Club is an annual trade fair, at which each member may rent a booth to display his company's product or service to other members and guests. Following World War II, as civic clubs began to expand away from downtown, additional Rotary clubs were organized in north, south, and west Oklahoma City, and in the State Capitol area.

In 1917, shortly after the United States entered World War I, Lions International was organized at a meeting in Dallas. Clubs by the same name had been organized throughout the country a year earlier, including an Oklahoma City Club. The local club participated in the first international meeting and was the third Lions Club in the world to get its international charter. Attorney Walter J. Lybrand was an international founder and became first president of the Oklahoma City Lions Club. An early leader was Edgar S. Vaught, later a federal judge, who served as local president in 1921, then became president of Lions International. So was Doctor Eugene S. Briggs. An early project of the Oklahoma City club was construction of the Lions Club Health Camp at North Eastern and Memorial Road. The camp, formed under the leadership of W. A. Brooks, provides camping experience for underprivileged boys and girls. It includes facilities for sports, swimming and outdoor living.

JOHN EMBRY	ROSCOE DUNJEE	RT. REV. THOMAS CASADY	NAN SHEETS
Legislator and	*Early Black editor,*	*Episcopal Bishop*	*Organized & developed*
U.S. District Attorney	*civil rights leader*	*for 26 years*	*city Art Center*

In 1958, under the leadership of Doctor Charles A. Royer, the Oklahoma City club formed a Lions Eye Bank, joining other clubs throughout the nation in this effort. A companion project is the Lions' effort to obtain Leader dogs for the blind. Oklahoma City Lions estimate that the program has resulted in more than 10,000 pairs of eyes being pledged and completion of more than 300 successful transplants. In 1973 Lions throughout Oklahoma were in the midst of another eye project — the raising of more than $300,000 to equip the Dean A. McGee Eye Institute in the Medical Center complex in east Oklahoma City.

Oklahoma City Lions Clubs have been expansion minded, and in 1973 there were twenty-five clubs in the greater Oklahoma City area. The original club now uses "Downtown" in its title.

The Oklahoma City Kiwanis Club was organized in April 1918, with more than two hundred charter members. Attorney Ed Howell was the first president. The initial project of the club was sale of $432,000 World War I Liberty Bonds. The Kiwanians led all Oklahoma City organizations in this effort. In 1919, the Kiwanis Club turned its attention to safety projects, one of which led to the organization of the Oklahoma City Safety Council. Six years later the Kiwanians organized the Kiwanis Junior Police among upper-level grade school children. This project quickly spread statewide. During the 1930s, the Kiwanis Club organized Key Clubs as high school student service groups. A Key club is now located in every high school in Oklahoma County. The Kiwanis Club has built three neighborhood service centers — in Mulligan Flats, McKinley Park and Walnut Grove. The idea for William Jennings Bryan School, Oklahoma City's first school for the handicapped, no longer operating, came out of a Kiwanis Club committee. The Oklahoma City Kiwanis Club has provided two international Kiwanis presidents. They were H. G. Hatfield, 1938-1939, and Edward C. Keefe, 1965-1966.

Serving as the principal men's civic club before formation of the international service organizations, was the Oklahoma City Advertising Club, revived in 1907. William H. Taylor was its first president. Past presidents have included newspaper editor Walter M. Harrison; developer and publisher W. P. "Bill" Atkinson; and agency founder Lowe Runkle, among many civic leaders. Although professionally oriented, the Advertising Club has played a major civic role, mainly in the area of promotion. It organized the Better Business Bureau of Oklahoma City in 1930. It provided promotional impetus to bring about public acceptance of the United Appeal. It launched and directed Oklahoma City's "600,000 in '60" campaign, as outgrowth of a talk by veteran publisher E. K. Gaylord before the Advertising Club in 1955.

The Civitan Club was organized here in 1921, with Earl J. Littler as its first president. "Builders of Good Citizenship" is its motto. One of the earliest projects of the club was planning and building the first nine holes of the Lincoln Park Golf Course without cost to the city. This established the city's first public golf course. Another project was developing Camp Don Shelley, with a clubhouse and camping area for boys, at Northwest Highway and MacArthur. This camp finally gave way to a housing development. The club sponsors a Civitan-Salvation Army Boys Camp each summer, presents annual Civitan Awards to high school students, and works with mentally retarded through the Dale Rogers School. In 1969 the Civitan Club started a new Boys' Club in Oklahoma City.

The civic club movement drew most of its membership from the over-thirty age group, and many eager young men in their twenties felt left out. This led to establishment, during the World War I period, of a Junior Chamber of Commerce in St. Louis, which eventually spread throughout the country. Its rules placed a maximum membership age limit at thirty-five. The Oklahoma City Junior Chamber of Commerce, now abbreviated to "Jaycees", was organized in 1927. Charles H. Moreau was its first president. The first local Jaycee to attain national prominence in the organization was Lee B. Thompson, an attorney, who served here as president in 1931, then rose to become national vice president. Another who became national vice president was David H. Bridges.

The biggest project undertaken by Jaycees was the building of Taft Stadium. Much effort of the Jaycees has been given to youth activity. The Jaycees organized the Oklahoma City Junior Symphony, one of the top youth orchestras in the nation. It organized and sponsors the State Fair band contest, which annually brings marching bands here from over the state. It conducts numerous projects for underprivileged children. Since World War II Jaycee chapters have been organized in several areas of Oklahoma City as well as in most outlying communities.

Another early civic organization here was the Sertoma Club. It takes its name from an abbreviation of its motto, "Service to Mankind." Robert M. Ecock was its first president. A major project of Sertoma is its "Service to Mankind" award, presented annually to an individual not affiliated with a Sertoma Club. Another activity is its "American Way" program, honoring school age youths who have made outstanding contributions in "promoting the American Way of Life." Six Sertoma clubs are now operating in Oklahoma City and others are active in outlying communities. The awards are prized highly.

The Hospitality Club of Oklahoma City had its beginnings in 1923, with philantrophy and service as its purposes. Mrs. James R. Armstrong was first president. Its principal early project was serving as a welcoming committee for distinguished visitors — hence the word, "Hospitality."

For many years the club has operated a dairy bar at the State Fair to raise money for its service projects. Other major projects have been an annual bazaar and a "Ladies in the News" fashion show. In its earlier years the Hospitality Club served as a planning committee for inaugural balls. During World War II, club members met troop trains and provided gifts to soldiers at induction centers. Today the club is active in providing aid for more than thirty different projects.

The Hospitality Club was instrumental in forming a Junior Hospitality Club in 1935, with Mrs. Betty Harwood as its first president. It was organized for daughters of Hospitality Club members but almost immediately began taking other members. It is no longer directly associated with the Hospitality Club, even though it still carries that name. Its best known activity has been the "Fabulous Follies," performed on stage by members as a money-raising project. The Follies celebrated a twentieth anniversary in 1973. The Junior Hospitality Club contributes annual proceeds from the highly successful Follies, as well as from its annual "Submarine Sandwich" booth at the State Fair, to a variety of local charities. The amount totals more than one-half million dollars since 1935. Junior Hospitality was instrumental in organizing the Oklahoma Foundation for the Disabled.

The Junior League of Oklahoma City was organized in 1927, with Mrs. Joseph Rumsey as president. Its purpose is to promote volunteerism and to develop the volunteer potential of its members in educational and charitable projects. In 1930 the league organized a Thrift Shop, selling used quality clothing. This shop has operated forty-three years and has been the league's principal money-raiser. It is now located at 1010 North Virginia. In 1931 the League started the Oklahoma City Charity Horse Show at the Stockyards Coliseum. This show operated until 1958, and helped to support charities of the League. One large early project of the league was the Walnut Grove Health Center, which it organized in 1932. Work of this center later was taken over by other organizations. The league has provided $82,000 in donations, plus many hours of volunteer work, to the Speech and Hearing Clinic of Oklahoma City.

The Cosmopolitan Club was founded in Oklahoma City in January, 1937. William O. Coe, who later was a major candidate for governor of Oklahoma, was its first president. This organization has devoted most of its effort to youth work. It has furnished books for school libraries and scholarships for students. The club erected bleachers at the old Indian baseball park at Northwest Fourth and Virginia for use of YMCA junior baseball players, and maintained them until the park was no longer used. Another Cosmopolitan Club was organized in northwest Oklahoma City, and an auxiliary organization, the Cosmopal Club, also is active.

The Optimist Club was founded a few years before World War II, but when the war began to strip men's civic clubs of their members, the Optimists merged into the Lions Club and disbanded as an independent group. It was reorganized in 1946 with new members. Its principal effort is in boys' work. The club sponsors baseball and football teams, along with other youth activity. Its civic projects are financed largely through the club's annual Christmas tree sales.

The Pilot Club of Oklahoma City was organized in June 1940, with Mrs. Morris A. Lyons as president. It is affiliated with the international Pilot Club organization. Its first big project was to develop a playground area, called Pilot Center. The first Pilot Center adjoined Washington School on Southwest Second Street, but the school was torn down during construction of Interstate 40. The club built a second center adjacent to Franklin School. The Center is operated by the Park Department. The club also offers scholarships for nurses and gives assistance to a number of charitable, health and youth organizations. There are now four Pilot Clubs in the Oklahoma City area.

The Exchange Club of Oklahoma City was chartered in March, 1941, with Burret A. Fost as president. Its purpose was to exchange ideas for community improvement. The club selects and honors a boy each month for outstanding citizenship. At the end of the school term it names a "Boy of the Year." The club also participates in Crime Prevention Week and in Junior Achievement Week. It has formed other Exchange clubs in northwest Oklahoma City, Greenbriar and Edmond.

No early history is available for the Loyal Order of the Moose. The present organization was founded in 1955 at the former Blossom Heath dance hall at Northwest Thirty-ninth and Grand Boulevard. Edward J. Smith was its first governor. It moved to Yukon in 1967, when its former meeting place became a victim of widening the expressway. The club has 1,670 members in a fifty-mile radius of Oklahoma City.

The Redbud Club was organized in 1962, with Mrs. Joseph W. Kelso as president. It promotes the civic, social and cultural life of the community, and is particularly active as a hospitality group for visitors to the city. This includes students in aviation.

Youth groups, as well as organizations benefiting youth, have played an important role in city history.

Hardly two hours passed after the multitude rushed into future Oklahoma City before a group of young settlers met in the temporary post office building to organize a Young Men's Christian Association. General F. L. Cramer was elected acting president and Doctor Angelo C. Scott was named temporary vice president. A few months later Scott was named the first permanent president of what is now the oldest organization in Oklahoma City.

No records exist of activity of the YMCA between 1889 and 1904, although it is known that the organization had a capital funds drive in 1891. Meetings during the 1890s were held in the first Overholser Opera House at Grand and Robinson, which was built in 1890. In the early 1900s the organization took quarters on the second floor of the Baltimore Building above a drugstore. This provided a room used both for a gymnasium and for religious activities. However, athletic functions in the gym often brought complaints from the drugstore below. A few years later the "Y" obtained leased quarters in the Hendrix Building on the south side of Main Street, between Harvey and Robinson, where the S.H. Kress store is now located. There it sponsored social and religious programs.

On October 29, 1916, a mass meeting of YMCA members and civic workers was held in the City Auditorium at Grand and Harvey to kick off a money-raising drive for a YMCA building. The goal was $300,000.

The present Main Library is in the same Third and Robinson location as its predecessor.

Judge C. B. Ames presided at the kickoff banquet. On Sunday, November 26, every minster in Oklahoma City was reported to have preached a sermon related to the YMCA drive. The campaign resulted in raising $255,000 with 4,500 subscribers participating.

A site was selected at 125 Northwest Second Street, between Robinson and Broadway. Construction of a building began in 1917. It included offices, worship space, activity area, living quarters for young men, and even an indoor swimming pool. The building was dedicated in December, 1918, by William G. McAdoo of California, a son-in-law of then President Woodrow Wilson.

Many older residents of the city can remember when, in dry years and with algae-laden city water almost undrinkable, a daily line of people with cans and bottles drew drinking water from a sidewalk faucet at the YMCA, from a sweet water well in the Garber sands. The Oklahoma Publishing Company had a similar well on Fourth Street. The indoor swimming pool at the old "Y" led later to creation of a Kerr-McGee employe swimming club, of competitive caliber.

The late 1920s produced the first camp for the YMCA. It was Camp Don Shelley, a forty-acre tract, near what is now the Northwest Highway. Land was given to the YMCA by W. N. Shellenburger, and was improved largely through help of the Civitan Club. Oil was discovered on the property. Mineral rights were leased to the Gypsy Oil Company. It resulted in income which made it possible to pay off indebtedness on the camp improvements and to purchase, in 1933, 220 acres on Lick Creek in the Arbuckle mountains. This was the beginning of Camp Classen, which now has 2,315 acres and is the largest resident camp in America. Early improvements at Camp Classen were made by volunteer convict labor. The Anton Classen family provided considerable monetary support — hence the name — Camp Classen.

The YMCA also played an important role in the early youth baseball program. One leader in the program was Roy Deal, father of Cot Deal, who moved from YMCA baseball to major leagues. Another was Roscoe "Bo" Belcher, who later created a baseball camp at Chandler and had a son, Tom, who also made it to a major league.

In 1952 the YMCA constructed a new, modern building on the northeast corner of Northwest Fifth and Robinson. It constructed an Eastside branch for black members the same year. The building which had served the "Y" since 1918 became an evening school for Oklahoma City University. Later the building was purchased by Kerr-McGee, which stripped the interior and incorporated it into what is now the full-block Kerr-McGee complex.

Today the YMCA of Oklahoma City has ten branches and 30,000 members. One-fourth of its members are now women and girls. Norman Macleod was metropolitan executive director of the YMCA from 1950, one year before its present headquarters opened, and directed YMCA activity in its greatest period of growth. He died in 1974.

The Young Women's Christian Association was chartered by 600 women in May, 1907. Mrs. J. F. Warren was its first president. Principal activity of the YWCA has been "to care for the health and emotional well-being of young women in a Christian atmosphere."

The YWCA first met in leased quarters in the Empire Building at 124 West Main. In 1912 it moved to the Gross Building at 112 Northwest Second Street, just east of the former Petroleum Club Building. During World War I, it was located in the Arcade Terminal Building, now Globe Life. Following the war it purchased its own building at 225 West Reno. In 1931 a new YWCA building at First and Hudson was opened, complete with living quarters for young women, several worship and activity centers, a small auditorium, and a cafeteria, open to the public. The cafeteria began business December 28, and four days later — January 1, 1932 — the offices and residential quarters were opened.

The YWCA has its Ione branch on a thirty-acre tract at 6103 Northwest Fifty-eighth, which provides both indoor and outdoor activity space. It operates its McFarland branch at 1701 North Eastern and its University Heights Center, a training class facility, in a former school (public) building on the southwest corner of Northwest Sixty-third and Western.

The Boy Scouts of America began to reach Oklahoma City, with the organization of scattered troops, not long after its 1910 incorporation. However, it was 1914 when an Oklahoma City Boy Scout Council was officially organized. J. G. Masters was the first council president, Oklahoma City's first professional Boy Scout executive was employed in 1918. He was Doctor James E. Pershing, relative of General John J. Pershing, World War I commander in chief of American armies in Europe.

Direction of the Boy Scout organization has been toward character development and the building of physical and mental skills. Much of its emphasis has been on camping and outdoor activities. The Oklahoma City Boy Scout Council in 1929 purchased 160 acres on the South Canadian River near Wheatland and began the development of Camp Kickapoo. This camp now has 360 acres, and includes a dining hall, swimming pool, and a large number of service buildings.

A merger between the Oklahoma City Council and the Canadian Valley Boy Scout Council, brought into the outdoor property Camp Sasakwa, near Holdenville. Another campsite was obtained following World War II on the Illinois River near Welling, downstream from Tahlequah. Known as Turner Ford, this has become a base camp for float trips on the river. Another Boy Scout camp, east of Arapaho, is known as Dripping Springs. The principal camp of the Scout Council is Slippery Falls, with 1,540 acres of wilderness land on Pennington Creek near Madill. Several small lakes have been developed in this area since the land was acquired in 1967.

Over the years local Boy Scout councils in central Oklahoma have merged. Today Oklahoma City is headquarters for the Last Frontier Council, serving 22,450 Scouts and leaders in a thirteen-county area. Headquarters is on the north end of the Fairgrounds. Principal donor for the headquarters building was Allen Street, one of Oklahoma City's earliest Scoutmasters. It was dedicated in memory of his son, Bob Allen Street, who was killed in an electrical accident in the early 1940s.

Girl Scouts were organized in Oklahoma City in 1935, with Mrs. George Reif as first president of the Oklahoma City Council. Playing a key role in the building of the organization was Mrs. Helen Stillman, who served as executive director of the council from the early 1940s until 1971.

The first camp owned by the council is a 110-acre site southeast of Oklahoma City. The camp is named "Cookie Land," since it was purchased from profits of Girl Scout cookie sales. Camp Red Rock, also bought with profits from cookies, covers 285 acres of land west of Binger, and was acquired in 1955. In 1965 the Girl Scouts leased twenty-three acres of land on Lake Eufaula for a boating base, naming it Camp Conover.

The council now covers Oklahoma, Lincoln, Logan and Pottawatomie Counties and is known as the Red Lands Girl Scout Council. Its annual membership is above 11,000. Its headquarters are at 121 Northeast Fiftieth Street.

The Oklahoma City Council of Camp Fire Girls was organized in 1926, with Neal O'Sullivan as first president. It was started at invitation of the Oklahoma City public school system. Its first part-time executive was Mildred Clark who now heads the home service department for the Oklahoma Natural Gas Company in Tulsa. The council purchased and began development of Camp Cimarron, near Coyle, in 1937, and Camp Dakani on Hefner Road, west of Frontier City near Interstate 35, in 1955. The council now has 9,000 members and leaders registered annually.

8

Culture, And Fun, Too

NTERTAINMENT FOUND ITS WAY TO Oklahoma City even in its earliest days. In the fall of 1890 Buffalo Bill Cody's Wild West Show came to the frontier town. The show played under a grove of trees on the North Canadian River, with 16,000 people crowding in to see it. This same grove shaded Governor Colonel Theodore Roosevelt's Rough Riders' reunion ten years later.

It was also in 1890 that Henry Overholser built the first Opera House on the southeast corner of Grand (now Sheridan) and Robinson. This later became location of the Commerce Exchange Building, which would house offices of the Chamber of Commerce, and also would be first home of the Oklahoma City Art Center. Still later the site would become the northwest corner of the Myriad Convention Center.

This Opera House in a frontier town was the vision of a man who declared, almost before dust of the Run had settled, "Every town needs schools, churches, hotels and a theater. I'll build the hotel and the theater."

The theater opened in September 1890, with John Dillon starring in "Wanted — The Earth." It was followed by "Uncle Tom's Cabin." The first floor of the building was occupied by a general store. The theater itself was on the second floor. It had a wooden outside staircase. The room was barn-like, lighted by kerosene lamps suspended from the ceiling. A bright red, calico curtain with a pair of Roman striped portieres in the center, supplied color to an otherwise drab surrounding. The curtain hung from a wire and was manipulated by two men who walked backward and forward, pulling at its front edges. Advertising was painted on the curtain. The seats were kitchen chairs. They were carried out often to provide necessary space for dancing. There were three dressing rooms. At other times these were the law offices of J. H. Everest, L. P. Hudson, and L. G. Puttmas. Since there was no backstage entrance actors had to go through the house in view of the audience.

In addition to shows, the main hall also was the scene of frequent charity balls, banquets, parties and community events. In 1891, for example, a Fourth of July celebration was held in the Overholser Opera House. It included concerts by a military band and by the Philharmonic Society. Tickets were twenty-five cents. This was higher than the price of most shows. The usual price was fifteen cents for performances, with ladies free when accompanied by gentlemen. The Al G. Fields Minstrels and Patti Rosa played there. Frederick Warde and his company once appeared in the theater in street clothes because a train hauling their baggage was delayed. The Overholsers operated this second story theater until 1903, when they decided it wasn't good enough for Oklahoma City. When the Overholsers moved out, the Stater Stock Company took it over and used it for one year before moving to its own theater in Putnam Park.

The second Overholser Opera House was constructed at 217 West Grand Avenue, and was opened in November 1903. It cost $100,000. The building was financed partially through sale of subscription tickets. It was a four story building of Roman buff brick. It had handsomely designed boxes and leather opera chairs. Capacity, including standing room, was 2,500. It had the largest stage in the west — being five feet wider than the Olympic stage at St. Louis. Height from the stage floor to the roof was seventy-two feet. A large music room opened to an orchestra pit in front of the stage. The building contained 720 electric lights and had toilet rooms on every floor.

Construction of the theater resulted in establishment of an Oklahoma Circuit for entertainment features. Fifteen theaters were on the circuit. Ed Overholser was circuit president. Towns in the circuit included Oklahoma City, Muskogee, South McAlester, Ardmore, Bartlesville, Vinita, Tulsa, Shawnee, El Reno, Guthrie and Enid. Sarah Bernhardt and Lillian Russell were among those who came to the Overholser in 1907. First performance in the new state of Oklahoma was "The Taming of the Shrew." Mary Mannering and Eleanor Robson came in 1908. Shriners presented an annual musical comedy in the theater. The Opera House was purchased by John and Peter Sinopoulo in 1917. The following year it was remodeled and the name changed to The Orpheum.

Remodeling took two years and cost $400,000. Only the outside shell remained in its original form. It reopened with "The Mikado." It carried entertainment from the national Orpheum circuit. The theater became famous for vaudeville shows. It also showed motion pictures. In 1926 it was the first building in Oklahoma City to be air conditioned. In 1930 it was remodeled again and this time renamed the Warner Theater. The Warner brought stage plays and first run motion pictures to Oklahoma City during its early years. In 1931 it was home of the unsuccessful "Warner Players." In its later years it was strictly a motion picture theater, lasting until the mid-1960s when it was torn down to create a parking lot.

Perhaps the grandest entertainment area in early Oklahoma City was the Delmar Garden, opened by John Sinopoulo and Joseph Marre in 1903. The garden occupied 140 acres of land leased from Charles Colcord and a partner. It stood on an area extending west from the corner of Western and Exchange, occupying much of the space where the Public Market now stands. Sinopoulo and Marre brought the idea with them from St. Louis, where Sinopoulo had operated a candy store and Marre, a saloon. They patterned it after the Delmar Garden in Forest Park at St. Louis. The Colcord organization constructed the buildings while the operators put in concessions. The partners later bought part of the land.

The Garden had a theater seating 1,200, a scenic railway, a ferris wheel, a dance hall and a swimming pool. There was a hotel and restaurant and an outdoor area where beer and other refreshments were sold under the trees. The Metropolitan Electric Railway Company had been organized in 1902 to serve the Garden. Ten streetcars were used to transport people

Delmar Garden refreshment area near Western and Exchange about 1903 was a popular spot.

to and from the park. It attracted people from many cities, and brought conventions here from other states. Many famous entertainers came to the Garden. Light operas, bands, musical comedies and dramas were booked. Lon Chaney, Senior played in "The Mikado." Madame Nordica sang there. John L. Sullivan performed in an exhibition boxing match in the Garden. Buster Keaton performed there with his parents at age three.

There was a race track at the park. Dan Patch, the famous pacing horse, raced there. Barney Oldfield burned up the track at sixty miles per hour. Quannah Parker and Geronimo often were there. Geronimo sold autographs for a dime. Silent movies also were seen. Best known was "The Great Train Robbery." Matinees cost a dime, and evening shows were twenty-five cents. Children were admitted free. Morris Loewenstein, who later developed his own motion picture theaters, was the press agent.

The glamour of Delmar Garden began to fade after statehood. Prohibition then prevented the sale of beer. Annual flooding of the North Canadian River brought hordes of mosquitoes. It closed about 1910. The scenic railway remained in operation several years.

The Empire Theater also opened in 1903 between present Park and Kerr at 216 North Broadway. It was then immediately north of the depot on the Rock Island railroad which ran through the center of downtown. Noise forced plays to be delayed whenever trains passed through. The Empire gave up in 1907.

Oklahoma City had an early open air theater, constructed in 1907, on the southwest corner of First (now Park) and Robinson. It was called the Lyric Air Dome. The theater was owned by Pete and John Sinopoulo, and offered vaudeville as well as silent motion pictures. Admission was ten cents. When noise of a dance hall built next door interfered, the building was enclosed and became the Lyric Theater. It had a spectacular white archway. Its acts came from the Orpheum circuit. The building went down in 1920 and the Perrine Building, now the Cravens Building, went up. Almost at the same time another "air dome" was going up, this one on the north side of Grand (now Sheridan) just west of the new Colcord Building.

The Folly Theater at 125 West Grand was built by F. M. Tulla, a furniture dealer, in 1907. It showed vaudeville and movies and later burlesque. In 1920 it became part of Midwest Enterprises, and continued as a motion picture theater until 1947, when it burned. It was rebuilt the following year as the Sooner Theater.

The Metropolitan Theater began operation in January 1909 with its own stock company. Lon Chaney, later the nationally-acclaimed actor known as the "man of a thousand faces" was a stage hand, and frightened the chorus girls with his grotesque facial appearances. An itinerate actor, Wayne Campbell, came there out of work and got a job as leading man. Later he moved on to become head of the speech department at Oklahoma City University. This theater became part of the Midwest group in 1920. It was the only nonunion theater in town in 1929 and received threats of being blown up if it did not unionize. It was dynamited shortly after midnight July 29, 1929, creating a four foot hole in the rear wall and damaging the rest of the building. It was condemned and in 1935 was torn down as a WPA project in Oklahoma City. It was on the site where the Mummer's Theater later was constructed.

The Colonial Theater opened in the autumn of 1909. It had an entrance with double stairs. Later it was called Majestic. Morris Loewenstein maintained his office in this building until his death in the late 1960s.

The Liberty Theater opened in 1915 at 19 North Robinson. playing vaudeville and motion pictures. The theater organized its own acting group, known as the Liberty Players. Best known was its bathing beauty chorus. Until 1930 it had both vaudeville and movies, then continued as Harbour Theater, showing movies. It was remodeled in the late 1950s for Cinerama. Today it operates as the Cooper Theater.

There were many owners of theaters in the first two decades of the Twentieth Century. However, as the second decade drew to a close, they were coming closer together, in part through self-defense against a problem threatening theater owners all over the country. In 1917 stage hands and actors unions arranged to strike for each other in a grievance against New York booking agents. In their fight for more favorable wages and working conditions, unions decided to try to close as many theaters as possible. John Sinopoulo, Oklahoma City's leading theater owner of the time, was finding acts stolen from his theaters as the actors arrived by train in Oklahoma City, and were hustled to the Palace Theater instead. As a result Sinopoulo bought the Palace to protect his acts.

There were, at the time, five theatrical groups, and the strike forced them to work more closely together. The groups were the Oklahoma Amusement Company, which owned the Liberty Theater; the Olympic Athletic Association, owning the Lyric Theater; Powell-Croak Amusement Company, owner of the Empress Theater; Folly Theater Company, owner of the Folly Theater; and the Metropolitan Building Company, owner of the Palace Theater. During the strike, Olympic, Powell and the Oklahoma Amusement Companies, pooled resources and acquired the Folly and Metropolitan Theaters. In 1920, they merged as Midwest Enterprises, with Sinopoulo as president.

Oklahoma City's first impresario was Hathaway Harper, who taught school, studied law, published newspapers and held political office before coming to Oklahoma City in 1895. In the late 1890s he brought the nation's highest pitch soprano, Ellen Beach Yau, to the Overholser Theater. In 1903 he brought Madame Nordica to the city to sing at Delmar Gardens. In 1909 he engaged the fairgrounds for a pilot named Charles F. Willard, employed by Glenn H. Curtiss, to make a landing. Approximately 500 persons paid one dollar each to see him land in a wheat field after a long delay, due to wind. Harper booked Sarah Bernhardt and Madame Schumann-Heink into the Orpheum on one-night stands. He brought many productions into city theaters during the 1920s before his retirement.

Although it was never owned by the city but so used, the building at 501 West California, which in its latter years housed the Utterback Type Shop, with the Trianon Ballroom above, was the scene of numerous entertainment programs and speeches, including one by the early-day socialist and labor leader, Eugene V. Debs. It closed as an auditorium in the early 1920s, but the building survived until the late 1960s when it was torn down during urban redevelopment.

The year 1921 marked the building of Oklahoma City's showpiece of theaters. It was the Criterion, on the south side of West Main between Robinson and Broadway. It cost $700,000. It was described as "a symphony in brick and stone." The stage area was of concrete and the building was five stories high at the stage end. There were thick, velvet carpets in the foyer and isles. Walls were of walnut and were nearly covered with paintings. The pipe organ cost $25,000 and was the largest in Oklahoma. The Criterion was built to be a motion picture theater for first run movies. Beginning in 1928, and for about two years, it tried legitimate stage, but went back to movies in 1930. It closed briefly in the early 1960s and reopened in 1964 as a burlesque theater, but soon returned to movies, continuing until it was demolished in 1973 for urban renewal.

When the Shriners began their huge temple on the southwest corner of Northwest Sixth and Robinson in 1921, they included the largest auditorium and theater in Oklahoma. It was completed in 1923 and opened with the new Oklahoma City Symphony — forerunner to the present Oklahoma City Symphony. The Shrine Theater hosted the principal meetings, plays and entertainment events of the city for several years. Will Rogers performed there. Harry Lauder was there twice. Ethel Barrymore performed in the theater. Numerous plays and musicals were offered. But hard times came to the theater as well as the Shrine organization, during the depression, and the Shrine lost the building. The former Shrine temple was acquired at public sale by the Home State Life Insurance Company, which operated the theater until 1951, when its area was converted into offices. It now is the American General Life Building.

The Stock Yards Coliseum, which opened January 16, 1922, climaxed a dream of many years. The project was initiated by Wilson and Company and Morris and Company (later Armour) when the packing companies gave $100,000 toward the project. A Chamber of Commerce committee headed by its president, George Frederickson, raised the remainder of $300,000 needed to build the Coliseum. When it was opened, it was described as "the greatest coliseum west of the Mississippi River."

It is located near the arch at the west end of Exchange Avenue. It was constructed to seat 5,175 people. There were 750 box seats. It opened with a three day run of "The Merry Widow." Dress was formal. John Philip Sousa's band played there during the first year. Wind damaged the building in the spring of 1923, and it was repaired with a smaller stage. During the 1920s the Coliseum was the scene of teachers' conventions, auto shows, livestock shows, and boxing matches, including an exhibition by Jack Dempsey. But in 1930 the Coliseum was destroyed by fire. At that time it was being used to store automobiles. Several people lost their lives fighting the fire and removing the automobiles. A new Coliseum was constructed in 1931 on the same site, financed by insurance money from the destroyed building. It duplicated the old Coliseum in size and design, with exception of a stage, which was omitted. Since then it has been used for livestock shows, automobile shows, charity horse shows, the Boy Scout Circus and wrestling. Completion of the all-sports arena at the Fairgrounds greatly lessened use of the Coliseum. It was sold in 1972.

In early 1937 the Public Works Administration-built Municipal Auditorium was completed, seating 6,000. This multi-purpose auditorium was designed to be used, not only for plays, programs and concerts, but for athletic events, displays, and dances. It included a main and a Little Theater. A second floor convention room, seating 1,000 was named the Mirror Room. It was the scene of the annual Gridiron Show for many years. For six years it served as the Mummers Theater. Another large hall below the auditorium was used for major conventions, dinners and display shows, called the Zebra Room.

Municipal Auditorium became Oklahoma City's major building for plays, concerts and special events. The Ballet Russe de Monte Carlo performed there several times. Oklahoma Cityan Yvonne Chouteau starred with that troupe in 1952. The musical "Oklahoma!" set a record for the auditorium in November, 1946 when 54,000 tickets were sold, and more than $30,000 in mail orders had to be returned. Reverend Bill Alexander, the colorful pastor of First Christian Church, held Easter services in the auditorium from the late 1940s through the 1950s, always with over-flowing crowds.

This auditorium was estensively remodeled in 1968, limiting its present use to productions on stage. This is because it was no longer in

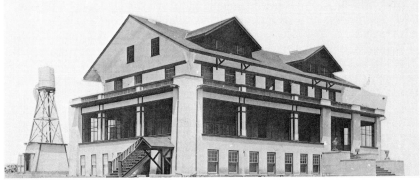

Social life was important in early days. This is the Oklahoma City Country Club of 1906.

The boardwalk cafe at Belle Isle Park was a favorite recreation spot during the 1920s.

demand for sporting events, circuses and other uses, with more adequate facilities available at the Fairgrounds. Upon being remodeled, it was renamed Civic Center Music Hall, holding 3,200 persons.

But something much larger was coming. It was Myriad Convention Center, a part of the city's Urban Renewal project, which would cover a four block area downtown, when cleared of its former buildings. This center was completed in 1972. It includes as its focal point an arena area which will seat 15,000 persons.

The first major outdoor amphitheaters of Oklahoma City were the result of WPA days. Projects were approved for Lincoln Park, on the east side, and Will Rogers Park, on the west side. Amphitheaters, following the natural slope of terrain, were constructed with concrete and considerable native stone by the Works Progress Administration. These facilities have been used throughout the years for programs, entertainment and meetings.

The largest event to be scheduled into the newly completed Lincoln Park Amphitheater was an annual community Easter Sunrise pageant, featuring the talent of local choral singers and actors, under the direction of Wayne Campbell of the Oklahoma City University fine arts department. The services drew increased crowds each year during the 1930s. Many persons from other parts of Oklahoma came to Lincoln Park each year to see the pageant.

Late in the 1930s, one Easter morning, the annual pageant was in full swing. Professor Campbell was pacing nervously as musicians neared the crescendo to signal appearance of the character representing Jesus Christ. Christ for several years had been played by a local Presbyterian minister, but this year he overlooked his cue, and was not in the wings ready to enter. Campbell could contain himself no longer. Just as the crescendo subsided, he blurted out. "My God! Where's Christ?," not realizing that an open microphone was nearby. Whether for this reason, the uncertainty of approaching World War II, or other causes, this was the last of community Easter Sunrise services at Lincoln Park.

The next major amphitheater was constructed at Northwest Thirty-sixth and Walker by First Christian Church in 1949, and has been the scene of religious services, concerts and musical plays. All these amphitheaters have continued to be used for entertainment and other events. Television, and later air conditioning, changed summer entertainment patterns, and all three amphitheaters have experienced less use in recent years.

Meanwhile, following World Warr II, a new type of outdoor theater was emerging. This was the drive-in motion picture theater. First in Oklahoma City was the Northwest Highway Drive-In, placed west of May Avenue and north of the Northwest Highway, shortly after war's end. Today most drive-ins are near major expressways and highways at the edges of the city.

Amateur theater got its start in Oklahoma City at the first Overholser Opera House in the early 1890s. There was one production in 1894 and two in 1895. One such play by the amateurs of early Oklahoma City was "The Octaroon."

Amateur theater has continued to be popular here. In 1925 a group known as the Civic Theater Association made the first major attempt to organize an amateur community theater in the city. It started with 225 members and grew to a high of 500 participants. The movement lasted nine years, dying in 1934 in midst of the depression. Doctor John Hubbard, an osteopath, was director of the group during the first seven years. He was succeeded by Joe Gifford in its last two years.

Gifford and others formed another group, The Theater Guild, in 1936. It presented plays at OCU and later in the Little Theater of Municipal Auditorium. It was forced to disband in 1939 for lack of support.

Another group was organized in 1931 in a vacant building at Northwest Tenth and Robinson, with Paul Anpault as director. It lasted only two years.

The WPA Theater was established in Oklahoma City in November, 1935, as part of the nationwide Works Progress Administration, a federal relief program. John Dunn, the director, combed relief rolls for former actors and performers. Rehearsals were held at 21 West Main, and later at 431 West Main, later moving to city offices on the northwest corner of Grand and Broadway. First performances of the WPA Theater were at Civilian Conservation Corps camps, under conditions offering no electricity or stages — usually the side of a hill. The group also collected Oklahoma folklore and wrote plays. Some plays resulted in a series of radio dramas over KOMA. The Federal Theater Project closed in 1939. Dunn later became director of the Oklahoma Educational Television system, retiring in 1972.

The Oklahoma City Playhouse started almost immediately after the close of World War II. It performed plays, including "Kiss and Tell," "Stage Door," "My Sister Eileen" and others, under direction of Lee Schirch. It closed in 1947 for lack of funds.

A stock company from the Clement Drama Festival in Clement, Massachusetts, came to Oklahoma City in 1949. The group, directed by Buddy Piper, was called the "Piper Players." It played the former Victoria (Movie) Theater at Northwest Seventeenth and Classen, but lasted only one season.

In 1948 a new theater attempt was getting underway, to be known as the Mummers, a name taken from an ancient traveling European minstrel group. Shortly before its creation one of the organizational leaders, a young, aspiring actress named Mayde Mack Jones, was killed in an automobile accident. Thus the name, "Mayde Mack Mummers."

The Mummers started in 1949 performing melodramas in an old carnival tent at Northeast Twenty-third and Eastern. The tent moved to Will Rogers Park the next year, and the third year the Mummers moved into the Mirror Room of Municipal Auditorium. As they moved upward in location, they did also in selection of plays and style of performances. By 1954 they were ready for a theater of their own. It was an old warehouse on West Main, which they remodeled themselves, using seats removed from a theater in Duncan and given to them by the late Henry Griffin. Mack Jones, Frisco Railway manager, was president during the first few years and Mack Scism, a high school teacher, became director.

In the mid-1950s, the Mummers became a professional Equity group, and shortly afterward many of its early participants, excepting Mack Scism, dropped out. In the mid-1960s the Mummers Theater received a Ford Foundation matching grant of $1,250,000 for a new theater building. It was constructed downtown with unfinished masonry exterior, with exposed utility and service pipes. The building cost about $3,000,000 — more

The cast for "Kimis," a home talent play presented in Oklahoma City in about 1890.

than had been allotted by the foundation. It included three auditoriums of different sizes. It was the first building to be completed in Oklahoma City's downtown Urban Renewal project, and its design caused considerable controversy. It opened in the fall of 1970. However, the built-in operational cost of the over-built structure doomed it to failure in less than two years. The Mummers died in 1972 after twenty-three years. The Oklahoma Theater Center, another amateur theater organization, headed by oilman and philanthropist John Kirkpatrick and John Belt, took over operation of the building and produces amateur theatricals successfully.

Other theater groups operated concurrently with the Mummers. The First Christian Church bought the former Edgemere Country Club grounds at Northwest Thirty-sixth and Walker in 1948 as a future church site, and immediately built an amphitheater on the grounds. In 1949, the church started outdoor "Twilight Time" productions under its music director, Tracy Sylvester. Performances included both music and drama. As a special event, for a number of years sponsorship of both the "Miss Oklahoma City" and "Miss Oklahoma" contests was included. This was the first and only time for a division of the "Miss America" competition to be sponsored by a church. In 1956, with building of the new First Christian Church, a theater in the round was constructed and used for dramatic entertainment, as part of the Twilight Time series. It is called the Jewel Box Theater. Amphitheater performances were dropped in 1962 but Jewel Box Theater shows continue.

The Miracle Playhouse began in 1958. Mr. and Mrs. Mack Jones, who left the Mummers when it became a professional Equity Theater, were its organizers. It opened in May 1958 in the former First Christian Church at Northwest Tenth and Robinson, and three months later moved to the old Ritz Theater. The repertoire included plays, melodramas and concert readings. The Playhouse continued through 1961.

The Lyric Theater was established in 1963 to offer a professional type atmosphere for trained young artists and to provide community entertainment. It was organized as a civic venture and as an extension of the fine arts department of Oklahoma City University. Doctor Jack Cogdill was in charge of production and Doctor Ray Luke was musical director. The University Theater was renovated, including new lighting and air conditioning, to accommodate the Lyric, which has become Oklahoma City's most popular local theatrical group. Playing a major role, both in the Lyric Theater and in renovation of the Fine Arts Auditorium of OCU, were Mr. and Mrs. John E. Kirkpatrick.

In 1966 a Warehouse Theater group organized in a former warehouse in downtown Oklahoma City. This group performs many off-beat, and sometimes controversial plays, and caters to a college-age audience.

Doctor Angelo C. Scott told of a group of settlers with musical inclinations who formed a chorus of sixty voices during the first year after the Run. Outside of church choirs, this was the first musical group known to have been organized in Oklahoma City.

The first music club to be founded in the new town was the Philharmonic, in 1892, with Doctor Scott as president. Its purpose was "to stimulate interest in things musical by presenting choral work." During its first four years, parts of "The Messiah" and "The Creation" were given, together with a number of variety concerts. Doctor Scott was organist for the club.

But even at an earlier date community bands and orchestras had been organized. The city's first uniformed band was founded in 1890. The first Oklahoma City Orchestra was put together in 1891 and continued throughout the 1890s. Louis Meier conducted the orchestra.

Appearance of the first Overholser Opera House in early territorial days helped to bring classical music and visits of professional musicians here. Grand opera came to the town at frequent intervals in early years. During the 1920s a continuous series of highest grade concert music was furnished through the Institute of Arts and Sciences and local musical organizations.

One of the most far-reaching organizations in the field of music was the Ladies Music Club, organized by Mrs. Ed L. Dunn in the spring of 1908. Mrs. C. B. Ames was its first president. This club has had a major influence in music over the years, and in 1973 had more than 300 members, divided into more than twenty special interest groups.

It is interesting that the word "Ladies," rather than "Women's" was the popular term in 1908, hence the name "Ladies Music Club." However, many years later it gained an auxiliary, called the "Men's Division," instead of "Gentlemen's Division," since at the time of organization the word gentlemen was not considered masculine enough.

Another organization which provided an early influence in musical life of Oklahoma City was the Apollo Club. This club was founded in the spring of 1900, with Charles M. Bosworth as its first president. For well over a quarter of a century this men's chorus furnished outstanding entertainment in Oklahoma City and other cities it visited. Another large club was the Sorosis Club, which studied music, literature, drama and art.

The first symphony here was organized in 1923, under direction of Dean Fredrik Holmberg of the School of Fine Arts of the University of Oklahoma. Oklahoma City at that time was one of few cities in the nation to support its own symphony orchestra. Instrumental in its founding was the Ladies Music Club, spearheaded by Mrs. George Forsythe and Mrs. Frank Buttram.

A second symphony orchestra was established in 1937. It gave its first concert in early 1938, under the conductorship of Ralph Rose. This orchestra was organized as a unit of the WPA Federal Music Project. Its first performances were in the Shrine Auditorium. Many of its musicians came from the earlier symphony.

In 1942 the symphony operation and sponsorship were taken over by the Oklahoma State Symphony Society. Later this became known as the Oklahoma City Symphony. After a short period under the direction of Rose, it was taken over by Victor Alessandro, who conducted until 1950. When he accepted another symphony post that year, Guy Fraser Harrison became conductor. Under Harrison the symphony attained national stature. For several years it performed weekly over the ABC radio network. In addition, its concerts were beamed regularly over Voice of America overseas as well as over the worldwide Armed Forces Radio Network. Harrison retired in 1973 and Ray E. Luke became interim conductor.

Gail Lawton was an early-day harpist in the Oklahoma City Symphony. Lawton moved from the Oklahoma City Symphony to Hollywood, where he became a "double" on the harp for Harpo Marx. Whenever difficult numbers were required, the music came from Lawton instead of Harpo. Lawton wrote his friends here to watch Harpo's playing to see if the fingers were long and bony, instead of stubby, whenever the films showed close-ups of fingers and harp only. "If the fingers are long and bony, they are mine," Lawton wrote. He never appeared in the movies but his fingers did.

An organization founded to support the symphony is the Symphony Society. In recent years the society has sponsored an annual series of pop concerts, featuring a portion of the symphony performing popular music, along with guest artists.

The Oklahoma City Junior Symphony, not associated directly with the symphony, was organized in 1951 by the local Jaycees. This orchestra, designed for high school age youngsters, attracted string musicians from several cities surrounding Oklahoma City, and developed into one of the top youth orchestras in the nation. It has played before the National Federation of Music Teachers in its annual convention, and in 1964 it performed at the World's Fair in New York.

The Civic Music Association was organized in the early 1950s to bring an annual series of professional artists to Oklahoma City. This organization is unique in that tickets are always sold for the coming season without a buyer knowing what artists will perform. When sales close in the spring, the board convenes and negotiates four or more programs to fit ticket sale receipts. All tickets are season memberships and no tickets are sold at the door. Programs are held in the Fine Arts Auditorium of Oklahoma City University.

Oklahoma City long has been known for outstanding high school choruses. Most prominent among these in recent years has been the Northwest Classen High School Cry-Slurs. Practically since founding of the school in the early 1950s the Cry-Slurs have won top musical honors, culminated by winning first place in the International Youth Music Festival at Graz, Austria, in July 1972.

Oklahoma City was one of the first three cities in the world to organize a chapter in a unique organization dedicated to barbershop quartet singing. The Society for the Preservation and Encouragement of Barbershop Quartet Singing in America, Incorporated (SPEBSQSA) started in Tulsa in 1938. The next two chapters were in Kansas City and Oklahoma City that same year. Hank Wright, Ernie Dick, and Grady Musgrave were instrumental in organizing the Oklahoma City Chapter. The city chapter held practice sessions in the Biltmore Hotel. Today the organization has chapters in the United States and several foreign countries, and an annual convention with national competition.

In 1940 an Oklahoma City quartet, "The Flatfoot Four," including Johnny Whalen, Britt Stegall, Red Elliott, and Sam Barnes, won the top national award in New York City. Shortly afterwards, Whalen died, and the club sponsored a show in Municipal Auditorium in 1941 to liquidate the mortgage on his home for his widow. The event was so successful that similar shows have become an annual affair in the auditorium, always

Making music was popular from the beginning. Here is the first community orchestra.

drawing capacity crowds. The society held its national convention here in 1948.

   While symphonies and vocal groups were providing cultural entertainment, orchestras were becoming popular for dinner music and dancing. A popular dance orchestra shortly after turn of the century was the Tomlin Brothers orchestra. Another early dance band leader was Harry Steinburg, who in later years would play with the WPA Symphony. He was popular at Belle Isle pavilion and the Euclid Ballroom. T. Holder had a well known black band which played the Oklahoma City circuit.

   One post World War I dance band group was Clarence Tackett's Toe Teasers. The Toe Teasers played city clubs and dance halls for about twenty years following the war. Joining the Tackett band in 1925 was a young former University of Oklahoma dance band director named Bonnie Spencer, who moved on to organize his own orchestra. This band was popular on the city scene for nearly thirty-five years. Out of the Spencer orchestra came Al Good, and others, who organized their own dance combines, which became more numerous as Oklahoma City grew in population.

   Several musicians went from the Spencer orchestra into major bands or into motion pictures. J. D. Wade, who started with Spencer at the university in 1923 before moving to Oklahoma City bands, went to New York to join Paul Tremaine, and later Eddie Duchin, before going to the West Coast as a musician for Republic motion picture studios. Dick Krueger left Spencer for the Henry King orchestra, later to be a tenor soloist at the Shamrock Hotel in Houston. Jim Harbert played piano for the Spencer orchestra in the 1950s, then went to the West Coast to accompany Peggy Lee. He then joined Frank Sinatra and began writing tunes which Sinatra sang. Harbert next arranged music for Ice Capades, then the Lido Show, in the United States and in Paris. Jack Teagarten studied music in the Central High School band under Floyd Kimes Russell, well known early band instructor. When the Orpheum Theater brought Paul Whiteman to the city for a show in the 1920s, Whiteman held auditions for his orchestra. Teagarten brought his trombone to the theater, tried out, and was hired. Teagarten played first with the Whiteman orchestra, then formed his own group. He toured the world, and often during his career was associated with Louie Armstrong in person, and in making records.

Another Oklahoma Cityan, Art Fowler, attended dances around Oklahoma City, and often played the banjo and ukulele as a sit-in. His later association with the crooner, Gene Austin, made him famous. He accompanied Austin in "My Blue Heaven," his most famous recording, along with many other tunes during the years the two were teamed.

The Blue Devils orchestra, a black Oklahoma City dance band which became popular following World War I, attracted several musicians who would go on to national fame. One was Jimmy Rushing, known world-wide as the "greatest living male blues singer," almost until his death in 1973. Perhaps the best known of his recordings was "Mr. Five by Five." Rushing got his training in Douglass High School before singing with the Blue Devils. He moved up to the Bennie Moten orchestra in Kansas City and to Count Basie's orchestra in New York. He later formed his own group which toured the world.

Charlie Christian grew up here and joined his brother's band in the city at age fifteen. In 1937 he organized his own band, featuring his electric guitar, then went to the Benny Goodman orchestra, where he was described often as the greatest of jazz guitarists. He died of tuberculosis in 1942 at age twenty-four.

The University Club at Northwest Third and Robinson was long popular for dining and dancing and was the city's first, large, downtown social club. The year 1924 saw building of the Oklahoma City Club, later the Oklahoma Club. The building is now the Tivoli Inn at Sheridan and Robinson. The Oklahoma Club later absorbed the University Club. It was the scene of some of the city's gayest dinner dances from 1924 through the 1940s. Another popular spot was the Savoy Cafe, which operated in the teens in a building on the northeast corner of Main and Robinson, which in recent years has been the Oil and Gas Building. The Savoy moved in 1920 to the basement of the Colcord Building, directly across the street north from where the Oklahoma Club would be built four years later. It operated as a cafe at noon and a club, with dance bands, at night. M. M. Norris was its proprietor.

L. E. Buttrick was Oklahoma City's top figure in the dance hall field for more than twenty years, extending from the mid-teens until about 1935. He had been a dancing teacher and operated the Buttrick School of Dancing in several locations during his career. He built the Euclid Dance Hall on the site of the present Oklahoma Theater Center downtown. He developed a summer pavilion in Memorial Park and one in Belle Isle Park. He and his wife, Myrtle, operated a dancing school and dance hall on the northwest corner of Northwest Fourth and Broadway, across the street from the Oklahoma Publishing Company. With Paul Braniff, who later would start Braniff Airlines, he built the summer pavilion at Springlake, the first entertainment feature in what is now Oklahoma City's largest amusement park. It was completed about 1922.

When the City Auditorium at Grand and Walker ceased to operate as an auditorium in the early 1920s, Buttrick developed the second story, converted from the balcony, into the Ritz Ballroom. He closed the Ritz after a shooting there in 1931. It remained closed for a period of time before reopening under new ownership. Its new name was the Trianon Ballroom, taking that from the million dollar Trianon in Chicago.

Buttrick owned a 16-cylinder Cadillac, easily recognized throughout Oklahoma City. This Cadillac carried Wiley Post when he paraded here after his record breaking flight around the world in 1933. Two years later Buttrick moved to California, where he lost the small fortune he had made in Oklahoma City.

The Huckins Hotel ballroom was the scene of dining and dancing for several decades. So was the basement of the Huckins until fledgling Radio Station WKY moved into this area. A popular dance spot beginning in the mid-1920s was the Continental Room atop the Skirvin Hotel. Its popularity was replaced by the Persian Room, constructed in the Skirvin Tower (now Continental) across the street west. When it was completed the Persian room, with its mirrored columns, was considered the finest and most beautiful ballroom in town.

Another well known night spot was on Northeast Fifth near the Santa Fe tracks. It was constructed as an indoor swimming pool. Buttrick took it over about 1924, covering the pool with a floor to form the Winter Garden Dance Hall. Later, in 1930, Billy Gragg took it over, and it became the Boga Ballroom. In 1932, the property was sold to Mistletoe Express, and Gragg moved to Blossom Heath on Northwest Thirty-ninth Street near Grand Boulevard. Gragg constructed his own home as part of the building. Blossom Heath became a popular spot for parties and conventions, although its popularity waned during the mid-1930s when a man was shot there in a dispute. The man recovered and the ballroom continued to operate until purchased by the Moose Lodge.

Another spot for partying was El Patio in the basement of the Perrine Building (now Cravens Building). It served fine meals and imported name bands but did not succeed financially. At that time Anna Maude Smith, who was operating the YWCA cafeteria on North Broadway, was persuaded to move in to start a cafeteria. Many of her friends discouraged her, declaring that "people will not go into a basement to eat." But she moved anyway. The result is Anna Maude Cafeteria, now the oldest cafeteria in the city, and known throughout the nation.

In addition to playing in hotel and public ballrooms, dance orchestras also were busy on the country club circuit — Lake View, Oklahoma City, Twin Hills, and Edgemere, in particular.

But the year 1922 brought a new market for popular orchestras. WKY, the first radio station west of the Mississippi River, was established in the living room and garage of the Westwood Addition home of its founder, Earl Hull. It later moved to the Shrine Auditorium building and

Trying out new automobiles has always been a popular pastime among Oklahoma City people.

still later to the basement of the Huckins Hotel. Local bands provided much of the entertainment. WKY later moved to Plaza Court at Northwest Tenth and Walker, and still later to the Skirvin Tower Hotel. This station was purchased from Hull by Oklahoma Publishing Company in 1928. The station is now located, along with WKY-TV, at a modern plant at 500 East Britton Road.

The second Oklahoma City radio station on the market was KFJS, later called KOMA. Other stations continued coming in until there were seven after World War II and eighteen in 1973.

Although early stations provided an important outlet for local bands, this importance gradually diminished, as recorded music and network dramatic and comedy programs took over. Still later, as network television took over the drama and comedy market, radio programming concentrated on recorded music and conversation, and local bands play à minimum role.

In June 1949, entertainment patterns were adjusted when Oklahoma Publishing Company placed WKY-TV, Oklahoma City's first television station, on the air. Originally, sets were expensive and few owned them. Those who did quickly gained in personal popularity with their neighbors, as they hosted TV-watching parties. Prepackaged TV dinners, wrapped in foil and ready to heat and eat, emerged as a popular dish, since they allowed people to eat their meals without missing a show. Within a few years, as prices went down, sets became more plentiful. Soon there were more television sets than homes in Oklahoma City. WKY-TV began receiving cable television from NBC in 1952. Other stations were soon to come. KWTV, a CBS affiliate opened at 7401 North Kelley in 1953. KOCO-TV began operations in Enid in 1954, later moving to Northwest Sixty-third and Portland in Oklahoma City. It is an ABC affiliate. All three stations

A downtown parade celebrated the arrival of Judy the elephant to Oklahoma City in 1950.

are VHF (very high frequency). Two UHF (ultra high frequency) stations started up, but failed. They were KTVQ at Northwest Seventeenth and Classen, and KLPR-TV, an affiliate of KLPR-Radio, at 128 Southwest Twenty-fifth.

Although networks control most night-time television and soap operas and re-runs take much of the daytime programming, television has provided an outlet for musical groups, particularly in the country music field, which always has found a receptive home in Oklahoma City.

Country and Western music have always been popular, but usually with a different audience from lovers of the waltz or jazz. Country music style has a natural home in an area as close to its frontier beginnings as Oklahoma. This is vividly proved each time the Grand Ol' Opry overflows whatever auditorium or arena it books in Oklahoma City.

Development of radio attracted country music combos here to play sponsored programs on the air during daytime and book dances at night. Jimmy Wakely had a trio, including Scotty Harrall and Johnnie Bond, called the Bell Boys. They moved on to Hollywood where Wakely became a motion picture star. Bond wrote popular hits, including "Cimarron," worked with Gene Autry, and later formed his own publishing company. Harrall joined the "Riders of the Purple Sage."

During the late 1930s feed companies brought country music stars to Oklahoma City. Hiram and Lavini Perkins, a man and wife team, had a country orchestra on the Superior Feed show. It was followed by Dixie Boy Jordan, a guitarist and singer, who worked with WKY staff musicians. Next came Wiley Walker and Gene Sullivan, whose "Wiley and Gene" country singing and comedy show played on radio, and later television, for nearly twenty years. Gene Sullivan, younger of the pair, was a music writer, who put together several million-record-sale hits. Best known of Sullivan's compositions was "When My Blue Moon Turns to Gold Again." Today Sullivan operates a recording studio in South Oklahoma City, and is the only Oklahoma Cityan ever to be named to the Nashville Songwriter's Hall of Fame, which is the highest honor given to a country music writer.

Bob Beckham, a city electrician who trained with Gene Sullivan in the mid-1950s, went to Nashville where he scored with such hit records as "Just as Much as Ever," and "Crazy Arms." He now operates Combine Music, a publishing company owned by Monument Records.

An attractive young girl from Midwest City joined the Sooner Shindig in the early 1950s before moving to Tulsa. After winning the "Miss Tulsa" contest she became "Miss Oklahoma" and one of the top four in the "Miss America" competition. Then she moved on to still greater things. Her name — Anita Bryant — is perhaps the best known of all singers who rose from an Oklahoma City beginning.

Harold Jenkins was beginning to attract attention as a rock and roll singer when he switched to country music and moved here. Although comparatively few people know him by his real name, his stage name — Conway Twitty — is a household word in country music. His "Hello Darlin'," was nominated for song of the year against "Okie From Muskogee." He is always near the top in the country music circuit.

In Oklahoma City, as well as in many other cities following the turn of the century, transportation, electricity and entertainment were closely entwined. There were few automobiles. Electric street car systems provided the means to reach places of entertainment. In Oklahoma City, the Oklahoma Railway Company maintained an inter-urban transportation system. The most popular line ran between Wheeler Park, on the North Canadian River, and Belle Isle Park and Lake, north of the present Classen Circle. From there later it continued to Guthrie. The transportation system owned the lake and area to its east. That area became the principal amusement park and picnic area of Oklahoma City. Use of the park for picnicking and boating was free. Commercial thrill rides, a dance pavilion, various concessions were operated in the park. A power plant was constructed east of the present plant, which served the electric railway system as well as rides in the park.

Although the street railway system did not own Wheeler Park at the other end of the line, the company was a big supporter of the zoo and other entertainment features there. The principal transfer station was at Northwest Seventeenth and Classen. Thus, persons living to the east of Classen — and most of them did — could take a streetcar west to the Seventeenth Street exchange, transferring south to Wheeler Park, or north to Belle Isle Park, in pursuit of entertainment.

The floods of 1923 brought considerable damage to Wheeler Park and to the zoo. As a result, a movement got underway to move the zoo. Largely through leadership of R. A. Clinesmith, an attorney and chairman of the parks and recreation committee of the Chamber of Commerce, the zoo was moved to Northeast Park (later renamed Lincoln Park). The move

This double wedding was held in Wheeler Park on the North Canadian River in May, 1903.

was not made without opposition, because automobiles were still scarce, and there was no public transportation to the park.

In 1928 Belle Isle Lake, park, and the electric power plant, were sold to the Oklahoma Gas & Electric Company, which promptly built a much larger power plant adjacent to the lake. For twenty-five years after purchasing the park, OG&E kept it open to the public free for fishing and picnicking, but the rides and other amusements were gone and the glamour of old Belle Isle Park diminished.

Several years before the Belle Isle amusement park was sold to OG&E, another park had started up on the opposite side of the city. Roy Staton had spent considerable time studying operation of a Denver amusement park. He bought a parcel of land across the street west of Northeast Park at auction from the state. He built a lake, a grocery store, and a swimming pool. Shortly afterwards a dance pavilion and a "dipper" ride went in. L. E. Buttrick and Paul Braniff operated the dance pavilion. It was the beginning of Springlake Park, which grew into the principal amusement park for Oklahoma City.

No public transportation was available to Northeast (now Lincoln) Park or Springlake at first, but businessmen in the area led by Cornelius Tuohy, a developer, secured right-of-way and induced the Oklahoma Railway Company to build a line out there.

Two other major amusement parks later were organized in Oklahoma City, only one of which is still operating. Wedgewood Park was formed in the 1950s north of the Northwest Highway near Portland, but closed in the mid-1960s. Frontier City, which mixes rides and concessions with a frontier atmosphere, was organized in 1958 by James Burge, who directed the Oklahoma Semi-Centennial Exposition of 1957. Although ownership and management have changed hands several times, the park is still operating on the Northeast Expressway near the Turner Turnpike.

There were probably no museums in the earliest days of Oklahoma City, because to people of the new territory, history was just beginning. Actually, the settlement of Oklahoma City, along with the other five original towns of the Unassigned Lands, was probably the most unique kind of history ever experienced by a town.

The Oklahoma Historical Society one block south of the State Capitol Building houses nine divisions of the Society, including an outstanding museum, the most complete collection of Indian archives outside the Smithsonian Institution, and an almost complete Oklahoma newspaper collection, mostly on micro-film.

Another imposing museum is the Science and Arts museum, built during the 1950s at the State Fairgrounds. It includes exhibits of a scientific nature, including the Kirkpatrick Planetarium, which conducts educational programs on a regular basis.

Best known nationally and most imposing of Oklahoma's museums is the National Cowboy Hall of Fame and Western Heritage Center on Persimmon Hill, overlooking U.S. 66 in northeast Oklahoma City.

The Cowboy Hall of Fame also is headquarters for the National Academy of Western Art, founded at the center in 1973, and hosts the annual Western art competition of this organization.

Oklahoma City also is home of the Oklahoma Firefighters Museum, founded by the Oklahoma Firefighters Association, and located in Lincoln Park in northeast Oklahoma City, not far south of the Cowboy Hall of Fame. The Firefighters Museum, completed in 1969, displays some of the old equipment used in the state. It is across the street from the National Softball Hall of Fame and Museum, completed in 1973.

The Oklahoma Memorial Association, founded in 1927 as sponsor of the Oklahoma Hall of Fame, changed its name in 1971 to the Oklahoma Heritage Association and expanded its activity to cover the broad field of Oklahoma Heritage. About the same time it was given the former home of Robert A. Hefner, who in his lifetime was a successful oilman, supreme court judge and mayor of both Ardmore and Oklahoma City. The home, at the northwest corner of Northwest Fourteenth and Robinson, occupies the remainder of a block otherwise taken up by St. Luke's United Methodist Church. Its furniture and other contents, all of museum quality, came from castles throughout Europe, and also were given to the association by the family.

Under the leadership of Stanley Draper, who had retired as Chamber of Commerce head, and with substantial gifts from C. R. Anthony, the Shepherd Foundation, B. D. Eddie, the Hefner family and others, the home was completely refurnished and enlarged. It includes the Oklahoma Hall of Fame on the top floor. To the west of the building are a library, galleria, chapel and formal gardens with statuary and fountains. The building is open daily, including Sunday, for public viewing, and had more than 10,000 visitors its first year.

Near the Hefner home — at Northwest Fifteenth and Hudson — is the Overholser mansion, owned by the Oklahoma Historical Society. It has been restored for viewing by visitors with assistance from the Oklahoma chapter of the American Institute of Architects. Both of these homes are in the vicinity of an area of fine old homes which have been restored by their present owners. These owners take pride in calling the neighborhood "Heritage Hills." These homes, all occupied by their owners, are occasionally opened to visitors on Sunday afternoons. They were Oklahoma City's mansions of the 1920s and are still beautiful today.

Oklahoma Heritage Center, former home of Judge Robert A. Hefner.

Many of the early-day cultural organizations gave attention to art. One was the Art Renaissance Club, organized in 1904 to study the history of art. The first major organization in Oklahoma to devote its principal effort to art appreciation and promotion was the Art League. This was formed in 1911 as a result of a consultation by Mrs. John W. Shartel, Mrs. Ed L. Dunn, and Miss Nellie Shepherd, who was, herself, an Impressionistic artist studying in Paris. The consultation took place in Paris, where Miss Shepherd was living and the other two were visiting. Formation of the league took place a few months later in Oklahoma City following a local art exhibit. Charles F. Colcord was elected the first president. The organization began with 150 members. Its membership ran into the hundreds by the early 1920s. Its purpose was to promote an interest in art, and eventually to establish an art gallery.

It was three years after the Art League was founded that Doctor Fred C. Sheets and his artistic wife, Nan, came from Bartlesville to Oklahoma City. They built a sprawling home at Northwest Twenty-seventh and Walker, which included a north side workshop and a south side gallery. Mrs. Sheets displayed the works of Oklahoma artists, including her own, in the gallery.

Each summer she would go East to paint. Soon she became acquainted with leading artists throughout the country, and was bringing many outside works to the Oklahoma State Fair. Later she supplied the state fairs at Muskogee and Topeka, Kansas. Her home became a meeting place for the Art League (still active in 1973), and was the scene of organization of the Arno Art Club, which is no longer operating.

In 1935 Nan Sheets was asked to organize an Oklahoma City federal art program under the Works Progress Administration. Through influence of the Chamber, she got free exhibit space in the Commerce

Exchange Building, where exhibits were shown for more than a year. Then the center moved to the Wirt Franklin Building between Broadway and Robinson on Second Street. In 1937 the center was moved to the fifth floor of newly completed Municipal Auditorium, where it remained until 1958. At that time it moved to the new Oklahoma Art Center at the Fairgrounds. Nan Sheets retired as its director in 1965.

Other art museums were springing up in the 1950s. Conservative artists and patrons started the Oklahoma Museum of Conservative Art on North Western, then moved to the former Nan Sheets home. Finally it moved to the former R.J. Edwards home east of Lincoln Boulevard and Northeast Fifty-fourth, where is was renamed the Red Ridge Art Museum.

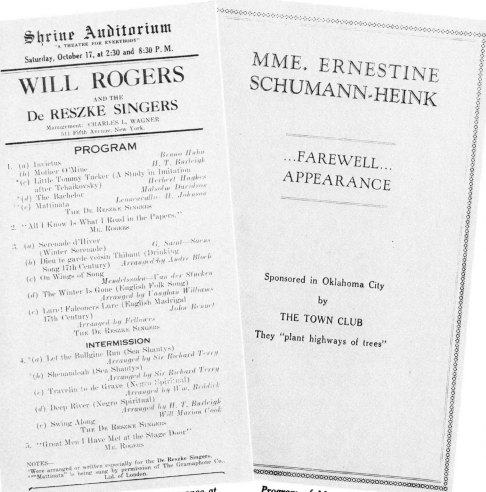

A program of Will Rogers appearance at the Shrine Auditorium in 1925.

Program of Mme. Ernestine Schumann-Heink's Oklahoma City appearance in 1929.

9

Sports Always Popular

IT SHOULD NOT BE SURPRISING THAT a city which had its beginning with the biggest horse race in history should become prominent in the field of sports. Certainly this has been true with Oklahoma City.

Although professional baseball did not organize on a sustaining basis until 1904, baseball began in Oklahoma City only a few days after the Run. The first ball park was located just outside the city limits on "Higgins' Forty," west of Walker Avenue, near where the Municipal Building stands today. The "grandstand" was constructed of beer kegs and two by twelves. The kegs were borrowed from a saloon at First and Harvey. One who helped build the stands was 16-year-old Eugene Barnes, who was destined to play a principal role in Oklahoma City baseball for the next thirty years.

The Oklahoma City Browns, one of three teams organized, played a Guthrie team once in Oklahoma City and twice in Guthrie, winning all three games. In addition the city teams played each other. The playing field moved in mid-season in 1889 when Higgins ran the players off. The new location was a block east of the Santa Fe tracks in the military addition.

Baseball was spasmodic during the 1890's, with several unsucessful attempts at organizing professional teams. The first professional team to play a full and successful season was the Oklahoma City Metropolitans. The Mets played in 1904 under the management of Barnes. Beefed up by remnants of a Galveston, Texas, team which had deserted in a player strike two years earlier, the Mets won first place in the Southwestern League, an all-Oklahoma circuit.

The following year the Mets joined the new Western Association, a Class "C" league, made up of larger towns of the 1904 Class "D" Missouri Valley League, with Oklahoma City and Guthrie added. Barnes bought the franchise and was principal stockholder in a corporate ownership with Seymour C. Heyman, clothing merchant and civic leader, as president. The pennant-winning Iola, Kansas, team moved here virtually intact. With some local favorites the team finished the 1905 race in second place to Wichita. It was managed by Jack Holland, long time central figure of professional baseball here. The Mets played in the Western Association until 1909 when they moved, along with Tulsa, into the Texas League. After three years there the Mets dropped out, later rejoining the Western Association. This first period of organized baseball ended with World War I and the team disbanded.

Following the war Heyman spearheaded reorganization of a

team. The Oklahoma City Indians owned by Holland and managed by Fred Luderus, in September 1923 battled the Tulsa Oilers for the Western League pennant until the big flood of that year forced them out of Colcord Park. Later a diamond in front of the State Fair grandstand was used. The Indians completed the season a half-game ahead for the pennant.

After the season Holland sold $100 multiple season passes to finance building a new baseball park for the city. Holland Park opened the 1924 season at Northwest Fourth and Pennsylvania, near the water works. Players moving to the new team included Emil Yde, southpaw pitcher, who later went to the Pittsburgh Pirates; George Harper, center fielder, who joined the Philadelphia Phillies; the great Carl Hubbell, left-handed pitcher who made such a record with the New York Giants. The team remained in the Western League through 1931, then returned to the Texas League, now moving into the Double "A" class. The Indians until Holland's death in 1936 were an independent stronghold in a growing network of "chain store" baseball. They became a farm club of the Cleveland Indians.

The biggest year in the history of the Oklahoma City Indians was 1934, when they won the Texas League championship and the Dixie Series. After Holland's death his son, John Junior, and Jimmy Humphreys became owners, with Jim Keesey as manager. The team finished first in the 1937 series but lost in the playoffs. During War II professional baseball again was suspended. Following the war, after a period of ownership by oil men Harold Pope and C. R. "Chuck" Virtue, Humphreys assumed ownership but financial troubles were setting in. The team folded after the 1958 season and the city was again without professional baseball.

Under a trust three years later the city built a $275,000 park at the Fairgrounds. In 1962, when Houston got its major league franchise, it formed a working agreement with a new Oklahoma City team to be called "The '89ers." In its second year, the new team won its division crown in the Pacific Coast League and went on to win the league championship. It repeated the same operation two years later. After several years in the Pacific Coast League, the team moved to the American Association in 1970. In 1972 it switched from a farm club of the Astros to the Cleveland Indians. The All-Sports Association has been prime sponsor of the revived activity.

Among '89ers who have moved up in major league circles were Astro centerfielder Tom Griffin and Montreal outfielder, Rusty Staub.

It is difficult to pinpoint when Oklahoma City's youth baseball program began. Youth baseball started on vacant lots near Main Street in 1889. However, in the first thirty years permanent youth leagues did not exist. An early Junior Baseball League was organized in the 1920s by the Rotary Club. The club built Rotary Park near Packing Town, largely for a baseball program. Gene Hemry, later a prominent attorney, was employed as a youngster to manage the league.

In the early 1930s the American Legion organized a national youth baseball project. Post 35 of Oklahoma City became very active in a high school age baseball program. Early leaders of the program were Granville Scanland and L. B. Wiggins. Teams were sponsored by local merchants. One of the outstanding earlier teams was Lewinsohn's Clothiers, which won state competition and participated in a regional tournament in New Orleans. Playing an important leadership role in the Lewinsohn team organization was Arlo Scoggin, who came to Oklahoma City with the Metropolitans baseball team in 1905 as an outfielder and bunting specialist, and later joined Heyman, then Lewinsohn, as a clothing salesman. Scoggin played a leading role in amateur and youth baseball leagues long after he retired from professional baseball.

The first state sandlot baseball tournament in the country on a state championship basis, took shape as a double elimination tournament in 1927, under sponsorship of the Oklahoma Publishing Company, with Charles Saulsberry as founder and manager. It eventually packed Holland Park with capacity crowds following hometown teams from over the state. It was good baseball — most of the time.

While the American Legion was taking the lead in organizing baseball programs among older youths in the public schools, other groups were turning their attention toward the pre-teen youngsters. In 1934 the Junior Chamber of Commerce began a program among grade school and junior high school age youths. Al Cook, Saulsberry, H. B. Lee, Frank Wolff, J. Wiley Richardson and Larry Wolf formed teams at the various schools. At that time they were handicapped because school regulations did not allow school ground to be used for organized sports. Therefore, as teams were organized, efforts were made to get permission to use privately owned vacant lots for practice and games. Late in the 1930s the YMCA, as an offshoot of the Y-Emblem Club, began organization of junior baseball leagues. Chester Hales and Roy Deal were among leaders in formation of these teams, which were, at first, sponsored by local business organizations.

Initially an "American" and a "National" league were organized, with player-age brackets determining league affiliation of the team. Through this program permission was obtained to use school grounds after hours and on Saturdays for practice and games. Although the primary purpose of this program was to provide physical exercise and teamwork experience for these young boys, the YMCA program eventually led to major league careers for a few participants. Among them were Frank Kellert, Cal McLish, Leroy Jarvis and Bobby Morgan.

In 1940, Oklahoma City got its first lighted park for amateur baseball. The park was built on land which later became part of the Oklahoma City Fairgrounds — just east of the present location of the Oklahoma City '89ers Ball Park. Roy Fisher, a Willys automobile dealer, along with Al Kellert, Deal and Saulsberry, were leaders in development of this park. It was used principally for games of adult commercial leagues, and to a lesser extent for the youth leagues.

YMCA continued to dominate the youth baseball program after World War II and into the 1950s. It continues to be the largest single baseball program. However, in the late 1950s and particularly in the 1960s, large neighborhood area leagues were organized by groups of citizens to sponsor baseball programs. Most of these leagues have acquired their own ground, and have built clusters of lighted baseball diamonds with grandstands. They play full seasons of both day and night games. Most

Oklahoma City's first baseball stadium was constructed in 1890 in Stiles Park.

of these organizations have also branched into other youth sports — particularly football and basketball.

A person cannot remain long in Oklahoma City before realizing he is in the softball capital of the world. The Oklahoma City Amateur Softball Association has more than 7,000 player members. This number does not count several thousand other players in unstructured leagues or miscellaneous participants who are not association members.

The softball program of Oklahoma City includes more than 400 teams. The number climbs each year. Leagues are divided into slow and fast pitch categories, with a half dozen sub-divisions in each department.

The softball program begins May 1 and ends Labor Day each year, with league games six evenings each week, plus exhibition games on Sundays and holidays.

Special events of the Oklahoma City softball program include an Indian Men's tournament and an Indian Women's tournament, both of which attract teams of Indians from throughout the nation. Many of these teams camp near playing fields during the tournament.

The Wheeler Park stadium has a covered grandstand for 1,500 people, and is considered by many to be finest of its kind in the United States. It is one of five diamonds in the Wheeler Park complex. Other fields can be found in City and private parks, as well as vacant lots throughout the city.

Oklahoma teams have traditionally ranked high in area competition and usually at least one city team reaches the national tournament.

In 1968 the International Softball Championship tournament was held in Oklahoma City.

The outstanding softball program of Oklahoma City played an important role in its selection as home of the Amateur Softball Association and Hall of Fame, which is also headquarters of the International Softball Hall of Fame. The association moved here from New Jersey in 1966, and in 1973 a Softball Hall of Fame and international headquarters building was completed and dedicated in the Lincoln Park area in Northeast Oklahoma City. Don Porter has been general secretary of the Amateur Softball Association since it moved to Oklahoma City.

Although softball has long been popular in Oklahoma City the organized program started its big climb after World War II. At that time there were about fifty teams. By 1951 there were 117 teams. In 1973 the number was up to 400.

Under impetus from the YMCA, with physical education director Rodney Palmer in a leading role, assisted by volunteer leaders Bill Hale and Cragin Smith, softball got a hold in the mid-1930s. Oklahoma City was one of the first to go almost all-out, with lighted parks and numerous playing fields. G. M. Byerley built a lighted softball park near the Capitol to enable girl players to host top national teams. Street's Ready-to-Wear was among the earliest to have a strong team.

A big factor in growth of the sport was introduction of slow pitch ball which came in 1963. This opened the game to boys, girls, men and women. The number of girls' and womens' teams grows constantly.

To Oklahoma City fans now the pinnacle of football lies twenty miles south on the University of Oklahoma campus. From there, the Sooners dominated Big Eight football most of the time since War II. For a while they loomed large on the national football scene, establishing an all-time consecutive win record.

But Norman has not always been the "football capital" for Oklahoma City fans. The first football game reported to have been played in Oklahoma took place on November 29, 1894. It was played at "Crocker 89" in Oklahoma City, now the intersection of Robinson and Seventh streets. The "Terrors," a team supposedly composed of players with previous football experience, were defeated by the high school "Boomers" twenty-four to zero before what was described as a "large crowd." By present standards equipment was poor.

The following year Oklahoma City High School had its own football team and defeated the University of Oklahoma thirty-four to zero. By the late 1890s, Oklahoma City High School was playing El Reno, Shawnee, and other nearby teams.

Oklahoma City University produced outstanding football teams in the late 1920s. OCU brought to the forefront a man who later became one of the nation's leading coaches — Lynn Waldorf. Waldorf came to OCU from an assistant's job at Syracuse in the early 1920s. He left in 1928 for then Oklahoma A & M College, from where he moved on to Big Ten coaching.

The golden age of OCU football began in 1928, when Vivian "Vee" Green came to the college as coach. Green had been a member of Illinois' famous, all-victorious Big Ten team, which featured the "Galloping Ghost," Red Grange, at halfback.

Installing what fans called the "Green System" at OCU, the new coach won thirty of his first thirty-eight games. The big years were 1930, when the team won nine games and lost one, and 1931, when they had a perfect season.

OCU continued to field good teams, but none equal to the 1930 and 1931 seasons. The sport was dropped during wartime for lack of players and resumed at end of the war, but after a short time was dropped permanently as the school concentrated on basketball.

In 1932 — the year after graduation of Goldbug greats — Oklahoma City had its first attempt at professional football. Signing a note to launch this project were Jimmie Humphries, business manager of the Oklahoma City Indians, and Saulsberry, then sports editor of the *Oklahoma City Times*. Most of the Goldbugs were in town and players such as "coffincorner" punter Bob Eaton; pro wrestler Ernie Webb and quarterback J. R. "Dummy" Anderson were signed. Also playing was Mike Massad of Sooner football fame. Pepper Martin, Cardinals baseball player, promised to slip into a game or two. Wes Fry, former Big Ten and National League player and coach of the Classen High School Comets, was coach. The team won eight of ten, losing to Memphis and St. Louis. There were box office problems. Saulsberry was ordered out of sponsorship by his managing editor. Coach Fry was told to get out by his school board. OCU guard Hal Halpirt became coach. Martin was fined $1,000 by the Cardinals for playing. Still, the team broke even for the season although players seldom made more than three bucks a game — when crowds were good. The team continued one more season then disbanded.

Professional football has had a sporadic record in Oklahoma City with successes in the field, but a poor financial record. A nucleus of former players from Capitol Hill High School, ramrodded by Tommy Pearson, who was coach and manager, organized a community football team in 1966, which played unscheduled games. In 1967 it scheduled a series of exhibition games. This season included competition with community and semi-pro teams in the Southwest. The team had a good record of wins. However, the season was marred by the death of Coach Pearson in the crash of a light aircraft while on a business trip for the team. C. B. Speegle, who had retired as coach at Capitol Hill High School, took over the team, which had named itself the Plainsmen. The squad contracted to join the Professional Football League of America with home games in Taft Stadium. The 1968 season, under Coach Speegle, resulted in victory for the Plainsmen in its first seven games. It was at this point that financial troubles were revealed to the players, and they learned they would not be paid for their effort. The season ended with losses on the field and termination of the team. Some of the Plainsmen joined another professional football attempt — the Midwest City Falcons. This team lasted only one year. It did not have a good season.

Another try at professional football began here in 1973. The Oklahoma City Wranglers were organized by State Representative L. H. Bengston, another former teacher at Capitol Hill High School. The team plays in the Southwest Professional League, which schedules contests in late spring and sumer, to avoid competing with college games. Labor disputes came up near the season's end but did not keep the Wranglers from winning the league championship in their first year.

High school football has enjoyed popularity in Oklahoma City and over the years traditional intra-city rivalries have built up between schools. At times rivalries have become so intense that police protection was needed in stadium areas following games.

In 1933 the Capitol Hill High School Redskins were mythical national champions, winning 12 straight games, climaxed by a 55-12 defeat of Harrison Tech, the city champions of Chicago.

The All-Sports Association has promoted an effort to maintain attendance at high school athletic events, and in 1957 began sponsorship of an annual football preview for thirteen City high schools. In this preview, each high school team played a portion of a game — usually about one quarter — and all profits went to the high school sports programs.

In the early 1930s the Oklahoma City high schools had no football stadium and no full-sized practice field. They played their games, and conducted a great deal of their practice, at the Western League baseball stadium. In 1936, the Oklahoma City Junior Chamber of Commerce started raising money to build a stadium as its major project.

Jim Warram was chairman of a money-raising committee, which also included Wilbur Vandergrift and Al Cook. Three year tickets to all home football games were sold for $8.16 each, in order to raise the ten percent of funds necessary to contract with the Works Progress Administration to construct the stadium on a 90-10 matching basis. In 1937 the stadium was completed on grounds of Taft Junior High School at Northwest Twenty-fifth and May. This has been since the principal high school football stadium in Oklahoma City, although with development of new high schools, there are now other football stadia. Taft Stadium was also the principal center for other outdoor sports events until construction of the outdoor arena on the Fairgrounds in the early 1950s.

In addition to high school football games, Taft Stadium has hosted both college and exhibition professional football. In 1943, when travel was limited by wartime gasoline restrictions, four major intercollegiate games were played in Taft Stadium including three of the Oklahoma A&M contests.

It was in 1936 that one of the leading annual sporting events of Oklahoma City was organized. It was the All-College Basketball Tournament, launched with sixteen teams, twelve of which came from Oklahoma. It began at 2 p.m. December 30, when Oklahoma City University tangled with Phillips University of Enid. That game was played in the Classen High School gym, and the OCU Goldbugs took an easy 49-35 win. Center Red Bryan and forward Chester Bryan scored thirteen points each for OCU. The final was an all-Oklahoma event, with Oklahoma A&M defeating Tulsa 40-17, with ten of Coach Henry Iba's Aggie team scoring. The contests were held in various high school gymnaisums.

The early tournaments were sponsored by the Milk and Ice Fund of the Oklahoma Publishing Company. However, not much milk or ice were purchased from proceeds of the first tournament, which lost $1,700. It was perhaps the only college tournament during the Christmas season, and was a money-loser for all the teams involved. But the coaches liked it and wanted it repeated. It was rescheduled in 1937 with twenty-two teams present. This time games were played at both Central and Classen High Schools, with final rounds in new Municipal Auditorium downtown. A throng of 4,864 at the final game, in which the Aggies beat the Southwestern Moundbuilders of Winfield, Kansas, made this tournament a financial success.

The tournament continued under sponsorship of the Milk and

Ice Fund until Oklahoma Publishing Company abondoned this program in 1957. But by that time it was too big, and too popular with both coaches and fans, to disband. The Sports and Recreation Council of the Chamber of Commerce met to determine fate of the tournament. Out of that meeting came formation of the All Sports Association. This organization continues its sponsorship of the All College Basketball tournament, but also sponsors other events, and participates in the promotion of numerous athletic activities.

Oklahoma State University dominated the All-College basketball tournament during its early years, although its last championship was in 1953. Still the Cowboys won eleven of the first thirty-seven All-College crowns, including eight out of ten between 1944 and 1954. Oklahoma City University is second in rank with five championships.

The All-College Basketball Tournament is one of the largest basketball events in the nation today. No longer is it open to all comers. Since the early 1940s it has been restricted to eight selected, outstanding teams. Even to be invited to participate is considered a big honor for a college team.

The tournament made its first move from high school gymnasiums to Municipal Auditorium when the auditorium was completed. When the All Sports Arena was constructed at the Fairgrounds, the tournament moved there. Its latest move was in the Christmas season of 1972 to Myriad Convention Center downtown. Total attendance at this event was more than 30,000.

Although the All-College Tournament has provided the highlight of Oklahoma City basketball history, basketball has been popular in the city since its earliest days. In the mid-1920s the Missouri Valley AAU Basketball League was formed, with teams from a several state Southwestern area. The Oklahoma City team was organized in 1926 by the Sterling Milk Company, owned by E. F. Comegys. The team included several former college players. One was Bill Haller, who retired in 1973 as Oklahoma County School Superintendent. The jump center was Henry Iba. Vic Holt and Bruce Drake played also. The team continued to be active under various sponsors well into the 1930s.

Numerous district and state championships have been won by Oklahoma City high schools, but the greatest award was in the early 1930s when Classen High School became national high school basketball champion. Besides drawing attention to the city and school, it marked beginning of a success story for a young coach named Henry P. "Hank" Iba, who moved on to college coaching, leading to Oklahoma A&M, where he had one of the best college coaching careers in the nation. Iba climaxed his career by coaching several winning U.S. Olympic teams. His only loss was on a disputed time decision to Russia in the finals of 1972 at Munich.

In 1948 Classen won the state round ball championship. This brought statewide attention to a star of the team and an all-stater, David Hall, who in 1971 became governor of Oklahoma.

Women's basketball had its heyday in Oklahoma in the late 1920s and early 1930s when the Oklahoma Presbyterian College Cardinals of Durant was the dominant team of the nation. The girls had been national champions, or near champions for several years, but fortunes of the college were not equal to those of the basketball team. In 1932, it was apparent that the struggling college could not support the team, so OCU and its supporters encouraged the girls to transfer. Good fortune followed the team to Oklahoma City, and in 1933, while the Tulsa Midcontinent-DX Oilers were winning the national men's amateur championship, OCU was taking the national women's crown. The two teams travelled together to Chicago to play exhibition games at the Century of Progress World's Fair that year.

The first attempt at professional hockey here was in the mid-1930s when the Oklahoma City Warriors was organized. The team was brought here by Tony Lyons and played in the Stockyards Coliseum. It played Kansas City, St. Louis, Wichita and other cities. The team starred flashy Bobby Burns and "Hub" Nelson. It was not backed too well financially and broke up after two seasons. Ice hockey skated back onto our sports scene in 1965 as the Oklahoma City Blazers, a member of the Central Hockey League, noted as tops in the minors. Competition was with Tulsa, Dallas, Fort Worth, Omaha, Kansas City and Amarillo. The Blazers were Number One farm club of the Boston Bruins.

Movement of hockey to Oklahoma City was a result of the city's general interest in sports, as well as the location of an All-Sports building at the Fairgrounds, which is especially suited to hockey.

A "Hockey Hounds" club, composed of about twenty-five civic leaders interested in sports, played a major role in promotion of company, civic and convention group attendance at hockey matches. More than one million fans passed through turnstiles during its six years of existence. But this wasn't enough for the Bruins, who dropped sponsorship of the city team at end of the 1971 season.

Meanwhile, something big was happening in downtown Oklahoma City. The Myriad Convention Center was being completed with an area seating 15,000. The Myriad had not opened when Ontario of the National Hockey Association announced that it would sponsor an Oklahoma City team in the Central Hockey League, beginning with the 1973 season.

Horse racing has always been a popular sport in Oklahoma. The question of pari-mutual betting on horse races is a regular one with the state legislature, but lack of betting has not killed interest in racing.

Most early settlers in Oklahoma City had horses. No doubt they raced them against one another, even though no official scores or records were kept. A newspaper report in 1893 shows that a horse race was held at the Fairgrounds, with a horse owned by Sutton and Dunbar winning the half mile dash, clocking fifty seconds.

Throughout the 1890s horse races were reported, with winners' purses usually running from $50 to $100. The Kramer track in Oklahoma City was described as "the" racing course of the Territory, almost equal to the Topeka track.

In 1900, a special series of horse racing events as well as a "cowboy's tournament" was held at Kramer's Park during the Rough Rider's Reunion for Teddy Roosevelt. An event of August 25, 1903, was described as the "greatest harness race meet ever held in Oklahoma, with the fastest mile ever made by a three year old in the state." The newspaper report also pointed out that one horse stepped into a depression in the track and caused a pile-up in the second heat.

Professional rodeo in Oklahoma City dates to the territorial period. The Colcord Baseball Park was the scene of rodeo events in the early 1900s. An example was a roping exhibition and contest at the park in December 1910, which drew a crowd of 8,000 and offered $1,070 in prizes. Rides were longer. Roping was on yearlings.

For years one of the major rodeos in the nation has been the annual State Fair Rodeo. But now Oklahoma City has two notable rodeos.

The National Finals Rodeo, bringing together the top fifteen cowboys and cowgirls of the nation in each of seven major rodeo events, found a home in Oklahoma City, beginning in 1965. This event, which closes the Rodeo Cowboys Association season each December, annually attracts to the city, rodeo fans from every state in the Union and several foreign countries. Chartered airplanes bring groups of fans from across the country. Most of these cross-country visitors stay to witness the entire ten-performance event. Attendance in 1973 was 84,000.

After money-losing seasons in Dallas and Los Angeles, the "world series of rodeo" came here under joint sponsorship of the Rodeo Cowboys Association, the National Cowboy Hall of Fame and Western Heritage Center, and the Oklahoma City Chamber of Commerce. The Rodeo Hall of the Cowboy Hall of Fame benefits from proceeds. This event has the largest purse, at $128,000, and attracts the largest combined crowd, of any rodeo in the world. It determines world championships in the six major men's riding and roping events as well as women's barrel racing. Broncs and riding bulls are nominated by finalists.

In recent years Oklahoma City has become scene of another important horse event. This has been the National Championship Arabian Horse Show, held at the Fairgrounds annually since 1969. Highlights of the one week event include special performance demonstrations, a national youth team horse judging contest, and a consignment sale which exceeds $500,000.

Freckles Brown rides Jim Shoulders' bull, Tornado, at the 1967 National Finals Rodeo.

Dog racing, virtually unknown in Oklahoma City today, was an important sport of the area in days before statehood. Greyhound races were held in the 1890s under National Coursing rules in an area just north of Council Grove. The golden year for dog racing here was 1903, when the National Coursing Association held its annual Waterloo Cup meet. Both dog and horse racing enthusiasm was at a peak in Oklahoma City at that time, and races were regularly drawing from 4,000 to 6,000 persons. Officials of the National Coursing Association as well as racing editors of sports publications made numerous visits to the city during the preparation period.

The big event was held October 31, 1903, with 250 dogs entered in national competition. D. K. Carter of Enterprise, Kansas, caused a sensation in a pre-race meeting by declaring that he used a twenty percent solution of cocaine as a stimulant, and defied officials to find a rule against it. It was agreed that a ten percent solution could be used. Three hundred rabbits and 250 dogs participated in the contest.

Oklahoma City, which helped produce such golfing greats as Charlie Coe, national amateur champion, and Sue Maxwell Berning, three times national women's open champion, may be developing new champions today through its extensive golfing program. More than 2,000 persons belong to Golf, Incorporated, which operates for golfers in metropolitan Oklahoma City. This organization records monthly computerized handicaps for all of its members and conducts the world's largest golf tournament each spring.

This fourball tournament annually attracts more than 1,800 players from the Greater Oklahoma City area. Players use nine courses in the tournament, which extends for six weeks, with flights determined by the computerized handicaps. A total of at least twenty-four flights is used in this match play tournament.

Its beginning was not nearly so glamorous. Golf started in Oklahoma City at the turn of the century when a few enthusiasts planted seeds of the ancient Scottish game in the vicinity of Northeast Twelfth and Stiles. They built a crude nine-hole golf course with sand greens during the spring and summer of 1900. The total cost was $15.

It created less than a sensation in Oklahoma City. There were not even any newspaper reports on its construction, although a year earlier a cryptic remark was printed that "Ponca City has a tennis club. Oklahoma City has become aristocratic enough to want a golf club."

There is no record to indicate whose idea the Oklahoma golf club was, but the first officers were J. H. Vosburgh, president; L. C. Tillotson, vice-president; R. K. Sleeper, secretary; and S. E. Laird, treasurer. Fred Patterson, R. J. and R. T. Edwards, C. B. Ames and Frank Butts also were involved in the organization. Butts was the club's first champion, holding the course record with a fifty-three — four strokes better than anybody else.

By 1910 there were four golf courses in Oklahoma City, including Lake View Country Club, in the northeast sector, which was forerunner to the Oklahoma City Golf and Country Club. Behind Lake View were George Frederickson, J. C. Clark and E. E. Westerfelt.

Lake View also was the first course to employ a professional — Leslie Brownlee, a native of Edinburgh, who came to America in 1904 and who was a golf pro in Fort Smith before coming to Lake View about 1910. Brownlee and other Scots he brought to Oklahoma, played an early major role in the development of golf, not only in Oklahoma City, but throughout the state. One was Bill Nichols, who went to Muskogee. Another was Art Brownlee, his half-brother, who came to Oklahoma City and Lake View. The clubhouse and grounds northeast of Oklahoma City were soon outgrown, and on July 6, 1911, the Oklahoma City Golf and Country Club was organized. It was incorporated in 1912. In 1921 it had 840 members.

Golf courses continued to spring up. In 1928 Oklahoma City had five major golf courses. They included Oklahoma City Golf and Country Club, Edgemere Country Club at Northwest Thirty-sixth and Walker where the First Christian Church complex now stands, Lincoln Golf Course, Twin Hills Golf and Country Club, and Lakeside Golf and Country Club. Housing took over some courses.

Big time professional golf came to Oklahoma City in 1928 when city courses combined to bring the first PGA tour event to the city. Bob Conliff, Senior, ramrodded the event. The tournament was continued for two more years before the depression knocked it out.

Twin Hills was the site of some important national matches, particularly during the late 1930s. In 1934 the Western Amateur golf tournament was held at Twin Hills during the heart of the hottest and dryest summer season Oklahoma had experienced. Local golfer Zell Eaton was winner. However, despite the heat, the club manager was credited with such an outstanding job that he persuaded the professional golfers association to hold its 1935 national championship on the same course. This time it was a raw and chilly October, with Johnny Revolta taking the title.

The Oklahoma City Fourball was organized in 1938, and is the state's largest single golfing event. It has a counterpart in Tulsa.

In 1937 national top professionals played a Fourball tournament at the Oklahoma City Golf and Country Club with Horton Smith and Harry Cooper winning. At Twin Hills in 1956 Fred Hawkins won his only tournament title. On the same course in 1959 Arnold Palmer won a PGA Event and in 1960 Gene Littler dethroned him.

In 1953, the Oklahoma City Golf and Country Club hosted the National Amateur Championship Tournament of the U.S. Golf Association.

Many golfing greats and near-greats have come from Oklahoma City. Two have been national champions. Western Amateur champion in the 1920s was Keefe Carter, for whom his father built Twin Hills. Although an Ardmore native, Charles F. Coe later adopted Oklahoma City as his home. Coe was national amateur champion in 1948 and again in 1958. He played on the Walker Cup team five times and was team captain in 1959. He was also a member of the first World Amateur Team in 1958. Susan Maxwell Berning started golfing as a child on the Lincoln Park golf course, and rose to national amateur champion before turning professional. As a pro, she has won three national championships, the latest being in July 1973.

The early 1960s brought a new major golf and country club —

Quail Creek — which has become a regular tour stop for the PGA. Others have sprung up in new developments as the city mushroomed into the suburbs.

Bowling is an active participant sport for all ages in Oklahoma City. Modern bowling establishments are located in every area of Oklahoma City. Both league and open bowling are available on round the clock schedules at Oklahoma City lanes.

The Southwestern Bowling Tournament had its birth here in 1925 and, now nearing its fiftieth anniversary, has grown to one of the nation's largest meets. A half-dozen city bowlers, meeting to plan the first state tournament, went for the regional idea instead. Most instrumental in this was O. E. McAfee, H. J. "Dusty" Rhodes and J. C. Connery, all leaders in early league formation in the city. The tournament moves each winter to one of several selected bowling cities, being held here about every five years. The National Congress is expected here.

The Oklahoma City Men's Singles Classic is held two weekends each January and the Women's Classic follows in February. Each of these attracts more than 1,000 top bowlers from several states, mainly in the Southwest. This originated as an *Oklahoma City Times* promotion with the men's event in 1933 and that for the women in 1940.

Several times the nationally televised men's professional tournament has been held in Oklahoma City, while women have bowled in the city once in the nationally televised meet.

Ruddy Bomar, an Ardmore native, bowled often in Oklahoma City, both before and after moving to top national fame as a professional. He was winner of many national professional tournaments and was National Bowler of the Year twice.

Three Oklahoma City women have won national championships. Toni Calvery was the 1973 all-events champion for the Women's International Bowling Congress, knocking down more pins than any of the 50,000 bowlers participating in a Las Vegas event.

In 1976 the American Bowling Congress tournament will come to Oklahoma City for the first time, setting up its own lanes in the Myriad. Approximately 80,000 bowlers will be participating in the three-months event.

Bowling as a sport in Oklahoma dates back to territorial days. In June 1901, two transients, Messrs Bohrer and Withar, put up a bowling alley under a tent on a vacant lot at a corner of California and Robinson. The following year a room in the Hendrickson building was rented to J. D. Stuart of Indiana for a bowling alley, and shortly afterward, an alley went up at Broadway and Main, probably in the basement of the Lee (later Huckins) hotel. The latter alley began holding ladies day events in mid-1902.

George Qualey was one of Oklahoma City's better early bowlers, setting a bowling record for the Southwest with a game score of 266 and a three game average of 225 in 1902. Later the same year, Oklahoma City claimed the team record of the Oklahoma Territory, with a victory over Perry. By the end of the year, the team had competed in a tournament of major cities and placed second to San Francisco.

Bowling continued to be popular, with the development of new and larger bowling alleys downtown, and even by the end of World War II, most alleys were in the downtown area. It was the postwar period which brought a bowling explosion. By 1950 downtown alleys were closing and new, larger and automated alleys were springing up in the suburbs. At one time there were sixteen alleys in Oklahoma County, but later the number shrank to about half that number — all of them large.

There have been many miscellaneous sports in Oklahoma City — some short-lived. For instance, in 1937 a municipal marble tournament was held here, with participants from El Reno, Moore and Bethany, as well as Oklahoma City. Trophies and plaques were awarded to young winners. Earlier there was a state tournament.

In 1941, under an agreement between the government of Mexico and the Chamber of Commerce, seventy outstanding high school and college athletes competed with Mexican teams throughout December in all major sports.

On three or four occasions — but never on a regular basis — a Soap Box Derby was held in Oklahoma City, with the winner going to Akron, Ohio, for the All-American Soap Box Derby. This organization never got a foothold in Oklahoma City, however, because sponsoring organizations seldom repeated sponsorship.

In 1956 Oklahoma City hosted the United States Open Chess Tournament, held in the Civic Room of the Biltmore Hotel. At that time national chess tournaments were unheralded, even in the city where the competition was held. All participants but one were adults. That exception was a thirteen-year-old named Bobby Fischer, who seventeen years later would catapult chess into world prominence in his world championship match with a Russian, playing in Iceland.

In 1956 the Jaycees constructed a drag race strip at the Fairgrounds in hopes of moving hot-rodders off Main Street. Races were held at the strip every Sunday afternoon. During the Labor Day weekend in 1957, national hot rod championship races were held at the Fairgrounds.

Chairman of the drag strip project was a young Jaycee engineer then working for the city, named Bud Carson. He had never seen an auto race when he took on the drag strip project, but it resulted in his eventually taking over stock car races here, renamed Mar-Car. The races now draw nearly 175,000 fans annually in weekly productions from April to September. Programs include stock cars, late model autos, midget and sprint cars, and motorcycle racing.

10

Division a Way of City Life

IT MUST BE REMEMBERED THAT although Oklahoma City sprang full grown upon the prairie, it could hardly have been called an adult. An adult has formal restraints imposed by his peers, and certainly in mores of the society in which he is a part.

For more than a year Oklahoma City had no formal government. Captain D. F. Stiles and his augmented infantry company had no role except to preserve something called "law and order," which sometimes was a disputable term between individuals or groups, each with its own definition.

This form of para-government was followed after the Organic Act of 1890 by an aldermanic system prescribed by the first territorial legislature. Later it became a commissioner form of government, with commissioners for branches of municipal services, such as finance, police and streets.

The city operated its first thirty-eight years under the aldermanic or commissioner forms, in both of which the mayor had administrative responsibilities and service performing duties, commonly called the "strong mayor" system.

The charter form of municipal government, has in its loftiest context, a mayor whose duties are almost exclusively leadership of the council as a policy making body, with the city's administrative functions handled by a city manager. Council members are elected by wards on a non-partisan ticket.

Here, as in some other cities, the charter form has proved difficult to implement completely for very long periods. This is due to the human element, the inherent political spoils system that varies with individual natures, and a historical ward cleavage that no protestation of civic brotherhood has been able to eliminate from our town. Activists seek office — activists like personal action.

In those thirty-eight years of aldermanic and commission government, the city had seventeen different mayors. In the forty-seven years after advent of the council-manager form in 1927, it has had eleven mayors and nineteen city managers, including one repeater. When the charter was adopted in 1927 there were 145,200 persons eligible to vote and 34,203 did so, giving the issue a favorable majority, while in the same election only 33,873 people voted in the four council races at issue.

Frank Buttram led a "Committee of 100" in pushing the charter election successfully to get the council-manager form installed. (We still have "Councils of 100," although largely as a watchdog committee to check

124

on general obligation bond expenditures, after first endorsing the elections). The first charter election called for choosing councilmen at large. In 1957 an amendment put nomination and election of those officers on a ward basis. The city clings to historic ward patterns.

It is an old saying that few people get interested in city government until they are unhappy about something. There is more than a cubic yard of truth sand in that remark. Perhaps he did not ever intend it to be interpreted that way, but the best philosophical treatise on our city government was written by Horace Thompson, for twenty-five years a City Hall reporter for the *Oklahoma City Times,* primarily, and for six years an administrative assistant to the city manager. Thompson was assigned to do a study of Oklahoma City government. His research went beyond the original 1927-57 outline, at that time the terminus. He found, as most serious researchers do, that to know the present is to study the past. Although forms change, the basic attitudes, concepts and intracacies remain almost constant. There is much truth to the ancient Grecian admonition to "study the past — all that is past is prologue."

Thompson found that: "In general, the public attitude toward city government centered on law enforcement. To a marked degree, public attention toward other aspects was determined largely by emotional reaction to the more sordid events which always have been common to the beginnings of frontier establishments. The actual existence of saloons and gambling halls, the potential evils of election irregularities and occasional official misdeeds, made excellent topics for conversation and headlines. The problems of municipal taxation, budgets, finance, administration of services, and analytical examination of municipal weaknesses in those fields, simply were forced to await the arrival of greater maturity in public attitudes.

"Consequently, the idea of municipal government as a system primarily designed to administer municpal services grew slowly, and in an irregular fashion down the years. The commissioner form of government was adopted under rule in 1911 and lasted until 1927. It was intensely partisan, its administration of services based upon political considerations. The inevitable result was inefficient and expensive performance. But it was not until an administration (John Calhoun "Jack" Walton) had packed the police and other departments with political favorites and protected them by mounting machine guns at strategic downtown locations, that people were awakened to the serious threat to municipal government. On further examination they discovered the city's financial condition in deplorable shape and those who had been in city office while this condition was developing were firmly entrenched politically.

"At such times, people demand a change. The change came in 1927 with adoption of a council-manager charter . . . the change marked a date when people became aware of the true import of city government as a service performing institution, rather than an institution for political amusement. Oklahoma City, like all cities, is people. So is city government. All three — the city, its government and its people, mature together. Sooner or later all three recognize several basic facts upon which the community's governmental organization and operation is based:

"First, municipal government is an instrument of public service; second, citizens are much more interested in results than in processes employed to provide municipal services; third, municipal government is 'good' or 'bad' in direct proportion to the degree that it provides maximum service at minimum cost, and interferes least with what citizens, as individuals, wish to do; fourth, municipal government is a political institution."

From 1927 to 1930, after the change to a charter form of government, prior excesses were overshadowed by events under the new system. Walter Dean was mayor and E. M. Fry city manager. General obligation bond issues totaling $9,029,000 were passed; the city deficit was paid; taxes were reduced; the city was put on a cash basis with the budget balanced. There was relative harmony between the council and mayor. This should have pleased all those who supported the change in governmental form. This was one of those rare times when idealistic conditions existed, even for former "aginners."

The euphoria did not last. C. J. Blinn was mayor for two years to begin the 1931-38 period, followed by tall Tom McGee for two years, then John Frank Martin (a former councilman) for four years. Under Martin bond issues of $1,280,000 were passed. Yet this was a period of turmoil with a parade of city managers that saw factional control grow quickly. There were eight city managers: L. D. Abney served seventeen days; John McClelland ninety-eight days (he died in office); A. R. Losh, 114 days; Albert McRill one year and 195 days; W. A. Quinn forty-eight days; Orval M. "Red" Mosier, three years and 149 days; F. G. "Bus" Baker, three and one-half months. Quinn returned for three years and ten months, serving through 1940.

This approximate ten year period saw some changes in city council each two years but most of the offices were held for four years or longer. Most of the power — and in this period there was council power — lay in combinations that most frequently were headed by Joe Campbell and Leonard Dickerson. Campbell went into office in 1935 and was reelected through 1943, but died in 1944. Dickerson started in 1936 and served twenty years, somewhat of a record, although Harlow Gers had ten and G. A. "Coxey" Stark had eight years. Percy Jones had six years, extending from 1937 into the mid-forties, and L. I. Baker had four.

This made for a continuity of a majority that the two-year councilmen could not match nor has it been equalled. There was not always unanimity but there seemed always to be a controlling majority. City jobs on a patronage basis were dictated by the council, in practical effect, especially in the police department. The parade of city managers attested that, contrary to the charter, the council and not the manager ran the city. Civic leadership realized this, also, and when there was a movement afoot requiring cohesion and support from City Hall to put a project across, support of the council leadership was courted. Usually it was obtained. Dickerson and Campbell, for instance, were cognizant of the city's municipal needs above actions of the council alone. So usually they went along. Never did they forget, nor let the public forget, that they were political people, elected through the political process, and that the vitamins of political life derive from patronage. Yet in his later years on the council, Dickerson was accused

ROBERT A. HEFNER
Mayor and Supreme
Court justice

GEORGE H. SHIRK
Mayor and Historical
Society president

JAMES H. NORICK
Only mayor with
non-consecutive terms

HARRY E. BAILEY
City manager and
creator of turnpikes

by some of his former supporters of being "a Chamber of Commerce man."

Beginning in 1939 there came a slightly different atmosphere. The times and the people were changing a bit, partially because the war period in Europe altered many things in civil life with uncertainties about America's role, and partially because the pendulum swings slowly but inevitably in the mores of a people and in their civic conscienceness. There was an element of "reform" since to use it otherwise implies perhaps more changes than actually resulted from multiple real, or fancied, misdeeds. Sometimes opinions differ on definitions.

The election of Robert A. Hefner as mayor was hailed as a reform. He brought to the office a record in the state judiciary, financial success in the oil industry, an interest in governmental affairs, and an unflappable attitude toward the public weal.

In this period there were city bond issues of $23,435,000 — a record then. The city's second and badly needed water reservoir was planned and was later to bear the mayor's name. Harmony was restored to the council, vis-a-vis the mayor's office, and the council's control as a factional element began to decline. Stability, more than transition, became a factor of the manager's office. Public confidence, that essential ingredient to good city government, gradually was restored. Much of this came from the mayor's attitude as a head pointer rather than knocker of heads. He had calm. He had patience to wait for the council to make its own decisions. His lack of a vote, as the rules then dictated, was perhaps at times more eloquent than a vote would have been.

Much of the harmony came through efforts of some councilmen previously accused of creating dissension, such as Campbell, Dickerson, Gers, Stark and Jones. Starting in 1941 Harry E. Bailey was city manager for three years, followed by C. F. Aurand for three and one-half years, then William Gill, Junior, for a similar period on his first hitch as city manager. Bailey's major achievement was utilizing his professional engineering background to supervise much of the dam construction for Lake Hefner. There were war scarcities. Contractors were bidding high. When bids appeared to be out of line the city did its own work by force account, meaning it was its own contractor, with Bailey supervising the project from the top.

Beginning in 1947 there were twelve years with Allen Street as mayor. Street was the son of a city official in early days, at an even more turbulent time, while Street himself had a break-in period as a councilman the four preceding years. He, as Hefner had exhibited, had a high boiling point and attempted to chair the council rather than dictate to it, with a fairly good reaction.

These were good years, in the civic sense of constructive effort, and citizenship cooperation. Bond issues for improvements amounting to $69,303,000 were passed. Ross Taylor, a professional engineer as Bailey was, but with prior experience as city manager of Enid, took the manager's post at City Hall and occupied it for five years. That remains a record for continuity. He was succeeded by Gill, who returned to the job for two years and three months, tossing enough energy around to hold dawn meetings with sanitation department workers and to respond to fire calls. Gill also backed creation of trusts as a means of financing a city equipment pool, for airport improvement, and later the Atoka water project — which he was involved in after resignation — in a joint venture contract with the low bid. Gill was succeeded by Sheldon Stirling, who had "adopted" Oklahoma City as a postwar returnee, and was an official of the Chamber of Commerce. He became city manager in mid-1957. Stirling found soon that he had multiple bosses; that one person, nominally gentle and a believer in the art of compromise, could not serve them all equally and constantly. He resigned.

Whether they be opportunists, businessmen with an urge to serve the public from a sense of civic responsibility, or persons who really enjoy the political infighting and alleged prestige of being a city councilman, most of the people who serve in that body soon learn that there is a different view looking out from the inside.

Walter M. Harrison was one of these. A very outspoken, somewhat controversial managing editor of the *Oklahoman and Times* from the War I period until 1946 — with time out for 1940-45 military service — Harrison was a city councilman and unsuccessful candidate for mayor. He posed a question in 1949, along with some observations: "Why should a mature, fairly successful guy, who enjoys privacy and freedom, deliberately choose to tie himself to an unpaid job in city service?

"Since April first I have managed to get the Park Department to scrape some dirt in Douglas Park. I have assisted in getting a sidewalk built for the Franklin-Kaiser school. I have succeeded in pushing through twenty-one 'hot-shot' calls for collection of garbage which drivers overlooked, and collected one trick cigaret lighter and one automatic ink pencil, which leaks furiously, from satisfied taxpayers."

Stirling served four years and nineteen days before being succeeded by Robert T. Luttrell, then city auditor, who lasted just more than two years. Robert Tinstman was the next city manager, and was to remain four years and two months. There seemed now to be a climate for longer periods than for earlier managers since Robert Oldland, who followed Tinstman, put in three years and six months. Nate Ross, who had been city finance director, became manager on March 1, 1971, and found a sudden termination July 24, 1973, after one of the quite common historic switchings in the "power bloc" of the city council. Pat Painter, head of the city planning commission was made acting manager. The year ended with Howard D. McMahan of Fort Worth, chosen as city manager.

Following Allen Street as mayor in 1959 was James H. Norick, to 1963; Jack S. Wilkes, 1963-64; George H. Shirk, 1964-67; Norick again, 1967-71; Patience Latting (Mrs. Trimble Latting) 1971-—. Mrs. Latting drew quite a bit of national publicity as the first woman mayor of a major American city.

Organized labor, as such, has not been a strong force in city elections. Its greatest strength has been reflected in council elections. For a time in the Dickerson-Campbell era labor was able to demonstrate more power. The war period with its aftermath had large numbers of citizens so intent on their own affairs they were quite willing to leave voting and city affairs up to someone else. Campbell was business agent for one of the smallest locals with the longest names in organized labor: The International Alliance of Theatrical Stage Employes and Moving Picture Machine Operators. Some of the stage hands, such as Pat Sterrett, also belonged to the bill posters union. It was Sterrett who, as a "Mr. Fixit" type, designed and built with little expense to the city, by using scrap for the framework, the changeable neon sign atop Municipal Auditorium (now Civic Music Hall) that announced coming or current attractions.

Labor has been of great assistance in getting general obligation bond issues passed, even when some results did not provide much work for skilled trades, which might often have been assumed to be a reason for labor's support. Unions were credited with helping to defeat a city earnings tax proposal in 1962, when the city was in an increasing crunch for operating revenue. Labor did not openly oppose a city sales tax in 1967, one of the first such measures that now are quite common in the state. Labor leaders have, from time to time, been in a high echelon of civic leadership when more push than normal was needed for a project.

In 1954 an illustration of citizenship interest in government, and active participation in it, was provided by Shirk, a native born attorney and history enthusiast, who that year was elected president of the Oklahoma Historical Society. (Nineteen years later he was still in that position). Shirk was called upon with others to prepare revisions in the city charter, later adopted, which featured a return to nomination and election of council members by wards, rather than at large. The non-partisan factor of council candidates was retained, meaning they could not run under any party label.

Shirk in 1955 headed a five-man study group on the city's water supply problem that came up with a recommendation to bring water from the more plentiful rainfall areas of Southeast Oklahoma. This created no immediate cheers but was to be implemented a decade later. In 1964, after the resignation of Jack Wilkes, to become president of Centenary College, Shirk was appointed mayor since he was acceptable to both council factions. He proved a good mediator, kept well abreast of city affairs, and enjoyed ceremonial facets of the mayor's position as Allen Street and James Norick had before him. Also as mayor, Shirk started the Community Relations Commission, named a Citizens Advisory Committee to keep an eye on bond fund expenditures that continues active, and in the 1970's continued an interest in city development by heading the Oklahoma Industrial Authority. Shirk also heads the Oklahoma City Historical Preservation Commission, that initially marked fifteen buildings important to the city's early life.

Oklahoma City government, regardless of its facade of operating under the charter form, has been so subject to cycles of council faction control and citizen interest that its course almost can be charted as to highs and lows, in relation to the paper principles upon which it is based.

One of the recurrent movements outside previously established entities such as partisan groups, the Chamber of Commerce and other civic organizations, organized in 1962 under the name of Association for Responsible Government (ARG). In its formative stage this group had in mind an attempt to get more urban oriented people into the state legislature, to offset dominant "rural" control which has featured that body from the first territorial session. That direction was of short length before emphasis switched to the city council.

From the end of War II some of the business community sought to get professionally trained men into the city manager's office, and to elect councilmen who would join in teamwork rather than be devotees of a political patronage system which, in practice, made a city manager ineffective. The purpose found skeptics.

In its own publication the ARG said, after stating the theme above as its dominant purpose: "... in 1962 ARG succeeded in electing four councilmen and a mayor. The association was disbanded immediately after election to remove any possible threat of pressuring, or lobbying for candidates elected by the movement. According to the by-laws, the association cannot be reactivated until six months before a primary election, at which time steering committees are elected following public meetings in each of the city's four wards.

"How are candidates selected? The ARG is a grass roots movement. The ARG now has more than 8,000 members. Capable candidates may be suggested by the membership to the executive committee of the organization in each ward. Five members from each ward constitute nominating committees, with the choice of nominees left to each ward.

"How are candidates financed? Each ARG endorsed candidate must pledge not to accept individual campaign contributions. Expenses are defrayed through $1 membership fees from citizens interested in obtaining competent, qualified men for office, who might not run otherwise. ARG candidates run as a group. ARG does not reveal the source of its funds to candidates."

ARG drew broad support from the League of Women Voters, Young Democrats, Young Republicans and some of the business community. It did not, at first, draw publicly stated support from the upper echelon of business and community leaders, while the Chamber officially remained in the neutral zone with neither obvious support nor disavowal. There was public interest manifested. An original ARG candidate, F. C. Love, was quoted in 1963 in an *Oklahoma City Times* editorial as saying: "I have lived here thirty years and did not realize that city government was such a big business. The city has $200 million in bonded indebtedness, thirty-three operating departments and $16 million in income each year. ... I say this is big business and should be run by dependable businessmen."

In a 1965 editorial *The Daily Oklahoman* spoke out strongly:

"The Oklahoma City council has been on dead center for two years. Anything proposed by the four ARG councilmen was certain to be opposed by the holdover councilmen. Previous to election of the ARG councilmen, any councilman could write a note to the city manager and tell him to hire a certain person or to fire another one. Instead of one city manager there were eight."

In the election of 1964 the ARG was successful in three of four city races and assisted in election of a reform minded mayor. At issue were metropolitan planning, urban renewal, and even retention of the council-manager form of government. As a result of the election, city government became briefly more centralized than at any time since adoption of that form in 1927. Citizen support for government increased to the point where, subsequently, a local sales tax was passed by a wide margin to bolster sagging city finances, and those who spoke about public improvement by general obligation bonds, no longer were bogeymen.

The *Oklahoma Journal* said editorially in 1966: "The revolutionary trend started three years ago when business and professional leaders took a look at their city government and did not like what they saw. Jobs were being bartered at the polls and some city councilmen paid their workers with municipal appointments despite restrictions in the city charter . . . the ARG moved into the polling places, spent money and elected four councilmen, all respected business and professional men."

The ARG backed persons served long enough to learn that being a member of the council is almost a full time job, too often thankless, and that preconceived ideas are buffeted by practical realism. This is not to infer that those who followed were any the less imbued with civic spirit.

The public interest aroused by ARG faded, in the historical cyclical way, and new faces were seen at city hall. Something really new for the city was added. Mrs. Latting, after serving one term on the council, was elected mayor in 1970. She exhibited strong interest in all aspects of city government, had equally strong opinions and ideas about how it should be conducted, and ran into essentially the same situation of council division that has characterized that body intermittently since 1927. The game was the same — only the players were different. There was talk of "blocs" while both a predictable majority and lack of permanence to a majority were evident in the familiar pattern.

After the election of 1972 a new "majority" forced resignation of City Manager Ross, amid charges of improper conduct by officials in building inspection departments, and other misconduct in departments under Ross' control, although nothing out of line was impugned to Ross himself. Some departmental officals resigned, some employes were charged with accepting bribes to issue permits and licenses, and Ross stepped out.

With other cities, ours has had difficulty at times in providing funds for essential governmental services and facilities desired by the people. Often needs are accelerated by population growth, business expansion and by advancing city limits, while revenues seldom keep pace with demands. By no means unusual but used here to great advantage in expediting government, industrial and cultural activity, and in providing those general increased services, is the method of trust financing. In most simple form this means providing funds for construction of facilities in which a governmental entity has a beneficial interest, as opposed to strictly private business, through sale of revenue bonds which are paid off through rentals or fees. Since trust properties and revenues are exempt from ad valorem taxes the whole idea is argumentative, but certainly this does permit getting things done more quickly than by conventional means. The "faith and credit" of the governmental agency that is ultimate recipient after bonds are paid off does not have to be pledged as in the case of voted general obligation bonds — which require promotional campaigns and voting — affirmatively. In a sense this financing method is typical of the sense of urgency which has characterized Oklahoma City since the day it was founded by people in a hurry.

Formally created on April 26, 1956, the Airport Trust was the first such venture. It was concerned initially with improving facilities and quarters at the Civil Aviation Agency, later Federal Aviation Agency, on the west side of Will Rogers Field. The original post-war construction there, after opening of the CAA installation was authorized, was done on a bidless joint venture by the Kavanaugh-Tankersley-Cowen-Murchison interests on a fixed fee basis, predicated on average cost per square foot of similar construction in the area. This was for administrative, instructional and warehousing facilities and included some renovation of War II struc- tures used by the light bombardment group stationed here for training.

There was inherent danger in possibly losing the CAA installation as it began expansion, nationally, although United States Senator Mike Monroney, the Chamber and civic leaders were working strenuously to retain and improve the facility. Basically needed were buildings and other improvements. It was a multi-million project. The federal government would lease the buildings but not provide construction costs. Spearheaded by Bill Gill, Junior, then city manager, and Phillip Rhoades, vice-president of First National Bank and Trust Company, a drive was made to create an Airport Trust. Business leaders backed the idea. Before revenue bonds could be issued by an entity other than the state, at that time, remedial legislation had to be passed. State Senator George Miskovsky authored and pushed such a measure through. Before New York bond buyers could be interested, details on construction costs and total bond indebtedness had to be secured. There being no funds available for preparation of architectural plans and specifications, or engineer estimates, Hudgins, Thompson and Ball offered to advance those costs and do such work on a speculative basis, with assurance of getting the architect-engineer con- tract on a fee basis, as a percentage of total construction costs, if the venture was successful.

Between 1956 and 1958 the Airport Trust sold nearly $10 million in bonds for the CAA project and related airport expansion. In 1961 more improvements were made with an $11.5 million expenditure. This was not without criticism of almost everything and everyone connected with the project by a minority of objectors, some of whom were almost professional at such an activity. Bond debentures issued by a trust must be approved by the state supreme court, which then makes them saleable if there is a market, but also permits a time period in which challenges may be made to the issue. That legal point was cleared up by intervention suit. The occupying agency by 1965 had more than 4,000 employes with an annual payroll of $32 million, was training air controllers for world wide dispersion, and additional activities were assigned here such as general aviation records keeping and air medical research.

Later the Airport Trust method of financing was used for expansion of Municipal Airport into Will Rogers World Airport, with subsequent improvements there, at Wiley Post Airport and at Cimarron Field.

The method was used also in 1960 to create the Oklahoma City Municipal Improvements Authority, better known as the Water Trust, to provide a new source of water for the city. As usual, the means and the methods were debated. Also, as usual, much of the spadework had been done years earlier by organizations and individuals who recognized that the time to assure a plentiful supply of municipal water was before the lakes went dry. Six years before formal creation of the water trust, what became its major project had been under planning for a reservoir near Atoka. A typical ploy was used here in obtaining right-of-way for a pipeline, similar to that used for land acquisition for Tinker Field, urban expressways and other projects — that of getting land options before all details were publicised and prices driven up.

This time about $4.5 million was advanced by the American First Title and Trust Company, with guarantees by businessmen signatories, to be repaid from a subsequent bond issue. There seemed to be no fear that a bond issue would not be ratified by citizens when they knew all the story and were made aware of a need for additional water supply. Water rates were raised to help retire the bonds. There was little general attention to the project until 1960 when plans and specifications had progressed far enough to provide estimates on construction bids. Then there was a tempest boiling in the non-existent water pot. Objections included the method of construction — how do you bring water 600 feet uphill over 100 miles of line? — who told whom to spend money that we haven't even voted? — and so on. Even a retroactive look at the city's two reservoirs, with memories of water shortages and projection of future needs, did not satisfy everyone. There was some division that has not yet completely vanished.

A Water Development Foundation, created within the Chamber, put itself into a neutral corner, regardless of its past help and interest, and remained there. It was joined by some business folk who did not want to oppose the apparent majority but neither did they want to support it. Some others fought the project in the courts. But the issue was approved, the bonds did pass, the line was put in.

In 1962 a slightly different form of trust financing was created with formation of the Oklahoma City Industrial and Cultural Facilities Trust. It differed from the others in that the city was not formally liable for commitments made in its name, although it had a beneficial interest and eventually would have the reversion, when bonds issued were paid off. Retirement of bonds was to be from rental fees. This trust was initiated by Oklahoma Industries, Incorporated, the industrial arm of the Chamber, which primarily was the agency available to provide sites for incoming industry against competition of other locations.

The new trust had one priority activity, which was to finance completion of construction for the National Cowboy Hall of Fame and Western Heritage Center, on Persimmon Hill in the city's northeast quadrant. After a preliminary phase dating to 1955 when the western shrine was located here, by trustees of the seventeen western states making up the traditional west beyond the big river, construction slacked off to be dormant after available funds were exhausted. The more than $1 million that Oklahomans put into the shrine in the fastest money draw in the West, had not been matched by enough other states, in ratio. In fairness, one wonders how much Oklahoma money would have gone into that project had it been located in Wyoming or Oregon? Of the thirty-seven acres at the site, the city owned twenty-five and the Hall of Fame had purchased twelve. To obtain new financing, trustees of the shrine deeded their acreage to the trust, with a reversionary clause when money advanced was paid off through rentals and the loan amortized, and received $1 million. By this method the shrine was completed and dedicated on June 26, 1965. By 1972 it was its own master while trustees and other supporters were as happy as a homesteader who survived the vicissitudes of nature and red tape to prove up on a claim.

The Industrial and Cultural Facilities Trust put a $1.5 million portion of its first $2.5 million amount issued to acquire a plant for Ling-Temco-Vought, first built by Oklahoma Industries through civic financing. This meant that the plant would be removed from ad valorem tax rolls. Therein, as Hamlet would have said, lay the rub. Like Hamlet there were many folk around with soliloquies, most of them sincere. Those opposed said lost taxes would endanger schools; that people should be allowed to vote on creation of trusts; that this all seemed to be illegal somehow.

Those in support replied that without ad valorem taxes better leases could be made with industrial users; that equipment, furnishings and processed inventories of industry were taxable; that the city's principal sources of income were derived from sale of services, not from ad valorem; that homes built by industrial employes are taxable as are their purchases; that more jobs meant more money turned into the economic stream. It was a year before the arguments were settled through an original jurisdiction ruling of the State Supreme Court and city council action. The trust won. The legal ruling did not change all opinion.

Something a bit new but akin to other trust financing was creation on January 7, 1958, of the Oklahoma City Development Trust. Bonds issued by this trust provided funds to purchase municipal equipment which the city did not have general revenue funds to acquire, in the quantity needed, and within a time period, because of expansion which accelerated the need for services that did provide revenue. The first issue was for $1 million. Bonds are retired from revenue. Local banks and investors took up this issue, meeting outside competition and acquiring a piece of the city's future at the same time.

11

Civic Power Structure

WHAT ANDREW T. BROWN IMPLIED IN HIS study of frontier Kansas City could well apply here: "Cities, as human groups, are depicted as possessing certain human characteristics, among them ambition and a sense of purpose."

The only constant factor in the development of Oklahoma City has been the inevitability of change, for change has been the growth pattern since the land opening.

An outstanding example of those who pushed for progress is found in the Oklahoma City Chamber of Commerce. As the general history of this city is somewhat different from that in many other areas, this group is far more than a business boosting, Pollyanna chorus. Its leaders since 1889, followed by the membership, have never hesitated to toss their money on the civic drum when action was needed, hoping to have it returned one day when the particular project was successful, but ready to lose it if necessary.

In some cities those who make up the visible power structure have been confused with those who form the real and often invisible leadership. In Oklahoma City the civic leadership structure is, for all effective purposes, the power structure, ranging from non-policital to apolitical and without elective office. Influence of this group in formulation of municipal policy is far stronger than that of public officials the city has had, with some variations.

A study in depth of leadership done in 1967 by Ronald L. Stewart as a master's thesis in political science, determined that "Oklahoma City has certain characteristics. . .that include existence within recent years of a highly decentralized political sphere, and the presence of a strong business organization which can act as a centralizing force for exercise of influence by the business community.

"A survey of these characteristics made it apparent that the preconditions for exercise of influence by businessmen exist in this community to a greater extent than in many other cities. . .business interests in Oklahoma City are centralized to a high degree, with projects being planned and coordinated through the Chamber of Commerce, a well organized institution with a history as old as the city itself.

"From past examples of the Chamber's influence in public affairs, it has been shown that the organization is capable of initiating projects which ultimately become public policy. . .the high degree of organization

VIRGIL BROWNE	JOHN A. BROWN	C. R. ANTHONY	LUTHER T. DULANEY
Coca Cola operator and civic leader	*Founder of largest department store*	*Established a major dry goods chain*	*Businessman and philanthropist*

exhibited by businessmen, coupled with their support of good government movements, increases their potential for political influence. This potential was most dramatically demonstrated by the role of businessmen in initiating changes in the character and personnel of municipal government. Political influence in this sense is not partisan but a relational quality enabling persons to control others in reference to policy making activities.

"This is not a political organization, per se, but the line between civic, economic and political matters may get a bit thin, sometimes due to personal feelings of dominant personalities (leadership) but not as a matter of consensus policy. Ten to twelve of the leaders are actively involved in every major project. The next group, up to some forty members, is active in more than one area. The next 200 to 300 members are active periodically in self-chosen areas."

One former city manager interviewed by the political scientist said, in reference to the role of businessmen in providing direction for elected city officials: "The Chamber and the business leaders who support it, are accustomed to resolving problems (such as putting the city on a sound financial basis). They are often more active than the city council because it has been so split from time to time. You need some continuity of planning on these things, which this Chamber group provides. You can't have a good city government without the support of citizens, however, under the council-manager form of government."

Among other interviews obtained by Stewart for his thesis were statements also explanatory. From one business leader came the comment that "the Oklahoma City Chamber certainly includes a wide diversity of members representing virtually every major firm in the community. The Chamber is unique in that it is 'big business' dominated rather than retail oriented as most are. It has been the prime mover in the community for decades on anything you can mention, whether civic or political, almost to exclusion of the city council."

Other persons expressed the view that, although it is the most influential organization on the local scene, its weight stems from influence of its individual leaders (directorate) rather than in an inherent power to solve local issues. "The organization tends to have little influence of itself but its members listen to the leadership; the organization functions to coordinate many types of programs and to secure support for the broader community."

Another: ". . .it is the leaders of the Chamber and not the organization itself. . civic leaders are active in the Chamber and its corporate board of fourteen is vital to forward progress of the city. The Chamber's overall board of directors, composed of more than sixty members, is the driving force behind the community on everyday activities for betterment of Oklahoma City."

And what was a noteworthy comment: "The leadership has been constructive with little direct self interst. Personal wishes have been largely subordinated; they have been as unselfish as you could expect this type of leadership to be. The public often feels that many of the leaders have profited personally — and some on the fringe have profited because of insider's knowledge in the past. For the most part, however, a self-policing technique is practiced, somewhat like the medical profession, and profiteers are forced outside the pale."

The opportunity for influence by an organized group, such as the Chamber has been provided historically by turmoil from the days of aldermanic and commissioner form of municipal government. Even after adoption of the charter form in 1927 this turmoil continued.

Support of elected city officials has not always been needed to put certain major projects across. Historical examples are removal of the Rock Island and Frisco tracks from the central business district; construction of Lake Hefner as the second large municipal water reservoir; construction of Lake Atoka and the 100-mile pipeline terminating at Lake Draper for the third large addition to the water system. In spite of certain official blocking attempts the key influence people won these conflicts.

Both city and county governments depend by necessity upon the Chamber to organize promotional activities — and provide financial support — for public bond issues which those officials desire voted, since neither of those branches of government can expend appropriated funds for such a purpose. They depend also upon the news media, both print and electronic, to promote public obligation bond issues.

Without question the publisher of *The Daily Oklahoman*, E. K. Gaylord, has been one of the prime leaders since 1903, having always been one of the first contributors or guarantors of needed funds, also providing editorial and news column support in that paper and, since 1916, in the *Oklahoma City Times.*

The informative function of the newspapers, in the view of other interviewed business leaders, probably has had more influence on city policies and projects than their editorial page views. A composite agrees with the newspapers, not excluding the box score on election of political candidates that they favored editorially.

The Chamber was organized on May 25, 1889, only thirty-four days after the opening, and then was known as the Board of Trade. It occupied donated quarters for a time and after changing its name to the Commercial Club, was housed above Wheeler's Bank, with Clifton George as the secretary-manager. Then it became the Oklahoma Merchants Club, and the Oklahoma City Club, before adopting the name Chamber of Commerce in 1902. It was incorporated in 1910 upon realization that members — in a pattern continued to the present — had pledged more than $1,600,000 for various civic and industrial projects. In the past fifty-four years the Chamber has moved but three times. First, for four years to the Oklahoma Club building (now the Tivoli Inn), then in 1928 when, with 5,300 members, it was seventh largest in the nation, it moved to the top floor of the twelve story Commerce Exchange building at Robinson and old Grand Avenue (now razed). It remained there for nineteen years. The Chamber moved in 1947 to the Skirvin Tower, leaving in July 1972 for its first ground level quarters on Santa Fe Plaza.

The Chamber has taken the lead in providing money for land options for various purposes and for promotional efforts to secure general obligation bonds, or for governmental and industrial complexes. This includes water and sewage systems; relocation of the State Fair of Oklahoma; acquisition of Tinker Field areas; expansion of the original Municipal Airport now housing the Federal Aeronautics Administration center; Will Rogers World Airport; outlying auxiliary airports such as Wiley Post, Cimarron and Mustang Fields; expressways; fire and police facilities; most of the industrial centers; Urban Renewal, including the Myriad area. Through its industrial arm it provided a means of completing construction on the National Cowboy Hall of Fame when it was stymied. It has provided leased facilities for a score of major industries.

Neither Edward Overholser, president-manager of the Chamber, nor any of the membership realized in 1919 that a new hand hired as assistant to Overholser eventually would be, in his way, about as great an influence upon the city leadership as the Chamber itself was upon civic affairs. It did not take them too long to catch on. Even after more than thirty years as managing director of the Chamber, until his "retirement" in 1968, Stanley Draper was indeed something different.

A native of Lasker, North Carolina, Draper was educated at Shenandoah College in Virginia and at the University of Chicago. After graduation he enlisted in the army and came here upon discharge from the service. If one were permitted but three things to attribute to him they would be, in order: an ability to dream large dreams and project them into the future; a driving power to accomplish almost any visionary project in a practical way; an amazing ability to get business and professional folk to pull each others' chestnuts out of a hot fire, without wearing gloves, and without knowing whose chestnuts they were saving.

Often this device was used to acquire land for acquisition later by an installation, or to create roads and expressways. Secrecy was often important because speculation would drive up option or purchase costs. There was a competitive angle, also, for hardly any major industrial related activity is without its competition elsewhere. Option on land in 1941 for the original Tinker Field project is a good example. City real estate men were asked by Draper to secure options on specific tracts of land, without being told what the intended use might be and only that "it's for the good of the city." Neither did one know what anyone else was doing.

The Oklahoma City Stockyards, when both the Armour and Wilson companies were producers.

That was a ploy often used by Draper. Another was to assure minimum funding for some activity from five or six willing backers, quietly, then to hold a large gathering at which people were asked to co-sign bank notes to get immediate action, with notes paid later from bonds or land sale. The history of projects which Draper inspired and helped secure, ranges through those first "rock roads" to the Frontiers of Science, water resources, industrial and cultural development. Each of them, in its way and in its time frame, are markers in the city's progress from the post-War I boom and bust to yesterday.

The one "gift" nature did not lavish upon Draper was that of patience. In time he did acquire some mellowing but even today in his retirement, a dominant hobby of historical preservation, and affairs of the Oklahoma Heritage Association, provide a release for a great amount of mental energy.

In its early days the Chamber absorbed a Civic Council as its Civic Committee. The first Oklahoma City Real Estate Association was a part of the Chamber. The Better Business Bureau started there as did the Oklahoma City Retailers Association, three tax limitations groups, at least twenty industrial foundations, and many cultural and educational facility acquitisition projects.

Draper used many variants of the admonition to "make no little plans" although his usual plea was more to the effect of "let's get it done." Many civic slogans were used but the most venerable one for years was that coined by Roy Christian in 1935 when, after a brainstorming session that included such things as "from stone age to steam heat" as a description of Oklahoma City's progress, Christian came up with "From Teepees to Towers." That lasted until the "Arrows to Atoms" theme of the 1957 semi-centennial celebration at the fairgrounds.

The combination of business leadership, action and ambition of the city had its first tangible result in 1910 when the community's first large major industry came into being. The procedure was typical of everything that has followed. This really began in October 1908 when Thomas E. Wilson, then executive vice-president of Morris & Company, a Chicago packing firm, came here on an exploratory visit. Wilson called upon Sidney Brock, a leading merchant and president of the Chamber, to say that his firm wanted to build a plant here but wanted no publicity at that particular time, a desire still typical of competitive business. What Wilson and Morris did want was a bonus of $300,000, which would represent ten percent of a three million dollar packing plant they would build. Also, they wanted some additional assurance of a livestock market.

Brock, like the other business leaders, was no hesitant companion to this sort of civic courting. With Anton Classen, John Shartel and E. K. Gaylord, he went into a huddle with Wilson in late afternoon and by one o'clock the next morning Wilson was satisfied with the assurance of those four persons, that the city would indeed meet his requests. Those four gentleman signed a formal contract with Wilson, representing Morris & Company, that they would guarantee the $300,000 would be raised. At that point in time this was a one-sided gamble but the city folk knew their people. The only other person let into the prospect at that time was George Stone, chairman of the Chamber's Industrial Committee, for Brock knew he needed help in securing land options. That money was advanced.

Cash was not all that Morris & Company wanted, Brock said later, although the bargainers got acceptance of a down payment of $150,000 on plant opening and the rest a year later. Morris wanted the city to extend its sewer connections to the plant area line, so that with other city effluent it would be carried to the North Canadian river bed. (As with other requests this was ratified later). Morris wanted the street railway lines extended to the plant area. With Shartel sitting in as a delegation member that was no problem. Morris wanted a belt line on rail to connect with the four trunk lines then in the area. That was promised. A Chamber committee purchased such right-of-way (being reimbursed later by the Oklahoma Industrial Company when surrounding business and residential lots were sold, much as the descendant Oklahoma Industries, Inc., does today). Morris would dig its own water wells for an initial requirement of 350,000 gallons a day. It asked also for exemption from·city taxes only, by being allowed to remain outside the city limits for five years as a reserved island, in effect.

Brock and Stone secured options on 575 acres of land in the area selected by Thomas Wilson — over arguments of the committee who wanted it east or west of the little city, to be out of the path of prevailing winds — but Wilson insisted. The public announcement came the next year. On May 19, 1909, the business community attended a mass meeting and pledged a total of $427,000 in capital stock for the Oklahoma Industrial

Company in less than two hours. In addition to the original principals to the agreement, those recalled later by two of them as attending that historic meeting and pledging funds for this, and some other anticipated needs, included: Charles B. Ames, Charles F. Colcord, Seymour B. Heyman, C. G. Jones, Sol Barth, Joseph Meyer, William Mee, J. L. Wilkins, Joseph Huckins, Weston Atwood, W. J. Pettee, O. P. Workman, J. M. Bass, John R. Rose, Oscar P. Halsell and A. L. Welsh. The stock subscribers later received eighty-two percent of their original investment back when the Industries arm was dissolved. The rest was. a donation. Again a typical gesture. O. J. Logan, a member of the state legislature at the time, said later that location of the packing plant here, and its accompanying facilities and services, had much to do with sentiment toward locating the state capital in the city.

It was October of 1910 when the packing plant and the attendant terminal market, the Oklahoma National Stockyards Company, was opened. On 197 acres of the optioned land the stockyards firm was built as the fourteenth major terminal market in the nation, after opening of the Chicago stockyards in 1865. Other land was sold for business use and for residential housing in the optioned area, initially some 140 acres for nearby housing. The packing plant required about 1,000 workers. Added to other supporting activities, including the stockyards, this meant some 2,400 jobs shortly, in a city of little more than 60,000 population.

About a year later Schwartzchild and Sulzberger, also came here and offered an adjoining plant for a similar sum, $300,000, for a $3 million plant. That also was provided. Within two months city bank deposits increased $2 million when two plants were operated. Later Armour and Company bought the Morris plant, while Thomas E. Wilson purchased the S & S plant. With a plant in Chicago, Wilson was one of the majors. Some sixty years later Wilson moved its corporate headquarters to Oklahoma City. Armour in the late 1950's closed its plant here, when faced with the necessity of almost complete renovation, while Wilson did make alterations and improved its facilities to modernize operations in 1964. Longest tenure as Armour manager was that of Tom Dee. W. W. "Bill" Martin was his long time counterpart with Wilson, being succeeded by Oliver Gaffney, and in turn by Floyd Olson. John R. Baker was long time manager of the stockyards company, succeeded by Oscar Holderby for many years, with Earl Schweikhard as current vice-president and manager. There are a number of independent packers operating here with a combined valuable assist to the economy in employment and purchase of livestock and other services.

The history of the terminal market is a story in itself. The first cattle arrived from near El Reno in 1910, being driven overland, and the last three months of that year saw total receipts at the yards of 35,093 cattle, 5,153 calves, 87,917 hogs, 5,065 sheep and 3,848 horses and mules. The first full year at the yards, in 1911, saw a total of 542,108 animals pass through. As a horse and mule market the yards reflect advent of the tractor age, for it dealt with draft animals. The War I years saw a spurt from 14,412 horses and mules in 1914 to a peak of 62,306 in 1917.

Oddly enough in the War II period, when most Americans were thinking only of mechanized forces, the market for equine draft animals

E. K. GAYLORD
Publisher and civic
leader for 70 years

DONALD S. KENNEDY
Head of OG&E for
more than 25 years

STANLEY C. DRAPER
City promoter and
chamber head

and their offspring undistinguished for anything but work, came back. From a total of 11,718 head in 1935 to 15,124 in 1938. Some of these later found their way to Greece and to Assam as pack artillery carriers, and even to the "mud, mules and mountains" campaign in Italy in 1943-44. The last mules from the Army Remount Station at Fort Reno went to the China-India-Burma theater in 1943. As a sheep market, the yards declined from a peak of 287,485 animals in 1956 to a small 26,412 in 1972. Horse and mule sales were discontinued in 1954. There were more than one million hogs marketed here in 1971.

The Oklahoma City yard has bloomed to be the largest feeder cattle market in the world. In 1972 there were 969,205 cattle and calves going through the yards. As a change from earlier marketing methods, where commission men met buyers in the stockyards alleys in a give and take bargaining atmosphere, the yards have gone to primarily an auction method with a limitation on the number of animals one shipper may send into the ring on certain days. This is to attract the largest number of buyers and expedite sales so that quantities, rather than single animals may be bid upon. Thursdays have been the largest market-auction days but now Wednesdays are added. There remains an option for individual dealing in the alleys if shippers or commission men desire that method.

A change in auctions was necessary since some of those Thursday auctions ran well into Friday. There have been more than 21,700 cattle go through the ring in one auction "day" that lasted nearly twenty-four hours. By putting a minimum on quantities it may be possible to hold down numbers to a more workable number and period of hours. That record day saw a total of $7,118,784 laid out for cattle on May 24, 1973, almost $1.5 million above any previous day, while several succeeding days almost equalled that. One commission firm alone of the fifteen on the yards, National, a cooperative formed during the depression 1930's, sold cattle grossing more than $1 million in its turn at the ring one day. And this, as with the higher total daily figure, was all done on a man's word and the nod of his head.

The Chamber has always been an advocate of improved streets and roads. In 1902 the only surfacing in the city was stone blocks from

HARVEY P. EVEREST
*Founder of magazine
distributorship*

JOHN E. KIRKPATRICK
*A leading
City philanthropist*

DEAN A. McGEE
*Co-founder and head of
Kerr-McGee Industries*

Broadway to Robinson on Main and on Grand, east to west, and two blocks on Broadway from Grand to First. Urban renewal projects in the 1970's that saw downtown streets torn up, could have provided a laboratory for civil engineering students — as well as certain types of historians — with the layers of stone, brick, concrete or asphalt. There were even some wood surfaces disclosed, as revealing as stratified geological layers of an archeological dig.

By 1916 the city had a number of surfaced streets, some of loose crushed rock, some of brick laid upon sand base, and a few topped by a substance called macadam, without capital letters of the surname of the Scot who invented the process. The Chamber that year proposed that a "rock road" be built outside the city to demonstrate the feasibility of lifting those Model T's, Stanley Steamers and Maxwells out of the mud so that they could get to town more easily to shop. By 1921 the Chamber had a "Good Roads Division," headed by R. A. Singletary, who doubled in providing rate information on common carriers, primarily railroads. At times he provided statistics to "prove" to an Interstate Commerce Commission regulatory body that it should lower freight rates.

State highways were improved but little after termination of surfacing at any city boundary. A numbering system gradually emerged after initial markers were used bearing surnames of persons who had the interest, zeal and money to place them, such as the Hockaday Highway across mid-America from the Dakotas through Texas. Traversing Oklahoma it had many zigs and zags for all early roads were laid out on section lines, where natural contours did not interfere. When federal designations came in, US 66, dubbed "the Main Street of America," was to run from Chicago to Los Angeles. It was largely unmarked and even untraced west of Oklahoma City. Singletary, with Joe Morse of Oklahoma City and Charles Tompkins of El Reno, loaded a Model T with camping equipment, shovels, boards to put under rear wheels when stuck in sand or mud, and such maps as were available and headed west.

The route they chose eventually became basically US 66, until later times when better earth moving equipment and construction methods became available, along with mileage reduction through use of straight line easements, fills, cuts, bridges and culverts. The Interstate system as we know it today, with its reduced mileage, would have been much appreciated in 1929 by the foot sloggers in C. C. Pyle's "Bunion Derby" from Los Angeles to Chicago, won by Andy Payne, later long time clerk of the Oklahoma Supreme Court.

By 1929 also, Oklahoma county could point with pride to hard surfaced roads, brick on a concrete base, that eventually went from the city north to Edmond, east of there to Bradbury Corner, thence north to the Logan county line, now Waterloo Road; south on Shields to the Cleveland county line; and west on Northwest Tenth street to the Canadian county line. Other main throughfares, now considered commonplace by some citizens, followed more slowly.

In 1949, in the manner by which it secured land for other purposes, the Chamber bought right-of-way for the urban highway and expressway program, in order to get that improvement moving. The method of using funds advanced by businessmen to secure some options in areas where public attention would jack up prices, later the co-signer method by which funds could be obtained from banks on a massive promissory type of note, was applied. The money was to be repaid later by bond issues but easements would expedite construction. "Deeds in trust" were given banks as additional surety on loans to satisfy federal or state bank examiners.

The later Tinker Diagonal resulted from similar action as did purchase of additional land west of the original base — also provided through the Chamber — to provide an industrial and building zone. After the east-west crosstown expressway to carry US 66 and a portion of US 77 traffic was assured, attention was given the Broadway Extension toward Edmond. In 1946 E. K. Gaylord purchased a strip of land 300 feet wide, extending north from Northwest Thirty-sixth street to the planned expressway, and donated it to the city for 'highway and park purposes. That parcel lay dormant for years although the Extension was four-laned north to Britton Road in 1962. Construction was begun on four-laning north from Britton Road to Memorial Road in 1972 and that section was opened July 20, 1973.

From its first underwriting in the city's youth to the major and sometimes grandiose projects of its first mid-century, in retrospect, Chamber leadership has depended upon a combination of volunteer and staff work to get things accomplished. Preparation and presentation of data is today more complex than it was when gathering information for Morris and Company, or when civic pitches were made at the Frisco railroad. The 1973 multi-million General Motors land acquisition and impending construction of a major assembly plant in the industrial area west and south of Tinker Field, is the largest project to date but fits a pattern established long ago. This project was two years in the process. Very few persons knew about it. That, too, is typical. Chamber staff people can guard certain information as zealously as industry does a competitive chemical process.

This "trade secret" was put to the epitome by Draper and is carried on by Paul Strasbaugh, now the executive vice-president, who combines some Draper teaching with ideas and ability of his own. Back of Strasbaugh, as they were for Draper through several decades, were persons such as Jack Hull, whose data compilation has been anonymous but weighed volumes; Glenn W. Faris, for years before retiring a key administration and organization man whose visual presentation in behalf of Oklahoma City — for one major contribution — was a major factor in the National Cowboy Hall of Fame being located here. There are others on the staff whom one might call the second generation, in the same category of professionals to whom work is more important than personal credit, in Stanley Draper Junior, Jess Matheny, Jack Byler, Clayton Anderson and Arch Jack, to name those of longest tenure.

12

Citizens' Services Expand

ALTHOUGH RAIL TRAFFIC IS NOT WHAT it was, especially in the passenger category, and Oklahoma City as a distribution point can boast of its large number of interstate and intrastate motor freight lines and air express, the city got its early day boost from railroads. Railroad promotion in that era was a way of life for some visionary speculators, other men with the financing ability to lay track had to be persuaded, or otherwise induced to venture across the new country.

Under federal land grants the Santa Fe built south from Arkansas City, Kansas, and by 1886 reached a hill north of present Oklahoma City, where the terrain sloped southward toward the North Canadian River drainage area. This stop was called Summit and had but a box car on a spur track for use as a telegraph office for rail crews. Then track was laid to Oklahoma Station, approximately where the Santa Fe station here is now. At the station was the depot, a post office with S. H. Radebaugh as postmaster (until succeeded by G. A. Biedler after the opening), a boarding house run by George Gibson, and a stockade owned by C. D. Bickford, a contract government freighter. There was an army quartermaster agent on hand, Captain C. F. Summers, concerned with supply for Fort Reno, and for Indian Agencies to east and west. The day before the opening Santa Fe hands completed a cottage for the agent's residence and arranged for two water wells, one at future Main and Broadway, the other south on later Grand Avenue.

A. W. Dunham, an eighteen year old Kansas youth who had been a "news butcher" on Santa Fe trains, then became a telegrapher, was made station agent. Also Wells Fargo Express agent, Western Union Telegraph Agent, and Stage Agent. The latter was rather an important transportation job at the time. A stage of the Concord type pulled by six horses, or at times mules, made the trip from Oklahoma Station to Fort Reno in four hours, each way. The stage had a boot in front and in the rear for small baggage. Larger items were placed on top. The fare was $3 one way or $5 for a rough round trip. Passengers were allowed forty pounds of baggage free and paid for any excess at express rates. It was not unknown for military personnel to be transported in a mule drawn ambulance. The Gulf, Colorado and Santa Fe built up southward from Red River to Purcell in 1887. A different name but same line.

That first east-west train of the Choctaw Coal and Railway Company chugged into Oklahoma City on May 10, 1891 in the heart of town, after altering its course slightly because of squatters in the first right-of-way. The Choctaw later extended west of El Reno, ending for a time at Weatherford, thence to Amarillo. It became the Rock Island in 1905, after reaching McAlester to the southeast.

The Atlantic & Pacific Railroad (now the Frisco) started ambitiously as a transcontinental line and reached Vinita, I. T., in 1870. In 1881 it got to what became Tulsa; in 1885 to Red Fork, now West Tulsa; in 1886 to Sapulpa, I. T. In 1895 the St. Louis and Oklahoma City Railroad was organized by Frisco interests in cooperation with the arm-twisting C. G. Jones and Henry Overholser, to build a road over the 103 miles remaining to Oklahoma City from Sapulpa. Delegate Dennis Flynn helped in Washington by getting some federal enabling legislation. The road was completed in 1898 at a cost to Oklahoma City citizens of $40,000 for land and other expense. Now four main compass directions were bisected for the trade center. That was important for growth.

Harry Gobel, an early day railroad fireman, said that engine crews (engineers and firemen, called hoghead and tallowpot, respectively) had their own private way of signaling their wives as they approached town, to get out the family buggy and be at the station to meet them at end of a run. They tooted the steam whistle, each with his own code.

Jones also was a primary organizer of the Oklahoma City and Western Railroad, from here to Quannah, Texas, some 183 miles, completed in 1903. The Missouri-Kansas-Texas Railway (the Katy), was extended from Bartlesville to Oklahoma City in 1902 over some 146 miles. A line to Atoka was put in by the Katy in 1904, extending that line about 136 miles on easiest grades. By 1907 Oklahoma City had a total of seven railroads which gave it a big asset in becoming a distribution center. When the last opening came, that of the Kiowa-Comanche country by lottery, a line of rail communication was already in place. A three-mile belt line within the city provided shuttling into teamster yards in various locations, away from freight depots on the main tracks. Some of them remain. Trucks, not teams, do the haulaway.

Eagerness of city leaders to secure rail transportation was a paramount factor. Most of them were dreaming rather large dreams of making the city grow. They failed to visualize just what location of tracks, passenger and freight depots through the main part of town would do, as the city did grow and street traffic increased — even in the wagon and buggy days — which after 1910 the advent of motor traffic magnified. By 1911 the Chamber of Commerce had begun a twenty year fight before the State Corporation Commission and the Interstate Commerce Commission, to force the Rock Island and Frisco to remove downtown trackage. The Rock Island passenger depot was where the Skirvin's "Sun Suite" pool is now, on the north side of the hotel, with a freight depot across to the west. The Frisco depot and freight shed were just east and west of Hudson. All this was in the area now known as Civic Center, one portion being named Couch Drive for W. L. Couch.

In 1914 the Corporation Commission ordered the Frisco and Rock Island to build "adequate" depot facilities. Three years later another order commanded the roads to put up a joint station at First and Hudson, where a larger right-of-way existed. Some private citizens demanded a four railroad, union station type of construction. Most city folk favored

Waiting for the last train to come to the Rock Island Station north of the Skirvin Hotel.

grade crossing elimination downtown, rather than a joint station, because there was daily complaint about long lines of traffic stalled by blocked crossings. In 1920 the Chamber was told that the Rock Island and Frisco "might" move their tracks to a location south of the business district if compensated for land they gave up. Judge C. B. Ames, chairman of the Chamber railroad committee, put the land value at $4 million.

In February 1927, Judge Ames reported definite encouragement for a plan to purchase the railroad property. On November 17 came another of many hearings before the Interstate and State regulatory boards, this time before J. B. Keeler, an Interstate Commissioner. Judge Ames said that no more legal proceedings would be necessary, that a citizens' committee and the railroads had reached an agreement. The next day one of those mass meetings typical of Oklahoma City was held and a whirl-wind campaign begun to raise a public improvement bond issue of $10,329,000, of which $4 million would be to purchase right-of-way, with that land to remain public park property or for other public use — not for sale. The issue passed. A Union Station was constructed, west of South Robinson on Southwest Sixth Street. The last train rumbled across Broad-way on November 30, 1930.

Settlement of the relocation argument in 1927 by no means ended the railroad story. Along with track removal and construction of the Union Station came a plan to elevate the Santa Fe railway through the main business district to eliminate grade crossings. In each of the forty-eight months of the four years following the 1927 agreement, the city could point to building permits representing investment of more than $1 million. Several months exceeded $2 million and one month saw a $4 million total. Since half of this construction spurt came after the economic crash of 1929, combined with opening of the Oklahoma City oil field late in 1928, the depression impact was lessened. In 1930 Oklahoma City led the southwest in construction.

The Union Station was dedicated in mid-1931 and was in operation nearly three decades before vanishing passenger traffic shut it down. In 1932 construction began on a $500,000 stone-faced station for the Santa Fe, approximately on its original historical site, with a $5 million track elevation program and acquisition of industrial trackage space and development area north of Northeast Twenty-fourth, bounded by appropriately named Santa Fe Avenue on the east.

Not the least result of railroad relocation was construction of the Civic Center buildings on vacated land. This included the County Courthouse, City Hall, Municipal Auditorium, City Police Headquarters and Jail. Depression was dragging the economy. The federal government created its various alphabetical, "pump priming" agencies, such as the Public Works Administration, (PWA) the Civil Works Administration (CWA) and the Work Projects Administration (WPA) as employment relief measures. An opportunity to do something about the Civic Center strip was not lost on a red-haired city manager, Orval "Red" Mosier, who held that post in a period when old City Hall needed a swinging door for its managers to go in and out.

Mosier was in office from August 1933 to October 1936. An Oklahoma City native, he had been executive secretary of a non-partisan tax payers' organization. He saw an opportunity and so did the city's business leaders. In 1935 the Chamber took the lead in a campaign to raise

Oklahoma City's Civic Center at night, looking west, not long after its completion.

a bond issue of $1,787,500 to provide fifty-five percent of the sponsor's cost in erecting the proposed Civic Center buildings. The federal government, through PWA, would provide the remaining $1,462,500 for the $3,250,000 consolidated project. The Chamber called it "The Bargain of the Century." The issue passed. The buildings were erected and occupied in March 1937.

Mosier, meanwhile, left the city to become vice-president of American Airlines in New York City, later being executive vice-president. To those who had been around since early days — and there still were many — there was a point of reflection in all of this. The city paid $65,000 to the east-west railroads to get them in here and $4 million to get them out. But what all that made possible appeared to be worth the cost.

The 45th Infantry Division Monument in Civic Center, built by 45th Division Association.

Couch Drive, the most narrow portion of Civic Center on the old right-of-way, now contains memorials fitting to the city and state. There is an Air Force monument, contributed by citizens, with a major assist from service and civilian personnel at Tinker Air Force Base; a monument dedicated to the 45th Infantry Division, from funds provided by guardsmen, and public campaigning support featured by the Business and Professional Womens' Clubs; a Navy memorial in the anchor from the battleship, USS Oklahoma, sunk at Pearl Harbor. This "hook" was obtained through efforts of former Rear Admiral John E. Kirkpatrick. Then there is a statue honoring the 89'ers, done by Leonard McMurry, and donated by the B. D. Eddie family.

(The USS Oklahoma was raised many months after the attack on Pearl Harbor and sold for salvage by the Navy. The ship broke its towing cable en route to the west coast and sank without the humbling end of being reduced to scrap. The anchor and the ship's silver service, the latter a gift from the state when the battleship was commissioned, were saved because they had been removed previously. The silver can be seen at the Oklahoma Historical Society.)

From earliest days need for municipal services was critical for the new city. Early in 1890 a contract was made with the Oklahoma Ditch and Canal Company, and J. F. Thompson of Houston, to install and operate an electric light system, substituting the incandescent lamp invented by Thomas Edison in 1879 for kerosene lamps in homes and to construct a water works. At that time water was of greater necessity than electric lights. It appeared that Thompson was a speculator for as late as March 1892 no progress was made. D. H. Scott then bought the franchise and put in a water works. About a year later one Henry G. Thomas, of Civil War star rank, bought Scott's interests and became also a social figure in the city.

In the early 1890's the Colorado Company had a small electric plant here which it operated until 1902. The Oklahoma Gas & Electric Company was formed then, with Judge C. B. Ames and Dennis T. Flynn as two of the leaders. The first office was where the Skirvin Tower stood later. Early in 1904 the local firm sold its principal interest to J. J. Henry of Denver, who later sold out to the Byllesby Engineering and Management Company of Chicago. The first plant at 20 West Noble Street by 1921 expanded to six generating plants producing some 30,000 units of power in separate cities. The company supplied gas later until 1928, when it sold those gas properties to Oklahoma Natural Gas Company. In early days OG&E also sold ice. It now is the state's major electrical utility with ten generating plants capable of producing 3,127,000 kilowatts in mid-1973. The company has had continual multi-million dollar expansions to keep ahead of domestic and industrial needs, a major portion of it under Donald S. Kennedy as president, later board chairman.

Oklahoma City now gets its principal domestic gas supply from Oklahoma Natural, based at Tulsa, but there's a story there, too. In 1901 near Red Fork, later West Tulsa, the federal government leased some land for oil and gas exploration along the Frisco right-of-way. There was a showing of gas at a well so Charles Colcord and C. G. Jones of Oklahoma

JOHN SHARTEL	C. B. AMES	SEYMOUR C. HEYMAN	SIDNEY L. BROCK
Developer of real estate and transportation	*'89er, lawyer and corporate organizer*	*Merchant; education and sports supporter*	*Merchant who helped bring packing houses*

City, with Robert Galbreath of Tulsa, pooled their leases and later prepared to pipe gas into Tulsa, about four miles away. Before they made much progress Glenn Braden offered them money and stock and bought them out in 1904. That deal resulted in formation of the Oklahoma Natural Gas Company in 1906 by Braden, H. M. Byllesby, Arthur Huey and others.

Water has always been a factor in Oklahoma City's domestic and even political life, since improvements have required bond issues with some objectors, and some skepticism about contract awards. The early citizens had to shift for themselves, almost, since in the first months there were only two wells available, primarily through courtesy of the Santa Fe Railway. The larger portion of the city was on a divide between the North Canadian and Deep Fork. There were several smaller creeks wending their way to those streams in the respective drainage area. Two of them were in the early city and later filled in as expansion made land more valuable. Creek water was a supply source but had disadvantages of transportation and for sanitary reasons.

The private firm that laid out a system from wells was not able to expand with needs. By 1893 the city acquired this facility. The supply then came from an original well dug by hand, and sealed with masonry near the Canadian, and several driven wells that required but a thirty-two foot depth in alluvial sands. Citizens by then had voted $80,000 in bonds for the system. Soon this, too, was inadequate and by 1907 a bond issue of $225,000 was put over and a new water plant constructed, which ran $30,000 above estimates. The filtration plant was hailed as "finest west of the Mississippi." It was believed adequate for 40,000 people. Population continued to grow. More wells were put down by the city. Private wells were utilized by many business firms, for much of the city was astride what later was identified as the Garber sands, one of Central Oklahoma's best aquifers.

Along with a growing need for potable water the city and its surrounding agricultural land had another problem. That was too much water at the wrong time and in the wrong place because of flooding. Some attempts at channel straightening failed because sandy banks were washed down and clogged the channels. By October 1914 the need for domestic water was such that for a time use was restricted to two hours per day. In July 1916 there was a two day supply at hand. One year later the first water supply crisis dominated both talk and civic action. Led by Ed

Overholser, there was action toward creating a "permanent" supply with a 1,700 acre reservoir on the North Canadian, to entrap what was, in that specific period, but a trickle. Water was cut off from the packing plants, from Wheeler Park and a ban put upon use of water outside homes for about sixteen days. On July 26, 1917, nature permitted those restrictions to be lifted by a three-inch downpour between Yukon and the city, on the Canadian. Restrictions had to be resumed, to a degree, after the flash flood subsided. More wells were drilled. On August 3, 1917, the city threatened to cut off water supply for any industry that consumed more than 100,000 gallons a day. Apparently some of them did not believe that drastic action would happen — but briefly it did — to nineteen firms. The city ordered drilling for ten new wells. Again nature gave an assist, two days later, with a heavy rain all over the watershed that sent a five-foot crest down the Canadian.

Construction of a dam on what was to become Lake Overholser was hampered by material scarcities during World War I but continued to completion in 1918. The now familiar site was a good selection geologically. There appeared to have been an old lake bed there in pre-historic times. A rather narrow gorge, just above Northwest Tenth Street, made a relatively short dam necessary and there were rock formations to stabilize the ends. The original dam was 1,100 feet long and fifty-four feet high. It would impound 17,000 acre feet of water from the Canadian. The foundation went down twenty-four feet to bedrock. The project required a $1.5 million bond issue. On April 22, 1918, there was a big celebration as the reservoir was dedicated and reports said that 10,000 persons viewed the project. Not the least part of ceremonies was a public marriage between Harvey Lee Hilton and Louise Nofsinger, who received all manner of housekeeping gifts from city merchants.

The lake filled slowly since drain off from consumption was steady. The capriciousness of nature exhibited itself on July 15, 1921, when 2.3 inches of rain fell in the immediate watershed in two hours, but within 14 months there was only a thirty day water supply impounded. In 1923 there were floods all over this region. Water from the North Canadian even reached West Main street. A new filtration plant was added to the system that year. The "dirty thirties" of regional dust bowl days, growing population and imbalanced supply for the demand, led to agitation for an additional water supply. Locations of a second reservoir were discussed, including possibilities near Fort Reno and in the Mustang vicinity. By 1938 Oklahoma City could participate in a Corps of Engineers reservoir project near Fort Supply, on Wolf Creek, which would permit release of water down the North Canadian channel. The city's share of the $7.5 million project was to be $2 million, with rights to 90,000 acre feet of water annually.

Then a Bluff Creek reservoir became an active issue. In February 1940 a bond election was to provide funds for construction of a dam and reservoir to impound 75,000 acre feet of water, to be connected with the North Canadian and Overholser by a canal; to make improvements at Overholser; to install a new pumping and filtration plant. All of this carried a $7 million tab. It was September 1941 before a 100-pound charge of dynamite replaced conventional ground breaking by shovel at the site of

Long-time Oklahoma City main postoffice at N.W. Third and Robinson — now a sub postoffice.

the Bluff Creek reservoir — later named Lake Hefner — and construction followed. Again that "permanent water supply" phrase was slightly understated as city growth continued. Spring rains of 1943 put the reservoir into service. (Lake Hefner was dedicated in June 1947).

Control of the North Canadian's flood waters as the stream wended through the city became more than an idea in early 1949 when hearings were held here. Channelization and bank stabilization was the favored method in contrast to a canal system. By controlling the stream better, economic benefits would be in preventing average annual losses of $400,000, possible loss of lives, some land reclamation with industrial sites, while added to that would be providing park and parkway areas. The cost was in excess of $16 million. It was authorized as a Corps of Engineers project by Congress, then appropriations followed, with first phase construction in 1953. The city had to provide a portion of funds for such things as utility line relocation. Work continued in phases for a five year period. The city's bond issue requirements for protection were less than the $1,850,000 required in the second 1923 flood, in October, that saw the river rise to a twenty-two foot crest, leave 15,000 persons temporarily homeless, and destroy bridges and property.

The Water Development Foundation of Oklahoma under Chairman William Morgan Cain, created within the Chamber, had prior to 1954 been looking into all phases of water problems and benefits for the city. Not the least concern was a larger and more permanent supply. By 1958 the foundation funded five separate studies on feasibility and engineering of acquiring water from heavier rainfall areas of Southeastern Oklahoma. Attention centered on the area near Atoka, where a bond issue in 1955 provided funds to construct a dam and reservoir on North (Clear) Boggy Creek, to impound 125,000 acre feet of water. With that were easements on right-of-way for the 100 miles to southeast Oklahoma City, to move water through a giant sized pipeline, with pumps to lift water up 601 feet in ultimate higher altitude along the way.

The Oklahoma City Municipal Improvement Authority was created to provide $9,204,857 through revenue bonds for the terminal reservoir, (now called Lake Draper) on Elm Creek, access roads, and to construct another filtration plant and other works connecting to the city system. Atoka lake began to fill in 1959 and in 1964 the first water poured into Lake Draper, constructed between 1961 and 1964. The Atoka project was not without its arguments and objectors, from almost every angle, including location and pipeline construction. The line, laid with five foot diameter pre-cast concrete pipe, was installed as a joint venture contract involving Gill Construction Company, Metropolitan Paving Company, A. J. Kavanaugh Trust, Cay Incorporated, Standard Industries, Tecon Corporation and Morrison-Knudsen Company. Contract cost was $33,265,402.

The city appears always to have had water troubles ranging from periodic scarcity to flooding, not the least of irritating streams being little Deep Fork as it traverses the near northern portion of the city, before leaving Oklahoma County. The first major attempt to tame the stream through the city was in 1959, after some five more recent periods of damage to homes in the fourteen square mile drainage area. In 1973 still another and larger project was inching along, combined with alteration of the urban expressway along the U.S. 66 route, as flood damage continued.

A storm sewer system for the city had been instituted in 1919 when the mayor and city commissioners, under urging of the Chamber, created a Public Sewage Board, with the dual charge to do something about storm waters and sanitary wastes. Early in 1920 the first cost estimates of the largest such project to that time were made. The survey showed that the city had an area of 17.28 square miles or 11,058 acres, but because of topography seven sewer districts were needed. (Fifty-three years later the official area was 645 square miles.) Storm sewers in use in 1920 were constructed between 1906 and 1909, as the city grew from 36,000 to 50,000 population and was proud of ten miles of paving. In a decade there were more than 90,000 persons and 173 miles of hard surface. In 1922 a bond issue of $1,098,000 was passed for storm and sanitary sewers. To show the magnitude of those storm sewers, at the outfall portion where water was dumped into the river, a Model T Ford was placed inside the sewer, which was eight feet in diameter and the first pre-cast concrete pipe used in the city, for a photograph. The Lee Avenue sewer was even larger with eleven foot diameter at end of its 6,400 foot length. Since then there appears to have been additional structures at periodic intervals and equally periodic unhappiness from some folk when heavy flash downpours temporarily flood city streets.

Sanitary sewer improvements also have been made, from time to time, with the largest project underway in 1973 for a treatment plant in the northeastern portion of the county. Opening of the McClellan-Kerr Navigation Project on the Arkansas has had a sustaining effect on the so-called Central Oklahoma Project, which by locks and canal would lift navigation here from Lake Eufaula, the gigantic silt trap for the river navigation channel, with a terminus surveyed near Arcadia. Feasibility studies have been made by the Corps of Engineers and preliminary planning funded as of 1973.

In early communications for our area the telegraph was no stranger. It appeared first in the future state on the east side in 1871 and on the west side, connecting the outside world, in 1876 from Wichita, Kansas, to Fort Reno. The first intrastate line, not on a railroad, was from Fort Reno to the Indian agency at Darlington, just north of El Reno.

The telephone was something else. The first line in later Oklahoma was constructed from Tahlequah to Muskogee in 1886, ten years after Alexander Graham Bell perfected the talking device, with its hand cranked, battery operated power. There was some trouble with the Cherokees until they learned that this mysterious thing could talk in their language as well as that of the white man. The Cherokee National Council gave permission for the line to be built, providing it took a route over rough ground to inhibit travelers from using it as a guide over their country.

The telephone made it appearance in Oklahoma City in late 1892 and early 1893. The first "hello girl" was Emily J. Hanson. It would be thirty years before a dialing system would begin to appear and thirty-five years before all the city had that device to use. The first local directory, printed in 1894 by the Times-Journal Publishing Company, contained 200 names. The directory was printed from handset type for the Missouri-Kansas Telephone Company. Telephone usage and printing improvements both developed to the point where, after forty-five years of continuous directory printing, the printing firm could say that it produced a book of 324 pages containing fifty tons of paper and 1,000 pounds of ink, in just twenty-two hours.

The Missouri-Kansas Telephone Company had its first exchange here and one at Guthrie. The Arkansas Valley Telephone Company began operation around Perry in 1897, including a toll line to Pawnee, where one of the firm's directors was Bird S. McGuire, at one time territorial delegate to Congress. Others included J. M. Noble and J. N. Coulter, both later connected with Southwestern Bell. The Arkansas Valley firm bought out a number of smaller firms and in 1902 became the Pioneer Telephone Company. It entered the M-K company field by buying exchanges from El Reno and Yukon with lines into Oklahoma City. Then Pioneer moved into the city itself as a competitor of M-K, so for some months business houses here had two telephones, two sets of bills, two sets of bells ringing — often at the same time — before Pioneer bought out Missouri-Kansas.

In 1904 Pioneer moved its main headquarters here from Perry. It picked up also a number of smaller companies. At that time there were 2,851 phones in Oklahoma City. In 1915 Pioneer was taken over by South-western Bell. Some people then were unhappy to hear that Bell, instead of giving each telephone subscriber a free line in the classified section, intended to put that addition to the directory on a paying basis.

The growth of Oklahoma City almost can be pinpointed by growth of the telephone company, which now has regional headquarters here. By 1907 its central city exchange was being rebuilt for the fourth time. No area in the nation of similar population had more miles of wire on first class toll lines. The city got its first automatic switching in 1922. In 1928

The Oklahoma City Floodway project strengthened and banked areas of the North Canadian.

Bell moved into its revamped $1.5 million building at Northwest Third and Broadway, the former Pioneer Building. By 1958 it had an additional major building at Northwest Sixth and Robinson, a $3.5 million initial contract. Long distance direct dialing started here in 1962 with the Sunset-9 exchange in the northwest quadrant. That year also Western Electric, manufacturing arm of the Bell System, brought here what was to be a plant employing at peak more than 3,500 workers. In 1964 Bell added a connected building to the first major structure at Broadway and Third, for a contract outlay of $4.7 million, which with equipment brought that investment to $9 million. That first telephone was about 371,268 phones ago.

13

To College on Streetcars

WHEN THE TWENTIETH CENTURY BEGAN the city that, almost like mythical John Henry of the Black River country, sprang full grown from birth, had much going for it. For one thing, this first year saw beginning of a transition to horseless carriages from the traditional means of personal transportation, when J. H. Everest chugged down dirt streets with his Steamer. It was a six-horse-power runabout with wire wheels, a "sport buggy without a horse."

The Western Directory Company was to compile statistics showing that the town held 14,369 persons (the 1900 federal census said 9,990). It said also, prophetically, that ere another survey was made a relocated City Hall would be occupied, the Carnegie Library opened, a sanitarium would be under construction, and Stiles Park dedicated.

That first year of 1900 saw "the greatest year in street improvements in Oklahoma City history," the *Times-Journal* proclaimed proudly in a special edition at year's end. The street commissioner had been given responsibility also for sidewalks. In a subsequent three month period there was laid 18,179 feet of board walk, 1,225 feet of stone walk, 4,150 feet of cement walk, 4,650 feet of brick walk and 550 feet of asphalt walk. Street improvement funds came from a poll tax but it was expected that an additional $5,000 per year would need to be appropriated to surface streets with gravel or macadam.

The post office could claim to have sixty percent more receipts than any other such office in the territory, with $8,727 for three months, more than $2,000 above a similar 1899 period. A municipal sewer system that would cost $45,000 when completed was under construction with the effluent going into the North Canadian. Instead of an all volunteer fire department there now was a basic salaried one, with John Marriman as chief. After being housed at the rear of business property since its inception, the department was looking forward to being in its own building at California and Robinson. "In 1900 the total number of runs was forty-four," the *Times-Journal* reported, "and the total damage of $3,305 was covered by insurance. Total cost of the department was $3,018, making it cost citizens about thirty-three cents each a year." The principal costs listed are interesting, in view of later times: $2,147 for salaries of regulars and $90 for volunteers; horse feed, $96.70; shoeing horses, $15.10; drugs and veterinary services for horses, $21.75; hiring extra horses and wagons, $46; washing bed clothing $6; one new hose wagon, $392 and plumbing, $1.50.

In contrast to today's temperamental weather, it is interesting to check that of the new town from 1890 to 1900. There was an annual mean temperature of 59.1 degrees. The maximum temperature in that period was 101 degrees on July 3, 1894, and again on August 1, 1896. The lowest was seventeen below zero on February 12, 1899. The average snowfall was 7.7 inches, with the greatest covering 14.8 inches in 1895 and the least, 0.2 of an inch in 1896.

There was a building boom that pivotal year of 1900 with construction valued at $1.2 million and an additional $300,000 under contract. Early wooden buildings were disappearing except for outer edges of the business district. There were more than 7,900 front feet of brick or stone buildings, including seventeen above three stories. There were both manufacturing and wholesale firms, from flour to beer to furniture to fabricated metal. There were three banks operating and another planned, along with a building and loan firm. The operating banks had total deposits of $1,369,595, which exceeded the three at Guthrie by more than $600,000, although government deposits were in Guthrie banks. The five-story hotel that Oscar Lee built drew from one visitor, Colonel William F. Cody — better known as Buffalo Bill — comment that "there is, in my opinion, no more perfect (sic) appointed hotel in any city of like size in America today." This was a $100,000 hotel, furnished for an additional $35,000, with space for some 300 guests. The early Grand Avenue Hotel had been expanded by owner Henry Overholser several times. But there were others such as the Northside Hotel, the Arcade, Planters, Saddle Rock, Hobson and Waverly. In one month, no doubt the largest, the town's hotel registers showed 6,543 signatures as an indication of Oklahoma City's drawing power. There was no competition to the west or for nearly 200 miles away on the east.

A cottonseed oil mill promised employment for 300 persons. The production of cottonseed meal stirred Anton H. Classen and F. M. Riley to build pens in which to feed up to 5,000 cattle. Most of them aside from local butcher shop slaughter, were shipped away, although H. O. Efer had started a small packing plant. Armour, Cudahy, Swift and Dold all had warehouses here for meat and poultry products, as distribution points, but major packers were ten years away for plant installation. It was claimed that Oklahoma City was the market for "the greatest variety of farm products of any city." Even barley grown nearby was of sufficient malt quality to be used in the two breweries. The Territorial Fair in 1899 offered a prize for the best exhibit of farm products grown on one farm of 160 acres. Six farmers competed and the winner displayed a total of 114 items.

Union labor came with the westward flow of skilled workers. After barbers the Typographical Union probably was next to make itself official. It had been chartered in 1894. The first statewide labor meeting, meaning both territories, was held at Lawton in December of 1903 when the twin Territorial Federation of Labor was created. Later, naturally, it became the Oklahoma State Federation of Labor. It did play an important role in the Constitutional Convention of 1907.

The first mill established for the dominant agricultural industry around Oklahoma City was that of C. G. Jones, which did most of its work grinding corn, the principal early crop brought by persons from eastern and southern states in 1889, which accounted for Jones' nickname of

"Gristmill." The first flour mill of size was that put in by George G. Sohlberg in 1904, president of the Acme Milling Company. He gained his first experience in Kansas and came here soon after the Run. He found financing here because the need for flour was obvious.

The educational and cultural aspect was not neglected. Reservation of Sections Sixteen and Twenty-six in each township for support of common schools, ordained in the 1890 Organic Act, provided a welcome addition to locally raised funds. The city had five school buildings with grounds for its pupils, valued at $128,000. Not the least support came from that gift of the 160 acre military reservation east of the Santa Fe tracks. The local district was bonded for only $48,000 and held $4,000 in building funds. It held $40,000 worth of mortgages on lots sold (from the reservation) and owned $6,000 worth of town lots. There were 2,400 pupils in late 1900 with plans to erect a new high school because of crowding.

Surely it could not have been antics and festivities stirred up by a reunion of the Rough Riders, but that first year of the new century saw formation of a strong Anti-Saloon League in Oklahoma City. The national league sent a representative here. A mass meeting against it was called for the Overholser Opera House and some 500 persons attended. The building owner was a leader of opposition to the dry movement, as a proponent of an open town situation, even while known as a personal dry. Former mayor J. P. Allen presided at this meeting and presented Henry Overholser to talk for the opposition. Which he did, to some length, saying that the national Anti-Saloon League people were not interested in Oklahoma City, per se, and did not understand its economic problems or business affairs. While this meeting was underway a rousing session favoring the league and its principles was going on at the Methodist Episcopal Church, South, where Doctor Delos D. Walker, who had been Prohibition Party candidate for governor in Kansas before making the Run, was the articulate spokesman. Underlying both of these meetings was the theme of an open or a closed town. Alcohol was to be an issue for years — even into our times — while the issue of prohibition would not be settled, legally at least, until adoption in 1907, then repeal in the Edmondson administration fifty-two years later.

The 1900 decennial census showed Oklahoma City to have 9,990 persons. Guthrie, also, was under the somewhat magical mark of 10,000 inhabitants, which the Organic Act said a city must have to vote bonds for public buildings. So Elmer E. Brown supervised a survey in 1902 that "proved" Oklahoma City had surpassed the minimum since the official census was taken, and carried his statistics to the Census Bureau in Washington. It was accepted and the first of almost continual public bond issues was passed. By 1903 the city claimed 35,000 persons but there is no official verification of that. Oklahoma Territory in 1900 had an official 398,331 inhabitants while Indian Territory held 392,060.

Beginning of what was to become one of the state's most important industries, or industry related activities, came in 1902 when the first refining was done in the Tulsa area. The first equipment was referred to as "teakettles," since a principle of boiling off lighter products was used on the crude. The main product was kerosene, for there were many more lamps and lanterns to fill than there were incandescent lights in use, while the heavier product was used for household fuel oil. The residue was sold, after congealing, for axle grease — for which there was also a large demand — and was used also on cattle as a smear to kill ticks or control lice and mange. There was even human medicinal use.

Oklahoma City jobbers "imported" these products from Tulsa. Growth of the total industry was years away. The city's own field was beyond the horizon a quarter century. Oklahoma City folk were more concerned with some recreational areas as that first decade slipped away. For parks they used Durland's Woods or McClure's Grove in timbered areas. Stiles Park was the first formal park. Developers of the Maywood addition provided a small, 200 feet diameter area at the intersection of Northeast Eighth Street, Stiles and Harrison Avenues, which was dedicated to the public. For five years this was accepted by the public as a rosy gesture but by the city council as a thorn. People clamored for it to be improved but money was tight for frills. By declaring this a childrens' playground for a nearby school some improvement money was found.

In 1902 James B. Wheeler, banker and developer, offered the city an area along the Canadian southwest of the city limits, provided that a minimum of $2,000 per year was appropriated to maintain and improve it. Local pressure almost literally forced this compliance. For several years Wheeler Park was the only zoological garden in the twin territories. Because donation of animals for a zoo came so rapidly it was quite difficult to secure funds to handle them properly. There was criticism of animal quarters and upkeep, added to other requests on the city purse by impatient folk. By 1920 the zoo contained more than 125 specimens ranging from bears to seals, with birds and water fowl. Earlier, in 1910, in one of those "let's look at the future" bond issue campaigns, $400,000 was voted to purchase land for recreational use, including 700 acres for Northeast Park, now Lincoln Park, and to buy land for a twenty-seven mile long, somewhat circular drive distant from, but encircling the city. This was Grand Boulevard. Visionary as he was about other things, Henry Overholser opposed the boulevard concept, saying that more small tracts inside the city for use as neighborhood parks should be secured instead.

It is important to remember that people in this era did not have multiple opportunities for spectator or participant recreation that exists in our time. For an overview what existed here by 1907 is of interest. Some facilities were public and some were operated on a paid admission basis. The first park for public use was small Stiles Park, donated by Captain D. F. Stiles and James Geary when Maywood was platted. Wheeler

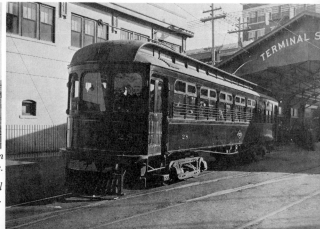

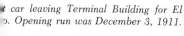

et railway cars of the Metropolitan
way Company on the University Line.

car leaving Terminal Building for El
. Opening run was December 3, 1911.

Park with its thirty-five acres came next. Riverside and Military Parks on the east side, carved out of the old reservation, made up about twelve acres. Belle Isle Park was the most elaborate, of 280 acres originally, with a large lake taking a great part of that, owned by the Oklahoma Railway Company. It had bath houses, a bathing "beach" with sand from excavated pits, and a "Coney Island" atmosphere.

Without doubt, next to becoming a railway hub and transportation center for the trade territory, the most important factor in early growth of Oklahoma City was its street railway system. In the century's first two-decades, and to an extent beyond them, there was a distinct need. Residential and some industrial growth followed the lines. In 1902 the Metropolitan Railway Company was formed with W. W. Storm as president and John Shartel as secretary. Other incorporators were S. T. Alton, E. H. Cooke and John Threadgill.

The first car moved on February 2, 1903, and it was estimated that 14,000 persons jammed streets to see the action. It was the first street-car in either territory. Within five days the company had five cars in operation.

In 1904 reorganization and more capital were needed for expansion. The Metropolitan firm became the Oklahoma Railway Company with Anton H. Classen as president and Shartel as vice-president. The lines ran up Broadway from Choctaw Avenue to Northwest Thirteenth street; out West Main to Western; from West Reno and Walker Avenues to Northwest Fourth Street; up Walker to Northwest Thirteenth Street; out on Fourth eastward to Stiles Park. There were ten cars on the single tracks with a capacity of twenty-eight persons each at time of the transfer.

By 1910 lines had been extended out on Classen Boulevard to Belle Isle Park, eastward beyond Stiles Park to the state fairgrounds, northward over what still remains as an extension of Classen to Britton and thence on to Edmond. A line out Northeast Thirteenth Street continued to Lottie. A line went west on Linwood Boulevard to Indiana, thence west on Northwest Twelfth Street and north to the Las Vegas addition. An El Reno interurban system was put in it in 1909, serving that town and Yukon, and in 1911 the Oklahoma Railway Company purchased this, operating its lines westward over Northwest Thirty-ninth Street. In 1913 lines were extended to Moore and to Norman. In 1916 the Edmond line was extended to Guthrie.

During the first few years of its operation the street railway company purchased its power from a local firm, then in 1908 built its own power plant at Belle Isle, which it used until 1928 before selling that facility to OG&E, from whom it then purchased power. The street railway company in 1928 purchased the Oklahoma Belt Line Railway, primarily an interline switching operation to serve spurs for industry, including the Packingtown area, over Exchange Avenue. This service or switching operation was leased to a subsidiary, the Oklahoma City Junction Railway Company. The company built a new $200,000 terminal in 1920 on Grand Avenue, between Hudson and Harvey. It put its first buses in operation in 1925. It has been estimated that as early as 1906, the street railway moved up to four million persons on its thirty-eight miles of internal track, with forty-eight cars and 150 regular employes, then serving 40,000 people.

Thousands of commuters, including students, can recall University Station in a jog on Classen Boulevard near Northwest Seventeenth Street. It was one of the last outlying landmarks to go eventually. Interurban service to El Reno and to Guthrie was terminated at midnight on November 6, 1946, but the Norman line was to last longer before it, too, was replaced by buses.

The Oklahoma Railway Company was intended to earn a profit in addition to providing a needed public service. Among those most directly concerned with its financing and operation those two factors were about equally divided. That assumption is borne out by statements and by illustration of their other civic activities. Overall it did not make money. At first it was continual expansion with cost of trackage and equipment. After that was amortized there was a period when it was in the black but it did not pay any dividends from 1911 onward.

It was placed in receivership in December 1924 with G. T. Lackey and George A. Henshaw as joint receivers. The company then had sixty-five miles of city tracks and eighty miles of interurban lines. When buses were added the company lost only $20,500, but started pulling out by making a profit in 1926, when it transported, one way or another, nearly 14 million persons. The receivership was lifted in December 1927. It was refinanced and reorganized with Hubert R. Hudson as president (he also was president of the Oklahoma City-Ada-Atoka Railway Company, once property of the Katy); G. A. Nichols, real estate man, as vice president; William Mee, banker, secretary and treasurer; board members T. C. Thatcher, A. E. "Doc" Monroney and A. O. Campbell, contractor and banker. There were some profit years and some losses. Street cars gave way to buses and in the late 1960's that fleet was taken over by the city under a trust, the Oklahoma City Transportation and Parking Authority.

For its impact upon the early times credit certainly should be given prime movers of the street railway company, Classen and Shartel, although they were engaged in other activities as well. Classen was a native of Illinois

University Station at N.W. 17 and Classen. In the background is Epworth University.

who left the farm at age sixteen. He graduated in law at the University of Michigan in 1887 and was author of a thesis that, for what it protended later, was almost prophetic. The title: *"How to Obtain Government Lands."* He homesteaded near later Edmond, engaged in real estate matters, and for a time after the death of its founder, Milton Reynolds, was editor of the Edmond Sun.

In 1897 Classen was appointed receiver for the United States Land Office at Oklahoma City and four years later its registrar. In 1902 he resigned to form The Classen Company, a real estate firm, which continued to modern times. He was president of the Commerical Club (predecessor of the Chamber of Commerce) for three terms.

Classen was not as wealthy as some of his contemporaries when he came here, or even later, but he had more vision than many of them. He put his resources to work in buying property at a distance from the more speculative development because of his faith in the future of the city. A believer in scenic beauty, he planted literally thousands of trees and ornamentals on his own and public property, when some people gave a very low priority to aesthetics. Youth organization camps here and in the Arbuckles are named for the family.

After Classen's death in 1922, Ed Overholser, president and manager of the Chamber of Commerce, who had been here since eight months after the opening, had this to say about Anton Classen: "It has been my good fortune to know intimately all the real town builders. Through association with my father I came in daily contact with them. . . . I have been in their councils. . . . I have heard them express their visions, hopes and fears. . . . I have seen results of all these things crystalized into the wonderful city that we have. . . . One man took a pencil and figured the area in square miles which this city must have to build upon, in the firm conviction that it would have 100,000 population. My father said that if he lived his alloted time he would see a city of 25,000. When that point was reached he raised the estimate to 40,000. I heard C. C. Jones make the prediction that the figure would be 50,000 in his lifetime. Only Anton Classen believed 100,000 after studying the areas needed for residences and business, and other details. Then he began to purchase surrounding land that, in his judgment, the city would require. His success was due to absolutely correct vision and working toward that vision."

John Shartel was a teacher in a country school on the border of later Oklahoma Territory at age fifteen. He earned money to continue his education at Kansas Agricultural College, from which he graduated in 1884. He also "read law" in the custom of that day, to become a lawyer. He came to Guthrie in 1889 and formed a law partnership but was interested also in real estate. In 1898 he came to Oklahoma City and was a builder, real estate developer, and an organizer of the Oklahoma Club, a combination of social and business affairs, with accent on the social, and was its first president. Shartel died in 1926.

Certainly a highlight of the decade was establishment of what became later Oklahoma City University. The move had its origin at the first territorial conference of the Methodist Episcopal Church here in 1892 with appointment of a committee on education. The initial committee report called for two or more conference seminaries for advanced grades.

The territorial legislative assembly in 1893 granted a charter to Oklahoma Methodist University, under control of the conference, and named a board of trustees for it.

In 1894 the conference heard a proposal to create a Methodist Hall at Edmond in connection with the normal school but did not approve. A similar proposal for an Oxford Hall at the state university in Norman failed. The matter came up annually and by 1900 gained more attention. Proposed then was a university under joint patronage of the two branches of Methodism, divided since 1844 into the Methodist Episcopal Church and the Methodist Episcopal Church, South. On June 22, 1901, a meeting was held in the U.S. Land Office here, after offering of that as a meeting place by Anton Classen, who represented both the northern branch of the church and the Commercial Club. C. B. Ames represented the southern branch. It was stressed that both branches would benefit from this act of union, that such a plan was both practical and feasible, and should be brought before both conferences that October.

One delegation went to Chickasha for the southern group conference and another to Shawnee to consult the northern branch conference. Ames, with R. Q. Blakeney, Ministers Broyes and Thompson and others, went to Chickasha while Joseph B. Thoburn, Messers Johnson and Blackwelder, with others, went to Shawnee. Each delegation was authorized to submit a proposition that Oklahoma City would donate 240 acres of land, of which about forty would be set aside as a campus, and the rest platted and sold for town lots to raise an estimated $100,000 for erection of the first building and creation of an endowment fund. Included was the idea that each branch of the church would give support, make solicitations, and share places on a board of directors for control of the institution. Several other towns were at the conferences seeking location of the school, including Enid, which offered 160 acres of land and $10,000 cash.

Reverend E. B. Rankin moved at the Shawnee conference that a joint commission of ten members be appointed to meet with a similar number from the Chickasha conference. Each was composed of five ministers and five laymen. Provided in commission guidelines was that this

Epworth University at N.W. 18 and Douglas, was the predecessor to Oklahoma City University. This building, erected in 1904 still stands, renovated as Epworth Methodist Church.

would be a joint endeavor, "to locate, build and equip" the university; that no location would be considered that offered less than $100,000 and forty acres of suitable land; that the commissions would meet in Oklahoma City in December 1901 to consider all matters; that any point of disagreement would be referred back to the respective conferences. Adoption of the proposal by both conference groups was the first successful effort toward unity since seventeen years before the Civil War.

There was opposition to locating the university at Oklahoma City. Enid wanted it and so did Methodist schools at Fort Worth and at Winfield, Kansas. The president of the Fort Worth school declared that the twin territories were sending 400 students to his institution then. It was historian Thoburn who suggested that the name be Epworth University, since the Epworth League was a success in both branches for young peoples' work, and the institution would serve young people. The name was adopted at the December 1901 meeting. Commission members also accepted a proposition from the University Development Company of Oklahoma City for an endowment of $100,000 and a campus site increased to fifty-two acres through "generosity of Mister Classen." The money was to be raised through sale of lots held by the development firm. The basic site was to be conveyed without being subject to sale or mortgage, to be used in perpetuity for higher education, without a reversionary clause.

More time passed. On May 6, 1902, the Epworth University Joint Commission met to hear the development company's proposition. This was a syndicate of city realtors and businessmen headed by Shartel. There were some concessions from both sides. The site acreage was dropped to fifty acres but the $100,000 in funds remained. The site selected was on the Colcord, Zeigler and Smith tracts, one and three-fourths miles from the city business center. Metropolitan agreed to run a street car line there. A boulevard (now Classen Drive) was to be constructed, 100 feet wide, from Northwest Tenth and Walker to the campus. Both conferences agreed that in 1902, each would contribute $75,000 for buildings and equipment in addition to that contributed by Oklahoma City folk.

Sale of lots surrounding the campus site was held on June 17, 18 and 19, 1902, to raise the $100,000 which was the city's gift. In October 1902, construction began and on April 1, 1903, laying of the cornerstone was a gala event. Banks and many business firms closed for the occasion to permit employes to attend. The first building of brick and sandstone was completed in September 1903 at a cost of $40,000. It had thirty-five rooms, including an auditorium, library and laboratories, "with all conveniences." A charter was granted to incorporators. Twenty representative men from the two territories were to form the first Board of Trustees. Selected as first president was Reverend R. B. McSwain, a faculty member at Southwestern University at Georgetown, Texas. Edgar S. Vaught, then an official of the city school system, and Doctor F. E. Day, pastor of the First Methodist Church, were named to select and purchase equipment for the university. On July 6, 1904, a faculty of twenty-seven instructors was selected for opening of the school in September with 175 students. The Chamber of Commerce raised $20,000 for opening semester operation expenses.

The Gold Star Memorial Building at right and chapel at left at Oklahoma City University.

President McSwain resigned for health reasons in the spring of 1905. Reverend George H. Bradford, D.D., of Kansas City, Missouri, was named to succed him with the title of chancellor. A USDA meteorological station near the campus, on land donated to the federal government by the school, not only performed its function there for decades, but offered assistance for instruction of students in several scientific fields. A dissolution of the joint relationship occured in 1911 and that interest held by the Methodist Episcopal Church was merged with Fort Worth University. The southern branch was on its own until 1929 when joint control was resumed.

The board of Epworth University, without consultation with the medical profession, decided in July 1904 to create a department of medicine. It appointed to its faculty physicians and surgeons including A. K. West, H. Coulter Todd, Lea A. Reily, U. L. Russell, F. C. Hoops, J. A. Ryan and W. J. Jolly. Doctor West was named dean and Doctor Todd secretary of that faculty. The medical school opened with three students, none of whom later ever obtained a degree in medicine. In July 1905 the executive committee established a four year medical college, which was a separate corporation from the university. To the faculty was added L. H. Buxton. Each member of the corporation subscribed $1,000 toward purchase of the Virginia Hotel, on the northwest corner of Northwest Sixth Street and North Broadway, for $19,000. It was to be altered and equipped for a medical school. The school grew rapidly. None of the instructors received a salary. Tuition went toward equipment. This was, at that time, the only medical school in the state area with a four year course. A College of Dentistry was opened in 1908.

The University of Oklahoma's College of Medicine, predecessor of its Medical School, first offered courses at Norman in 1898 and by 1900 could give a bachelor of science degree with a major in medicine. From 1904 until 1910, when it merged into the School of Medicine, the Oklahoma University College of Medicine was within this adjunct of Epworth University. Epworth offered all its pre-medical courses at its home campus while those of the University of Oklahoma were at Norman. The burden of financing Epworth's medical school proved too great. In 1910 trustees made an agreement with regents of the University of Oklahoma, which took over, and the Epworth College of Medicine became the School of Medicine for the University of Oklahoma. Property of the Epworth institution medical department was sold for $30,000 and the separate corporation dissolved. With the college went some twenty instructors and a student body of forty-seven.

By 1909 Epworth could boast of a College of Liberal Arts and schools of fine arts, law, business, civil engineering, pharmacy, dentistry, and medicine. For years the university had a hard scrabble. At times, for financial reasons, it had to drop some of its more ambitious courses, in addition to seeing the medical school spun off. The name became Oklahoma City University and locations were changed twice before the university moved to its present campus in 1922. It now has four principal branches; The College of Arts and Sciences, the School of Business, School of Music and the School of Law. It offers undergraduate baccalaureate degrees with master's degrees on the graduate and professional level, in addition to a Juris Doctoral degree in law.

In 1962 the city business and professional community raised $2 million to help OCU launch its "Great Plan, designed to transform the institution into a regional center of academic excellence," as the brochures described it.

This was effected through assistance of a consulting group from Massachusetts Institute of Technology, and a fiscal transfusion of $2 million from the Ford Foundation as a matching grant for locally and state raised funds. That campaign was a success, primarily local.

Resulting was upgrading of faculty, improved instructional facilities, honors courses, an expanded scholarship program, and some innovative approaches to teaching methods and curriculum. The university is on a semester basis except for the School of Law, which uses a year around quarter system.

A 1972 enrollment of 2,417 included seventy-five percent undergraduates; seventy-one percent were county residents, thirteen percent were from elsewhere in the state, fourteen percent came from out of state and two percent were international students. Slightly more than one-half of the enrollment is of day students while others attend night classes. A feature of the program is a continuing education phase, and pursuit of a major in a different field than that in which a person studied previously. This program includes also many seminars, short courses, or workshops for special interest groups.

The university also is a center for many metropolitan area activities. Included are the Civic Music Association, Chamber Music Association, the Junior Symphony, the Lyric Theater and similar offerings using facilities of the Kirkpatrick Fine Arts Building.

Heating plant serving the University of Oklahoma Medical School in east Oklahoma City.

The university is not tax supported. Students pay, on an average, about fifty-five percent of the cost of their education with the balance provided by the business community and Methodist church groups. The physical plant is placed on fifty-five acres of ground and is valued, as of 1972, at $20 million. Business researchers say that the institution generates about $24 million annually in economic activity for Central Oklahoma.

In 1972 the Kerr Foundation gave the university a $750,000 grant which will be used for the first phase of a three part School of Law complex on the campus. During the past twelve years the Oklahoma City community has invested, through donors, more than $6 million in the institution. In 1973 a capital fund drive was planned for May 1974, to seek $2.8 million. When seeking approval for the campaign, President Dolphus Whitten said this was necessary for OCU to meet its objectives through 1980.

14

Statehood, But Satan, Too

FOR YEARS THERE HAD BEEN agitation for single statehood. The west side included the Panhandle, which dropped its attempt to create the Territory of Cimarron when made a part of Oklahoma Territory in 1890. The east side, as represented by Indian Territory, gave up on its proposed State of Sequoyah. At last they found themselves joined in the State of Oklahoma on November 16, 1907.

In the fifty-ninth Congress of 1906 there were several Omnibus Statehood bills passed. The House wanted one state composed of Indian and Oklahoma Territories, and one state composed of the Territories of Arizona and New Mexico. The Senate went along on the first portion but objected to the second. A compromise was reached, providing for single statehood for Oklahoma, with citizens of Arizona and New Mexico to hold a plebiscite to determine their own future. This they did later on single statehood for each in 1912.

Our bill was passed on June 14, 1906. It called for delegates to a constitutional convention to be elected in November. The interesting "Con-Con" under leadership of its president, William H. Murray (Alfalfa Bill), held its sessions and on September 17, 1907, the constitution was adopted. It was a most interesting document, at ninety-five pages and 45,000 words one of the longest in history, with a strong Populist and Agrarian flavor. It contained one feature that would be used repeatedly over the years to amend its provisions: the initiative and referendum.

Historian Doctor Arrell M. Gibson says that President Theodore Roosevelt "detested the Oklahoma constitution." He thought it too restrictive. Murray at least scrupulously followed provisions of the enabling legislation — along with ideas of his own and those of others. President Roosevelt approved the constitution and proclaimed Statehood Day for Saturday, November 16, 1907. In reference to the total scene, Grant Foreman wrote that "probably no other section of the American people in all history required, in the same length of time, so much federal legislative consideration as Congress gave the Indian Territory (all the region) in bringing about translation of the country from a near chaotic condition to a state of the Union."

So a state it became. At that time Oklahoma ranked eighteenth in area of all states, was larger than the six New England states combined or any state east of the Mississippi, and had half as many people as the original thirteen American colonies contained. It was the last of twelve states carved wholly or in part from land of the Louisiana Purchase of 1803. The population then was 1.5 million. Oklahoma Territory had experi-

J. F. OWENS	CHARLES N. HASKELL	HUBERT L. BOLEN	W. B. ANTHONY
OG&E head & national	*First governor of*	*State treasurer;*	*Carried State Seal to*
Chamber director	*Oklahoma*	*tax commission head*	*Oklahoma City*

enced eighteen years of self government while Indian Territory had a background of more than seventy years. That is why, for many decades, the political power of this state was dominated by the east side.

Hailing signing of the statehood proclamation, *The Daily Oklahoman* echoed sentiments expressed by other papers and by most citizens in an overline across Page One: "Oklahoma, so long a maverick of the Southwest, finally has achieved the coveted brand of statehood, and has been admitted to the corral."

The recognition of statehood and its broad implications are most interesting but we are concerned here primarily with Oklahoma City. When Inauguration Day came at Guthrie there was a symbolic wedding of the two territories, with C. G. Jones representing Oklahoma Territory and Mrs. Leon Bennett of Muskogee (a Cherokee) representing Indian Territory. The Chamber of Commerce rounded up people to buy 1,000 railroad tickets it had optimistically pledged the Santa Fe for special trains to the inaugural. State officials chosen in the same election that approved the constitution were to be sworn in, also.

Oklahoma City then had a population of 32,451. Muskogee was second with 14,418; Guthrie third with 11,643, followed by Shawnee and Enid. Tulsa came ninth on the list, followed by Lawton, Ardmore, McAlester and Chickasha. There was a patina of gloom over the economic picture. On October 28, 1907, the city had the first bank "holiday" in its initial fifty years. A flow of money from eastern financial centers nearly dried up. There was perhaps over expansion of credit in this growth area. Banks remained closed for about a week. As E. K. Gaylord was to recall later: "We had a meeting at the home of one of the bankers and decided to issue scrip certificates to be used as money. We had to have something to meet payrolls in the community and we all had confidence in the basic solvency of our banks." To bolster such confidence at the time, the paper announced that it would accept checks on the closed banks for subscriptions. Circulation lists increased.

What was the general situation, otherwise, in burgeoning Oklahoma City in 1907? There were nine financial institutions here — five national and three state banks and one building and loan company. The aggregate capital and surplus of these was more than $1 million while total deposits amounted to more than $6 million. This was far distant from that day on April 22, 1889, when T. M. Richardson accepted a small check from an eager depositor for the Bank of Oklahoma City, while his associates were unloading lumber for a bank building.

The city had four directional trunk line railroads and three feeder lines that opened new territory for its trade and distribution territory. The city had a bonded debt of $748,500. It had manufacturing and processing plants that grossed $10 million in annual production, of which flour led the list, but included a long list of products from furniture to cigars. It had the state's largest broomcorn warehouse with stocks of 1,200 tons, and a five acre cotton compress that processed around 100,000 bales valued at $5 million. There were 116 miles of cement, stone or brick sidewalks, with some fourteen miles of paved street. There were thirteen miles of storm sewers and forty-three miles of sanitary sewers. A new waterworks was completed. The street railway company had a $1 million investment.

Epworth University and Hills Business College offered varied instruction. Natural gas was brought to the city. John A. Northrop proved that the day of the "horseless carriage" really was here when he made a round trip to Edmond in his "Los Angeles Tourist Special" in four hours. There were sixty conventions in the city that year, three of them national in scope. St. Anthony's Hospital had grown to a $100,000 valuation while Rolater Hospital enlarged to a capacity of twenty-five beds. Pilgrim Congregational Church provided a free dispensary — with donated physicians' services — for the indigent. There were ten public school buildings serving 6,000 students. *The Daily Oklahoman* put out an eighty-eight page special edition — largest seen in the state — as its color comics featured "Happy Hooligan." "Peck's Bad Boy" was quite a draw at the Overholser Opera House. Social clubs were plentiful.

Prohibition had been a controversial subject since early days. After the Organic Act of 1890 saloons were licensed. The Enabling Act for statehood required a vote on the subject, which by direction of the territorial legislature was placed on the same ballot as the constitution, with the result that statewide prohibition was voted in the first of many elections on that subject. (After national repeal in 1933, under President Franklin D. Roosevelt, Oklahomans voted that beer with an alcoholic volume not in excess of 3.2 percent was nonintoxicating.)

There were strong forces on each side of the liquor question. Since 1903 there had been a recurrent local fight on an "open" as opposed to a "closed" town because of its status as a visitor, convention and distribution center. Among the open town advocates were W. J. Pettee, Charles Colcord, Seymour Heyman and Roy Stafford. Ironically, Colcord was personally more attuned to the dry side. He thought open saloons were good for the economy, yet in his role as a peace officer he enforced ordinances and laws to which he was opposed. City advocates of opposition to prohibition claimed that a shutdown would mean substituting "thirty saloons for 3,000 bootleggers," and were rather prophetic in that assertion. Actually there were forty-six saloons in the city then.

In the last territorial legislature Senator Richard A. Billups of Oklahoma City, trying to please both sides of the liquor question, proposed a system of "medicinal whisky" to be procured on a physician's prescription (the Texas system), and the measure was adopted after being dubbed "the Billups Booze Bill." It, too, was repealed by the later prohibition vote.

Billups was a personal dry. The last saloon here closed its doors at 11:50 p.m., November 16, 1907, after a local brewery poured $27,000 worth of beer and unknown quantities of mash into storm sewers and street gutters. Most of the city's female residents remained at home that night. Male citizens, taking advantage of both a lowered price and last chance at booze, hauled it away in every type of conveyance. They got a small break from incoming Governor Charles Haskell, who told Sheriff George Garrison to permit saloons to stay open until day's end, although formally prohibition went into effect at 10:16 a.m. that day, when President Roosevelt signed the statehood proclamation. Brawls were common that evening, reaching a climax when Fred Norris shot and killed Robert Johnson, a bartender at Ed Donley's saloon on First Street, after an argument over a jug.

That year of 1907 saw also beginning of an institution that has kept abreast — or even out-paced the state in its growth — in the Oklahoma State Fair. It is forty-one days older than the state, as a matter of fact, and it also is a matter of fact that it has never received any direct state support appropriations. There is no official state fair in Oklahoma. As people have done since the trade fairs of antiquity in the Near East, Oklahoma City folk planned and conducted a Territorial Fair in 1893, held in the business district and supported by merchants, as part of the emergence of varied cultural and entertainment activities. A premium book for the second fair in 1894 is still extant. These fairs continued until 1907.

Early in the statehood year that energetic promoter, C. G. "Gristmill" Jones, sold a number of persons on the idea of a permanent fair. The first campaign for funds resulted in but $17,000 when $100,000 was needed to purchase 160 acres of land (including a small lake) on ground at Northeast Tenth Street and North Eastern Avenue. At that time it was one mile outside the city limits. The Katy ran shuttle trains there on a fifteen minute schedule the first year or so, before the street railway company could lay track to the site. Henry Overholser put more money into the original fair plant construction than anyone else. It was — and remains — a non-profit association. There were times during depression

Looking east on Grand Avenue during an Oklahoma City street fair in the late 1890s.

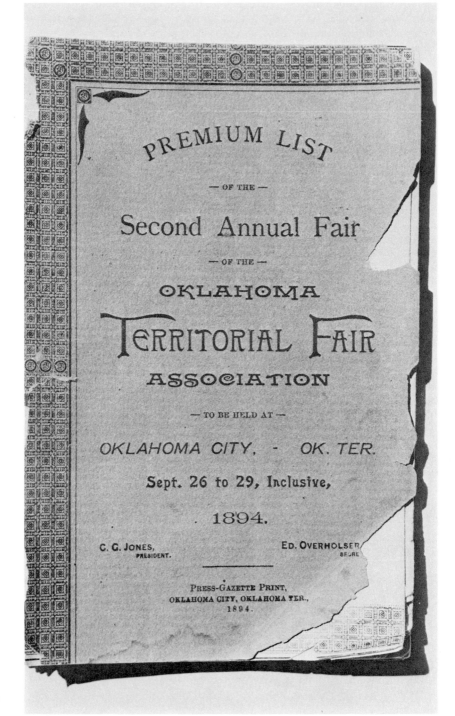

This is the only known premium book for the second annual Oklahoma Territorial Fair.

years when that "non-profit" was accentuated. The first buildings included a grandstand by the racetrack, the main exposition building, an office, music hall and various exhibition buildings for manufactured and farm products, livestock and poultry. The first premium list totaled $10,000. There were 75,000 persons in attendance. Jones was president and Ed Overholser secretary of the first board.

The financial condition of the fair was always somewhat precarious. After Overholser the next secretary-manager was I. S. Mahan, of Iowa, succeeded by Ralph T. Hemphill, also of Iowa, then C. G. "Pete" Baker and later by Orval O. "Sandy" Saunders. Advent of the city oil field in late 1928 had some effect on the fair. After an arrangement was made with the city to take the land over as a park, wells were drilled on the south portion. The city for several years contributed some $35,000 annually for premiums. This was the only outside assistance the fair has had. From its revenues it had to pay for maintenance and upkeep of the buildings and grounds, and its small permanent staff, along with temporary employees during Fair Week.

In 1954, in a rather involved transaction, the Oklahoma City school board and city purchased a school land section on North May Avenue, between Reno Avenue and Northwest Tenth street. The board traded a quarter section to the city for the 160 acres of old Fair Park, turning that property into Douglass High School, with only the Livestock Coliseum building removed. The city took the rest of the land, citizens passed a bond issue of $4.7 million, and the best fair plant in the nation resulted, with its title changed to the State Fair of Oklahoma. There has been continual expansion, most of it paid from fair revenues, with the city having charge of buildings during eleven months of the year and the fair the other month. There have been many innovations as the fair grew in attendance toward the 1,000,000 mark, including a monorail, new exhibit buildings, and International Exposition status, with wares exhibited from a number of other countries.

Through philanthropy of the John E. Kirkpatricks the Oklahoma Art Center and the Kirkpatrick Planetarium, as part of the Science and Art Center, have added to attractions at the park on a year around basis, as has the bond-built Arena. A portion of the section became a site for All Sports Stadium, now home of the 89'er Baseball Club. A quarter went to Oklahoma State University's Experiment Station, initiated by a different type of "Run," when on a "farm in a day" display conservation practices were applied in a mass demonstration, with noted speakers such as Louis Bromfield on a program. The County Extension Center now is located there, along with a branch of the OSU Technical Institute and a Firemens Training Center. A Reserve Armory and softball park are on the Reno Avenue Strip.

Prior to statehood and through early years the immutable pendulum that clocked city affairs continued to swing. It timed changes and arguments for change, in mores of the citizens. Things that jar public conscience of a city are more likely to be on the bawdy side than on the beautiful. Certainly this has been true here in many instances, beginning with the first "open town" arguments and first conventions held, with periodic cleanups that have continued throughout the city's history. The

The Exposition Building of the State Fairgrounds at N.E. Eighth and Eastern, constructed shortly after statehood. The Douglass-Kennedy High School now occupies these grounds.

The vegetable and grain exhibit at an Oklahoma City street fair in October, 1898.

pendulum swings, varying from sweet music at one terminus to a discordant bonging at the other, as public concern is reflected in soft or hard law enforcement.

With forming of the territory there was more enforcement than under provisional government, some by internal process, the rest by deputy United States marshals. There were licensed saloons and a lingering presence of sporting characters on the civic stage. In 1903 the city was host to the Panhandle and Southwestern Stockmen's Association. It was noted by open town advocates that these visitors not only appeared to enjoy burning the candle at both ends but had no objection to paying for the tallow. Naturally money was spread around town no matter where it originated.

A big parade was turned out for the stockmens' meeting which included a military unit from Fort Sill. Some exuberant person, either a visitor or native, joined in the excitement by firing a wild shot that killed a soldier. Some persons demanded that newspapers ignore the story since it would inhibit the city drawing other conventions. *The Daily Oklahoman,* with Roy Stafford as editor, did not print the story. E. K. Gaylord, then a minor partner, was quite put out at this omission and the next day ordered the story printed. A new and non-related shooting that same day doubled the necessity for news.

If some early day news was on the sordid side there were lighter items in contrast. There were many laughs among people not engaged in the hotel business in 1908 when the legislature, acting upon a bill by Speaker William H. Murray and Representative George C. Whitehurst of Beckham county, passed an act requiring all hotels — and all railroad sleeping cars — to provide bed sheets long enough to fold back three feet over the top covering.

This was referred to as "the nine foot sheet bill," and allegedly resulted from Murray not having enough sheet to cover his feet when he pulled covers up around his neck. Included in the same measure was requirement that each hotel room would have a knotted rope fastened inside, long enough to reach the ground from a second story, with an iron fire escape outside for hotels of more than two stories.

Prohibition in 1907 took saloons out but a market for booze remained. William J. Creekmore was ready to supply demand. For a decade he had one of the strongest combinations to control whisky distribution of anyone until the post-war bootleg era came in.

Starting out as a gambler around 1895, Creekmore had an illegal whisky business in Sapulpa, in dry Indian Territory. He moved to Tulsa, bought out the biggest dealer there, then branched out to control the southeast portion of the state. With statehood his base shifted to Oklahoma City. He appeared to have such control that no one could touch him. Raids on bootleggers were frequent but seemed to be against Creekmore's competitors. Attorney General Charles West, with enforcement attorney Fred S. Caldwell and support from Governor Haskell, took after Creekmore. Not until Oklahoma County Attorney John Embry got into the act did the local enforcement establishment nail Creekmore. Eventually he was charged with conspiracy to violate the liquor laws, jury tampering and bribery. He was convicted February 22, 1917.

There had always been agitation to get laws enforced rigidly and movements for "blue laws" to effect Sunday closures of all business, with emphasis on prize fights, gambling, horse racing and such offerings. The movement had success during the revulsion to such openly known activities as Creekmore's. Beginning almost with the first legislature there were periodic attempts at closing movie houses and other similar entertainment on Sundays. This usually resulted in members of the legislature receiving free passes to use or give constituents.

In 1914 there was an event here that has become a part of the historical heritage. It brought the young city more national publicity than it desired — of that type — and added the name of "Queenie" to the dubious list of characters who had their brief moment on our civic stage.

As Albert McRill told it, the Chamber of Commerce, newspapers and business interests went all out to secure a stockmens' annual regional convention — the episode in 1903 being now but a memory — and they did get the meeting. This was to be one of the largest gatherings yet seen here. No one later admitted being an activist in providing presumed entertainment requirements of the big spenders. On hand were 10,000 bottles of illegal beer; six prize fighters whose anti-climactic exhibition also was illegal, and Queenie (born Theo Buchanan) from Chicago.

Queenie was not illegal — per se — but her performance as Salome, without even one veil, definitely was. Queenie not only stripped to the buff, casting bits of wearing apparel to the cheering masculine audience, she was borne up and down the aisles for benefit of those in rear seats of the auditorium. Paper money and silver were tossed into a cowman's large, volunteered hat, for "the little girl."

Delegates left town a bit lighter of wallet and heavier of head. Some of the home folk who helped make up a crowd estimated at 3,000 could not resist telling about the affair to stay-at-homes. The first day after the exhibition only a brief mention of the convention was published in papers, one saying merely that the cowmen "ended a most delightful convention with a smoker at the City Auditorium last night."

At *The Daily Oklahoman* a press association stringer put a story on the telegraph wire. Papers near and far from Oklahoma City had a great time playing up the account. The *Oklahoma City Times*, then in separate ownership, castigated the *Oklahoman* in print for putting out the story, saying "respectable people in Oklahoma City feel that there was disgrace enough without parading it in outside newspapers. There has been a demand for publication of details in the Oklahoma City papers, but mainly it has come from those who were not present and who presumably would have enjoyed witnessing the nastiness."

Womens' clubs, the Ministerial Alliance and others asked authorities at all levels to investigate and punish those responsible, suggesting a variety of charges. An appointed Board of Inquiry found that Queenie did indeed appear and dance at the smoker, "sans veils, sans beads, sans everything." A charge of conspiracy "to procure indecent exposure" was levied by information on three men, two of whom were named, the other a "John Doe." Twenty-seven businessmen signed their bonds. The case died in a Justice of the Peace court where it was filed, but the memory lingered on, to be told and retold to succeding generations.

In after effect, and specifically in 1914 "l'affaire Queenie" changed the political situation at City Hall and helped provide impetus for a general cleanup in town and county. In closing days of Mayor Whit Grant's administration, interest grew in law enforcement, then became a crusade without equal in city history to that time. As with some other victories of this nature, after the election many decent persons thought changes would be permanent and turned to more personal matters, as beneficial aspects eroded. "Reform" movements have short lives.

The cleanup campaign did make the civic cauldron bubble and three ministers aided prominently in the stirring. They were Doctor H. H. Hulton of the First Baptist Church; Doctor R. A. Chase of the First Methodist Church, and Doctor Aaron Prince Aten of the Southside Christian Church. They were aided greatly by "The Central Hundred," a committee headed by Attorney Embry, a federal district attorney before becoming a county official.

There were ten candidates for mayor in the Democratic primary of 1914, all declaring for law enforcement. They were Herbert M. Peck, Dan B. Welty, J. S. Coates, L. E. Patterson, John H. Myers, D. A. Bennett, Jasper Sipes, Lee Van Winkle, M. K. Galleon and W. D. Gault. The lone Republican candidate was Ed Overholser. Reverend J. B. Norton, a Presbyterian minister, filed as an Independent. The "Central Hundred" endorsed Peck but Gault was nominated with about one-third of the primary votes. He was supported by the city administration and those favoring an open town. It was apparent, McRill wrote, that if Democrats split their votes, Gault, son of the city's first mayor under territorial status, would be elected.

Overholser, son of Henry Overholser and like his father identified until then as an open town advocate, would get any straight Republican votes. Reverend Norton might get help from either party and particularly from church groups ignoring party labels. So a committee called upon Overholser, who told them, according to McRill: "...you can report to your group and to all people of Oklahoma City that Ed Overholser, as mayor, will do all in his power to enforce the laws of the state and ordinances of Oklahoma City. That means against all forms of vice.

"It would be hypocracy for me to try and sidestep or alibi as to my record on prohibition. I was against it in 1907 and again in 1910. I honestly believed it would be a bad thing for the city. My views have changed and I was wrong. Vacating the sixty-odd saloon buildings did not bring disaster. Clean, reputable businesses have taken over those buildings. We're a cleaner, better city because saloons went out. I'm for prohibition now," he added.

"But — in any event — I am for law enforcement. What my personal views of a law may be doesn't enter into it. You can tell your people I will enforce the law and all the people in Oklahoma City who know me will tell you my word is as good as any bond."

That did it. Overholser was elected mayor by 327 votes. Doctor J. G. Street, father of later Mayor Allen Street, was elected commissioner of property; Mike Donnelly was chosen commissioner of accounting and finance. Overholser's first official act was to appoint W. B. Nichols, "the fighting deacon," as chief of police.

The new regime started a cleanup and it was a tough one. County Attorney H. Y. Thompson died suddenly in April 1915 and, although all three county commissioners were Democrats, under the law then a Republican had to be appointed county attorney. In quite a tense situation Embry was selected, and said: "I will stay in office until I have accomplished what I came here to do."

Roadhouses were raided, illegally shipped liquor was seized at the express office, property owners who permitted their leased premises to be used for unlawful purposes saw themselves sued for a sum of $1,000 per day for such usage, after notice was given them to terminate rentals.

The midway has always been the most crowded area of the State Fair of Oklahoma.

The Jim Norick sports arena at State Fair Park seats 8,900 people for sporting events.

Embry began gathering evidence against Creekmore, "king of the bootleggers." Embry used undercover men to obtain evidence, men who had worked for him in the United States District Attorney's office, and paid them out of his own pocket. He got from County Judge William H. Zwich orders that no shipment of liquor could be delivered to the consignee unless he showed in writing that he was a person of good character and the liquor was to be used for a lawful purpose. That, for a season, pulled corks from the jugs. It resulted also in the 1917 conviction of Creekmore, one of his chief agents and a Wells-Fargo Express employe, on conspiracy to evade the liquor law.

Embry also broke the syndicate that controlled gambling, epitomized by operations at the Southern Club on Grand Avenue, and a string of other houses, the last remnant of the Turf Club interests downtown. (There was to be a counterpart of the Southern Club later in "The Big House" on West Reno.) The "Big Four" combination then was composed of Jake Barnes, Cecil Proctor, Jim Dupree, and either Red Cameron or Bill Monnahan, dealing for fourth place in the combine. The raid that wiped out the Southern Club saw these principals and twenty-eight other men arrested and all the plush fixtures demolished.

There followed raids on the Olympic at 105½ West Main; Red Cameron's place at 24 West Main and the Monte Carlo at 114½ North

Robinson, which for eleven years had been an Oklahoma version of the place in Monaco for which it was named. Chief Nichols led many of the raids personally. On one of them, in a more affluent part of the city, he got quite a bit of static from some prominent persons arrested, who insisted they knew too many leaders of the city administration to be taken to jail.

Nichols' comment, as related by McRill, is something of a classic: "My best friends in this town have double-crossed me time and time again since I have been chief. I may not be chief longer than tomorrow night — but while I am chief I'm going to be one. And it doesn't make any difference if I catch my own brother in one of these raids, he'll have to come to jail. Millionaires and hod carriers all look alike to me. I've started to do something and I'm going to carry it through."

Organized bootlegging had been broken up — for a time. Gambling houses and resorts of the madams and their soiled courtesans closed for the first time since opening of Oklahoma Country. Embry, having done what he wanted to accomplish, served his appointed term and did not stand for reelection. Nichols lost out when Jack Walton became mayor and the city started creeping back into a less rigidly enforced status of crime control, as the pendulum swung the other way, aided as always by enough persons willing to push, by paying those ready to supply an illegal demand.

There was someone around to take over remnants of Creekmore's leaderless empire, as it was fragmented during the next few years, in the form of Orban Chester Patterson. For nearly two decades Patterson was called "the crime octopus of Oklahoma County," although there were said to be tenacles reaching elsewhere. At least for nine lurid years after 1931, Patterson seemed to write his own rules, without serious opposition from city or county officials.

Patterson came here with a law degree when the city was almost wide open again, in the general letdown of the War I period. He started practice in the office of Moman Pruiett, then the best known criminal attorney in the Southwest, who defended more than 200 accused murderers without a death penalty. Patterson had a political alliance with Jack Walton, former public works commissioner, who was elected mayor in 1919. Walton's firing of Nichols as police chief changed the lock on the vice door. That gave Patterson a boost toward getting control of things. He knew how to use law to help defeat some of its basic aims. Editorial campaigns and speeches before civic clubs caused him no worry. He was generous with tips to newsboys and with contributions to charity. He was quiet, well mannered, and unobtrusive of person.

Patterson knew when and how to lose money at poker, and to whom, in sociable games at his apartment. A bribe? Not at all, one former member of the city vice squad said later, "you just got lucky at poker." No prosecutor could have proven otherwise had a private game been raided. But who would have made such a raid then?

It was not the city or county that finally got Patterson, but the federal income tax people, through Charles Dierker, United States District Attorney, and Federal District Judge Edgar S. Vaught. The trial was in January and February 1940. The government subpoenaed fifty-four witnesses to testify for its tax case that Patterson from 1933 to 1936, had

The electric monorail at the State Fair of Oklahoma at N.W. Tenth and May.

an income of $89,464, while reporting $14,704. After testimony backing charges of his being a "fixer" for a car theft ring and boss of a liquor syndicate, before other waiting counts were brought up concerning call girls, dope and open gambling, Patterson changed his pleas to "no defense."

On March 2, 1940, Judge Vaught sentenced Patterson to five years in federal penitentiary and to $5,000 fines on each of five counts, with sentences to run concurrently. He was released in late 1943 on a conditional parole and died in Utah the next year.

15

Air Age Slip Stream

LTHOUGH MANY THINGS OF STATEWIDE interest underlined 1910, for Oklahoma City itself this was the first multiple
highlight year of its history to that time. It saw three events
which were to have a cumulative effect down through the years and lay
a foundation for many things to come. They were capital removal from
Guthrie to Oklahoma City; beginning of major industry with a packing
plant and the terminal livestock market; the fledgling flight of fabric
covered, open cockpit biplanes as our air age began.

We were not far behind that phenomenon called flight, that was
a visionary but designed idea of Leonardo Da Vinci, which in the twentieth
century became both an absorption and a competitive event worldwide.
In December 1903 one of the Wright Brothers got off Kill Devil Hill at
Kitty Hawk, North Carolina. The distance flown could be marked inside
a 747 passenger plane today. Louis Bleriot made it across the English
Channel, from Calais to Dover, in July 1909. Glenn H. Curtiss, who made
the first "ship to shore" flight, a hop from a barge on Lake Keuka in Western New York State to shore, got the first big air prize in America when
he won $10,000 offered for a continuous flight from Albany to New York
City. The distance of 137 miles was flown in 152 minutes, on May 29,
1910. Our town then got air minded.

In March that year Curtiss sent Charles F. Willard to Oklahoma
City to make a demonstration flight. The first airplane to lift off our soil
attained an altitude of fifty feet and made a distance of 200 yards. That
was better than the Wright flight. It was made in a pasture near where
Capitol Hill High School stood later. An exhibition flight was scheduled
here in August 1910 but failed to take place because the Wright Brothers
had obtained an injunction against the intended pilot, a French national
named Louis Paulhan, for patent infringement. Then the "International
Aviators" were booked here for an exhibition. They were headed by John
B. Moisant and included a Swiss named Audemars and three French fliers:
Ronald Garros, Rene Barrier and Rene Simon. They wanted a guarantee
of $7,500 for a three day exhibition which included some auto daredevils
such as Barney Oldfield and "Wild Bill" Doolin. A Chamber of Commerce
committee headed by Sidney L. Brock, Seymour C. Heyman, John
Sinopoulo and J. H. Leavitt raised $7,000 and the Oklahoma Railway
Company came in with the other $500. The day after the contract was
signed Moisant crashed and was killed at New Orleans. When the "flying
circus" did get here it was in January 1911. They did their best in a sudden

Early Birds were Joe Neyer and C. F. Gilchrist.

but typical "norther." People here saw their first monoplanes then for the fliers had two small, single wing, Bleriot craft. One of them even raced Oldfield around the Fairgrounds track. No speed argument was settled.

There was something of a lull in the aviation era for a few years until the United States Army Signal Corps went into the flight training business. Post Field at Fort Sill was activated. A number of Oklahomans who were later to make a contribution to flight were in service or training in the war period. These included residents Bennett H. "Hun" Griffin, Joe Neyer and B. S. "Cheebie" Graham. A small field, Westwood, was established in the Packingtown area. Two Army men, Lieutenants T. S. K. Reed and J. W. Jamison set a record by flying the seventy-two air miles from Fort Sill to this field in twenty minutes net flight time. There was even talk of airplane service between Oklahoma City and Tulsa in mid-1920, yet that was about eight years away. There was need of space for an air field. The Chamber, spurred to "think aviation" by Stanley Draper from 1919, leased an eighty acre plot on the Oklahoma-Cleveland county line, between Stops Ten and Eleven on the interurban line, two and one-half miles south of our city limits, for an airport. Griffin and Mart Adams had a distributorship for Lincoln-Standard airplanes and put up a hangar at the field. Griffin flew the first plane into it on September 1, 1923,

Tom Braniff, left, developed Braniff airlines. *Paul Braniff, right, started the lines.*

with H. C. Martin, chairman of the Chamber aviation committee, as a passenger.

This was the age of the barnstormer or exhibition flier. It saw many persons active in our area who were later to make contributions to the age of flight. You had to interest people in aviation to sell planes. If you had an idea for a plane of your own, as Sam Coffman did, you made expenses meanwhile by flying folks off cow pastures for a fifteen minute adventure at a price of $3. Later he produced the first airplane made in Oklahoma City. With Jimmy Mattern, Griffin was to make a record flight across the Atlantic in 1932 on a round-the-world flight attempt, only to wash out in Russia. Burrell Tibbs was a barnstormer and one of the instructors for Wiley Post, who used compensation obtained from an oil field accident that took an eye, for flight instruction.

Tibbs later claimed — and this claim has not been disproved by documentary evidence — that he had more small craft hours than any other man in America. As late as 1953 he flew one of the last Curtiss open cockpit jobs from Dayton, Ohio, to Grand Prairie, Texas, with his usual box of cigars, a flashlight and a Rand-McNally Atlas — in six days. The attraction of Oklahoma City aviation brought a young grease monkey named Johnny Burke down here from Wichita, to remain as manager, then owner, of the original Wiley Post Airport at North May and Britton Road. James Brazil, Bill Bleakley and Clint Johnson were in all air activities they could get into. Bennie Turner was writing about aviation for *The Daily Oklahoman* and flying in anything that would get off the ground.

The Southwest Aviation Park came into being at Southwest Twenty-ninth Street and May Avenue, in December of 1924, backed, as usual, by the Chamber. It was a quarter-section tract. National Air Transport, Incorporated, obtained an airmail contract with the government and Oklahoma City got on the first "transcontinental" line, even if this segment was Dallas-Fort Worth to Chicago, with Wichita, St. Joseph, Missouri, and Davenport, Iowa, as intermediate stops. There were specifications to meet at the airport, such as grading and drainage, perimeter and runway lighting, with a revolving beacon to indicate the field with its sod runways.

The first air mail from here was lifted off at 11:10 A.M. on May 12, 1926, all 314 pounds of it, in an NAT plane appropriately named "Miss Oklahoma City," which made a circuit over the city before landing. It was christened then by Augusta Johnston, daughter of the postmaster. The Chamber had underwritten a guarantee of at least thirty pounds of air mail per day for a ninety day period, or 1,300 average letters each day, at a rate of ten cents an ounce or fraction thereof, to terminal points such as Chicago. Five cent increments were laid on for more distant points such as New York, with a twenty-five cent charge from Oklahoma City to Boston. It was two years before night air mail flights were authorized since beacons at ten-mile intervals had to be installed across the country. For approximately six years the Army then flew airmail before that service was returned to private contractors. Braniff obtained the contract through here. NAT was to become a part of United Air Lines later.

Meanwhile, both commercial and general aviation continued to grow here. NAT started an express and passenger service on September 1, 1927, with charges for people of ten cents per air mile, or $78.80 to Chicago. Earlier that year a gentleman named Charles A. Lindbergh captured the world's fancy with his epic solo flight to Paris. Later he came through here helping to lay out the transcontinental train-air combination route of Transcontinental and Western Air.

The Ford Trimotor became the airlines' work horse as the DC-3 was to become later. Erle P. Halliburton of Duncan started Safeway Airlines through here. Coffman started his plane factory in the old Midland Motor Company building on Westwood, near the airport, in November 1928, and on March 28, 1929, there were 8,000 persons around the airfield to see the test flight of the first Oklahoma City made airplane, the Coffman Monoplane. It was quite an improvement over that old Curtiss Jenny of Coffman's barnstorming days.

In August of 1928 Oklahoma City had some recognition as an aviation center when it was made a stop for the transcontinental air race from New York to Lost Angeles. In July of 1929 the city's airport could claim proudly that in a month it had 1,582 inbound craft and 1,592 departures. Braniff Universal was the largest commercial line, but Curtiss and Safeway used the field with a growing number of private planes. Cheebie Graham operated the Curtiss Flying Service and also there was Burrell Tibbs' Flying School. Arch Dixon made history with the state's first glider flight. Clem Sohn, the "Batman," was here.

The line that became Braniff International began here on June 20, 1928, when Paul Braniff took off in his five place, Stinson-Detroiter, for Tulsa on the first scheduled flight. Following the Oklahoma City-Tulsa run flights were expanded with stops at Duncan, Wichita Falls, Breckenridge, Abilene and San Angelo, while instate service here included Seminole-Wewoka. In 1929 Braniff merged with Universal of St. Louis and went to tri-motors. In one year Braniff grew from that one aircraft, with one combination executive-employe-pilot and 160 route miles, to a $3 million firm with thirty-two planes, twenty pilots, seventy-five other

An assortment of styles of Braniff passenger airplanes, beginning with the 1928 Stinson.

employes and 5,000 route miles. It severed from Universal later and Thomas E. Braniff joined his brother in the airline. At the end of its first decade Braniff had 270 employes and 10,000 route miles. By 1944 Braniff was an international line with routes in Latin America. Its domestic routes were extended almost yearly, to Amarillo, then to Wichita, Colorado Springs and Denver by 1945. Tom Braniff was killed in the crash of a small, ice laden aircraft while on a Louisiana duck hunting trip in 1954. Fred Jones then became chairman of the board. Braniff later was sold to Ling-Temco-Vought which divested it in 1971 under court order. It now is operated independently.

It was in this style airplane that the first airmail flew in and out of the city.

Already gaining a place in the burgeoning air age, Oklahoma City in 1930 got more attention from the nation, when Wiley Post won the National Air Derby from Los Angeles to Chicago. The 1,740 mile flight was made in nine hours, nine minutes and nine seconds, beating by twelve minutes the time of Art Goebel, later winner of the Dole Flight to Hawaii. Post, after learning to fly rather quickly even for those days, started doing commercial flying for independent oil operator F. C. Hall here in 1927. After a few months Post went to Burbank, California, as chief test pilot for Lockheed-Vega Aircraft Corporation. In late 1930 he returned to Oklahoma City as pilot for Hall. The plane used in the derby was a high winged Lockheed-Vega monoplane, powered by a 420 horse power, Pratt & Whitney Wasp engine. It was a seven place aircraft with special fittings and had a rated top speed of 235 miles per hour. The plane was named "The Winnie Mae," after Hall's daughter, Mrs. Leslie Fain.

In 1931 Post and Harold Gatty made the best time on a global flight to that time. Post used some of that experience, while working out some other ideas of his own the next two years in high altitude flight, to take advantage of "pusher" favorable winds. He developed a pressure suit that would permit a pilot to stay alive in thin atmosphere — warmed from the engine manifold. This is essentially the basis of pressurized clothing worn by today's astronauts. Post in July 1933 set a new globe circling record. And solo at that. He flew the Winnie Mae 15,400 miles in seven days, eighteen hours and fifty minutes, better by twenty-one hours than the flight made with Gatty. When he climbed out of the plane at Floyd Bennett Field in New York his first request was for a replacement for his lost eye patch. An ambulance surgeon made one for him.

The International Aeronautic Federation awarded Post the second Gold Medal given an American (Lindbergh was first) based not only on his record solo flight, but upon his developments for high altitude flight. Pressurized cabins on today's commercial aircraft, taken so matter of factly by air travelers, grew from Post's ideas. The world knows that Post, with his passenger, Will Rogers, was killed at Point Barrow, Alaska, in August 1935 when their round-the-world plane crashed. A memorial air show was held here for Post in 1937 under direction of Moss Patterson. In 1961 the former Bethany, later Tulakes Airport, was named for the famed one-eyed pilot. It is more than a "secondary" port now.

Even young folk got into spirit of the expanding air interest here in the early 1930's. Part of that was participation in a model plane contest based on models of actual planes. Post gave an award for the best scale model of the Winnie Mae, while Patterson put up a similar monetary prize for a model of his Great Lakes plane. Roy Hunt, of Oklahoma City and Norman, in 1932 won the National Air Race from Los Angeles to Cleveland. In 1930 Hunt, with Bennett Griffin, flew more than 300 hours above our skies testing refueling methods for an endurance flight, in preparation for an intended world flight. Their chief helper was O. M. "Red" Mosier. They wanted a global flight to end at the Chicago "Century of Progress" World's Fair. "Uncle Jim" Brazil loaned them his Buhl airplane to fly to Chicago to talk to Rufus Dawes, chairman of the fair, to seek financing. None of the three had enough money to get to Chicago and live without assistance. There was a depression on — remember? But Dawes knew it, too, yet after two months of keeping the trio's hopes high, and admitting their plan was feasible, the plan was dropped. Roy Hunt, meanwhile, set a world's record for consecutive outside loops in an aircraft. Inside loops were old hat with barnstormers. Later Hunt "bought the farm" in Missouri while flying a small plane for the Hightowers and Johnsons.

By 1930 there were a number of lines operating out of here. In addition to Braniff there was Bowen Airlines, flying an Oklahoma City-Dallas-Fort Worth route. Transcontinental Air Transport and Western Air Express had terminals here with coast-to-coast connections. National Air Transport continued its schedules to give the city five airlines. By 1931 it was obvious that more space was needed for the air industry. The Chamber backed Air Park, or Municipal Field, was far too small. A second field, Curtiss-Wright, had some commercial traffic. A bond issue secured 640 acres for a new Municipal Airport, now the west section of Will Rogers World Airport, which began operations in 1932 with thirty-two daily inbound and outbound passenger and express schedules. Oklahoma City now

Wiley Post, champion pilot, stands beside the Winnie Mae, named for Oklahoma Cityan Winnie Mae Hall (later Fain) by her father, F. C. Hall, Post's financial backer.

Air view of the Federal Aviation Agency Aeronautical Center complex in Oklahoma City.

was but twelve hours from either coast. In December 1932 Braniff moved its headquarters from Kansas City to Oklahoma City, where it remained until recent years, before shifting to Dallas.

In the early 1930's there were Chamber sponsored state air tours, for in many communities aircraft remained a spectator attraction. One of the five day tours involved twenty cities. What became Trans-World Airlines had routes here from 1930 to 1934, but lost out on a shuffling of airmail contracts and left, to return in 1956. In 1961 TWA had the first commercial jet flight from Will Rogers Field. American Airlines started its schedules here on June 15, 1934, which with Braniff and Bowen gave the city eight daily schedules. In 1956 Slick Airways, with Del W. Rentzel as president, rounded out ten years of cargo service here. There were more than 100 firms using air cargo services from here, the Chamber reported. This was aided in 1966 by opening of a "port of entry" customs service for air freight.

Growth of Municipal Field after mid-1935 had overtones of what later was to be defense preparation and War II training. It became Will Rogers Field and was approved by the Army Air Corps for reserve pilot training in January 1936. This was not without its price to the city airport budget for a basic improvement program ran to $430,000, in addition to an $181,000 allocation from the War Department, and some $1 million in funds from the Works Progress Administration. The field's lighting system was completely revised, runways lengthened and strengthened, cross-runways established, all runways paved (some had been graveled), taxi strips added. In June 1941 the airport was dedicated as Will Rogers Air Base by the Air Corps. For the next two years improvements were almost constant with more than an additional $1 million spent. As home of a light bombardment group parts of it were closed to civilian aviation until late in 1945. On May 1, 1946, control of the field passed back to the city. There were thirty-five buildings and five hangars in place. The original 640 acres had been expanded to 1,272 acres by the Chamber's Industries

Foundation, then leased to the army. Before war's end it held 10,000 aviation personnel.

To commemorate the person for whom Will Rogers Airport was named, prior to a major rennovation of the terminal building in 1954, Sylvan Goldman presented the city with a bust of Will Rogers done by sculptor Jo Davidson, creator of the full length Rogers statue at the memorial in Claremore. On November 25, 1954, an American Airlines flight from Los Angeles to New York became the one-millionth aircraft to land at the port here. In 1957 a $7,497,000 bond issue was passed to expand the airport. Civic leaders put up the money to underwrite acquisition of a protective zone around the expanded field. The present Will Rogers World Airport was opened and dedicated the first days of December in 1966. It has a planned, protected area.

Its mid-American location and the para-military structures at Will Rogers — with the protected space — were a natural for post-war development of some sort. In typical fashion city leaders and the Chamber had not been waiting this long to court some possible "damsel with a dowry." As early as 1938 there was contact with the Civil Aeronautics Administration about having some sort of installation here. Advent of the war naturally altered that picture but it came into clear focus again in 1946. Earlier, in 1941, the city airport became one of thirty-nine in the nation to be an aerial traffic control point, with the CAA having jurisdiction over both civilian and military air traffic. In March 1946 the Chamber persuaded the CAA to move its Standardization Center from Houston to here. This was a training center for CAA inspectors and was headed then by Bennett Griffin, who later for years managed Washington National Airport. Also to be here was a maintenance and overhaul base for CAA aircraft and a signals division for training in maintenance of navigation aids. The city had to provide about $150,000 in expansion funds, primarily two hangars and a headquarters building.

Then, in June of 1946 the CAA, having already put so many activities here, went to the extent of making this the official Civil Aeronautics Administration Center. A Veterans Hospital at the base was turned back to the city. The twenty-three "temporary" buildings were sold and cleared off. A CAA Training Center to cost in excess of $13 million was authorized, including one warehouse to encompass fifteen acres. There seemed to be an air of urgency about construction. A survey of local construction costs of similar buildings on a square foot basis was made. A consortium composed of Dan Tankersley, Link Cowen and Al Kavanaugh of Oklahoma and Clint Murchison of Texas took the contract at the local average cost per square foot.

Later the installation became the Federal Aviation Center of the Federal Aviation Agency, which on May 15, 1959, took over control of all the nation's air space. In 1961 the FAA Aero-Medical Research Center was made a part of this installation. Traffic controllers from all over the world were trained here. In one year, from September 1960 to that time in 1961, there were 327 men from fifty nations trained. From Shannon to Seoul it is not unusual for a pilot to hear a bit of Oklahoma slang from a control tower. Expansion has been fairly steady as services increased, including transfer here of the personnel records of all certified pilots in the nation in 1964, requiring a new housing structure, and a new $2.5 million training systems building in 1968. In addition to location of the CAA facilities here in 1946, there were other aviation highlights that year. National Skyways Freight Corporation located here: Continental Airlines put Oklahoma City on its Tulsa-El Paso route; Braniff began cargo operations with DC-4 aircraft; American Airlines started operating DC-4 aircraft out of here on its transcontinental route from east to west coasts — the first four engine jobs — later replaced by the DC-6 and 6-B and DC-7, before the jet age.

Leasing of Will Rogers facilities to the military in 1941 spurred activity in providing more fields for civil aviation. The original Wiley Post Airport on North May was used by light civilian aircraft. The city secured land on the north side of Bethany for a second municipal airport and for an outlay of around $1.5 million made it usable by commercial craft. Later it was called Tulakes. Federal money was secured, too. The Civil Air Patrol was based there. By 1960 Tulakes was termed, with apparent justification, "the best secondary airport in the nation." By 1964 an expanded airport, now renamed Wiley Post, was in being. In 1966 Cimarron Field, near Yukon, which had been a primary training field for War II pilots, was enlarged for another auxiliary airport for Oklahoma City. In 1973 still another general aviation airport, in the northeastern sector, was discussed.

Oklahoma City was host to the National Air Clinics of 1943 and 1944, the first one being the initial domestic aviation planning session held on a nationwide basis. This was repeated in 1945, with the added bit of interest in Tinker Field being "dedicated" as a permanent installation. Former Durant resident, Lieutenant General Ira C. Eaker, who as a young officer set an endurance flight record in the "Question Mark" and commanded an Air Force in the European Theater in War II, was the principal brass at ceremonies. In May 1945 Continental added direct service from here to Hobbs, New Mexico, which became a sort of commuter plane for city oil men as play developed in the New Mexican areas around Hobbs and Jal.

May 11, 1945, one of those interesting human stories began to unfold when Central Airlines, formed by Keith Kahle, got a "certificate of convenience and necessity" to start serving more than a score of state cities from here, as a feeder line. The first aircraft used was a four place Bonanza. Kahle had been editor of a small publication called "Taxi Strip." He was one of the most severely aviation "bug" infected persons around the local aviation scene. Central, after inter-state expansion, moved to Fort Worth, and still later was absorbed by Frontier Airlines.

Aero-Commander began making aircraft at Tulakes with twin piston engine planes in 1951. The first production plane was purchased by the *Chicago Tribune*. To prove merit of the aircraft, one took off from here with one engine sealed and flew to Washington, D.C., in seven hours and fifty-five minutes, landed, took off and returned here with the engine still sealed. This impressed the Department of Defense enough so that Aero-Commanders were added to the White House fleet for short to

The Federal Aviation Agency Aeronautical Center trains air control personnel worldwide.

The FAA Aeromedical Research Institute can simulate various altitudes and temperatures.

Jerri Cobb, test pilot for Aero-Commander, who set national flying records.

medium length flights. By March 1955 there had been 200 Aero-Commanders produced here. They were distributed world wide. The later development of a Jet Commander was sold to the Israeli government. The company, meanwhile, in 1961 passed in ownership from the Pew interests of Pennsylvania, R. T. Amis, Junior, and others of Oklahoma City, to Rockwell-Standard, now Rockwell-International. Chamber members underwrote $352,000 for land acquisition for the original plant but only $180,000 of that sum was needed. Jerri Cobb in April 1959, set a new world speed record for light, twin-engined planes in an Aero-Commander, taking the record from the Russians. Later she made a bit of additional history with a world flight. She now is Mrs. Jerri Cobb Mock.

Oklahoma City in 1956 had the only approved National Air Show in the country. Some of the jet jockeys, cutting in afterburners to break through the sound barrier, really gave an indication of what was to come in 1964 when a planned series of sonic booms was laid down over the city as the country swept into the space age — even though super-sonic transports still are not produced on this side of the Atlantic whale pasture.

In late 1973 a consultant for the Oklahoma City Airport Trust said that one of every six persons here had some direct relation with the aviation industry. Indirectly that affects the complete economy.

16

High Tide Toward War

THE TOWN WAS BEGINNING TO feel that it was a city before the blessing of statehood came. There were enough young bachelor type businessmen around, tired of living in boarding houses and small hotels, to form the Pickwick Club in 1904. They rented a house, hired a cook and other servants, and became quite a factor in social life as member Oscar Dietz recalled later. He said also that one of the sharp carriage drivers for Sunday afternoon excursions to Shepherd Lake was E. K. Gaylord.

Business was picking up. In 1906 city jobbers handled $28 million worth of merchandise, not only within the twin territories but in neighboring states, too. Commercial building took a spurt with $2.5 million gross in one year as stone and brick replaced wood. Most elaborate was that of Pioneer Telephone Company with its gingerbread facade at Northwest Third and Broadway.

Residential building was said to exceed a construction rate of two houses each day in 1906. Already some of the fine homes now marked for historical preservation began to appear, along with the Mount St. Mary's seminary at 2801 South Shartel. Henry Overholser was somewhat in the lead on private homes, with the near classical Victorian architecturally styled mansion at 405 Northwest Fifteenth, out "in the country," in 1904. It is marked for national as well as local historical preservation. A campaign backed by the Oklahoma City Chapter of the American Institute of Architects made this possible. The AIA group will use the carriage house as an office while the interior, after the limited restoration needed, will be open for tours.

Frank P. Johnson built a massive stone house at 439 Northwest Fifteenth, somewhat Grecian in design and ornamentation, now the home of Mr. and Mrs. Frank Johnson Hightower. The Oklahoma Publishing Company in 1909 erected a five story building at Northwest Fourth and Broadway that remains an example of classical Greek revival in its trim and in construction design. It remains one of the most solidly built structures in the city. This was designed by Sol Layton and Weymis Smith, whose contribution to local architecture included Central High School and the State Capitol.

The Baum Building at old Grand Avenue and Robinson, with its outstanding adaptation of trim used on the Doges Palace in Venice, was a subject of study by architectural students for years, before falling to urban renewal in 1973. Saved from that modernization was the Colcord Building across the street to the west, the city's first "skyscraper" of twelve stories. It was designed by William A. Wells, a student of Louis Sullivan of Chicago, whose students of "modern" skyscrapers included Frank Lloyd Wright. The Chicago School influence also was seen in the Pioneer Building. The mansion built in 1916 by W. T. Hales at 1521 North Hudson, for which the architects were Hawk and Parr, remains another fine example of our early period. In 1939 this became headquarters of the Roman Catholic Diocese and residence of the bishop.

Statehood had its effect on Oklahoma City construction. The city itself went into 1908 with a bonded debt of $748,500. This included funding for previous issues and more funds for water and sewer services and city hall expense. Fines of $5 to $25 for cigaret smoking, decreed by the state legislature, raised little revenue in the law's short life. Sensational charges of murder by arson, involving "Big Anne" Wynn's establishment, created a flurry, but the general tone of news stories was dominated by reports of progress. Currency payments were resumed by banks following a brief financial recession of 1907. There were four new church buildings under construction. Four days in April of 1908 saw an area of twenty-two blocks sell for $226,000. The Majestic Building of seven stories at Main and Harvey was announced. W. J. Pettee expanded on Main Street and the First State Bank opened.

There were some fire casualties. The Oklahoma Broom Company plant burned at a loss of $30,000. The Lee Hotel, the city's finest, fell to fire, but Joseph Huckins announced a month later that a new Lee-Huckins Hotel of ten stories in fireproof construction, with 443 rooms, would rise from the ashes. By another year it would represent an investment of nearly $1 million. Oklahoma City folk gave members of the legislature a big banquet and made no bones about intention — again — to seek location of the capital.

Flood waters twice cut the gas mains, the second time in December for ten hours when temperature stood around twenty degrees. Also during the year the Moss Brewery was raided by sheriff's deputies, the second time involving some heavy labor as $8,000 worth of illegal beer was poured into gutters. Mayor Scales called a mass meeting to oppose a commissioner form of government. Floods also submerged Delmar Gardens and Wheeler Park for a time. The Chamber began its state "good will" tours.

A new post office was a big event in 1910. Years later, in a "flash-back" presentation E. K. Gaylord was to say: "One of the biggest disappointments to downtown property owners was location of the new post office. The Chamber agreed unanimously that it should be located on the west side of Harvey, between Grand and Main. This area flooded frequently because of insufficient storm sewers. We sent a photograph of that area under six or eight inches of water to postal authorities in Washington. No one else knew this. When an official came to select a location he was given a recommendation for the Harvey location. To astonishment of those sponsors he rejected it, and on his own motion, selected a corner on the hill at Third and Robinson. I didn't tell anybody about this for twenty years."

Civil rights protest movements in Oklahoma City began in 1910 with Roscoe Dunjee's "Black Dispatch." It provided the first means of direct publicity by the black community and affiliated national organizations, to awaken both black and white citizens to discrimination at the polls. The legislature proposed a "grandfather" clause amendment providing that no person could be registered to vote unless he passed an examination demonstrating his ability to read and write certain portions of the state constitution. He was exempted from this requirement if he was a lineal descendant of a person elegible to vote on January 1, 1866. This had the practical effect of excluding almost all Negroes from voting. The amendment carried by 35,000 votes.

The campaign did not end there. In 1915 the United States Supreme Court in Guinn vs. the United States, held the "grandfather" clause invalid. Some state election officials were charged with violation of federal election laws, were tried, sentenced, later pardoned. In August 1958 Oklahoma City had the first civil rights "sit-ins" for a Southern or border state, seeking to desegregate eating establishments downtown, at stores and cafeterias. There had been protest marches here before but not the sit-ins. These were mainly youth groups led by Clara Luper and others. Subsequent national court actions broke down all historical barriers on public accomodations.

In 1911 the state, under Governor Lee Cruce, set up the first highway department with Sidney Suggs of Ardmore as chairman. Cityans saw the first road building tax, or excise tax, of many yet to come, with a $1 fee per licensed vehicle. One fellow who paid little attention to that — since he did not own an auto — was Jess Willard, who worked some on construction of the original dam at Lake Overholser. But he found pleasure in working out at the Oklahoma City Athletic Club, about where the Cooper theater was later on Robinson. He did become world's heavyweight champion later by defeating Jack Johnson in 1915, losing to Jack Dempsey in 1919. Willard had no major fights here.

On February 3, 1913, the city had the heaviest snowfall that it had seen, to then, when seven inches of snow covered the landscape. Ground was broken for the state capitol building July 20, 1914, with Governor Lee Cruce swinging a pick and W. B. Anthony a shovel. It was the incoming 1915 chief executive, Governor Robert L. Williams, who was to have more influence on the construction. Governor Williams appointed himself head of a revamped State Capitol Commission and was quite articulate about his desires in design, materials and other factors, as the $1.5 million structure developed under architectural supervision of Sol Layton. There were arguments about the type of stone to be used and almost everything else. The legislature authorized a building of three stories but by having a basement, and mezzanines between the generously spaced floors, the equivalent of several more stories was added. There was original planning for a $300,000 dome, for which supports were prepared, but materials scarcities incident to World War I and lack of funds, kept the building domeless. There were six bidders on construction, including A. O. Campbell and Holmboe Construction Companies of Oklahoma City and Manhattan Construction of Muskogee. The contract went to James Stewart & Company of New York, builders of the Utah and Idaho capitol buildings. Governor Williams did not wait for completion of the building in mid-1917, he moved there in January, while later state offices scattered over the city were installed. All of them. This freed space in commercial and school buildings for other usage. The State Supreme Court, for instance, was on the sixth floor of the Lawrence Hotel.

War clouds were darkening the European landscape but in 1914 there was little direct interest here. You could get a room with a bath at the new Lee-Huckins for $2.50, maximum, with a club breakfast for twenty-five cents, a noon meal for forty cents and a table d'hote dinner for seventy-five cents. The hotel gave its guests a little pocket notebook with some information printed on the back cover, including such details as the railroad distance from the city to Choctaw being fourteen miles. W. B. Skirvin was ready to give Joe Huckins some competition with the first unit of his hotel, a block north, beside the Rock Island passenger station. The large number of nearby truck farms resulted in opening of a Public Market out on Exchange Avenue at Reno in 1915. That year also saw Oklahomans given the pleasure of a state income tax. When the price of bread here rose from five cents to six cents a loaf there were comments about "what is the world coming to?"

The county assessor did report that in July 1915, automobiles outnumbered horses in the city, with 1,900 compared to 1,353. The McClelland-Gentry firm offered Dodge cars; Wallace Campbell acquired the Buick agency from one Chrisman; Sandy Brooks had the air-cooled Franklin to offer; Ray Stapleton sold Reo models; M. H. Randall provided Chevrolets and Baird H. Markham was the Chandler dealer. Touring cars and roadsters were the main models — each provided with side curtains to put on when rains fell. Henry Ford opened an assembly plant for Model T's on West Main, near the dead end of Classen Boulevard, which gave quite an impetus to employment for the area with that $5 daily pay rate. Flivvers were driven away from the plant by state dealers. Engines were so tight that for some distance the cars had to be driven in low gear, from that floor pedal, before loosening up enough to chug along in high gear. The last Model T came off, nationally, on May 31, 1927, after 15,007,033 were produced. The Model A with its gear shift appeared in 1928. One of the early Ford plant employes here was Fred Jones, later a major dealer, with other varied interests including manufacturing auto components.

Potential of the city as a livestock market impressed Frank L. Kenyon, who came here from Dallas in 1900 to open a brick plant, and organized a stock show. To get the $3,700 needed for premiums and to hold the show, he walked the street raising money, most of which came from the city's seventy-two licensed saloon keepers. By March 1916, when you could have bought a high-wheeled buggy for $33.50, city businessmen and stockyards interests started the Southwest American Livestock Show at the yards. The first event drew entries from Oklahoma, Kansas, Texas, Missouri and Ohio. There were 343 cattle, 152 hogs and forty sheep. After a few years the open show was replaced by the Oklahoma 4-H and FFA Junior Livestock show, although the original organization remains as sponsor.

Now, as the largest purely junior show in the nation, the annual event draws more than 4,000 animals, 2,500 youths and a $70,000 total in premiums and bonus money. For years the Chamber has provided $7,500 in its annual budget for premium support. The Sirloin Club of Oklahoma, supported by business and professional folk with $100 annual memberships, provides other expenses of the show and a premium on every animal exhibited, in addition to fancy prices paid at auction for the top animals. This replaces direct solicitation and permits assistance to many other youth activities. The Junior Show was held at the yards for years, where it outgrew the Coliseum and tentage, and in 1958 moved to the fairgrounds.

Oklahomans participated in the curtain raiser for involvement in War I when the First Oklahoma Infantry regiment and some smaller units were mobilized for service on the Mexican border, in the punitive retaliation to Pancho Villa's escapades. Oklahoma City had regimental headquarters and the band, under "Doc" Flynn, which earned the dubious nickname of "The Old Gray Mare Band." The city also had Company M of the regiment, a field hospital corps and Troop B of a cavalry squadron. The border experience provided many tall tales but little else. Units were returned in February but had only twenty-nine days before being mobilized again for the real war, declared five days later, on April 6, 1917. This time, when they entrained for Fort Sill, the atmosphere was a bit different than it had been in July the year before, when some 12,000 persons gathered at the station to bid them farewell, after a ringing patriotic speech by later Federal District Judge Edgar S. Vaught. One departure seemed almost beginning of a lark — for who was afraid of that Mexican bandit? The second was most serious and a voyage into the unknown.

Units were under strength. Efforts were made to increase the rolls. In Oklahoma City Governor Williams, Adjutant General Ancel Earp and Captain Raymond S. McLain, commanding Company M of the First Oklahoma, all made appeals. Oklahoma City folk put on a mammoth parade but it was not until the later draft that units were filled up to strength. More than 7,000 men registered in the city for the draft. In July the first drawing took place with 300 from Oklahoma City being tabbed. In August the National Guard was federalized. On November 30, 1917, the first all-Oklahoma company reached France.

During early weeks of the war the city had its first campaign for sale of Liberty Bonds and reached its quota of $2,100,000 with Will S. Guthrie as chairman of the campaign. In November 1917 a drive for YMCA funds to provide field workers and supplies to troops in France saw $65,000 raised. The bond and stamp program went so well that a special shanty at Main and Broadway was constructed — the first such in the nation — to encourage participation. Business people paid for it. The idea is said to have originated with E. Richard Carhart. Making speeches here were William Gibbs McAdoo, secretary of the treasury, and Champ Clark, speaker of the U.S. House of Representatives. For the second Liberty Loan drive the quota was $3,060,000. There was $3.5 million subscribed, under chairmanship of Judge C. B. Ames. Along with Carl Williams, editor of the *Oklahoma Farmer-Stockman*, they headed a statewide campaign as well and instituted the $1,000 Club.

Folks listened to Herbert Hoover, national food administrator,

MAJ. GEN. ROY HOFFMAN
*A longtime National
Guard leader*

MAJ. GEN.
CHARLES F. BARRETT
Father of 45th Division

LT. GEN.
RAYMOND S. McLAIN
*Businessman and
Guard leader*

MAJ. GEN. FRANK CANTON
*Adjutant general
of state*

and began to observe "meatless" and "sweetless" days. The War Mothers Association was organized with Mrs. R. L. Drake as president. There was a large patriotic gathering in Wheeler Park. There was some unhappiness over the rising cost of food. Milk was an especial target of housewives. The price went to fifteen cents a quart. Henry Gray, an assistant county attorney, threatened to put dairymen out of business for profiteering. He said a "reasonable" price was twelve cents. There were twenty-five women registered the first day after a call for Red Cross volunteers and a drive started to raise $125,000 for that organization. Backyard and vacant lot gardening became a major movement. Awards for this endeavor were provided by the Oklahoma Publishing Company and the Chamber. D. C. Mooring of Oklahoma Agricultural and Mechanical College, Stillwater, was engaged to be an on-site advisor for home gardens. John Boardman headed this movement. It was claimed that 10,000 gardens were planted in the city.

The national impetus to get emotional about all things German reached a high point in Oklahoma City. This was almost the focal state point of patriotic demonstrations, speeches by national figures, and the like, because it was the capital. A number of organizations sprang up including a "Minutemen" group and the American Military League, of which George D. Key, an attorney and prominent state politician, was commander. There was talk of weeding out school textbooks that contained "Germanism." A Home Guard was organized. The International Workers of the World, or "Wobblies" as they were called, were accused of socialistic activities, anti-draft movements and other hindrances to the war effort. They approached the end of their influence — always negligible — in state politics after the "Green Corn Rebellion" in the Seminole area. A consignment of books of the International Bible Students Association, entitled "The Finished Mystery," was confiscated on an attorney general's opinion that they held "dangerous propaganda." It was a typical, emotional, wartime syndrome.

In other ways city folk aided the war effort and thought of servicemen. There were 2,000 families who signed up to entertain soldiers from Fort Sill on Thanksgiving in 1917. They managed to secure some 1,500 service personnel for dinner. There was talk about need for more school buildings, dating to a committee recommendation earlier that year for a $541,000 bond issue to erect three junior high schools and a new ward school. Magazines and books were collected to be sent training camps and, hopefully, overseas. In early 1917 the Chamber's directorate, thinking of the cultural atmosphere, went all out with a pledged $25,000 guarantee to bring the Chicago Civic Opera Company here. In October the company came to bring the city's first grand opera, with performances of "Faust" and "Lucia de Lammermore," featuring such artists as Melba, Galli-Curci, and Muratori. The influenza epidemic of 1918 took its fateful toll. The economy spurted as scarcities began to appear. Oil went to $2 a barrel in August, setting a record for the Mid-Continent, and wheat went to levels it would not see again until another war, and yet another time, in 1973. Bank clearings in October reached the highest mark, ever, with $32,-362,000, more than $9 million above the previous year. War's end, when it did come on November 11, 1918, found the city as deliriously happy as any place in the nation, with ringing of bells, tooting of whistles, firing of every type of weapon, shouts, and a wave of momentarily excused vandalism upon public property. There were 7,000 men who left Oklahoma City during the war for military service or to do non-combat work connected with the effort. At end of the war there were 100 vacant living units in the city. There were some person wondering about how the situation of returnees would be met.

Roads occupied attention of the Chamber early in 1918. A "good roads" committee was organized with C. A. Schweinle as president and Judge J. H. Burford as vice-president. In May a $300,000 bond issue was passed to buy the quarter section of state school land upon which the Oklahoma State Fair was located, as a lessee.

Jack C. Walton was elected mayor in April 1919. One of those things that amuse people later — and perhaps even some at the time — came with his issuance of an order on June 17 that all sixteen horses used by the city's mounted police would be equipped with rubber shoes so that criminals could not be warned audibly that police were in the vicinity.

The $1 million school bond election proposed earlier, was passed easily by a six-to-one majority. More persons voted for bonds than voted for candidates in the city election, by 354 ballots. Provided by the election was funds for three junior high schools and improvements for eleven of twenty-eight grade schools. The American Legion was born and the first statewide meeting was held here. Horace H. Hagan, a city lawyer, was first commander of the state group. Mayor Walton proposed an ambitious municipal bond election to provide improvements totaling $2 million. The largest items were to make sewer extensions costing $750,000; $200,000 for a "Victory" auditorium; $400,000 for improving the city jail, and $350,000 for water main extensions. The proposition was defeated.

The year 1919 saw the peak of a period of prosperity, with prices driven up by the war era, which would carry over briefly until the inevitable letdown occured. Food was high. There were $18 silk shirts available for young gallants, $3,000 motor cars with a Stutz Bearcat or a Pierce-Arrow as the ultimate, but a high labor return for workers. Food prices, as usual drew much attention. More than 100 residents petitioned County Attorney Robert Burns to call a grand jury and investigate both retail and wholesale prices. Sugar reached a price of twenty-one cents a pound; best hotel rooms jumped from $2.50 to $5; house rentals went from $25 monthly to $65; lumber from $16 a thousand board feet to $45. Salaries were up, so were wages, but in typical American fashion no one wanted that aspect investigated. A teapot tempest that boiled for a time — but little else. There was some attention paid to the less fortunate. A Welfare League was formed, by ordinance, with John Boardman as chairman to help the unfortunate through voluntary means, and a small increment in city funds. Amid all this came one of those periodic crime waves in the city, which later sociologists were to blame on a general letdown of morals following a war, but which was not conducive to presenting a pleasant picture of civic purity to the world.

17

A Different Decade

LTHOUGH IN SOME ASPECTS OKLAHOMA City shared
major historical events with the rest of the nation in the decade
after 1920, there were highlights more local in effect, some of
which were of a state nature but hubbed on the capital city.

There were several labels applied to this period nationally. "The
Mauve Decade," was the F. Scott Fitzgerald appellation. "Flapper" was
a common term for the bobbed-haired, short-skirted female who danced
the "Charleston." The term "lost generation" reflected antics of youth,
who were but following lead of their elders in sampling bathtub gin or
other spirits, as prohibition enforcement broke down and created the first
massive lessening of public morality in our history.

The decade began with a highlight in wartime economy but in
1920 a slackening was apparent in indices that sharp observers did not
believe would go away. A mild recession followed in the early 1920's —
mild in contrast to that great depression to follow in 1929 — but painful
enough at the time. There were strikes and business failures. There were
also some business successes. Even before discovery of oil in the Oklahoma
City field in late 1928, the state on August 4, 1920, became largest oil producer of the nation with more than nine million barrels monthly. California
and Texas trailed. As Charles N. Gould pointed out a bit later, rather
prophetically, Oklahoma City without trying was center of the action.

First year of the decade saw a social highlight in February when
General John J. Pershing, commander of the American Expeditionary
Force in War I, paid the city a visit. Hardly had that excitement died down
when there was a storm of public protest over establishment of a smoking
room, "for women only," at the Automobile Show to be held in March.
Oklahoma Railway Company announced plans for a new $200,000 terminal
on Grand, between Harvey and Hudson; Chamber directors endorsed a
$500,000 water improvement bond issue as they made arrangements to
move into new quarters at the Oklahoma Club, when it was completed,
near the southwest corner of Grand and Robinson. Oklahoma City, as the
decade began, held 91,258 persons, an increase of 54,168 or forty-two
percent since 1910.

The national election in late 1920 saw the young state's first major
swing to the Republican party. There was some filtered down opposition
to the Democratic ticket because of President Woodrow Wilson's plan for
a League of Nations. Isolationism took hold politically, even though
economic unhappiness created by the recession was a more personal voters'

way of expressing desire for a change. This was the first election in Oklahoma where women were permitted to vote. There were 391,813 of them eligible to do so. The state, aided greatly by the large Oklahoma City vote, went Republican for the first time by giving Warren G. Harding 243,831 votes to 217,753 for James M. Cox of the Democratic party. An oddity, of sorts, was that Socialist Eugene V. Debs received 25,716 votes in Oklahoma. John W. Harreld became the state's first Republican United States Senator; Alice M. Robertson of Muskogee became the first (and only) Oklahoma woman to serve in the United States House of Representatives and, at that time, second in the nation, as five of the eight house seats went Republican. The Oklahoma House of Representatives had a Republican majority for the first time by fifty-five to thirty-seven.

The early 1920's saw Oklahoma City a focal point of matters both political and economic. Nationally Knights of the Ku Klux Klan had a revival to reach an apex and slide away in 1924. Oklahoma City and the state were hot spots for the robed organization. Here it was said cynically that "the KKK‚ uses violence to protect its politics and politics to protect its violence." The organization was strong. Factions aided in splitting the Democratic party wide open. Emerging as champion of anti-Klan forces was John Calhoun "Jack" Walton, who was to make his own mark on city and state.

An engineer by profession, Walton came here from Kansas City, allegedly from a high post in the Pendergast machine. He was public works commissioner in 1917 and mayor in 1919, under the "strong mayor" commission form of government, which Walton interpreted literally, basing his political control on patronage and handling of the police department. Adopting the mantle of the Oklahoma Farm-Labor Reconstruction League, Walton ran for governor in 1922 against John Fields, editor of what became the *Oklahoma Farmer-Stockman*, and won. Walton's inaugural barbecue at the fairgrounds in 1923 was the largest gathering in the state to that point of time, estimated at 150,000.

Quite soon afterward, and through first months of his administration, the bloom faded from Walton's political rose. His actions as governor drew criticism that grew to open opposition. He began to use state militia by gradual martial law decrees. He tried to shut down the State Fair the last week in September, to hit at Oklahoma City business leaders, and did slap on a martial law type of curfew, causing people much trouble about passes for late workers. Walton tried to take over the Oklahoma City police department completely by placing machine guns by its headquarters at Maiden Lane and Wall Street. When a grand jury was called in October to probe his administration, Walton placed machine guns at the County Courthouse, then located where the Downtown Holiday Inn now stands.

After not quite eleven months as governor he was impeached by the state House of Representatives. The State Senate sat as a court. Walton was convicted of eleven charges, including illegal collection of campaign funds, padding public payrolls, suspension of the writ of habeas corpus, excessive use of gubernatorial pardoning power, and general incompetency. He was removed from office November 19, 1923, to be succeeded by Lieutenant Governor Martin E. Trapp, who settled in Guthrie on the "Run," and had held the state's second office since 1914.

Walton earlier had an effect on city elections in 1921, as mayor, for the issue became more an anti-Walton campaign than a political one. City Commissioners Ollie S. Wilson and Mark Kessler announced for re-election. Administration opponents quickly charged them with being dominated by Walton, of aiding unionization of the police department, of approving issuance of thousands of "courtesy cards" which were said to be special police commissions, and of creating an "unnecessary" mounted police force. In opposition to the two commissioners, both Democrats, Republicans Robert Parman and Warren Moore became candidates. They were supported by media and by enough persons to win their seats by 2,500 votes.

There were many disputes to follow, Historian Kerr wrote, among which was a call for resignation of Charles Ruth, Municipal Counselor, who asked for a vacation to let things cool down. The Board of Commissioners with the two newly elected Republicans and Mike Donnelly, commissioner of accounting and finance, outvoted Walton and took the police department out of the mayor's control, placing it under Donnelly, whose first official act was invalidating all those courtesy cards. C. T. Linve was replaced as police chief by M. C. Binion, a former sheriff. Walton challenged the change in police administration but a district court opinion said commissioners acted legally. Walton appealed and the State Supreme Court reversed the lower court decision. Walton again had the police department and appointed Carl Glitsch, then manager of New State Ice Company, as chief. Glitsch determined soon that he could not properly enforce prohibition laws and left the post, being replaced by W. J. Clark, an early day policeman.

City schools' enumeration in 1921 showed 20,700 children of school age, an increase of 3,000 over the previous year. In April there were complaints made to the Health Department that people were violating an ordinance restricting ownership of cows to one per residence. Flooding along the Canadian bottoms added more impetus to plans for control. On the economic front the city was growing in importance. Oklahoma City, although its own field was seven years away, gained importance as an oil industry center. Persons active in opening pools elsewhere made their headquarters here during these years. More than 100 firms had their base here or established major regional sales and distribution centers. Investment for grain and milling facilities exceeded $2 million, with equal payrolls, by five flour mills and five feed mills. A new six-story Cotton-Grain Exchange Building (later Leonhardt Building) was a regionally important home for brokers. Yet with all this the recession caused many commercial business failures as commodity prices dropped along with oil prices. A "panic" form of public psychology developed. Breadlines appeared. St. Anthony's Hospital began its soup line for indigents that would open and close with cycles of the economy for several decades.

American Legion Post 35 acquired a permanent home at Northwest Tenth and Robinson; ground was broken for the Masonic Temple four blocks south; the Tradesmens National Bank emerged at the northwest corner of Main and Broadway.

What Albert McRill called "the Open Shop War," antecedent to "Right to Work" modes, resulting from efforts of the Chamber to secure employment for people jobless because of the recession, in opposition to organized labor, had a fateful culmination in December 1921 with a strike against packing plants. Some 500 strikers paraded through the downtown business district. A small riot erupted later in Packingtown when several persons were injured. Things smoldered for about two weeks until nine union labor white men, McRill said, went after Jake Brooks, a Negro and a nonunion worker at a packing plant, and lynched him. A mass meeting at the Chamber resulted in a request to Governor J. B. A. Robertson to declare martial law. A limited action resulted. State Adjutant General Charles F. Barrett blamed both the Chamber and unions for the trouble. Charges were filed against nine men implicated in the lynching. Three pleaded guilty and drew life sentences while the others were released.

There were activities on the civic scene in 1922. An Oklahoma County Tuberculosis Hospital was organized with an advisory board headed by E. K. Gaylord, with John R. Boardman, Dr. L. J. Moorman and J. F. Owens as members. The first long stretch of county hard surfacing highway, extending ten miles east of the city on Northeast Twenty-third Street, was dedicated. John A. Whitehurst of Oklahoma City and Cyrus Avery of Tulsa tossed a bit of earth with a gold shovel used by the governor of Pennsylvania in 1916 when he opened eighteen miles of his state highway. Residents were asked to house teachers here for the Oklahoma Education Association meeting at a rate of $1 per person, since there was not enough hotel space to accomodate them — a feature that existed for many years due to size of that convention. The Thomas E. Braniff Company announced plans for its ten-story office building at Northwest Third and Robinson, which would be open a year later.

Early in 1922 the Chamber proudly announced that a project underway for more than two years was achieved. The State Corporation Commission upheld the Chamber's contention that Oklahoma Gas & Electric Company charged too much for natural gas. The Commission relied upon a Chamber committee to appraise value of the firm's gas distribution facilities, for rate fixing purposes, which was set at $1,280,660. A rate increase was denied and the burden of paying for more than a ten percent leakage from lines was to be paid by the company rather than consumers. During the contest the Chamber's Public Utilities Committee was headed by three men as chairmen: H. G. Snyder, Fred D. Bearly and T. C. Thatcher. Members included Joseph Huckins Junior, John R. Boardman, John A. Brown, J. A. Deignan, A. E. Monroney and I. Frank Roach.

Unemployment still was a factor. The United Provident Association put cots in a building at 127 West Grand and provided meal tickets for jobless males. The Chamber continued its employment services as Southwestern Bell provided free telephones at the Chamber for volunteers to use in job searches. One set of volunteers, as a group, was the Women's Missionary Society of St. Lukes Methodist Church. Yet there were people who had traveling money. The city prepared a tourist park for them, with sanitary facilities and concrete ovens, just east of Belle Isle Park on Grand Boulevard. Madame Schumann-Heink gave a concert at Central High

School for a 1922 entertainment highlight.

There were bright tones in the city's economic picture. Home building spurted in the Winans-Harndale-Hawes Capitol Addition, after somewhat of a slowdown for eight years, largely because of the war and recession. G. A. Nichols took a forty acre tract west of Classen Boulevard, between Northwest Seventeenth and Twenty-first Streets (original Epworth property) and built seventy-five homes in addition to selling lots to people who desired to construct their own. Another forty acre tract north of Northwest Sixteenth Street, owned by Margaret McKinley, was purchased by Nichols and named Gatewood, as homes were built. An outdoor market, similar to an original one at Grand and Harvey, was put in across the street from the YMCA Building on Northwest Second Street.

By April 1922 the Chamber released impressive figures to show that Oklahoma City was both the industrial and political capital of the state. In gross amounts there were 227 firms making nearly $70 million worth of products, including value added by manufacturing. OG&E had become the state's largest utility firm. Bank clearings totaled $78,754,546 for the month of March. The nine national banks held $46,811,199. Harvey P. Everest, who began distributing magazines here in 1914 with receipts of $610 his first month, by 1922 attained monthly receipts of $20,174. Weekly and monthly magazine sales in Oklahoma City totaled more than 120,000, through ninety-three local dealers, as Mid-Continent News Company expanded to 456 dealers in other state towns, 397 in Kansas, eleven in Arkansas and Texas. One of the most popular was *Captain Billy's Whiz Bang*, in the oil fields particularly, while *Cosmopolitan, American, Ladies Home Journal* and *Saturday Evening Post* were best sellers in Oklahoma City. It was the latter two Curtis publications, and its *Country Gentleman*, with which Everest began his magazine distribution business.

What else was Oklahoma City at about one-third of its first century? It held an area of 17.295 square miles with 150 miles of paved streets, 155 miles of water mains and nine fire stations. There were two vaudeville houses, one musical stock company and twelve motion picture theaters. Previous year's building permits totaled $8,171,153. There had been more than $1 million in postal receipts. There were 367 industries; wholesale and jobbing interests valued at $145 million; retail business with $85 million in value; manufacturing valued at $111 million and 22,857 telephone subscribers; five trunkline railroads served the city with nine routes out and there were 68.64 miles of electric interurban; there were 2,100 acres in parks with 1,500 of that improved; a Better Business Bureau was established; fifty-three of the industries were newcomers.

WKY Radio made second history by broadcasting successfully from a moving train (with cooperation of the Frisco) from zero miles to 100 miles to Lawton. Radio was so new that the Chamber published a list of towns, ranging from Mexico to North Dakota, from which letters came telling about reception of this scientific marvel.

R. H. Hansen, superintendent of mails at the post office, compiled a report in late 1922 for President-Manager Ed Overholser of the Chamber, that was well publicised. In it the official pointed out that city delivery covered only ten square miles of the city's incorporated area. A comparison was made that data secured within the delivery area in 1922 disclosed 12,770 occupied residences with 282 vacancies, whereas in 1918 there were 10,960 residences occupied with but forty-eight vacancies, although of the larger number most were for sale and not rental. The residence tally did not include 1,765 rooming houses, some of which sheltered but two or three extra persons. There were 1,516 retail establishments within carrier limits and 127 outside foot delivery zones. The official arrived at a census figure of 112,006 by listing capacity of residences at 76,963; apartments, 12,333; shacks and tents, 2,810; hotels, 5,700 and rooming houses, 14,200.

Backing its claims as a convention city — a claim continuous in nature — the Chamber could point out that the new Coliseum had an audience capacity of more than 5,000 with 50,000 square feet of exhibit space; the City Auditorium could handle 2,000 persons on the first floor, 2,200 on the second floor and 150 far up in the balcony. The Elks Club House had an auditorium seating 400. The new Masonic Temple (Shrine Auditorium) under construction would provide various halls and rooms for gatherings of a few hundred to 2,500 in the auditorium. Designed by Layton, Smith and Forsyth, this limestone building cost $1,250,000 exclusive of ground. The building committee included A. E. Monroney, as chairman; Fred D. Bearly and W. J. Pettee. It would offer, in its time, everything from opera to Earl Carroll's Vanities.

The Huckins Hotel had banquet halls varying from 150 capacity to 325 while the Skirvin had rooms ranging from forty persons size to 300. Smaller hotels, such as the Lawrence and Kingkade, also had meeting space. Largest in theater seating was the Orpheum, with 2,000 on Grand, (once the Overholser Opera House, then Orpheum, later Warner Theater) with the Criterion's 1,800 and the Liberty with 1,600 capacity. Victor E. Harlow was chairman of the Chamber Convention Committee, with assistance of E. M. Snedeker. They announced proudly that for number of conventions scheduled for 1923, Oklahoma City stood third in the nation, preceded only by Chicago and New York, in that order. There were 119 conventions signed up for our city.

The summer of 1922 was the hottest in the city's history with temperatures up to 105 degrees. Autumn saw the first Community Chest organized with Judge C. B. Ames as chairman of the committee.

What Claude Weaver, the city's sixth postmaster, called "a million dollar post office and federal building," approached completion in 1923 in its block long front on Northwest Third Street, with a depth of 140 feet on Robinson and on Harvey. The location, purchased previously for $159,000, was considerably more valuable than when covered by $200 lots in 1890. The first building appropriation was $500,000. It was built of Oklahoma granite, Bedford stone and marble. Federal appropriations were secured at various times by Congressmen Dick T. Morgan, Joe B. Thompson and Weaver. Only five post offices in the nation were said to rank in a higher class than that in Oklahoma City. In 1923 Edwin Starkey, second man at Mid-Continent Life Insurance Company to R. T. Stuart Senior, was equally bullish on importance of the city as a life insurance center. Using the volume of insurance in force for Oklahoma, by legal reserve life insurance firms only, Starkey said there was $545,251,769 worth of policies in force — a 5.5 percent increase in a decade — and that the state's business centered in Oklahoma City, with an estimated seventy-five percent of the business written, and premiums paid, of the state total. Mid-Continent today is the state's oldest legal reserve life insurance company. Two other major "native" firms are Standard Life and Accident Insurance Company and Globe Life and Accident Insurance Company.

Hailed as "the finest filling station in the southwest" was the Marland Oil Company facility in a triangle of land between North Western and Classen Boulevard, roughly between Northwest Sixteenth and Seventeenth Streets, opened in January 1923. Marland later became Continental Oil Company but as a Conoco station this remains one of the longest continuously operated stations in one place in the city. A tangible reminder of the "king" role in agriculture of cotton, was the Traders Cotton Compress, across town to the southeast, with its $1 million plant that was largest west of the Mississippi then. Which did not impress Sir Harry Lauder at all when that Scottish singer strutted in place while singing "Roamin' in the Gloamin'" and other songs for a Chamber luncheon that packed a hall and left hundreds milling around outside. The fact that the city had 102 churches, forty-three modern school buildings and issued more than $4 million in residential building permits the previous year, might have been more impressive to the visitor.

The Western Union Telegraph Company in 1923 had its main office here at 14 North Broadway and seven branches around the city, including those at the Capitol and Stockyards, which were handling a total of nearly one million messages per month. This was the third largest traffic center of the Gulf Division, including Texas, Louisiana and Arkansas. The company operated its own cleaning, pressing and repair shop here for its fifty-nine uniformed messengers, among some 300 employes. An organization to cast a long shadow was organized in 1923 when the Town Club, a women's group, sponsored "Oklahoma City Beautiful," to push for landscaping, cleanups and such improvements of home and commercial areas. A contest started off the campaign with winners including the Marland Service Station at Classen and Northwest Seventeenth; Morris Packing Company; the home of Phil Baird Junior; Sparrow Park and Park Congregational Church. Mrs. Charles N. Gould was president of the sponsoring club at that time. In 1973 an "Oklahoma City Beautiful" organization continued active under Kenneth Dew of Fidelity Bank as president.

As secretary of the Oklahoma City Motor Car Dealers' Association early in 1923, Edgar T. Bell said that of the 244,883 vehicles registered in Oklahoma, ninety-five percent were distributed through the city, the largest distribution point between Kansas City and Dallas. For seven years city dealers and branch offices held annual automobile shows. Not only were models of vehicles available for viewing, but also there were "models" of feminine pulchritude to see, and hear, since entertainment was an added feature of the shows. As an example, that year there was Dorothy Lang, a former Ziegfeld Follies beauty, who danced; Mary Ellis, another New York importation, who sang; the Tripoli Trio, vocalists and instrumentalists. The Sooner Serenaders, a student dance band from the University of Oklahoma, provided dance music for those venturing on a floored arena at the Coliseum.

After the Walton regime a city election in April 1923 was relatively tame for voters, if any city election through the city's history could be labelled tame. O. A. Cargill, then county attorney, was elected mayor over Allen Street, his nearest opponent. Commissioners elected included Robert Parman, Warren E. Moore, Joe H. Patterson and W. F. Vahlberg.

The city became somewhat of a center for business colleges in 1923 with four of them, training more than 2,000 students, as Oklahoma City College (Epworth) drew those seeking academic degrees. So did Central State Teachers College at Edmond, fourteen miles away, which President John G. Mitchell said now served more than 2,500 students, after its start in 1891 as a normal school with one instructor and twenty-three students. Typical of women's organizations that have prodded civic consciousness throughout the city's history, was the Federated Patrons Club. In 1923 under leadership of Mrs. Cora M. Miley, the club put on a campaign to beautify city school grounds. In the Capitol Hill area Mount St. Mary's Academy, operated by the Sisters of Mercy, trained young women in cultural, academic, musical and dramatic courses. A campaign to raise $300,000 in the city and $100,000 outside to enlarge the Baptist Hospital at Northwest Twelfth and North Walker was instituted. The purpose was to increase its thirty-five beds to 200. The name was changed to Oklahoma City Hospital — later Oklahoma City General — and still later to Mercy Hospital.

In June 1923 the city, for the first time, established a supervised playground and community center for blacks. This was a coordinated effort by the Board of Education and various committees. The center was located at Douglass School on South Walnut Street. There were two paid supervisors and many volunteer helpers. Rotary Park, sponsored by that civic club, meanwhile became a demonstration park for such youth public facilities. The first effort to secure a form of municipal stadium here surfaced in mid-1923 when a committee headed by Robert K. Everest, with W. M. Longmire and John A. Brown as members, talked up a park project in the northwest sector, bounded by Eleventh and Fourteenth, McKinley and Douglas streets. They envisioned a large playground and a 40,000 seat stadium. Taft Stadium today is the nearest approach to that venerable idea. State Fair of Oklahoma directors in late 1973 authorized a feasibility study for a stadium at Fair Park.

Desire to assist in broadening the trade territory as the auto age became apparent, for personal short trip use as contrasted to the rails, led city interests to join other forces in securing money from all sources including federal, for a bridge across the South Canadian River at Newcastle. The cost was $435,000. The original structure, with improvements, now is a one-way lane southbound. Establishment of a Federal Reserve Branch Bank here was quite an economic boost in addition to bringing the city some national attention. This was largest in the nation in ratio to member banks. Early in 1923 in one month it handled more items than did similar banks at Atlanta and San Francisco. The Skirvin Hotel added an east wing to its original structure, doubling room capacity of the hotel.

A twelve-story Physicians and Surgeons Building — later Medical Arts — was placed diagonally across the street at Broadway and First, with the Security National Bank on the ground floor. The Stockyards National Bank became ninth of members in the Oklahoma City Clearing House Association.

John A. Whitehurst, president of the State Board of Agriculture, said that Oklahoma City was hub of the state's valuable wheat industry. What may have interested civic leaders a bit more, at the time, was a long awaited declaration from the First Assistant Postmaster General of the United States, that as of July 1, 1923, this post office address would be "Oklahoma City" officially. Local folk had since 1890 called it that, but to the federal establishment it was first Oklahoma Station, then simply Oklahoma, which was too much for Walter Lybrand, who kept importuning officials for the little four letter word addition. He even got a third assistant postmaster general here for a round of personal promotion over the matter. The issue was not that simple. A petition with 20,000 signatures was procured. United States Senator John W. Harreld and Representative Fletcher Swank of the Fifth District, also lobbied for the change.

The city could claim five daily newspapers in 1923. They were *The Daily Oklahoman, Oklahoma City Times, Oklahoma News* (Scripps-Howard) the *Oklahoma Livestock News* and the *Daily Legal News.* Not the least of industrial plants was that of the Ford Motor Company on West Main, turning out up to 244 vehicles daily from its assembly line with a monthly payroll of $80,000. It served all Oklahoma and twenty-six counties in Texas, including the state's Panhandle. There were 461 employes and all executives here had moved up through the ranks. A massive tree planting across the city was successful, after a campaign by the Oklahoma City Beautiful group sponsored by the Town Club, with cooperation of the Oklahoma Nurserymen's and Oklahoma Florists Associations. This aided success, also, of the city's first Flower Show at Merrie Gardens, which drew displays from across the nation. Exhibits were valued at $300,000.

Need required a school building program of $1,900,000 for substantial additions to existing schools and some new ones. The first Community Fund drive in December 1923 had a goal of $216,998. Apportionments were made to the Fund office itself, to the American Red Cross, Boy Scouts, Holme's Home of Redeeming Love (for unwed mothers), Oklahoma Children's Home Society, Public Health Nursing Bureau, Salvation Army, Sunbeam Home, Tuberculosis Society, United Provident Association, YMCA, YWCA and an "emergency fund."

Earlier in the year some of the more notable movie personalities were seen on city screens, silent, of course, since the first all talking picture came into being July 6, 1928. (It was "Lights of New York," shown at the Strand Theater in New York City.) At the Criterion here one could see Harold Lloyd in "Safety First;" Richard Barthelmess and Dorothy Gish were in "Fury" at the Empress; at the Capitol Milton Sills and Anna Q. Nilsson were starring in "Adam's Rib" while at the Liberty, Pola Negri was again being the great vamp of her time in "Mad Love."

18

— and Then Came Oil

I N COMMON WITH ALMOST EVERYONE else in the nation, and in fact most of humanity worldwide, Oklahoma Cityans suffered through a great depression triggered by the stock market crash of October 1929. So far as the city area was concerned, effects of that dire economic period would have been much worse except for four things: discovery of oil in the Oklahoma City Field on December 4, 1928; removal of Rock Island and Frisco tracks from the heart of the downtown area and their relocation; four years of more than $1 million per month in building permits; and construction of four public buildings on the Civic Center strip vacated by railroads.

From the standpoint of economics and stimulation to growth the oil field probably was most important. Several test wells had been drilled around the city and in Oklahoma county before the discovery.

Actually there had been dreams of oil for many years. The city area was hardly a year old when some now unknown wildcatter started a test about where Northeast Fourth Street and the Santa Fe tracks are, then some distance from the business area. A prayer picnic was held. A minister asked a blessing for the drillers, their crews and cable tools, but the hole was abandoned later at about a 600 foot depth.

Geology should be given credit for discovery of the city field. George D. Morgan and Jerry B. Newby were among the first geologists to observe favorable structures here, with their work between 1917 and 1919. This was mainly surface geology. Geophysical probing was in the future to become a more efficient finalizing method of indicating oil and gas possibilities.

In the autumn of 1919, L. E. Trout studied the same area that Morgan and Newby walked out, and mapped what is now the southern part of the Oklahoma City field. In 1925 L. E. Trout, Claude Dalley, S. H. Woods and L. R. Trout drilled a well near the Cleveland county line to a depth of 4,480 feet, but found only traces of oil. That year also, John R. Bunn worked out a surface high north of the capitol for a "deep" test at 7,180 feet. That well, drilled in 1926 by the Cromwell Oil and Gas Company, disclosed some oil showings. (Calling it deep was proper for those times at more than 7,000 feet, where in 1973 there are wells probing the Anadarko Basin in Western Oklahoma at contract depths beyond 25,000 feet.) There was enough oil interest here in April 1926 that the Rock Island laid on an overnight "Oil Special" between Amarillo and the city.

Much credit for the Oklahoma City field should go to G. E. Anderson, then on the faculty of the University of Oklahoma. He was employed on a consulting basis by the Indian Territory Illuminating Oil Company, a glamorous name later absorbed by Cities Service. Anderson found a southward projecting nose, outlined on the Garber sandstone-Hennessey shale contact, and extending through Oklahoma City. The ITIO's geological department mapped the area, resulting in the leasing of more than 6,000 acres.

The Foster Petroleum Corporation of Bartlesville joined the ITIO in drilling the Number One Oklahoma City well on land purchased from Mrs. Celia Hall. The site chosen for the test was about six miles south of the city, in the SE-SE of Section Twenty-Four, Range Eleven North and Three West near present Southeast Fifty-ninth Street and Bryant. Drilling began June 12, 1928. As the well was drilled it gave up several oil and gas showings, the most important from 3,997 to 4,012 feet, where a flow of 47 million cubic feet of gas was encountered.

In late November the Arbuckle limestone was found, saturated with oil, and casing was set. While drilling the plug with cable (or standard) tools, gas pressure forced tools up in the hole, creating a bridge. For two weeks crews tried to remove the bridge. At 3 P.M., on Tuesday, December 4, pressure broke through, sending tools into the derrick and a flow of oil above the derrick top. In the first twenty-four hours a total of 4,909 barrels of forty gravity oil was produced. Ten days later the well was deepened to 6,455 feet. In its first twenty-seven days the Number One Oklahoma City produced 110,496 barrels of oil at a price of $1.56 per barrel. The mother lode of "black gold" was tapped.

The ITIO-Foster interests controlled all the new field within a radius of two miles of the discovery well for about 6,500 acres of leases except a few large tracts owned by Tom Slick, Sinclair Oil and Gas Company, Coline Oil Company, Roxana Petroleum Company and W. R. Ramsey. Only a Wirt Franklin lease on the Robert Lord section cornered the half-section under the discovery well on the southwest.

On December 12, 1928, the Empire Pipeline Company completed a line from the well to a railroad loading rack five miles away. Total drilling cost of the first Oklahoma City well was $57,000, exclusive of the pipe and rig, or derrick. Drilling time was five months and twelve days from spudding in until the well was completed.

Announcement of the new field brought thousands of people here. Shanty towns sprang up near the producing area. Bodine City was built south of the well and Emerson City flanked in on the east. South of the well, also, the Sutton townsite was laid out. Soon half a dozen townsite offices were extolling their offerings. All of them folded within a year.

Oklahoma City thus became the new oil center. From the hour that radio broadcast to the world that a major field had been discovered, another Southwestern metropolis experienced adolescent growing pains. Daily its hotels, particularly the Huckins and Skirvin, buzzed with promoters, lease hounds, brokers and speculators. Exuberance and optimism sparked a Chamber dinner soon after the well came in, in the course of which a five year building program designed to save Oklahoma City from boomtown chaos, was formulated. A prediction was made that the city might have a population of 400,000 by 1940. The Skirvin Hotel announced

The Oklahoma City Oil Field crowded with derricks, as it looked from the air in January, 1930.

plans for a 150 room addition and WKY Radio quickly went big time by signing for a National Broadcasting Company hookup.

On June 20, 1929, Sinclair completed the second producer in the field. Coline brought in its Number One Olds seven days later for a 5,400 barrel well, in the lower Simpson sand, thereby convincing everyone that Oklahoma City did indeed have a major field.

Lease by lease, development spread northward. As it approached city limits of that time, the city council invoked an early day business zoning ordinance to create limited drilling areas, to prevent encroachment. The first zone, "U-7," north of Southeast Twenty-second Street on the east side of the city, was established on May 10, 1929. A second zone, north of Grand Boulevard, with North High Avenue on the west, was designated on December 3.

There were few restrictions within a permitted zone. Derricks, slush pits, steel and earthen tanks, invaded industrial and residential areas. March 4, 1930, the U-7 zone, along with a strip across the south edge of the city, was opened under regulations. Five months later still another zone was opened between Southeast Fifteenth and Southeast Twenty-ninth streets, and between North Byers Avenue and the Santa Fe tracks on the west. A fourth zone was opened November 25, 1930, between the Santa Fe railroad and Santa Fe Avenue, north of Grand Boulevard, while still others came later.

By summer of 1929 the Oklahoma City field had grown with several new wells flowing 15,000 barrels daily. By September 12 there were fifteen producing wells in the field, making 60,000 barrels a day, while nineteen other wells were drilling. An oil man's committee had asked the state Corporation Commission for a thirty day shutdown because oil was being produced too rapidly on a declining market. On September 11 the commission, heeding the pleas, issued Order Number 4,804, applicable to the city field, which had reached 67,507 barrels daily on September 11 and 12, declined to 12,935 barrels for a twenty-four hour period.

The Oklahoma City Producers Association, under the presidency of Wirt Franklin, played a vital part in meeting over-production and field control problems. Franklin, head of his own petroleum corporation while vice-president and manager of the Cromwell-Franklin Oil Company, was a large acreage holder in the field.

On September 25 the association employed Otto B. Bradford as field umpire, and set up a system similar to that in the Greater Seminole field, with Bradford serving as liaison officer between producers and the Corporation Commission. When the field was reopened on October 12, many wells were better producers than they had been at time of the shutdown. A small lesson in conservation.

The producers association and oil company representatives had a simple proration ready when the shutdown was lifted. Producers were divided into "A" and "B" classes according to section lines and to prevent overloading the pipeline gathering system at one end of the field. (Four classes were needed a year later.) Each class was permitted to flow its wells four days in succession during November, up to forty percent of each well's potential, with the allowable increased to fifty percent in December. On January 27, 1930, production in the field was decreased to twenty-five percent of the potential. This plan was effective temporarily. At 1929 year's end there were fifty-three producing wells in the field, 161 drilling, twenty-six shutdowns due to operational difficulties, and twenty-seven shutdowns because of proration. By March 1930 there were 135 completed wells and 173 drilling wells on location.

Many temporarily wild wells were caused by strong gas pressure. Sand produced with the oil flow caused much cutting of control fittings to create more problems. A fire came early in March when the Sinclair-Amerada Kinter Number Five well, on the east side of the field, blew out and burned 1,200,000,000 cubic feet of gas in twelve days before it was brought under control.

The most awe inspiring spectacle — and the only one most people remember — was staged by the "Wild Mary Sudik" on March 26, 1930, when it blew out tools from a well producing 20,000 barrels of oil daily with about 200 million cubic feet of gas. The Sudik Number One, an ITIO-Foster well in the south part of the field, had penetrated the top of the Wilcox sand formation, second of the prolific pay sands found. Strong winds from the Wild Mary blew a film of oil as far as Norman before typically reversing wind direction.

There was neither a control head nor master gate left to shut in the well. There was only enough surface pipe to make a connection remaining. After a struggle of five days, a master gate was swung into place and anchored over the surface pipe, but it would not hold. Finally, on April 6, the well was brought under control. H. M. Myracle, with a crew of mechanics and engineers from the American Iron and Machine Company, built a special connection that was put on a rig and swung from lines inside the derrick. The die nipple was swung over and enough new threads cut on the surface pipe to permit the new control head to be screwed on and hold. It was a most difficult job but it was done well under human pressure of urgency. Two other wild wells were tamed later in the year when the Sigman Number One and the Morgan-Stout Number One wells went berserk, but they were not as wild as Mary Sudik. So far as public attention was concerned they were anti-climactic.

On May 27, 1930, the Hall-Briscoe-Holmes Number One well was completed for 17,000 barrels, to be first to reach the southeast edge of the city, as it existed then. By June 21 the Continental Oil Company had extended the field into Cleveland county with its own Sudik Number One well.

It was drill bits nibbling toward the city limits that created what became quite a civic movement over extension of the field into the city. There was to be division among city leaders that involved more than the "haves" and "have nots" of oil and property interests, residential lot owners and guardians of public lands, such as city ownership of Fair Park, east of Eastern Avenue.

March 4, 1930, the city council created an ordinance prohibiting drilling within the corporate limits, except in a "U" zone — one north of East Reno Avenue and another across the south edge of the city — and drilling within those zones was limited to one well per city block, with royalties unitized for property owners in that block, since no one could tell from under which portion the oil came.

During 1930 there were attacks on proration orders of the Corporation Commission made by the C. C. Julian Oil and Royalty Company and Champlin Refining Company, before the State Supreme Court and Federal District Court, but the suits were denied. Market demand for oil was a major factor in shaping the commission's order. Not only was there a depression that affected almost everything, but by July 1931 lush production in East Texas caused crude prices to tumble as Humpty off the wall, to a chilling sixteen cents for 34.0 to 34.9 gravity oil. At that point in time, Oklahoma City and East Texas could have provided world needs of oil outside the United States if they could have produced to the possible potential.

This was too much for Governor William H. "Alfalfa Bill" Murray. On August 4, 1931, he proclaimed a state of emergency and declared martial law within a 50-foot zone around each well, and ordered the National Guard to take control of twenty-nine Oklahoma fields having 3,106 wells, and to close even all prorated wells until the price of oil rose from its abysmal depth to at least one dollar a barrel. In October he relented a bit. Control was lifted to the extent that wells could operate at a five percent allowable of their potential.

That was the situation for about eight months. Meanwhile, there were accusations that "hot oil" was being produced in subtle defiance of the governor's orders. It was alleged even that, if an inspector came around to check if a valve was open permitting flow of oil into a gathering system, he could "tighten" a valve which was of a reverse, or "left-handed" nature, and effectively open it for a flow.

On June 6, 1932, military control was invoked with a bang of rhetoric and Colonel Cicero Murray, a cousin of the governor, was placed in charge of the city field which, being newest and most flush at the time, was Number One target of the governor's ire. The operation-proration committee and the advisory committee were abolished and their records seized by the militia. The martial law zone was extended about tanks and pipe lines, in addition to wells, and meters were installed to prevent "hot oil" from running. The meters intensified talk of reverse valves. The field was closed down entirely from March 4 to 14, 1933, except for wells that were having salt water troubles. They would be worthless if attempts were not made to correct that situation.

The state legislature on April 10, 1933, enacted House Bill 481, a proration law. This law became a pattern for other states. It created a proration staff within the Corporation Commission and had much effect on reducing illegal over-production.

Allegations that "hot oil" runs were being made from the field, in defiance of legal proration, to a degree verified in the minds of some persons that rumors of "reverse valves" were true.

Howard E. Cole, a certified public accountant, in 1933 had a contract with the city providing that he could receive one-fourth of all money that he could collect for the city, on hot oil runs from wells on city property. (This had a precedent: tax ferrets in state government worked on a percentage basis, locating and disclosing tax evasions.) The agreement with Cole called for secrecy on identity of oil firms involved until April 1934, to give Cole a free hand in locating evaders and collecting from them. He claimed that he could recover a quarter million dollars, at least, that otherwise would never be paid in royalties.

In January 1934 an initial payment of $52,000 was made by an oil firm through an Enid bank, to Francis G. "Bus" Baker, city auditor. Cole then received a payment of $17,662, the overage being on assurance from the payer that more was forthcoming. Councilman Frank Martin demanded that the oil firm's identity be disclosed in open meeting. Naturally other firms not connected with the instant case came out with similar demands. This circumstance clouded Cole's efforts but the issue flamed out like a gas flare on a well in time. An old shield was held up by all potential or suspected hot oil runners in refutation of charges, direct and indirect — "not proven."

By October 1935, the "Governor's Mansion" area east of the state capitol was opened by the British-American Oil Producing Company, with its Mary Green Number One, northeast of the mansion. A rather bitter city election saw adherents of drilling within city limits win out, although even before that, the city's right to forbid the state drilling on its own land within the city was debated hotly.

What amounted to the discovery well of this new area around the capitol was most unpopular to many residents of northeast Oklahoma City, particularly those owners in Lincoln Terrace. They envisioned wells from outside the city on the southeast making their way across their lots to state owned land, including the University of Oklahoma Medical Center, north and south of Northeast Thirteenth Street. The mansion area well gave the state ideas, for it seemed to indicate a geological fault that extended from the original field northwestward.

On March 25, 1936, an election was held under a city ordinance to create a new one-mile square drilling zone immediately north of state property on Northeast Twenty-third Street, and west of the older zone.

Voters approved the measure and operators promptly staked fifty-three locations in the new zone.

Additional controversy developed immediately over the possibility that wells in this zone would drain oil from under state property — this time the state being involved rather than residential property owners. Governor Ernest W. Marland, taking a leaf from Governor Murray's book, called out the Guard briefly to halt exploration until the state could act in its own defense.

The State Board of Affairs awarded leases on sixteen separate tracts to the Sunray Oil Company and one tract to Anderson-Pritchard Oil Corporation. Governor Marland, who once had been an oil man himself, rushed the start of five wells near the capitol and had Guardsmen patrolling the area to keep city authorities from interfering. The city tried to get an injunction against the state land drilling but Marland refused to accept service of a subpoena and made that attempt fruitless.

The Sunray-State Number One well, east of the governor's mansion, was the first state well to find production and established a potential of 11,263 barrels in June 1936. At this time Phillips Petroleum Company bought a half-interest in the state tract from Sunray. The Capitol Site Number One well, directly south and across the street from the capitol, was completed by Phillips on June 8, 1942. A special act of the legislature was necessary to permit angle, or directional drilling of this well, to a point beneath the capitol building itself. It is said that the bottom of the hole is 431 feet north of the top of the hole. The well was drilled to 6,618 feet in 171 days. The well's initial production was 545 barrels of 39.1 gravity oil in twenty-four hours. This well produced a total of 1,460,377 barrels of oil to January 1, 1973, with present daily production of thirty-five barrels. The state has a royalty of one-fourth of the income from this well, in contrast to the usual one-eighth. It has recovered $671,499 in royalties and obtained $103,619 in taxes from this one well.

State capitol area leases produced a total of 8,290,934 barrels to January 1, 1973. As of that date, the state has received an income of $14,-792,666 from wells in the capitol area. There is no way to estimate value of the tourist attraction that the wells, specifically that just south of the capitol building, with details about it displayed in the capitol first floor rotunda have provided, but they are a tangible asset so far as visitors are concerned.

The same legislation that permitted the Capitol Site Number One well also allowed the Lincoln Terrace Number One well, by British-American, to be drilled directionally under that residential area, from the Oklahoma Historical Society grounds. This well produced 412,292 barrels before being closed down in January 1960. The Society later was able to obtain the derrick as a gift. In 1963 the legislature assigned an area around the derrick to the Society for development of an oil museum. Efforts have been made since 1964 to collect materials for the outdoor portion of the museum. More than a quarter of a million dollars worth of equipment has been donated by various oil companies, drilling contractors and individuals. Plans have been prepared for a museum building to contain smaller items, dioramas, a library and meeting rooms.

The well north of the Capitol was lighted to celebrate the new capitol office buildings.

In late November of 1936 a "Pageant of Petroleum Progress" was held here, coincident with a meeting of the Independent Petroleum Association of America, complete with receptions and a parade. Not the least attraction, so far as the non-oil public was concerned, was bringing in an "instant gusher" in the city field. This was accomplished satisfactorily, and under controlled timing, by piping gas into a small producer and through high pressure, sending a stream of oil up over the crown block of the rig. It was not coincidental that photographers for national newsreels, Paramount and Fox-Movietone, were on hand to film this spectacular for nationwide distribution in movie houses.

The city field in early 1973 had 294 wells producing 5,200 barrels daily. With recovery of more than 730 million barrels to that time, it is

CHARLES N. GOULD
*"Father of state
oil development"*

WIRT FRANKLIN
*Founded Independent
Petroleum Association*

FRANK BUTTRAM
*Oilman, civic leader
and philanthropist*

ROBERT S. KERR
*Oilman, governor,
and U.S. Senator*

ranked as a great oil field, one with a potential in excess of 100 million barrels. According to late statistical reports, it is ranked ninth in the nation in total recovery. The prolific East Texas field ranks first in the states, followed by several California fields and the Sho-Vel-Tum district in Southern Oklahoma, which really is a consolidation of several fields.

There are some unusual characteristics about the city field. It has produced from at least thirty different zones. It was the first major field in the Mid-Continent area in which producing wells were more than one mile deep, and where development was with rotary tools, although some rotary rigs appeared at Tonkawa and Three Sands in 1921.

The Phillips Petroleum Company community leases in Section Three, Township Eleven North, Range Three West, have recovered more than twenty-two million barrels for the largest recovery in the Oklahoma City field. Our field was more widely spaced than many earlier flush fields, such as Spindletop near Beaumont, or Three Sands in our own state, relative to total land area. Also, its limits were defined with a smaller percentage of dry holes than many fields, a far cry from pure wildcatting.

More than 1,650 wells were drilled in our field and 1,545 were oil and/or gas producers. The field could be said to extend in a generally northwesterly direction from the original well, which might include the West Edmond field, brought in by Ace Gutowsky in a willow wand witching type of location staking, after almost every geologist in the country discounted the chance of finding any oil in the area. After every imaginable attempt to raise necessary drilling costs, Gutowsky made them all look foolish, although in the oil business there are more tales to the contrary.

Extending drilling through Oklahoma City itself, Jones & Pellow Oil Company, in the latter part of 1972, drilled to a depth of 7,021 feet by the Baptist Children's Home near Northwest Sixty-third and Pennsylvania. After the well was plugged back to 6,750 feet it flowed 300 barrels per hour with 180,000 cubic feet of gas. The second Wilcox, Simpson and Oswego strata were tested before production was found in the Viola limestone. This was the first well inside the city in twenty years.

This well is considered part of the Belle Isle field which was opened in 1963 by Robert A. Hefner III, with his Belle Isle Number One, just east of the Oklahoma Gas & Electric Company's generating plant. This was a dual completion in the Cleveland sand and Oolithic limestone. The Cleveland was perforated from 5,756 to 5,776 feet, while the limestone was perforated from 5,886 to 5,891 feet. As of January 1, 1973, this well provided 206,205 barrels of crude.

Development of any major oil field is due to a large number of people who form the leadership, make decisions on behalf of themselves or their employers, and often add a touch of glamor through their own personalities. This level is known. It is patently unfair to call them completely responsible for bringing in wells that, in total, make up a field. There are thousands of persons involved after scouts, geologists and leasers do their work: rig builders, drillers, roughnecks, roustabouts, pipeline crews, truckers, dozer operators, tool pushers and so on. Some of these folk are personalities, in their way, too. Unlike the other level, most of them pass through a field and go on to the next El Dorado, leaving little of written record behind them.

There are quite a few people who left their mark in some fashion on this field. At the normal risk of leaving some unrecorded here one can identify these persons at least:

Jerry Newby, the consulting geologist, has said also that George D. Morgan was the rock hound who made first observations of the city field area, in 1917. "In the fall of 1917 the Oklahoma City Chamber of Commerce and Frank Buttram, my brother-in-law, employed me to check north of the capitol building and the area east of the city," Newby once remarked about his own activities.

"I found what I now know was an unconformity and the east slope of a massive sandstone. All of this was north of the North Canadian River. Frank held the rod for me while I did the checking. I never did learn what they did with my information," Newby added.

Homer Keegan, who operated the Triangle Royalty Corporation, was employed in the land department of the ITIO. In late 1927 Keegan was allotted $42,000 and told to start obtaining oil and gas leases in Oklahoma county.

"That really wasn't much money," he said once. "We didn't have any trouble getting leases. Some geologists had said there would never be a drop of oil in Oklahoma county. Personally, I wouldn't have spent a dime of my own money. Leases were going for $5 an acre on a five-year term." Keegan did his bit of leasing for four months.

Schoenfeld & Hunter drilled the discovery well for the Indian Territory Illuminating Oil Company on a cost-plus contract, with two five-man crews working twelve hour shifts, called tours in those days and pronounced "towers." The drillers were Charles H. Rupe and Sidney Hodges. The well produced more than a million barrels of oil before 1934. It was shut down from 1934 to 1937, then produced gas for a few years before being converted to gas storage.

The Indian Territory Illuminating Oil Company, was started by H. V. Foster of Bartlesville in 1904. It was purchased by Cities Service Oil Company in 1941. Burdette Blue, vice-president and later president, was very active in company affairs of that firm with a colorful name.

Other chief ITIO officials in the Oklahoma City district in 1928 and later were Art Hoenig, vice-president for production; W. Pat Sutton, superintendent of production; C. E. Wright, chief petroleum engineer and W. W. Clawson, district geologist.

December 9, 1971, Cities Service Oil Company donated the first well rig and two-thirds of an acre surrounding it to the Oklahoma Historical Society. The well was plugged but casing in the hole and the wellhead fitting were left. The Historical Society also was presented the original well log, a map of the tract, the original daily drilling report, and a plaque commemorating the discovery.

Among other personalities in the city field was the colorful Tom B. Slick, called "king of the wildcatters" because he opened more pools in the Mid-Continent area than any other individual operator. At his death in 1930 at the age of forty-seven, Slick was perhaps the second largest operator in the city field, with forty-five producing wells in which a majority interest was owned, exclusive of those shared with Prairie Oil and Gas Company. Slick sold a half-interest in his holdings to Prairie in 1929 for a reputed $40 million. This included 8,000 acres of leases. Prairie later was absorbed by Sinclair.

J. Steve Anderson and Lev H. Prichard, who organized Anderson-Prichard Oil Corporation, were active in early field development. In 1923 and 1924 these men leased several thousand acres which later became a part of the field. When the discovery well was being drilled, Anderson-Prichard still held a portion of leases secured five years before. Immediately they started buying more leases. In 1929 they contracted with Tom Slick to develop the Hooper lease for a one-half interest. Eight producing wells were drilled there. By November 1930, the company had eighteen completed wells with eight more drilling.

W. R. Ramsey and W. E. Ramsey, with money from the Carter county fields that created Ramsey Petroleum Corporation, were quite active in early attempts to discover oil in Oklahoma county. When the discovery well came in their firm had considerable acreage and began drilling two wells on the Fortson lease. Before they completed either well, Mid-Kansas Oil and Gas Company of Tulsa offered the Ramseys $2 million for their holdings in the field. This deal was consumated in February 1929. Mid-Kansas was a subsidiary of the Ohio Oil Company, of Findlay, Ohio, now known as Marathon Oil Company.

The Ramsey Brothers were victims of an oil field oddity. L. E. Trout, one of the city field's first geologists, assembled a block of leases and drilled a test to 3,500 feet. He was able to go deeper only by selling an interest, quite a frequent occurrence in those days. He prevailed upon W. R. Ramsey to take over the test. It was drilled to 4,500 feet, only to get a dry hole. Later, Sinclair Oil and Gas Company obtained leases in the same general area and got a producer less than 100 feet from the Trout test, by drilling 2,000 feet deeper. That well was completed for around 40,000 barrels per day in August 1930.

The Coline Oil Company, a subsidiary of the Santa Fe Railroad, was one of the first operators in the field. The company acquired a block

Looking south from the Oklahoma State Capitol at the oil wells in east Oklahoma City.

of leases in the south part in 1926. Its first well as started on December 28, 1928, and completed on June 27, 1929. H. L. Briggs was general manager and E. A. Paschal was chief geologist. Paschal in 1926 recognized presence of a fold south of Oklahoma City and recommended purchase of the leases acquired by his company.

Wirt Franklin, also from Carter county's fields, was president of the corporation bearing his name. (His Palacine brand name will be recalled by persons who can remember that mammoth statue of an Indian that stood at crest of the winding drive on US 77, over the Arbuckle mountains, and elsewhere). He also was head of Cromwell-Franklin Oil Company in association with Joe Cromwell, in drilling the first deep test north of the state capitol, leading to defining the city field.

By 1931 these two firms had about fifty wells in the major Oklahoma City pool. Active in all matters concerning proration and conservation, Franklin also was an organizer of the Independent Petroleum Association of America. Frank M. Porter was vice-president and production manager for the Franklin interests. Later that Ardmoreite, too, was president of the Independent Petroleum Association. From his earlier activities in the Seminole area a pool he opened was named after Cromwell.

Shell Petroleum Corporation was one of the first to buy leases in the city field in 1926 and completed its first well on September 11, 1929. Connected with Royal Dutch Shell, a major part of this firm's stock traces to the royal family of the Netherlands, through Queen Wilhelmina, and to Sir Henri Detering, its long time president.

Although Phillips Petroleum Company was a pioneer in the field, so far as acreage was concerned, it had only five oil producers as of November 1, 1930. However, due to the astuteness of Dean A. McGee, then district geologist for Phillips, the company obtained choice leases in the northern part of the field, under which lay the prolific Wilcox sand that became a major producer. L. B. Holland was production superintendent for Phillips.

McGee now is chairman and chief executive officer of Kerr-McGee Corporation. That firm, now involved in processing of fossil and nuclear fuels in addition to worldwide drilling operations and other activities, had its beginnings when Anderson-Kerr Drilling Company moved its two drilling rigs from Ada to the city field in 1930. In a short period the company, composed then of Robert S. Kerr and his brother-in-law, Jim Anderson, acquired part ownership in fourteen producing wells in this field. McGee became a partner of Kerr's later.

Sinclair obtained school land leases in the field in 1928. By November 1930 Sinclair had fifty-three producing wells. Glenn Harroun was district superintendent while John E. Van Dall was district geologist. Van Dall was one of the rock hounds who worked out the structure north of the state capitol, with John R. Bunn, in 1925.

Among large independents in our field was the Skelly Oil Company, founded by W. G. Skelly of Tulsa. By 1930 that company had sixteen producing wells and five drilling tests underway.

Forrest Harper and Roy J. Turner became active in the field soon after its discovery in December of 1928. They formed their firm and throughout that winter personally tramped the slush, buying and trading for leases and shares of leases, eventually to have interests in twenty-three wells in the Walnut Grove area and an interest in four wells east of there. When the city area between Northeast Fourth and Northeast Eighth streets was developed, Harper and Turner worked out arrangements with Phillips for interests in twenty wells. They also had interests in several wells north of Northeast Twenty-third Street in the mansion area. Turner later sold his interests.

With advent of town lot drilling in the north end of the field — for which Phillips was one of the most actively visible supporters regarding municipal elections on drilling zone extension — many independent operators and promoters flocked to the city. The older zones were controlled largely by majors or the most affluent independents.

Some newcomers included Acme Gas and Oil Company, Blackstock and Mabee, California Operating Company, Century Petroleum Company, Cunard Oil Company, Denver Producing and Refining Company, Don Leon Oil Company, Glidden Oil Company, Gant and Garvin, Government Petroleum Company, Huddleston and McKeehan, L. C. Hivick, Morgan Petroleum Company, Oils Incorporated, Plains Petroleum Company, Russell Petroleum Company, C. E. Stout, Traders Oil and Gas Company, Larkins and Warr, and Wrightsmith Oil Company. Other drilling contractors active in the field included Helmerich & Payne, John Mabee, P. C. Perry, Jack Shaffer, Patrick Drilling Company, Spears Drilling Company and Sultan Drilling Company.

19

Growth Before Groans

I N LATE MARCH 1924 A NEW thirty-inch water main from Lake Overholser to a new water filtration plant for the city was laid, one just like those of major cities in the nation, which impressed those who voted bonds to pay for improvements. It pleased health officials, also, for they blamed flooding of the year before and inadequate water treatment for causing illness. The city now had 198 miles of water lines.

Construction from the mid-1920's to end of the decade was a city highlight for it marked many major developments in structural size and financial outlay. In ratio the pace would not be duplicated again until the decade of the 1960's in building or building planning. Kerr's Department Store rose beside the streetcar terminal station with eight stories. B&M Clothing Store (Barth and Myer) moved into new quarters. The Halliburton Company, under R. D. Halliburton, made its third move in twenty years, ending at Main and Hudson as Gloyd-Halliburton. Now the structure holds city offices as an annex to City Hall.

A new supplier for construction material, Midwest Steel Company, opened its plant at 1424 West Main. The Elks Lodge had a new $500,000 home on the northwest corner of Northwest Third and Harvey, later the Key Building, still later the Oklahoma Natural Building. An art exhibit was the first big public event in the Elks Building, a civic enterprise headed by Frank Buttram, with the local Yunt Galleries bringing in the major art show. Interest in visual arts grew rapidly.

Building permits for the first six months of 1924 totaled more than $4.6 million, which those quick to offer growth statistics pointed out was more than a million in excess of similar permits in Tulsa. The National Editorial Association held its annual convention here in May, with Walter M. Harrison as general chairman. Many visitors added tours into Texas and Mexico.

New industries employing 830 persons added to the city's activities in 1925. A convention economic impact was noticeable when 75,000 visitors attended the 228 meetings offered. City voters turned down a $1.75 million sewer bond issue, but did vote more than a million dollars worth of street improvement which included a viaduct on South Walker over the river and railroad tracks.

The Daily Oklahoman built an "ideal home" at 2741 Northwest Seventeenth Street, in Crestwood, and put out a special edition to tell all about its marvels. These included the latest in lighting and furnishings and a push button door for the attached garage. Unlike many other innovations the door was made here by the Overhead Door Company. Governor and Mrs. Martin E. Trapp were first guests at the official opening. The Crestwood addition was developed by John J. Harden with G. R. Veeder in actual charge. Harbour-Longmire furnished the house. The Crestwood addition was so new that the paper gave directions about driving there by auto, out Northwest Sixteenth, or making a trip by the Las Vegas streetcar. Which a majority of people did.

In March 1926 the city got its second radio station in KFJF which featured activities of American Legion Post Thirty-five among its other programs. Not only was this the first Legion "sponsored" station, it had much to do with that post in little more than a year becoming the nation's third largest with 2,500 members. Famed wildcatter Tom B. Slick moved his residence here in the spring of 1926, purchasing the Bass home at 327 Northwest Eighteenth Street. Slick's local oil interests were handled by Charles F. Urschel.

Buick Motor Company built a new building on the northwest corner of Broadway and Northwest Tenth Street that would, in its time, house many other varied activities. Downtown building construction saw a big spurt in 1926 with most of it completed the following year, as more than $16.8 million in new construction was underway. Included was the Petroleum Building at Northwest Second and Robinson, later the Republic Building, now the Midland Mortgage Building; the Perrine Building, a block south and across the street, now the Cravens Building; a seven story auto hotel on the south side of First Street, built by Reinhart and Donovan, later demolished in the First National Bank expansion; the Mid-Continent Life Insurance Building at Shartel and Classen Drive; and the first planned apartment hotel, the Aberdeen, at Northwest Fifteenth and Robinson. The University of Oklahoma Medical School and the Governor's Mansion would emerge in 1927 after legislative appropriations. St. Anthony's, Wesley and Oklahoma City General Hospitals all expanded; Southwestern Bell added a nine story building; OG&E built its home at Northwest Third and Harvey, of six stories, later adding an additional six as planned originally; the Wells-Roberts Hotel was added to the downtown area.

The business community noticed that the J. B. Klein Iron and Steel Foundry had grown considerably since its founding in 1909 as the J. B. Klein & Company Iron and Wire Works. The name was shortened in 1912 and after 1926, when Klein met with accidental death, management was under R. W. Robberson, whose own firm succeeded Klein later. In 1926 Klein got a competitor when American Iron and Machine Works moved here from Tonkawa. In mid-1926 R. L. Polk & Company published a city directory that reported population at 144,415, almost a 4,000 increase over the previous year. A similar directory gave Tulsa a census of 126,090. The first half of 1926 saw eighty new business firms or industries settle here with addition of 200 new families. Victor E. Harlow announced that his publishing firm was seeking authors to make the concern truly Southwestern in character.

W. J. Pettee, the city's first hardware merchant, was pointed out as a premier example of making a success in the American way. Floyd Lamb told a story about Pettee, who liked to work the floor of his store, selling a saddle and waiting to day's end to mark up the charge account. He could not recall to whom he sold it so charged a saddle to three men. "Two of them paid for it," Lamb recalled in 1934. Oklahoma Hardware Company, now the state's oldest and largest, became a major wholesaler in this period. It had been founded in 1901 by S. E. Clarkson and A. W. Boyd, later joined by W. H. Vick. For years it had a major competitor in Richards and Conover Hardware Company, a branch of its Kansas City operation. In 1973 Oklahoma Hardware expanded to 200,000 square feet of operating space and diversified.

Tibbs-Dorsey Manufacturing Company was producing marble bank fixtures which were distributed over the southwest. George G. Sohlberg's Acme Mills produced flour for wide area marketing after steady growth since 1893. Under E. S. Malone the Alexander Drug Company was a major wholesaler to the region. It began operations in 1900. The Oklahoma City Library System was called a reflection on the city's progress. It had in 1926 the Main or Central Library, eight branch libraries and twenty-two stations in grade schools, the Community House and the new University Hospital.

A rather interesting commentary on the times came in a 1927 issue of *The Daily Oklahoman*, in a story about the bootlegging situation: "Just as starving wolves, driven by fear from the pursuit of prey for a time finally return to the chase, Oklahoma City bootleggers are beginning to emerge from their hiding places and resume business at the same old stands," the story began.

"About fifty speakeasies were closed when the new city council took charge of the city's law enforcement. The business got very uncertain about that time and most of 'the boys' took to the timber until they could ascertain lay of the land under the new order. Thus far they have discovered nothing, except that the police department means business, but cupidity and jealousy have lured them back to their old haunts and most of them were in shape for business Sunday, according to reports from a number of citizens.

"Prices remain about the same. Corn whiskey is selling for from $2 to $3 a pint; alcohol for $22.50 a gallon, and labelled liquor $12.50 a quart. An immense amount of caution is being displayed by those who have returned to the trade. Liquor is harder to get in Oklahoma City than in any time the last four or five years. The supply is plentiful, but dealers are particular in their selection of customers."

In February 1927 the city acquired the third largest bank in the midwest with consolidation of the American National and First National Banks, into the American First National, under brothers Frank P. and Hugh M. Johnson. Previously they were competitors. Only St. Louis and Kansas City of this region had larger banks. With capital and surplus of $3,200,000 this one led banks in thirty-three states. A business industrial subsidiary of the Chamber, Oklahomans Incorporated, acquired a new executive early in 1927 in William S. Key, who as warden of the State Penitentiary at McAlester made its industries almost pay for operation. A former retail hardware man at Wewoka, Key went from a company commander in the First Oklahoma Infantry, and a battery commander of the first artillery regiment in the original 45th Infantry Division, to division commander by 1941. He was later Provost Marshal General of the European Theater, commanded the Iceland Base Command, and was military governor of Hungary near the end of World War II. He also headed the state Works Progress Administration, where he put emphasis on building combination armories and community centers, bridges on school bus routes and other public improvements. As a candidate for governor in 1938 against Leon C. "Red" Phillips, Key was defeated narrowly in the primary.

An obvious highlight of city history was the change in 1927 from commissioner type of government to that of a charter form with a city manager and council. The mayor would not have administrative duties. This movement actually began in 1923 with preliminary discussions. Walter C. Dean headed a committee to study charter government in other cities. By early 1925 mass meetings were held to explain the idea to citizens, first at the Chamber, with Campbell Russell presiding, then at First Baptist Church Tabernacle. There a "Committee of 100" was named with Frank Buttram as chairman to get steam behind the movement. Hubert L. Bolen was chairman of the charter sub-committee. In September 1925 the first draft of a charter was submitted to the general committee, amended, then circulated. City commissioners refused to call a special election in December but promised to submit the charter at the regular November election in 1926. The charter carried at that time, was challenged in court, upheld by District Judge Tom Chambers, and appealed to the State Supreme Court, which on February 28, 1927, handed down a decision favoring the charter.

In March the "Committee of 100" endorsed a ticket for councilmen and mayor that pledged support for the manager plan. In the primary all endorsed candidates won except one who lost by seventeen votes. Elected mayor was Walter C. Dean. Councilmen elected were: First Ward, P. W. Tibbs and Fay Thompson; Second Ward, W. M. Baughman and Claude Stephens; Ward Three, Oad Colbert and Jesse Todd; Ward Four, Frank J. Quillin and J. G. Binkley. The council on April 15, 1927, employed Edmond M. Fry, city manager of McAlester, as city manager here at a salary "not to exceed $1,000 per month." Fry lasted four years, which for two decades was the record, until Ross Taylor's five years.

In mid-1927 there were but nine cities in the nation with a population between 100,000 and 300,000 that had a lower per capita bonded debt than did Oklahoma City, according to the Detroit Bureau of Government Research. The outstanding debt here then was slightly more than $16 million for all types: general improvement, schools and utilities. Tulsa then had an $18 million bonded debt. Construction of the Commerce Exchange Building began at Grand and South Robinson. In September thousands turned out on Wednesday of State Fair Week to see Charles Lindbergh, who had made his epochal non-stop flight to Paris earlier in April. Governor Henry S. Johnston, Mayor Walter Dean and United States Senator Elmer Thomas were credited for getting "The Lone Eagle" here, with many other cities anxious to have that honor.

One business landmark was changed for what became another

in autumn of 1927 when Barth and Myer Clothing Company, started in 1897 by Sol Barth and Joe Myer, was purchased by Rothschilds of Kansas City and St. Louis. Movie houses began moving away from the downtown area to keep touch with people. One of the first was the Victoria Theater at Northwest Eighteenth Street and Classen Boulevard. It was considered very outstanding in an architectural style of modified Gothic. Later it housed a broadcasting studio, a Players Group, and in 1972 became an office building. An indication of more things to come in the aviation industry was shown in October 1927 when the Oklahoma Aero Club purchased a six passenger Stinson-Detroiter monoplane. Members of the club were Tom E. Braniff, president of Braniff Investment Company; L. H. Prichard of Anderson-Prichard Oil Corporation; Harvey P. Everest of Mid-Continent News Company; Virgil Browne of the Oklahoma Coca Cola Bottling Company and Paul R. Braniff, of the investment company. This was the plane that started Braniff Airways a year later.

In one day the city raised $28,000 for Mississippi Valley flood relief, in answer to a call from President Calvin Coolidge and the American Red Cross, when its quota was $10,000. J. R. Barton was superintendent of city schools, with an enrollment of almost 30,000, nearly $8 million in school property, and a total of fifty-one schools of all types. Setting policy was what Barton termed "The Business Men's Board." Earl E. Leech was senior member in point of tenure. R. F. J. Williams was next in service; Frank McCall was board president; Thomas E. McGee, J. O. Crawford, G. A. Reeves, G. C. Harrell and Day Fezler were the other members. The budget for 1927-28 was $1,983,657.

Many things were to happen here in 1928, although some of them resulting from generally high economic indices would fall upon tough times a year or so later, after the 1929 stock market crash. Year's end would see the Oklahoma City oil field come in as activities in that industry combined to make an uplift during the year. A new auditorium of the Civic Theater Association at 211 Northwest Second was offered as an additional lure for convention planners. Spurred by T. M. Jeffords, agricultural agent for the Katy Railroad, Fred H. Ives, the project supervisor, and the Chamber, plans were made to open a "poultry colony" at Nicoma Park. G. A. Nichols was the developer. The general appeal was living in a pleasant community setting while making poultry raising either a vocation or avocation. In January the first night air mail service from Dallas to Chicago, through here, was begun. Crippled Childrens Hospital in the medical school complex added to the city's impetus toward a state center. With almost 100,000 annual visitors need for a large Convention Hall was emphasized. The last Model T's rolled out of the Ford assembly plant.

Joe D. Morse was chairman of a committee to provide a welcoming reception at the Fairgrounds on Friday, April 13, 1928, for ninety-eight survivors of C. C. Pyle's cross-country "Bunion Derby." One way that Promoter Pyle raised funds was to charge admission to a tent where weary, sun and wind burned trotters and walkers were bunked. Football player Red Grange was another attraction but Oklahoman Andy Payne, the foot-slogger leader, was of equal interest.

In the first quarter of 1928 the city had 2,110 retail establishments in sixty-two categories, with sales of $146,477,291 and 14,121 employes. Many of the city's more affluent residents began to hear about a development called Nichols Hills, a 2,380 acre project north of the city. Three fire insurance firms were organized here; Prudential Fire Insurance Company, capitalized at $500,000 with Tom Braniff as president and E. E. Doggett as secretary; Globe Fire Insurance Company, capitalized at $1 million with Ed Semans president and Henry Ludlow secretary; American Standard Insurance Company, with capital of $500,000, headed by Robert M. Eacock, president, and Hubert L. Bolen, secretary. A half-million dollar Public Market was opened in undeveloped territory along the Oklahoma Railway freight line on Exchange Avenue, by John J. Harden, complete with a dance hall upstairs.

By mid-1928 all designated state highways in Oklahoma county were paved, under construction, or let, except 1.4 miles on US 66. It may be difficult to envision it now but in 1928 the state's largest flour mill was located here, in the Oklahoma City Mill and Elevator Company, while forty-one percent of the state's flour milling capacity was located here or within twenty-five miles of the city.

In July 1928 one of the largest building projects yet planned for the city emerged in a major hotel on Grand Avenue named the Oklahoma Biltmore, later Sheraton-Oklahoma, later Hotel Oklahoma, still later Myriad Plaza. The board of directors was headed by Charles F. Colcord and included W. T. Hales, W. R. Ramsey, P. S. Janeway, J. W. Hawk, P. W. Tibbs, R. J. Edwards, M. J. Reinhart, John Sinopoulo, Leon Vorhees and D. I. Johnson. It was planned for twenty-five stories, designed by Hawk and Parr, Architects. It was built in 1929-30 to thirty-three stories but a planned eight story automobile "hotel" connecting to the east was eliminated. Property west of the Oklahoma Club to Harvey Avenue was purchased and buildings on those lots torn down. The hotel was to have many financial problems, beginning with the depression, and extending to present times. This new hotel venture did not deter W. B. Skirvin from making $2 million worth of improvements and expansion of his hotel. Skirvin did lose the University Club of Oklahoma City as a tenant. It moved to top floors of the new Oklahoma Savings and Loan Association Building at 300 North Robinson.

California Avenue was dressed up with a new "white way" lighting system from the Santa Fe depot west to Walker Avenue. Merchants who aided in providing the $10,000 cost, and other business firms, were so pleased with the project that $2,000 worth of merchandise prizes were given away as bands played and spectators viewed the "modern" illumination. Organization of Consolidated Gas Utilities Company was completed in August of 1928 and opened headquarters here to serve territory in western and northern Oklahoma and south central Kansas. Properties of Midwest Gas Company and some other small companies were acquired. Logan W. Cary, formerly of OG&E, was president of the new firm.

Construction of a new Unitarian Church at Northwest Thirteenth and North Dewey brought church property evaluation in the city to $7 million. Scott Ferris purchased the Cotton Exchange Building and announced an addition. This is now the Leonhardt Building. The Osler

Building at Northwest Eleventh Street and North Walker Avenue was built by physicians to become one of the city's best known professional buildings. Wesley Methodist Church completed its structure at 1401 Northwest Twenty-fifth Street in October as 1928 building permits reached the $18 million mark. The city was growing up. In 1928, deposits in banks here passed the $100 million mark for the first time, a gain of $14,015,000 during the year. Deposits in the six national banks at year's end totaled $101,989,299 for the major amount, as American First National led the state with $54 million.

By 1929 changes in public transportation were becoming noticeable. A Union Bus Station and a Union Truck Terminal here were indicators of the coming trend, along with highway improvements, as 211 towns in the city trade territory had overnight truck service and 110 bus schedules were operated in and out of the station. Service to Fort Smith permitted use of an "interstate" label. In January 1929 the first of several organizations which would continue under various names and scope was formed by the Red and Arkansas River Conservation Association. Tributaries of those streams were included. The first of many federal appropriations for studies followed with $15 million. Inter-agency, inter-basin surveys, reservoir dam construction for the state's major lakes and bank stabilization (continuous) of the Arkansas, and the McClellan-Kerr Navigation Project, followed for nearly four decades.

Quite familiar to Oklahomans through mail order catalogues, the first quarter of 1929 saw Montgomery Ward and Sears Roebuck establish retail outlets here. Ward bought property at Main and Walker, east of the county courthouse, and erected a building, using it until recent times when Ward joined in development of Penn Square. Sears first leased four floors of the Grain Exchange Building at Grand and Harvey, then took the rest, for its store. After Sears became the first commercial establishment on the Shepherd homestead at Northwest Twenty-third Street and Pennsylvania Avenue, the downtown building was used for a time by Sears, and later housed the district Internal Revenue Service office and other tenants, before falling in near instant demolition under urban renewal. John J. Harden, developer of what was then outlying areas, opened up Creston Hills on the far east side, below Northeast Twenty-third Street.

Early 1929 saw Oklahoma City designated on the route of "Carlsbad Cavern Highway," one of the last uses of a name rather than a numerical designation, although such sub-titles as "Main Street of America" for US 66 were publicized. Oklahoma City University proudly opened its new College of Fine Arts building, with a 1,500 seat auditorium and fifteen soundproofed practice studios. Journalism students of the university, thirty-five in number, made a trip to Washington to witness the inauguration of President Herbert Hoover.

General Mills purchased the Oklahoma City Mill and Elevator Company and made expansions. Related was construction of a $100,000 feed making facility for Superior Feed Mills. In May the new $450,000 Capitol Hill High School was projected to be ready for use by autumn. Polyclinic Hospital was constructed and opened on Northwest Thirteenth Street and now, with remodeling and additions, is Doctor's General

Oklahoma City Railroad Yards — 1920

Hospital. Tankersley Construction Company put the first large apartment building in Lincoln Terrace, on Culbertson Drive.

In August OG&E announced plans for a new steam generating plant at Belle Isle lake, almost tripling power output of the older plant there, with an additional 30,000 kilowatts. Work began on the $500,000 Oklahoma Historical Building in the capitol complex. Midwest Enterprises was building a theater and office building downtown, one of the first such ventures there in several years. Oklahoma Publishing Company put in a $1.5 million mechanical plant, east of its building at Northwest Fourth and Broadway, and separated from it by a park. The two were connected with a third floor level, covered ramp, with pneumatic tubes carrying news copy to the composing room. In 1963 a new multi-million building connected the two older ones.

On October 12, 1929, almost 1,000 persons gathered at the Chamber to hear a talk by famed economist Roger W. Babson, who told them: "In the last analysis the future of Oklahoma or any other state will not be determined by its banks or its railroads, by its hotels or its stores, by its factories or its farms, but rather by what the power is that those tools produce; and the first step in analyzing any state is the recognition that these things are mere tools — tools which can upbuild or destroy according to the purposes, the motives, and the ambitions of citizens of that state.

"When we came to examine the southern states, or especially a group of twenty states which we selected for this purpose, with the idea of ascertaining which one of these states has the greatest latent power, Oklahoma was one of two or three of the twenty which stood immediately and outstandingly in the forefront."

Babson was indeed a prophet when early that October, he told this audience: "When a New York banker tells you that the day of the cycle is over and that there will be no more panics, don't you believe him." The big stock market crash that preceded the depression came near month's end.

Grand Avenue — 1923

Included in Babson's "Magic Circle" of economic growth areas later, Oklahoma City folk in late 1929 remained optimistic. A report from the Chamber proclaimed that the city was responding to President Hoover's business stabilization and employment program by continuing its record breaking building and development pace, with prospects for even more activity during the winter months. October's building permits, the Chamber said, were more than $1.5 million, which placed it fourth among leading cities in nineteen southern and southwestern states. For ten months of the year the city ranked fourth, again, with nearly $22 million in permits. This did not include railroad removal or station construction. It was led by Washington, D.C., Houston and St. Louis, in that order.

Graham-Paige Motor Company was building new quarters. So was Greenlease-Moore Chevrolet, Norton Buick and Fred Jones Ford. The Park-O-Tel, the first "modern" drive-in motel in the city, was completed just north of the state capitol on Lincoln. The Maria-des-Cygnes Apartment Hotel was under construction. Announced was a thirty-five story bank and office building, following merger of the American First and Security National Banks, as the First National Bank and Trust Company, at Robinson and Northwest First, now Park Avenue. Some other major projects were announced then but never constructed. A difficult decade lay ahead.

20

Climbing From Depression

WHATEVER ELSE 1930 HAD FOR people of Oklahoma City, the first month was a real chiller-diller, for residents saw the most prolonged ice and snow condition in city history with temperatures below zero, and little relief for six weeks.

This storm began with a front moving down from Canada that made thermometer mercury plummet on January 6. Snow began soon after that and by two days later there was more than twelve inches on the ground atop an ice sheathing. Not since 1918 had there been such a heavy snow with temperature, for a spell, that averaged twenty-five degrees per day. In 1930 the average for January was 23.3 degrees while there were days of sub-zero temperature.

The Salvation Army, churches and some private businesses opened doors for the jobless and needy, where they could be warmed and fed. Many workers got temporary jobs at fifty cents an hour to shovel snow and ice off walks and from weakened roofs. Some awnings collapsed, one causing injuries to four persons downtown. It was January 24 before temperature rose above thirty-two degrees and February 8 before it swung up to sixty-eight degrees. (The winter of 1972-1973 was compared to the 1930 condition but was neither as prolonged nor severe.)

A warm-up by nature was exceeded by business folk who, upon urging by Chamber leaders, adopted the slogan "Let's Go!" to indicate a counter offensive to growing decline in economic conditions making a tortoise approach from Eastern banking circles. Although much of it was planned previously, more than $230 million in construction for the state was proclaimed for 1930, with $43.5 million of it in the city itself, $38.5 million in its trade territory and the rest elsewhere, led by $34 million in the largest state highway program. Oklahoma county would get about $1 million of that. The city also would benefit from about $8 million of more than $33 million to be expended by railroads in this area. Downtown track removal, track elevation, and passenger and freight stations, were the large items here.

Almost all manner of utility improvements from transit to power were underway. Public and private schools would expend more than $2.5 million, most of it in the city resulting from a bond issue. A number of expensive homes began to rise in Nichols Hills. The first permanent home for the YWCA was financed by a subscription campaign for $700,000. Many pledges were depression faulted. There was an evident attempt by almost all segments in industrial concerns to improve facilities or expand. The oil field, little more than one year old, created a demand for steel products, led by steel tanks. The Boardman Company and American Tank Company, the latter now renamed and owned by Black-Sivalls and Bryson, went into large scale tank production. Specialty products of American Iron and Machine Works got extra publicity dating back to its fabrication of a hood that successfully capped the "Wild Mary Sudik," and the field's second wild well, the Sigmon Number One. Devices to tame wild wells were not a stock item. They had to be designed, fabricated, and applied. Construction contracts begun in 1929 made a rising if jagged effect on the city's skyline.

In March 1930 the fifteenth Southwest American Livestock Show, now turned into what became the nation's largest Junior Livestock Show, broke all previous records for number of entries at the Coliseum and former horse and mule barns at the yards. Public attendance was estimated at 40,000 persons. Warming earth became host to 3,000 trees on city street easements as the Junior Chamber of Commerce put on a beautifying project. Preliminary population figures of the decennial census added another rosy glow to the city's claims of growth in May, to be revised by the Census Bureau later to show 185,383 residents, placing the city forty-third in the nation. Ten years before it stood eightieth in rank. Under Chief George Goff the city fire department had 200 trained men who, in addition to being fire fighters, did almost all municipal motor maintenance work, street lighting system installation and maintenance. There were now twelve fire stations — three of which were built by the departmental force itself.

By midyear work began on a Union Station for the Rock Island and Frisco. A $1 million plus addition to the federal building was put under contract. The Better Business Bureau was reorganized to protect consumers, an outgrowth of the first endeavor created some sixteen years earlier, at urging of a Chamber committee headed by Tom Baugh. H. G. Mitchell was general manager of the bureau. The eleven story Black Hotel at Grand and Hudson had its $600,000 construction underway. By August the city's jobbing and wholesale business reached a $250 million crest. The city was host to some 6,000 physicians and surgeons from this and surrounding states at a conclave sponsored by the Oklahoma City Clinical Society in September.

The thirty-one story Ramsey Tower construction began for a building in excess of $2 million. Later it was the Apco Building, Liberty National Building, and now is the City National Tower. With Charles M. Dunning as chairman, a civic committee proposed a $9,391,286 general improvement bond issue, with a recommendation that only local residents be employed on multiple municipal projects. Included on the committee were John A. Brown, A. O. Campbell, Walter C. Dean, E. K. Gaylord, Frank P. Johnson, Carl C. Magee, G. A. Nichols, J. F. Owens, J. M. Owen and Robert M. Rainey. The bond issue did not materialize — a sign of the times.

Underground long distance cables were laid between the city and Tulsa and to Dallas in autumn. Construction began on the Skirvin Tower Hotel, across the street from the original hotel, with a tunnel under Broadway connecting the two. While the city council argued about a permit for the tunnel workmen dug it out. The Exchange Avenue viaduct neared completion. The year 1930 saw fifty-eight new industries and more than 400 other firms established here as the city claimed major activities in thirteen categories outside professional listings.

Principal speaker at the annual Chamber banquet in January 1931 was a young University of Oklahoma student, from Pittsburg county, a national oratorical contest winner in high school and but recently announced as successful winner of regional Rhodes Scholarship to Oxford University. He was Carl Albert, now speaker of the United States House of Representatives, highest federal post yet for an elected official from Oklahoma. His talk was broadcast on WKY, pioneer radio station of the southwest and third licensed in the nation, which had moved its studio from downtown to Plaza Court at Walker and Classen Drive, the city's first planned shopping center. With Gayle Grubb as manager then, the station would go later to the Skirvin Tower, after that to Britton Road east of the Broadway Extension.

A most definite sign of the times as the city began to feel depression effects was a notice that appeared in a Chamber publication on February 5, 1931, which asked residents not to advise their relatives and friends to move here unless they had guaranteed jobs or business connections. It was explained candidly that home folks came first in employment. Oklahoma City University had 1,460 students, an appreciable increase over the 117 just a decade before. Many collegiate males, athletes particularly, had jobs with the city fire department. In late April the Chamber promoted its first "Senior Day" with invitations to state high school graduates to make a tour of industries, the Capitol and Oklahoma Historical Society. Wilson and Morris packing plants joined by providing a barbecue luncheon for visitors. On April 21, 1931, Ed Overholser died. There is little doubt that he topped the list of civic leaders during the decade just passed.

In mid-1931 the first "local" administration of OG&E came into being upon death of Arthur S. Huey, Chicago, president of the city utility and board chairman of the controlling H. M. Byllesby Company. J. F. "Jack" Owens was made president after being general manager since 1918; W. R. Emerson was named a vice-president as was George Ade Davis, who later would be president; Frank J. Meyer, vice president in charge of operations, and B. M. Lester, secretary. St. Anthony's Hospital added a five story addition to increase capacity by 100 beds to 375. An extension of US 270 gave the city its tenth federal highway outlet.

Plans were drawn and a forty acre site purchased between Grand Boulevard and Northwest Sixty-third Street for a major cathedral of the Episcopal Church, under Bishop Thomas Casady. One novel food product produced here, heading for regional and national distribution, was a carrot syrup made from that vegetable and flavored with maple, made by the Carrot Food Products Corporation. The last huge draft horses used for cartage disappeared from city streets as O.K. Transfer Company was completely motorized. Beginning as a one-horse dray outfit under G. W. R. Chinn in 1889, the firm was taken over by A. C. Weicker in 1899 and was both the largest and oldest continuously operating transfer company in the city. From 125 horses, teams dwindled to twelve before their disposal, including a six-horse hitch that made city parades more interesting. Work neared completion on the administration building of Municipal Airport, with its 640 acres, as nearly four years of $1 million a month in construction ended. The city in 1931 ranked twelfth in the nation for permits and second only to St. Louis in this region.

More indication of the times was evidenced in the 1931 Community Fund budget, which allocated $338,092 of its $450,565 total to various relief agencies, principally in food orders, clothing and housing for destitute families. Fund Director Wilbur J. Adams reported that 46,393 men, women and children had been aided in prior months of the year. They were fed, clothed and in many instaces sheltered, through the Salvation Army, United Provident Association and Red Cross. Yet a mixture of low unemployment and reduced income did not appear to affect total area economics in some ways. During 1931 there were 367 new business firms established here employing 2,730 persons. There were 344 conventions, or meetings, with a total of 136,000 persons in attendance. In number of such affairs the city ranked fourth in the nation.

In 1932 a commercial transaction that involved much city history occurred when John A. Brown and John Dunkin (of Tulsa) bought the interest of Anson Rorabaugh in the Rorabaugh-Brown Dry Goods Company. The original firm was that of Sidney L. Brock, member of a townsite

The First National Bank and the Ramsey Tower (now City National Bank) going up in 1931.

company on opening of Oklahoma Country, and for many years a civic leader. In 1915 Brown, with Rorabaugh, bought the Brock store, although Brown was able to put up but twenty percent of the total outlay required. He was manager of the store and a prominent figure in civic life through the years. With Dunkin he had a department store at Tulsa, also, and for some forty years shared honors for the state's largest department store volume. The familiar downtown structure, spread over its Main Street location and to suburban centers over the years, now is a property of Dayton-Hudson Corporation of Minneapolis. Mrs. John A. (Della) Brown operated the firm for many years after her husband's death. Kermit J. Hardwick was store manager many years.

In April the second largest mass feeding project (second to the Walton Barbecue) happened when the two major packers, Wilson and Armour, hosted students from 126 state high schools at the second annual "Senior Day." This touring visit became, in time, a state tradition, but sheer size finally prohibited a free lunch, just as hosting exhibitors at the annual 4-H and FFA Junior Livestock Show outgrew a reasonable contribution of that nature. In May the Ford Motor Company plant announced that it would put 1,000 men to work, following a decline, boosting its monthly payroll from $40,000 to $150,000. Naturally this was seen as an indicator of business upturn after lean depression years. August saw construction underway on a $50,000 4-H Club Building at the State Fair, after some litigation. The organization's "State Fair School" originated in 1910 with creation of a "Corn Club." It was not until 1939 that the Future Farmers of America had their fair building. Through money raising events by state FFA chapters and sale of souvenir brass coins with an inscription, "I Put a Gold Brick in the FFA Building," the sponsor's share of cost was provided. The building was constructed under the Works Progress Administration with Charles H. Tompkins as project manager.

The Boy Scout organization announced an active membership of 2,000 youths, as eighteen new troops were established, Cub Scout and Sea Scout programs created. In August, also, the active Junior Chamber put on a "Made in Oklahoma City" show that featured ninety-one firms with displays in fifty-five donated retail store windows downtown. The young mens' group also was quite proud of having 562 entries in its "backyard playground contest" as another activity. The *Oklahoma City Church Press* began operation here, becoming the *All-Church Press* later, with editions for various churches. W. P. "Bill" Atkinson, then a journalism instructor at Oklahoma City University, was an advertising salesman for the church paper group before becoming a builder of homes in the northwest city area, then developing Midwest City, and in the postwar II era establishing the *Oklahoma Journal*.

The second local radio station, KFJF, went on the air in October 1932 as KOMA, a Columbia Broadcasting Company outlet, owned by Texas interests. For several years it operated out of the Biltmore Hotel. In December, headquarters of the Carey, Lombard and Young Lumber Company, after being in Chicago for forty years, moved to the city with C. J. Carey as vice-president and manager.

The year 1933 had four memorable events of quite different

nature. First was the city's first "bank holiday" since 1907, which to an extent affected everyone; the second and third happened on the same day and captured wide interest among citizens although few of them were involved personally; fourth was a crack in the state's prohibition dike that widened under voters' declaration that beer of no more than 3.2 percent alcohol by volume was not intoxicating.

Governor William H. Murray decreed a bank holiday March 22, 1933, because business failures (including some weak banks), home foreclosures and other critical economic matters concerned him greatly. His action was predicated on a Thursday starting point, but President Franklin D. Roosevelt called for a national "bank holiday" for the following Monday. In Oklahoma City the Cash Reserve Association put about $135,000 worth of scrip in circulation. It was printed on a special "safety" paper stock, in slightly larger size than regular currency, and was sold to business firms in blocks of $1,000 face value with a $10 charge for operations. Murray said the scrip plan was illegal and not reliable but for several days, before the holiday was lifted twelve days after it began, the scrip was accepted. Denominations were $1, $5, and $10. One side had a photo of the Oklahoma City skyline and the words: "City of Progress." When real money came back scrip was redeemed at face value — except for $729 worth that went into souvenir scrapbooks — and the redeemed scrip was burned with proper public ceremonies.

On July 22, 1933, Wiley Post brought the monoplane "Winnie Mae" down at Floyd Bennett Field near New York after the fastest solo flight around the world. He made the 15,400 mile aerial journey in seven days, eighteen hours and fifty minutes. There were 25,000 persons at the field to welcome him.

That same day — or to be more exact thirty minutes before it began — Charles F. Urschel, trustee of the Tom B. Slick Estate and husband of the former Mrs. Slick, was kidnapped from their home at 327 Northwest Eighteenth. They were playing bridge with Mr. and Mrs. W. R. Jarrett, associates in the oil business. Jarrett, also taken away, later was released to bring back a ransom demand for $200,000. The ransom was paid and Urschel released near Oklahoma City. He had been detained in a shed at the Texas farm home of parents of Katherine Kelly, wife of George "Machine Gun" Kelly, later identified as one of the three kidnappers with Albert L. Bates and Harvey Bailey. Urschel was able to help authorities pinpoint his place of capture by noting at what time daily an airliner passed over the farm. When people there were identified names of the actual kidnappers were disclosed. Later captured, they were tried and sentenced in federal district court here, by Judge Edgar S. Vaught. The men got life. Mrs. Kelly was sentenced to a long term, her parents to shorter terms. Pretty, auburned-haired Katherine Kelly, left prison gray and facially lined.

People voted on beer in 1933 through a special election, a majority of nearly 90,000 votes. State Attorney General J. Berry King said that beer was legal when results of the election were announced but that licenses for sale first must be procured. Governor Murray, who had timing power because of his control of the Oklahoma Tax Commission on the licensing matter, took things a bit slow and proclaimed a form of martial law in

JOHN L. PETERS	FRED JONES	WILLIAM S. KEY	WALTER M. HARRISON
Founder and head of	*Ford dealer and*	*Prison, WPA and*	*Editor, Oklahoma*
World Neighbors	*components mfgr.*	*National Guard leader*	*City Councilman*

railroad yards to prevent suds from seeping out of loaded freight cars. The stalemate lasted briefly. For the first time since November 15, 1907, beer sale and consumption was legal.

As 1934 began there was a general feeling that worst of the depression was over. Making an important impact on local economy and providing some unusual structures — especially for those who could recall the railroad tracks and stations there — was the Civic Center development pushed by City Manager Orval "Red" Mosier. More than 2,000 items were displayed from local manufacturers and processors at a trade show. The Chamber sponsored an international goodwill trip to Mexico City and had fifty-seven persons along to boost relations. The ten day excursion, by rail, had a tab of only $144 for transportation, hotel rooms and meals.

At the annual Chamber banquet in January one of those things happened that demonstrate the frailty of man. Edwin Markham, renowned poet best known for his "Man With the Hoe," and his scholarly Lincoln tribute, was the unwitting witness as speaker. This was a Tuesday evening. Markham on Monday talked for two hours to another interested audience. The 80-year-old, bearded poet, had an audience of 750 persons at the Chamber banquet. He had suffered a slight illness that day but this was unknown to his listeners. His first rambling introductory story brought some laughter as he returned, again and again, to the beginning. People who thought that was a presentation gimmick soon realized that he was having trouble and grew silent. Markham would say something with the brilliancy for which he was famous, then lapse into incoherent mumblings.

It was at one of these points that, as Paul Kennedy wrote it for *The Daily Oklahoman* in one of the best examples of descriptive writing in our years, Markham "rose to the most dramatic intensity probably ever witnessed by a banquet audience . . . he had been handed his own poem on Lincoln. As the first line flashed through his mind he began a recitation that brought the audience to edge of their seats.

"Stanza after stanza thundered from his lips. With his snow white hair and beard and his giant stature, he made the picture of a patriarch of old pronouncing the eternal truth. Then, with his climax in sight, his memory forsook him again.

"He fought to bring back the picture; fought harder than a giant oak fights the tempest. But the picture wouldn't return. The tragedy of the giant oak crumpling was the last scene as Walter M. Harrison, toastmaster, stepped in and finished the lines.

"Helped to his seat, his head slumped over on his folded arms as Harrison began reading the poem that had made Markham one of America's foremost men of letters:

"'Bowed by the weight of centuries he leans,' began the poem impressively, and the leonine head of the poet came erect as if he were putting his last ounce of strength into the effort.

"'And on his back the burden of the world,' and as if the sentence — his own sentence were the pronouncement of his suffering — he slumped again, this time not to rise until the audience was dismissed."

In four months, with better prices and less restricted flow, the Oklahoma City oil field produced crude valued at $59 million, which was $6.5 million more than the value of twice that much oil in eight months the previous year. From twenty-five cents a barrel, oil now reached $1.04. Macklanburg-Duncan was getting known over a national and international market for its weatherstrips, basis of the company that began at 211 Park Avenue, now producing many products at a large plant on North Santa Fe. Bank calls over the past four dates showed a steady increase with $72 million in deposits in March 1934. The Board of Education found funds to complete Taft Stadium by autumn, with a major assist from the Jaycees, whose membership raised a major portion of the cost. The Real Estate Board said that more than one-half of residential property for whites which was vacant a year earlier, now was occupied, and one-fourth of closed industrial property of the previous year now was in use. A similar comparison of Negro residential property showed more than eighty-seven percent occupancy.

Debaters Jack Durland and Alice Sutton, representing Central High School, won first place in a national speech tournament held at Topeka in May. City Manager Orval Mosier was able to report, at end of his first year, that the city had no tax levy; showed a $400,000 revenue gain; had no outstanding warrants; owned property valued at $80 million; there had been but a $70,000 fire loss on property evaluated at $108 million; park attendance had been 2.38 million; the water department turned a million dollars to the city treasury; there was $1,565,000 of bonded debt retired and the city had $3 million cash in banks. That was the best city economic report citizens had heard for quite some time. It was made in August 1934

Among activities in other areas, the Men's Dinner Club and Ladies Music Club arranged a concert and reception to honor Joseph Benton of Norman, who as Guiseppi Bentonelli was well and popularly known on the operatic stages of Europe for nearly twelve years.

In late 1934 Harbour-Longmire, a partnership that began in 1910 with a handshake and now is vanished from the business scene, was said to be the second largest furniture store in the nation, after one in Los Angeles. It was a manufacturer, distributor and wholesaler, in addition to having its own sale rooms.

On December 20 Charles F. Colcord died. A man of many parts here since 1889, a law enforcement officer, builder and oil pool developer, he was one of the city's dominant figures for more than forty years.

Progress Brewing Company, taking its name from one of President Roosevelt's pet themes, was opened here by John Kroutil of the milling family at Yukon. Eventually it would become an affiliate of Lone Star, San Antonio. Where but so short a time before there had been a surplus of housing, largely due to persons living with relatives or otherwise delaying home purchases, the Real Estate Board in April declared there was a shortage of 1,100 units for a population the size of Oklahoma City. There were 200,000 residents claimed. The Ramsey Tower sold to Connecticut Mutual Life Insurance Company, principal mortgage holder, in July, for the first major business transaction since the depression began. Something that would be welcomed by some city administrations as a revenue producer, condemned by merchant patrons and imitated in various forms, made its appearance here in mid-1935 with the Park-O-Meter. This little device, originating from an idea of Carl C. Magee, former editor of the Scripps-Howard *Oklahoma News* here, would bring more national attention to the city. It eventually would be accepted widely across the land. From Magee's ideas and sketches engineering staff and faculty at then Oklahoma A&M College, at Stillwater, designed the meter and drew the specifications. It was produced in a commercial plant at Sand Springs. Magee held the patent.

Most shocking news of 1935 was the crash death on August 16 at Point Barrow, Alaska, of Will Rogers and Wiley Post. Both, in their way, were international figures and especially beloved in Oklahoma where they were born. Oklahoma City lost one of its own first citizens that same week in C. B. Ames.

In October a "Silver Jubilee" recognition was given Armour, Wilson and the Oklahoma National Stockyards Company, which originated here in 1910 to create a major and continuous industry for the city. Remember Major Bowe's National radio program with amateur talent? Oklahoma City was "saluted" by the program the last of October but several local amateurs who sought tryouts did not make the grade.

It was in the 1912 campaign for the presidency that Thomas R. Marshall, running for vice-president on the Democratic ticket led by Woodrow Wilson and miffed at some things the opposition said this country needed, gave his long used retort: "What this country needs is a good five cent cigar." Here in 1935 Patterson & Hoffman tried to supply that need with a locally made "P&H" stogie, selling for five cents, packed twenty-five to a red metal can.

21

Scandal Topped By War

LTHOUGH THE CITY HAD LINGERING ties with the War Between the States as late as 1936, with the Union Soldiers Home on North Eastern (later home of the State Health Department) and Confederate Home at Ardmore, one of the last direct relationships was lost in March. Colonel R. A. Sneed, Confederate States of America, by now accustomed to a title of higher rank commonly used — died at age ninety. A former secretary of state for Oklahoma, he had also commanded the national Confederate Veterans group. With his full beard and imposing figure Colonel Sneed had a resemblance to Robert E. Lee, under whom he served.

Mechanical air conditioning, now so commonplace, made its first appearance in the city in April 1936 at larger theaters. Prior to that time a system of forced air from blowers fanned persons in front seats but did little for those in back rows. From theaters to other commercial establishments this feature of modern living finally spread to homes, hotels, and later to automobiles. Radio by now was in its golden years but those "prophets" who said that music over the air would kill the phonograph record business had to back down a bit. Record sales mounted steadily.

In May, a benefit for the 1936 Milk and Ice Fund was sponsored by the Oklahoma Publishing Company. Assistance to the needy was disbursed through the United Provident Association. The affair was an "Olympia Circus," put on at the Lincoln Park Amphitheater, and produced for the fund by Ralph T. Hemphill, state fair manager, with assistance and talent supplied through Mike Barnes of Barnes-Carruthers of Chicago. For years this organization provided grandstand shows at the fair.

At one performance an unscheduled event brought gasps from the audience. A feature was the Blondin-Rellims Troupe, which did a high wire act with two men walking the wire, two more standing upon their shoulders, and still a third above the second pair, standing on a rod supported by shoulder harness of the couple.

At successful conclusion of the act, after the men reached a platform at one end of the wire, it was customary to grab a piece of bicycle tire (to prevent hand injury) and slide quickly down a rope, to take bows. When the first man grabbed the rope it came loose and he fell thirty-five feet to the sawdust ring, just inside a wooden curb for Denny Curtis' horse act. The performer suffered a broken pelvis. A knowledge of how to take a fall prevented more serious injury.

Pushed primarily by the city oil field, Oklahoma county was leading other counties of the state in production, with Greater Seminole next. Local fields produced more than 54 million barrels in a year, or in excess of thirty percent of state production. Industrial movements kept inching westward and southward from older sections of the city in 1936 as other indicators continued an economic buildup. Dust bowl days of 1935 and 1936 put a pulverized pall in our land and even filtered into psychology of the people. City dwellers were less injured economically from severe drought.

The first six months of 1936 saw 4,000 persons, enumerated in 836 family groups, become new residents. A splurge of spending by War I veterans who received varied sums in "adjusted compensation," or bonus, failed to materialize. With memories of a recent depressive past, most recipients put their money into banks and savings institutions, a Chamber report stated.

The first year of parking meters made the city finance director happy, at least, as the device spread from first usage here to other states with 8,000 ordered and 5,000 installed by July in Texas, Florida, Kansas and Pennsylvania. After all that drought and dust — the first three days of the State Fair were rained out — but rain drew blue ribbons.

Early 1937 saw municipal officials and employes report to a splendid $650,000 structure in Civic Center, as other buildings on the old railroad right-of-way competed for attention. Reservations already were being made for Municipal Auditorium after its completion at mid-year. Radio Station KTOK opened in April for the third outlet, bringing programs of the Mutual Broadcasting System here, following the other two major national outlets. It was key station for a state network. Kerr Drygoods Company put in its Uptown store — way out at Northwest Twenty-fourth and Walker, which like downtown Kerr's now is gone — but that location now is rather popular with many persons as the district office of the Social Security Administration.

The city's first "iron lung" for benefit of those with severe respiratory and other ailments, appeared here in February 1938, largely through activity of the Jaycees who made that acquisition a major project. The device was turned over to the city fire department for custody and delivery, as needed, to hospitals. A spurt of office building construction by early 1938 resulted in 1.5 million square feet of space being available and almost all of it occupied.

Without much fanfare a variety store called TG&Y was opened on Northwest Twenty-third Street, near Walker, with the second to appear a year later at 825 North Broadway, near a warehouse serving twenty-five similar stores in the state. R. A. Young was manager. The state born chain now is national in scope with ownership elsewhere, although Young remains board chairman of the organization.

For Oklahoma City the year 1938 had internal sensationalism connected with the school board. Since 1933 there had been rumors of hanky-panky concerning the board. Civic leaders and patrons that year got a measure of control on the board by adding some members. The board then was composed of Edward Spivey, Day Fezler, E. E. Dorsey, Earl Foster, Fred Jones, Dell Miller, Mrs. J. S. Poole, Roscoe Price and R. A. Bryant. Thad Wells of the First National Bank was treasurer. In May, Wells was succeeded by Ray M. Scruggs, also a First National vice-president. Bryant resigned and Otto Rose, a prominent Capitol Hill political figure and businessman, was appointed to succeed him. Prior to the 1933 elections Spivey headed a majority on the board which included Dorsey, Foster, Jones, Miller and Bryant. The latter's resignation and Rose's appointment first put Spivey back in control, backed by Fezler, Price, Rose and Mrs. Poole. There were some changes in succeeding years but from 1935 the majority faction, now headed by Rose as president, included Earl Johnson, Mrs. Poole, Price and Spivey.

It was almost like a bomb bursting in 1938 when John Prigmore, school district auditor, discovered that treasurer Ray Scruggs' account was short by $757,751, primarily in bonds purchased as an investment and believed to be in the board's safe deposit box. Scruggs was charged with embezzlement, tried, convicted and sentenced to the Federal Reformatory at El Reno. He soon became editor of the inmate newspaper.

There were charges of other malfeasance. District Judge Ben Arnold called for a grand jury investigation of board members' actions. The jury's report and indictments followed in July 1938. There were near amazing allegations of kickbacks on board purchases, from building sites for new schools to floor cleaning materials. Board members Spivey and Price, board attorney Frank Wilkins and L. H. Capshaw, an oil royalty dealer, were indicted on bribery charges. The grand jury removed Rose, Price and Mrs. Poole from the board. Spivey and Johnson resigned before ouster proceedings against them began. In October Wilkins was convicted and sentenced to seven years at state prison. County Attorney Lewis Morris brought Spivey to trial. He was convicted in December and sentenced to ten years.

At Spivey's trial it was disclosed that he received a $6,829 payoff on sale to the board of a $73,710 site for Northwest High School. The vendor was the one responsible for blowing the whistle on Spivey, after marked money was passed to him in a furniture store rest room. Waiving a jury trial, Capshaw was found guilty and sentenced to three years. Price was tried last, was convicted, and given a five year sentence. Mrs. Poole, nick-named "Mother Poole" because of her activities with youth, was penalized most by publicity connected with her actions as one of the board majority manipulators.

That was not the end of the school board scandal script. Investigation by the Internal Revenue Service and the office of Federal District Attorney Charles Dierker led to indictments on Spivey, Price, Rose, Johnson and Wilkins for income tax evasion. Wilkins, by then a broken man, agreed to "sing" about board members and income tax evasion charges on him were dropped. His story, told on the witness stand, was little short of fantastic at scope of the majority operations and concealment practiced. Wilkins said he had to kick back a portion of his own salary to retain his position as board attorney.

On April 24, 1941, Rose was found guilty on two tax evasion counts and sentenced to ten years in federal penitentiary by Federal District Judge Edgar S. Vaught in May. Also found guilty and sentenced were Price, three years and Johnson, eighteen months, since he testified also for the government. Price and Johnson took a guilty plea without standing trial.

For the 1939 spring school board election all eight members of a new board had to be selected. A Citizens League, which had become active earlier, drafted Roy J. Turner, J. Wiley Richardson, Dave McKown, Al Robinson, Ed L. Hisel, Sam A. Rice, Earl Miller and Warren H. Edwards as nominees for a "reform" board under the old operating system. But there was more "reform" in the air. An ordinance proposed by the Citizens League and drafted by Albert McRill, who had served as municipal counselor in addition to being a former city manager, proposed that the school board system be reorganized. This would result in election of a five member board on a non-partisan ballot, one member to be nominated from each of the four wards and one at large, but all to be elected at large by district patrons. Some dissent remained.

By a vote of four to three the city council rejected offering the ordinance to voters at the regular election November 8, 1938. Against it were Leonard Dickerson, Joe Campbell, Percy Jones and G. A. Stark. In favor of it were C. T. Lockwood, L. I. Baker and A. J. Moore. An initiative petition with some 16,000 names, twice the number required, was secured and held valid to set an ordinance election on April 4, 1939. The measure was adopted by more than two-to-one. Elected under the McRill-League ordinance in December 1939 were Richardson, Ward One; Turner, Ward Two; McKown, Ward Three; Hisel, Ward Four and Edwards, at large. The voting margin was again about two-to-one.

The new board instituted many changes to the old system. A budget reduction of eighteen percent was necessary to keep within available funds and that was made. Reforms on bidding and purchasing were provided with open meetings. A monetary saving was made by having the district's non-payable warrants invested in its sinking fund. A most important change was getting the board, as such, out of direct personnel hiring, letting those in charge of administration and instruction employ people. Operational and custodial supervisors hired their personnel. A purchasing agent did that large chore and was responsible to the board.

The "openness" of such a system as contrasted to former closed door meetings, board controlled patronage and purchasing, was quite apparent. The taste of politics that being on the board gave to Turner, who regarded it as a public service, was indirectly responsible for his seeking and winning the governor's chair in 1946. One hears at times today that there is "politics" in the Oklahoma City school board and administration. If this does exist it is but a mere trickle compared to the flood that broke the dam in 1938.

City folk early in 1939 had no definite knowledge of what would happen in Europe before year's end and their own inevitable involvement in another war. Some of them should have — for since late in 1933 there was someone trying to tell them. This was Everett Haynes, a local man who began riding on sprint tracks at Minco and went on to be one of the nation's leading jockeys, riding for such stables as that of August Belmont. He then went to Europe and became the most famous international jockey of that era in the booming sports age.

First, in France, he rode for Pierre Wertheimer, whose money came from the "Evening in Paris" line of toilet items. Haynes' first successes were with Epinard, "the wonder horse," that won almost every major race in Europe. Then Haynes went to Germany and became a gentleman jockey, owning his own stables as he rode also for the Stahl Halma Stables. He won the Berlin Derby and Hindenburg Trophy three times.

Haynes and Max Schmelling were heroes in Germany. Traffic police stopped vehicles to permit them to cross the street. But when Hitler came to power in 1933 everything changed. Haynes' horses and property later were confiscated. Fortunately he was able to foresee some of this. He converted some assets to international currency and jewelry which Mrs. Haynes carried out to places like Copenhagen and put in safe keeping.

The Haynes' boys were herded with German youth to mass gatherings of the Hitler Jugend and some evidence of mob psychology effects was apparent. Waiting almost to the limit when they could avoid detention the family finally came home.

Haynes attempted to tell city folk, including those of the news media, what was happening and what was going to happen as Hitler's strength grew toward dictatorial status. But no one was listening. Times were too good after what we had been through here and Europe was far away. Almost the only ones willing to sit and hear Haynes, and believe his prophesy of potential war, were his two lifetime friends in Oklahoma City, Orval "Red" Mosier and Nate Jackson. Each, in his way, also made history. Mosier rose to executive vice-president of American Airlines. Jackson would have been welterweight champion of the world had he been on the giving — instead of receiving end — of one final blow.

City folk did have another radio station to tune in when KOCY went on the air as the fourth major outlet. People also had big ideas about celebrating the golden anniversary of land opening in Oklahoma Country on April 22, 1889. Leaders began the year beating the civic drum, doing legitimate bragging to that accompaniment about progress of the city that was born grown, but still had ability to add to its stature. There had been forty-eight banks here since that first one in a tent, and seven healthy ones survived. Two-thirds of the different banks could be traced into those remaining. There had been $104,545,183 in deposits the last call, not including thirty-three cents to the right side of the decimal. Assessed valuation exceeded the deposit figure as size of the city was put at 25.12 square miles.

The city had two big parades celebrating its anniversary and used as a theme "From Teepees to Towers." It was easy to prove both indicators. Police estimated that 100,000 persons witnessed the two parades, one downtown in the city, the other in Capitol Hill. Mayor Robert A. Hefner, disregarding his sixty-five years, rode a horse in both processions. *The Daily Oklahoman* printed 200,000 copies of a huge special edition of 292 pages, consuming 870 tons of newsprint, which if extended in a strip seventeen inches wide would have covered more than 10,000 miles.

Trains still were competing with the maturing air industry as the Santa Fe offered to put a person into Kansas City after a seven hour journey. The Frisco offered to add but fifteen minutes to that time by way of Tulsa. Number of automobiles was increasing although the county registered but 7,000. The oldest locally owned dealership was that of C. J.

Myers, a Dodge dealer on Robinson, almost downtown, who as other firms did, offered to provide free instruction on driving to auto purchasers.

A familiar project was pushed by the Chamber as 1940 began. It was adequate water supply — a recurrent theme almost since that first windlass well on Main Street in 1889 — but even more of a priority item after duster days and prolonged drought that saw the federal government buying cattle that were little more than bones held together by a hide. In somewhat of an ironic but factual counterpart there was demand for more flood control projects. These two factors were, and continue to be, of paramount importance to the city and state. A municipal election February 20, 1940, was to offer also a proposal for a reservoir on Upper Bluff Creek to contain 75,000 acre feet of water; new pumping and filtration plants; expansion of the distribution system and improvements at Lake Overholser.

The 1940 decennial census put the city's population at 204,517 persons, in contrast to the 185,389 ten years earlier, which in turn nearly doubled that of 1920. Draft registration was followed by inductions late in the year with Oklahoma City designated the receiving center. City units of the 45th Infantry Division in September joined fellow Thunderbirds at Fort Sill as one of the first four National Guard units to be called up as the nation went on a defensive footing. An advance detachment of sixty officers and 700 men of the 37th Air Base Detachment reached Will Rogers Air Base on Municipal Airport, to handle ground operations, and prepare for activation of the 48th Light Bombardment Group with more than 3,000 total personnel.

Although war still was more than a year away the military establishment was spending more than $300,000 here in intervening months on vocational education for national defense training. This included a Civilian Pilot Training Program and a variety of skills training for both high school youths and adults in the public schools. Anticipating more involvement, and concerned about space for potential military training or industries connected with "lend-lease" efforts, was the Chamber's National Defense Committee headed by Virgil Browne. A special sub-committee led by L. H. "Lofty" Mann concerned itself more directly with training. Local contractors found opportunities here in a $2 million expansion of Will Rogers Field facilities while others held defense contracts elsewhere. In all, seven firms held more than $30 million in construction contracts.

One hundred and twenty-three manufacturers and wholesalers in the city, including sub-contractors, received what was called National Defense contracts. In one month, as the year faded, more than $3 million in supplier contracts were issued. Repair shops of the Civilian Conservation Corps (CCC) in the state were consolidated here with some 600 mechanics, in shops built on a ten-acre tract given to the federal government by the city. A new Northwest Highway cut distance to Woodward by nearly sixty miles. Bluff Creek reservoir (Lake Hefner) bonds passed. Much of the $350 million in new wealth from agriculture passed through city financial channels. More than 300,000 visitors attending 681 meetings continued to uphold the city's third rank nationally for convention numbers, to provide an estimated $7,345,000 ambulatory dollars. By any standards the city's economic pulse was strong and on the upbeat.

Early in 1941 the shift of much general aviation to the city's alternate port near Bethany resulted also in housing expansion of that area. Warr Acres originally sprang from a sixty acre tract developed by C. B. Warr with 122 homes programmed. Later he would develop the Mayfair Addition. A $300,000 Industries Foundation to expedite defense construction here and elsewhere grew quickly after a preliminary infusion of $20,000 from Phillips Petroleum Company.

The new Variety Club Health Center was dedicated on the south side in June to provide more medical services for those less able to pay. By July the first of many campaigns to salvage and conserve strategic materials appeared with emphasis on aluminum. A newly organized Defense Council set up collection points. Additional push from defense related industry aided in shoving city bank and savings deposits to the highest point with $125 millions total. Department store sales topped all previous records, too, with a twenty-four percent increase over a similar period the previous year. By agreement between the government of Mexico and the Chamber, seventy high school and college athletes were to engage in an "international" sports competition the month of December. But Pearl Harbor intervened.

With the rest of the nation Oklahoma City was shocked and angry at the blitz over Hawaii, the Philippines and elsewhere in the Pacific on Sunday, December 7, 1941. Then came a declaration of war on Monday following President Franklin D. Roosevelt's "day of infamy" request of the Congress. On Thursday Congress responded to a declaration of war against us by Germany and Italy in voting a similar formal declaration against them. All speculation ended. Now we knew what the game was but not the rules, time limits, or eventual score. That was for national history books later.

In Oklahoma City parents of men in the 45th Infantry Division, now at Camp Barkeley, Texas, wondered what would happen to them. At Will Rogers Field, Colonel Earl H. DeFord, base commander, cancelled all leaves and furloughs for personnel of the bombardment training group. After threats from some young men the Japanese Bazaar at 115 Northwest First Street, even though protected by two officers sent there by Chief of Police Frank Smith, decided to close up shop. Gunji Tada and his wife had owned the shop there for thirteen years. Gunji had lived in this country forty-three years and his wife twenty-five years. Their assistant, Motoko Hirose, was born in America. That was the temper of the times. The less restrained wanted to strike back at someone and a visible target would do — no matter what background — a feeling that reached its epitome on the West Coast in an over-reaction with a resultant bleak page in our nation's "melting pot" history.

The local Civil Service office asked for volunteers in more than seventy skilled trades to go to Panama and rush completion of defense facilities there. Police and private guards laid on strict security surveillance of city industries and utility plants. Lake Overholser was closed to visitors. Joe S. Morris, postmaster, added extra guards to postal quarters and at the main office restricted passage to all but public spaces. The county chapter of the American Red Cross opened an enlistment campaign for military

ROY J. TURNER
*Oilman, civic leader,
and governor.*

A. P. MURRAH
*Judge now heading
Federal Judicial Center*

JOHN R. ABERNATHY
*Preacher and Chamber
forum leader*

EDGAR S. VAUGHT
*Educator, attorney,
federal judge*

service nurses. The Second Air Support Command was activated here under Colonel Hume Peabody, at Will Rogers Field, in February. The twelve-year-old city oil field, as third largest producer in the nation, took on more importance with its monthly yield in excess of three million barrels.

Oklahoma City in February 1941 was treated generously in a National Geographic magazine story on the state, as it would be again nearly thirty years later. Under President W. E. Hightower the Chamber went all out seeking defense industries, stressing the high percentage of "native born" people, geographic location, transportation, power and fuel, and the lack of industrial labor competition. There was talk of making Lake Overholser a seaplane training area after Captain R. S. Fogg sat an amphibious craft down there to check out possibilities. The major prospect centered in a huge air depot which by March was off the "dream list." H. E. Bailey became the new city manager and $30 million worth of defense construction was underway or under order here.

In January 1942 Oklahoma City University began offering night classes in defense work specialities as vocational training classes in the city's public school system swelled. J. F. Owens retired as president of OG&E, to be succeeded by George Ade Davis. A former chief of staff of the 45th Infantry Division, Davis served without pay as the state adjutant general, after the National Guard was federalized. W. P. "Bill" Atkinson announced plans for a "Model City" planned community at Midwest City, envisioning homes for 2,500 persons, primarily those employed at the adjoining Midwest Air Depot. (Later Tinker Field). Lieutenant Colonel W. R. Turnbull was the newly arrived base commander. Fred Jones, who had been a dollar-a-year man in Washington for the war production program, became regional coordinator for the Office of Emergency Management and chairman of the Chamber's Industrial Division.

Eager to do something for the defense effort, citizens responded quickly to a "Victory Book Campaign" for reading material in military installations. Boy Scouts made the collections. The sunrise Easter Pageant at Lincoln Park became a civic activity casualty. Stanley Rogers organized an air raid warning system. A top project of the Jaycees encouraged flying the national flag at city homes. The city learned that, due to influx of defense plant workers, it had the lowest housing vacancy rate in many years.

New families arriving in March included persons from thirty-four states, West Africa and the Canal Zone. "Victory Gardens," reminiscent of an earlier World War, became popular again.

In April 1942 Frank A. Sewell became president of the Liberty National Bank as Ned Holman, identified with that institution nearly thirty years, stepped up to chairman of the board. Starting at Texhoma, Sewell retained his interest in a Clinton bank when he came here. Decades later his daughter, Mrs. Patience Latting, would become the city's first woman mayor. Gold stars began to appear in city windows as the United Service Organization (USO) recruited young ladies to join in social events for servicemen. Campaigns for sale of war bonds and war stamps found a responsive citizenry. Business firms joined in an effort to stagger working hours to make mass transportation more evenly spread. The Rotary Club purchased a $2,000 mobile canteen for use by the American Red Cross in December.

By 1943 gasoline and tire rationing demonstrated an effect on mass transportation as monthly revenue of the Oklahoma Railway Company nearly doubled that of a year earlier. The streetcar firm could switch from red ink to black on its ledgers for current operation. In January the Ramsey Tower became the Apco Tower, after its purchase by Anderson-Pritchard Company and by C. R. Anthony, whose mercantile interests were expanding also. In February the city was acclaimed first in the nation for lowest traffic fatality rate of cities between 100,000 and 250,000 persons. The second "war loan" drive in April had as its theme raising money to replace the battleship, USS Oklahoma, sunk at Pearl Harbor. Neal Barrett, manager of KOMA, was drive chairman. Lawrence J. "Smokey" Hilbert replaced Frank Smith as chief of police. Smith, who made his early reputation with the Federal Bureau of Investigation during the "Osage reign of terror" in 1926, went back to the FBI. The Baptist Children's Home on Northwest Sixty-third Street was enriched by a $100,000 gift from the Frank Phillips Foundation.

A highlight of early 1944 was launching at the Philadelphia Navy Yard of the light cruiser, USS Oklahoma City, with Mrs. Anton H. Classen as sponsor to christen the ship. City and county folk, joined by Cleveland county, raised $45 million in the second victory drive, part of the impetus being a substitute for the lost state named battleship. The cruiser's formal silver service also was donated. With most public interest on the war a campaign was put on seeking $125,000 to support the Oklahoma City Symphony, with Reverend William H. "Bill" Alexander as drive chairman. A public salute here and assistance in a war bond drive was an April event featuring Lieutenant Earnest Childers of Broken Arrow, an Oklahoma Indian, first of eight recipients of the Medal of Honor in the 45th Infantry Division, for action at Oliveto, Italy.

January 1945 began with city banks nudging the $300 million mark in deposits, which they would exceed by $2 million in March. A reflection of that was receipt of more than two million animals in 1944 at the stockyards for a record in its thirty-four year history. Dan W. James, owner and manager of the Black Hotel, in March took control of the Skirvin Hotel properties from O. W. "Bill" Skirvin, son of the founder, and his sisters, Mrs. Perle Mesta and Mrs. Marguerite Tyson.

Our people will long remember, although for varied and most personal reasons, the year 1945, since conflict in the European Theater ended in late spring and that in the Pacific in early autumn. Surrender of Japan created here — as the headline on a roundup story in *The Daily Oklahoman* by Ray Parr put it — "City Calmly Goes Nuts at Big News." As Parr wrote: "Nobody who saw and felt it will ever forget it — Oklahoma City's reception to end of the war. There will be nothing to match it in this generation.

"First there was the heart tug, so poignant it hurt down deep. Then there were tears, and prayers of humility, offered to Him who had guided loved ones through the terrifying nightmare of history's most cruel war, so that they might come home. There were tears for those who won't come home.

"But after tears and fearful tenseness came the realization that it was all over. The dam of courage that held pent up emotions for nearly four years finally broke.

"Oklahoma City was engulfed in a flood of hilarious happiness that swept through the streets in a wild torrent of joyful humanity."

Ceilings on wages, prices, rent and transportation remained for a time but except for meats, fats and oils, butter, sugar, shoes and tires, all other rationing was off. Many of those stamps and coupons could be burned gleefully or pasted in a memory book. Construction, held back by scarcities and controls, would bloom again soon. Problems of jobs after demobilization and curtailment at defense plants would in the next few years challenge the city's leaders and planners.

22

How Tinker Happened

I N AUGUST 1940, WORLD WAR II had been underway about a
year in Europe, after German invasion of the Low Countries, but
United States participation in a punitive way was yet more than
another year beyond an ominous horizon.

In common with much of the nation Oklahoma City folk were
apprehensive. They did not like the idea particularly, but there was a
feeling that, as was the case after 1914, we would be drawn into the conflict. Words or phrases like "lend-lease" and "Bundles for Britain" were
tossed around. Mistletoe Express trucks carried requests for "A Fin for
the Finns" emblazoned by two-sheet posters on their sides, in a campaign
to raise funds for the only nation paying off its War I debt to America.

The various continental army commands were having maneuvers,
the largest of any in peace time, as the 45th Infantry Division bore the
muggy heat of Louisiana as an element of VIII Corps, unknowing that planners were working on a Thunderbird call to active duty in September.
There was a feeling here that the city's major activity, in event the nation
got into the war, might be aviation related.

The Army Air Corps also was making plans, that August, and in
Washington R. A. Singletary, the "third senator from Oklahoma," representing the Chamber and primarily a roads and transportation man, was
knocking on doors trying to learn what his city could do — and get — in
connection with the defense effort.

He learned that the Air Corps wanted to take over a portion of
Oklahoma City Municipal Airport, get some additional land, build barracks
with support and operational facilities, and use it for training a light bombardment group using A-20 aircraft. That appeared to be positive. Among
other rumors that Singletary picked up was one about the then War Department desiring to construct as many as thirty aircraft plants, to produce
cargo and fighter craft for our allies, and for our nation. Singletary, in his
stolid, unexcited way, got on the phone to Stanley Draper at the Chamber.
That organization had no funds, of itself, with which to buy land. The city
had no money for such a purpose. Yet, if plants were a potential, it was
obvious that land would be needed. In a maneuver typical of such actions
since 1889, fourteen business leaders responded to Draper's call and met at
the Chamber on October 16, 1940, to form the Industries Foundation of
Oklahoma, Incorporated, a trust type of organization that could acquire
land and erect facilities for lease or later sale to the government.

Present were Samuel W. Hayes, Chamber president; Frank
Buttram, immediate past president; Harvey P. Everest, vice-president, and

Dan Hogan as another trustee. Included was an advisory committee headed by E. K. Gaylord with members Ben Barnett, Tom E. Braniff, W. C. Dance, W. E. Hightower, Ned Holman, R. B. F. Hummer, W. M. Longmire, L. A. Macklanburg and J. F. Owens. Articles of incorporation were filed on December 10, 1940. There were 291 men who subscribed $294,500 to fund the foundation. "Beneficial interest" in units of $500 were issued to subscribers without any guarantee of repayment of principal. Two years later, after citizens voted a bond issue, they did get their money back with five percent interest. Land previously acquired by the foundation was purchased by the city, through a bond issue, at its original cost. The first land acquired was adjacent to Municipal Airport, a 1,219 tract to be used for an air base. Jack Hull of the Chamber staff did the planning work on acquisition. The highest price paid was $175 per acre.

Then the boiling pot bubbled over. In late December Singletary learned that the Army Air Corps was considering location of an air depot in mid-America, along with one on the east coast, and one in the western states region. It was mentioned, almost casually, that Oklahoma City might be considered. Talk was that these would be permanent installations, with 2,000 to 2,500 employees annually; that they would cost anywhere from $10 million to $15 million and would require from 800 to 900 acres of land, of which 640 preferably would be flat.

Oklahoma Cityans were proud of their surrounding prairies. They were air conscious and had been since barnstorming days. They bragged about the large amount of flying time available here. They quoted statistics to prove that we had an average 328 flying days per yer, and more average hours of sunshine out of available hours of daylight, than even Miami, Florida.

So interest grew here, as James N. Eastman Junior described it later in the "Chronicles of Oklahoma." But a slight damper was put on some of the larger plans and dreams of Draper and others, after they were told — through Singletary based upon his information — that the city could not have both an aircraft plant and an air depot. The latter appeared to offer more permanency so it was decided to go after a depot with all urgency. The light bombardment training basis by now was affirmed.

Tulsa was found to be in the running for a bomber plant to be operated by Douglas Aircraft Company of Santa Monica, California. The Oklahoma City Chamber tried to help land it for the east side of the state and, perhaps, lessen any potential inter-city conflict for an air depot. Special legislative action was required, and secured, to eliminate state sales tax on materials to be used by Douglas. This was a temporary barrier. The Tulsa plant was announced January 31, 1941. Also in January the tempo of ground to air interest was heightened by a War Department announcement that Cimarron Field, west of the city, would be used for a primary training base. Clarence Page, B. S. "Cheebie" Graham and J. B. "Jerry" Sass, lost no time in securing a contract to operate that base, with civilian instructors and maintenance personnel.

In February 1941 the Air Corps asked the Chamber for data on a possible depot site of 960 acres, with details on labor, transportation, etc. Tentatively one was selected on SH 74, near Norman, and one on

Southeast Twenty-ninth Street, five miles east of the city limits then. In a rather secretive maneuver the Chamber started getting options on land with funds provided by business leaders.

The public, which had not been told all that was going on in order to keep land prices from zooming and speculators fogging the atmosphere, began to catch on February 26 when congress released testimony from a house appropriations sub-committee, made by Army Corps of Engineers at a hearing February 13.

Included was: "A board of officers is now out planning location of these (air) depots, being careful not to go into towns where factories are planned, so they will not upset the labor situation. However, I will say there will be a northeast depot, a mideast depot, and a midwest depot. To approximate that more closely, I will mention Albany, New York; Atlanta, Georgia; and Oklahoma City."

Oklahoma City, and specifically the Chamber and civic leaders, were going all out to secure a depot. They were aided by discovering that they had a friend at court, so to speak, in then Colonel Fred S. Borum, a native of Muskogee and chief of the field service division, Air Materiel Command. He was believed to favor Oklahoma City's location. Assistance on the Washington scene was provided also by Senators Elmer Thomas and Josh Lee and Representative Mike Monroney, along with that of Fred Jones, an official of the Office of Production Management at that time.

On March 8, 1941, a site inspection team representing the Air Corps and Corps of Engineers, came here. Heading the team was Colonel Frank M. Kennedy for air and Colonel H. A. Montgomery for the engineers. They inspected the Southeast Twenty-ninth Street site on the next day, a Sunday. On Monday an emergency meeting was called at the Chamber with the inspection team, the Chamber group, Mayor Robert A. Hefner, City Manager Harry E. Bailey, members of the City Council, and county officials. There was no publicity.

Colonel Kennedy told the group that Wichita and Muskogee were competitors for a site and offered to provide one without cost. The Oklahoma City group countered by offering up to 960 acres free and to meet any and all other requirements. This included removal and relocation of pipelines and utilities, providing rail sidings and improving roads, both arterial and access. The foundation had its subscribed funds to accomplish all this. There would be no delay pending passage of a bond issue. The inspection team asked for and received a binding agreement. Speculation was not a scare word to Oklahoma Cityans. Between Sunday noon and Monday morning was some of the fastest and most orderly "frenzied" data gathering that Jack Hull and the Chamber staff had ever done. To put it lightly, the inspection team was amazed.

John Ingersoll in Philadelphia, who controlled the Oklahoma City, Ada and Atoka Railroad, agreed to lay down spur tracks from that line to the southeast location. The City Council, not quite accustomed to speed, nevertheless went along by agreeing to call a bond election for a water line. Oklahoma Gas & Electric Company and Oklahoma Natural Gas Company foresaw no problem in extending their services. The word now was that 960 acres might be needed.

March 10, 1941, an appropriation bill for the three depots was passed and on March 18 President Franklin D. Roosevelt signed it. That appeared to finalize everything but it was not until April 8 that it became official when Robert U. Patterson, then Assistant Secretary of War, signed the project orders. Estimated cost was $14,036,215 and civilian employment was estimated at 3,500.

Prior to that, feeling very sure of the ultimate location and knowing that a civilian work force would be required but that hardly anyone in the city knew what an air depot was, or what people did in one, Draper, with the advice of Publisher Gaylord, felt that an informative newspaper series on depots was needed to help recruit labor.

The only Air Corps Depot at that time was at Duncan Field, San Antonio, which served the continental United States and the Caribbean area. We were told to go there and do a series for *The Daily Oklahoman*. Security at military installations already was in effect. Permission was secured from the War Department and excellent cooperation obtained from Colonel Royden Williamson, then public relations officer for the VIII Corps Area, at Fort Sam Houston.

This was done on April 5. The next day we went to San Antonio and spent two days interviewing personnel, both military and civilian, inspecting operations and taking photographs with an Army supplied photographer.

The evening of April 8, busily engaged writing on the intended series in a hotel room, we had a call from the city editor of the *Oklahoman*, Olin Archer, who asked: "How is the series doing?"

"Very well," was the reply. "About one more day and we should have it wrapped up and ready to start in the Sunday paper."

"You don't have that much time," Archer said. "The wires have just announced Oklahoma City as a location, so we need a story from you now to run alongside the piece from Washington."

The base was an assured fact. The land was under option but had to be purchased. Under Mayor Hefner the city council called for a bond issue of $982,000, most of which was for the depot land requirement, some

B-29 aircraft were repaired at Tinker Field in the post World War II period. This facility was used in the manufacture of C-47s by Douglas Aircraft during the war period.

A TF-33 fanjet engine is overhauled at the Oklahoma City Air Logistics Center at Tinker.

for purchase of land for general aviation airport use at Bethany, later Tulakes. With the bomber training at Municipal, and its space limitation of that day, commercial and private use taxed the city airport. The bond issue passed by a margin of nineteen to one on April 29.

(The installation when activated carried the name of Midwest Air Depot for nine months, then was renamed Tinker Field, for Brigadier General Clarence Tinker of Pawhuska, a part Osage, who was lost near Midway in the Pacific on a bombing mission.)

Contractors on the depot were Charles M. Dunning and Guy H. James of Oklahoma City, and Patterson Steel Company of Tulsa, as a joint venture. It was a cost plus, fixed fee job under a $14,270,000 contract, because a sense of urgency did not permit time for multiple bid letting. Actually, the prime contractors began work before the construction contract was signed. Ground was broken July 30, 1941.

In September the army said it would purchase an additional 480 acres to obtain a total of 1,440. There was a near $7 million expansion beyond the original plan, for a project cost in excess of $21 million. First 2,800 civilian personnel were trained at Duncan Field, others in city high schools and at the Twenty-third Street National Guard Armory. Among other things they had to learn to say "deppo" instead of "deepo."

In the summer of 1941 Fred Jones heard some scuttlebutt about a possibility that three more bomber production plants would be located in the interior of the nation for security reasons. That stirred city folk again.

After more rapid data gathering the Chamber submitted briefs on three possible locations: one near Will Rogers Field, one near Tulakes Airport, one adjacent to Tinker Field. The foundation wasted no time securing options to purchase land at all three proposed sites. At an informal suggestior. attributed to the White House, a group from the city composed of Virgil Browne, Chamber president, W. E. Hightower, E. K. Gaylord, Fred Jones, Draper and Hull, went to the Los Angeles area on October 22 to confer with Donald Douglas, to see if his firm would be willing to put a bomber plant here.

Early in January 1942 a group from Douglas came here to inspect proposed sites. They wanted no mass gathering. After being met at the airport by Mayor Hefner they first wanted to talk only to the mayor, as representative of the city, and Hull, representing the Chamber. In addition to data which Hull already had prepared there were other requests. Following a near all-night session by the Chamber staff this was provided. Involved was 480 acres east of the Air Depot, with the now expected committments about pipelines, utilities, rail and highway transportation arteries. Later others joined the conference. Included were County Commissioners Grover Pendleton, R. L. Peebly and Mike Donnelly, who agreed to improve county roads to the site. A call from Federal District Judge Edgar S. Vaught to Philadelphia, concerning extension of spurs from the Oklahoma City, Ada and Atoka Railway, got another favorable result. A two hour session with all data requested, and approvals needed, ended that exciting day. City Councilmen then were L. I. Baker, Joe C. Campbell, Leonard Dickerson, "Salty" Fullerton, Harlow Gers, Percy Jones, G. A. "Coxey" Stark and A. P. Van Meter.

There was a county bond issue of $1,225,000 for roads and highways to serve the plant and its workers, outside the base area, while the city had a tab of $864,000 for land and $685,000 in bonds for relocation of pipelines and extension of a water service line. All issues passed easily. C. C. Pearson came here as general manager for Douglas in June and on July 4, 1942, the ground was broken with more unspoken patriotism than florid oratory. The Austin Company was prime contractor for the "black-

B-52 aircraft being modified and overhauled at the Oklahoma City Air Logistics Center.

out" plant, with 1.75 million square feet in the main building, which was three-fourths of a mile long and had a maximum width of 850 feet. Later total plant space was about three million square feet.

Preliminary construction for the Douglas site began March 23, 1942, for there was much to be done before buildings could be erected. It was a $20 million facility, employing at the peak nearly 24,000 persons, of whom almost fifty percent were women. Many had preliminary training in the Oklahoma City school system's vocational education classes. As portions of the plant were completed they were turned over to Douglas. The first C-47 cargo plane rolled out in March 1943 after the first unit was released to the plane builder, being assembled from parts made elsewhere. Later the plant would do some manufacturing, too.

Plane Number 1,000 came off the line just a year later and its cost was paid by school children of the community as a contribution to the war effort. Number 2,000 came off in June 1944, Number 3,000 in October 1944, and Number 4,000 in January 1945. The plant produced a total of 5,355 C-47 planes and subassemblies for 400 C-54's, 900 A-26 bombers, and so on. The plant was phased out June 28, 1946, now is utilized by the Oklahoma City Air Materiel Area, more popularly known as Tinker Field.

Tinker during wartime reached a peak of 15,000 civilian employes. During that period it served as the parts supply depot for a large region, and was busily engaged in its second activity of a dual mission as a maintenance depot. It had a maintenance role on the B-29, after Boeing delivered the first big bird to the Air Corps in July 1942. Tinker modified the Enola Gay, the bomber from which the first atomic bomb was dropped on Hiroshima in 1945.

Tinker Field, in its twin roles, continued to play an active part in the nation's defense capability after War II and saw it increased in 1950 when the Korean War flamed south across the thirty-eighth parallel. It served as a home base for various services and functions of the renamed United States Air Force, after creation of the Department of Defense in the early 1950's. Troop carrier and other reserve units have used its facilities and services, particularly during the "Berlin Callup" of the Kennedy administration.

It is the nation's largest jet engine overhaul facility. OCAMA in 1973 was one of the largest logistical centers of the Air Force, supplying, maintaining and otherwise servicing weapons systems on a worldwide basis, along with aircraft. It manages materiel valued at almost $2 billion inventory value, in 26 million units, and handles more than two million requisitions annually, through automatic data processiong.

The Chamber began planning for the so-called Tinker Diagonal highway in 1951, with William Morgan Cain and Major General F. S. "Fritz" Borum as the front men in their respective Chamber and Air Force roles. It later would connect Interstate 35 and Interstate 40, being a portion of the latter since opening to traffic on May 18, 1962, when John Kilpatrick was Chamber president.

The installation has had some variations in function and employment over the years but on the whole has been rather stable. As jets took over from piston engines more than a decade ago, except for light aircraft, increased air speeds demanded longer runways for take-off and, particularly, for hotter landings than older planes required. Both Air Force and civic leaders saw a necessity for additional land. Another foreseen handicap was encroachment. Under the Chamber administrations of Donald S. Kennedy and Ray J. Spradling in the 1954-56 period the Chamber, with community support, provided 638 acres in 1955 (another eighty-three acres in 1968) for base expansion to the west. This was primarily for personnel housing and a hospital.

It was necessary to borrow $352,350 of the amount needed for this and later acquisitions, which made the total that citizens underwrote come to $1.2 million, provided on signatures alone by the First National and Liberty National Banks, pending later bond issues and sales. Some Chamber subsidiary funds were used. (A portion of this land in 1973 provided a site for General Motors that will become a major assembly plant.) Chamber presidents during this important growing period were H. B. Groh, Ancel Earp and Edward L. Gaylord, in addition to those cited above.

Additional protection the Chamber and community secured included 3,700 acres to the west and south, a portion of it acquired by the industrial arm of the Chamber for selective sale to air related and non-conflicting industries, while 10,465 acres to the south and east were brought under control. The city placed Lake Draper, a reservoir used for storage of municipal water, as terminus of the 100 mile long Atoka Lake pipeline, just south of the air base, to protect that approach.

The north approach to north-south runways — most commonly used in this area due to prevailing winds — was a problem. A housing area called Glenwood Addition was placed there when the area was outside limits of Midwest City and therefore there was no zoning control. There have been three accidents there, two in the immediate Glenwood area, where two persons were killed and much property damage resulted. Another occurred nearby when a jet pilot diverted his powerless plane just enough to miss Glenwood School. He died in the crash.

This situation in 1973 became quite an issue. In the face of base closings in various parts of the nation in an economy reduction, there was much talk from the state's delegation in congress, and from some Air Force officials, that unless the flight pattern was cleared of housing and other structures, there was a strong possibility that Tinker would be shut down. Nothing official — just strong talk.

That became quickly a matter of utmost civic concern. Not only is Tinker the state's largest employer, with some 22,500 civilian workers in addition to around 3,000 Air Force personnel, the near $300 million annual payroll and $50 million annually in procurement contracts let in the state is of greatest economic impact locally, regionally, and in some aspects, statewide.

After the Glenwood area was taken into Midwest City's limits an attempt was made to get an urban renewal area voted in, so that it could be cleared of its 836 homes and an elementary school, but that attempt failed. It was alleged the issue was not "sold."

Later, as seriousness of effects of an economic loss that might be forced on the area by base closing became more evident, Oklahoma county

A jet engine sub-assembler makes final adjustments on a stator vane at Tinker.

A powerful J-70 jet engine used in the F-4 fighter is being overhauled at OCALA.

commissioners, with support from the Chamber, business community and residents of the county, called for a bond issue of $10,800,000 to clear the area. In addition to removing housing, and reimbursing the school district, thirty-two vacant lots would be acquired. The whole approach pattern would become a green space with other uses.

On May 8, 1973, the "Save Tinker" bond issue drive, headed by Edward Cook, passed by a majority of eight to one, with 80,716 votes for it compared to 10,250 against the proposition, in one of the largest turnouts for a special county election yet produced. A sixty percent margin in favor was required. The result was 88.7 percent. Although the Air Force and administration guaranteed nothing, action by the community should have some effect on admittedly difficult decisions on base closures.

The city's activities in relation to origination and continuation of the complex now known as Tinker Field, was rather well summed up in 1964 by Major General Lewis L. Mundell, after three and one-half years here as commander of OCAMA, when he said:

"Support rendered by the civilian community is without parallel in the Air Force today. Although this support appears to be known and acknowledged throughout the country, I don't believe that unselfish and courageous actions toward the common good taken by this community and its leaders, are yet understood and appreciated."

(The designation "Oklahoma City Air Materiel Area" was scheduled to be changed to "Oklahoma City Air Logistics Center" in April 1974.)

23

Growth Has Many Faces

LWAYS OPTIMISTIC, EARLY IN JANUARY 1946 E. K. Gaylord proposed to the Chamber that the city's slogan should be "300,000 by 1950," and directors of that group went for the idea. At that time the city population estimate was 220,000 and that of "greater Oklahoma City," or metro area, was 267,000. By 1950 census figures, four years later, the city was credited with 243,504 persons and the metro area with 325,352. A major portion of the latter count came from growing Midwest City, which like the air depot it was intended to serve originally, grew instead of declining in post-war cutbacks as did some other defense oriented installations. Other surrounding cities also grew although major suburban buildup was more than a decade away.

In February 1946 alumni of the University of Oklahoma Medical School began a drive to raise $3 million to hasten creation of a medical research center. Plans and hopes for the Oklahoma Medical Research Foundation had been of concern since 1944. The idea spread across the state. It was not until mid-1949 that construction began with completion a year later of a basic $800,000 building adjacent to the medical school. For the groundbreaking Oklahomans had a distinguished visitor, Sir Alexander Fleming, a Nobel prize winner for discovery of penicillin, which he told us here in an interview came while he was "rabbit hunting" in the laboratory. He came at the invitation of Governor Roy J. Turner for the first of two visits the British scientist made to the city in a few years. Efforts to get a Veterans Administration Hospital here, which began also in 1944, were culminated in the autumn of 1946 when a 500 bed hospital was authorized by President Harry Truman. It also was in the Medical Center area.

Meanwhile the city was having growing pains and changed ownerships of "landmark" buildings. With Ike Hall, R. D. Cravens purchased the Perrine Building at North Robinson and First Street (later Park Avenue) and then a bit later Cravens added the Petroleum Building a block north, which later was called the Republic Building (for the oil well supply firm that was a subsidiary of Kerr-McGee after that firm purchased it) and before being sold to Midland Mortgage.

In April 1946 Representative Mike Monroney received the Collier's Trophy for the most outstanding national contribution to aviation. The Variety Club of Oklahoma received a national award for most outstanding charity work in the previous year in competition with similar clubs. The National Governor's Conference met here, as it had in 1938, to set some sort of mark at that time, since only five cities had twice been host to such a meeting. Outboard motorboat racing, absent from waters of Lake Overholser during the war, returned in June 1946 seeking a portion of $1,120 in prize money in fourteen racing events. For those with a lingering memory for other times, there was a touch of nostalgia in November when interurban service to El Reno and Guthrie ended.

Governor Turner took the lead in proposing to Oklahoma City and Tulsa business leaders, and to members of the legislature, that a four-lane, limited access highway be built between those two terminals as a toll road. It would reduce mileage by more than fifteen miles and aid highway safety as two-lane US 66 carried an increasing traffic load. This would be the first turnpike west of the Mississippi. Later it was assured, constructed through sale of revenue bonds, and carried Turner's name. He carried Turnpike Pass Number One and, years later, said privately that this was the only such thing that came out of his administration.

"I don't mind using the pass occasionally," he confided to us, "since it cost me personally $55,000. There was no other way to finance some studies and trips back east to talk to bond buyers — and I believed in value of the turnpike to the state."

In March 1947 the city's sixth radio station began operation in Capitol Hill as KLPR, a 1,000 watt station. April of 1947 saw a devastating tornado hit Woodward, with a lesser but damaging flick of its tail at Leedey, with 106 persons killed and millions in damage. In May hundreds of city folk, led by scores in construction trades under a Turner proclamation for a "W-Day," went to the stricken city to help in reclamation work. In June a benefit rodeo for Woodward and Leedey was put on at Taft Stadium, with services of contestants, livestock producers and arena help, all donated. There were some celebrities here from Hollywood including Western star Johnny Mack Brown, who provided a laugh to the crowd and got a painful back bruise for himself, when tossed by a trick mule. In June the Jaycees had reason to feel proud — for the second time in two years the local chapter was declared most outstanding in the nation.

Oklahoma Industries, Incorporated, the business development arm of the Chamber, in January 1948 acquired an additional thirty-five acres of land in the Santa Fe industrial area to go with 146 acres that it had purchased from Doctor L. J. Moorman, which began soon to fill up with plants and distribution facilities north and south of Thirty-sixth Street. KTOW began operating from the top floor of the Apco Building as the seventh city radio station. Later it became KJEM in another location and in 1973 changed to KLEC. There was some pleasure in May of 1948 when Oklahoma City was declared a Grand Award winner in the National Safety Contest for the previous year. It was first in traffic safety for cities in the 200,000 to 500,000 population rank and shared an overall rating with Wilmington, Delaware, for the top spot. With Tulsa, Oklahoma City was among ten cities that exhibited a business gain in excess of ten percent the previous year.

With some of its building condemned, the Salvation Army in early 1949 turned to the city for help in securing $148,000 with which to build a new Citadel and Family Recreation Center. W. S. Key headed the drive that provided funds. In May 1949 one of those things that captures public interest happened when children put nickles and dimes into a fund to buy a baby elephant for the Oklahoma City Zoo. The 1,000 pound creature, shipped from then Siam, arrived with a great display of enthusiasm. A "naming contest" by letters resulted in the female elephant being named Judy. She remains queen of the herd at Lincoln Park.

The zoo got much national attention in 1950, also, when "Leapy the Leopard" took French leave. A few big game hunters and a number of other out-of-state volunteer types, some with dogs "trained to hunt down mountain lions," descended upon the area as local volunteers walked the hills. Leapy brought himself back and died from an overdose of tranquilizer in some "bait" meat left out for him at the zoo. In 1951 a Hokkaido bear was sent to the zoo by men of the 45th Infantry Division, then training in Japan after the Korean War callup. Friends of the Zoo, organized in 1954, and the Oklahoma Zoological Society, both have aided in making Lincoln Park Zoo one of the nation's finest. Passage of improvement bond issues by citizens helped greatly in providing physical facilities.

Television arrived in Oklahoma City in June 1949, at WKY-TV, the first of such stations in this part of the nation, later the first local station of all to initiate color telecasting. The station equipped the Little Theater at Municipal Auditorium for a sound studio and offered three hours of television daily — except Saturdays. Opening the first telecast were Governor Turner, E. K. Gaylord (whose sale of a Denver radio station provided funds for WKY-TV), Father John Walde, Rabbi Israel Chodos, Doctor Henry G. Bennett, Senior, Doctor John Abernathy and station manager, P. A. Sugg.

A major transaction in city banking circles happened in August 1949 when the First National Bank and Trust Company purchased the Tradesman's National Bank. The First then sold the Tradesman's ten-story building at Main and Broadway to City National Bank. With that merger the First became the state's first $200 million bank. That August was a month for bank activities. Central State Bank (the former Morris Plan) headed by L. D. Lacy, announced that it would build a half-million structure at 304 Northwest First Street.

September saw a shift of three Oklahoma Air National Guard units from Norman to the northwest side of Will Rogers Field. Initially part of a fighter unit, the base later would be headquarters of the wing, then shift to troop carriers and cargo craft, retaining headquarters in the state. The cargo fleet was upgraded.

The year 1950 began in Oklahoma City with all indications of a building boom that by December would surpass any previous year with more than $50 million in building permits. This upward trend continued the previous year's volume of $33 million and was in advance of the Korean War, with its construction material scarcities, which would not be noticeable for some time after the blitz across the thirty-eighth parallel in June. The U.S. Postal Service instituted a new method of delivery from the office here to state towns with a "mobile post office" which replaced vanishing rail deliveries to the trade territory.

The first of annual science fairs for city high school students was held in April and has continued. Under reminders of the city's growth over sixty-one years and its ability to "make great plans" and then live up to them, citizens were asked to vote $36 million in general obligation bonds in May, for a large number of improvements. Heading the list, as it did historically, was water resource development, followed by street improvements, sanitary sewers, and a new fairgrounds, for major items. An important portion was the city's share of an $18 million North Canadian floodway project, with the largest contribution coming through the U.S. Corps of Engineers.

T.G.&Y. Stores, heading toward becoming one of the nation's major chains, constructed its general headquarters and warehouse in the Santa Fe industrial area. The U.S. Army Reserve found a new home at Northeast Thirty-sixth Street and Eastern Avenue, near the National Guard's Lincoln Park Armory. In June the new home of the Oklahoma Baptist Convention was dedicated at Eleventh and North Robinson. St. Ann's Home for the Aged, at Northwest Sixteenth Street and Portland was dedicated. By July, C. R. Anthony Company was in its new headquarters at Northwest Sixth and Broadway and talking about four new stores in California — its first on the West Coast — quite a distance from those in the Rio Grande Valley. Oklahoma Publishing Company made a $1,700,000 expansion in its productions department by bringing in a multiple unit press, capable of printing a sixty-four page paper, including sixteen pages of color, at the rate of 600,000 copies an hour.

The city by year's end saw 1950 surpass all previous years in construction underway, more than twice the volume of the "boom" year of 1929. Deposits of $401,000,000 in the city's eight banks also was a record — an increase of twenty-six percent over the previous year and the largest increase of any other major city in the tenth Federal Reserve District. Bank debits also showed the largest reserve district increase with a sixteen percent rise over 1949. In August there were special forums and civic club meetings to honor men of the 45th Infantry Division, including the large number of city units, that for the second time for many of them were called up for federal service. They were to report at Fort Polk, Louisiana, September 1, in terrain quite familiar to many Thunderbirds who were there on maneuvers in 1940 and 1941 prior to an even larger war. In the face of things unknown to come, the recruiting slogan was "Go with the men you know." Major General James C. Styron of Hobart, a veteran Thunderbird, was division commander.

Early in 1951 Midwest City folk and the original developer of that community, W. P. "Bill" Atkinson, had reason to exhibit civic pride. In a contest sponsored by the National Association of Home Builders, with thirty-six communities across the land competing, Midwest City was declared the "best and most completely planned city." For those in Oklahoma City concerned with cultural aspects, there was pride in an announcement that a new central library at the corner of Northwest Third Street and Robinson, would replace the venerable Carnegie Library there.

The near quarter-century old city oil field was accepted as a routine fact as 1952 began, although excitement had long since crept away, while most of the speculators departed. The Chamber, in an attempt to remind folk of the industry's importance to the city, told them that more than

30,000 persons were employed in our immediate area by the petroleum industry. Something perhaps more familiar to many persons — the soil that supports all plant life and the livestock industry — was brought into focus in May 1952 with the first National Land Judging Contest. Sponsored by WKY and WKY-TV, with a score of cooperating agencies, the contest grew to international scope and continues to the present. Teams from across the nation compete here annually in a contest comparable to that of livestock judging, through evaluation and description of soil profiles, capabilities and nutrient needs.

The month of May also saw dedication of two new church structures here in Westminster Presbyterian at 4400 North Shartel, and Crown Heights Christian Church at 4020 North Western. Doctor Walter H. Judd, then a congressman from Minnesota and former medical missionary in pre-War II China, was dedicatory speaker at the latter church in the first of many appearances he has made here. In June 1952 the United Fund of Greater Oklahoma City was formed (now United Appeal). It was designed to combine fund raising of all voluntary, character building and private welfare agencies into one drive. (Some fragmentation led later to creation of the Appeals Review Board, which passes on all major fund solicitations in the city, for official sanction.) The original United Fund had C. R. Anthony as president. Harvey P. Everest headed the study group whose recommendation resulted in creation of the organization.

One could say that 1953 revealed plans and specifications on drawing boards that were to shape many things to come for the city. One was removal of four miles of track from the fairgrounds area, except for the main line of the Rock Island heading west and some spur trackage; removing some fourteen miles of other rail lines for creation of industrial districts, and for a fifty-four mile system of urban expressways and the crosstown system of limited access highways. The old fairgrounds on Eastern Avenue would undergo quite a face lift as it was adapted for Douglass High School. Bendix-Westinghouse late in the year broke ground for a plant in the Willow Springs industrial area — where it would be seventeenth in two years to build in a special location — and sixty-fourth industry to do so since the industrial area project idea was shaped up in 1946.

In April 1953 the first major store outside the downtown area came as Sears Roebuck put in its 174,000 square feet facility on Northwest Twenty-third and Pennsylvania. This was the first major commercial construction on the original Shepherd homestead. Plaza Court at Northwest Tenth Street and North Walker was the first varied shopping center, of any size, opened in the city, but Sears was the first "giant" to move out and set a now familiar pattern. Sorey, Hill and Sorey drew Sears' plans and Manhattan Construction Company was the contractor.

An enterprise along other lines was development of Southwestern Bible College, near 5000 Northwest Tenth Street, an affiliate of the Pentecostal Church. L. D. Lacy headed a fund drive for $100,000 to equip classrooms for students, trainee ministers and missionaries, for the school founded in 1946. Now it is Southwestern College and general academic in nature rather than being strictly Bible oriented. From 250 students it has grown to some 1,000. Prior to the 1953 fund drive some classes of the college were held in a remodeled mule barn. A long needed link between Oklahoma City north of the river and Capitol Hill was a bridge on South Agnew, opened in July 1953, with other improvements on the thoroughfare between Southwest Twenty-ninth and Reno.

In July 1953 the city got its second television station, also in the VHF or very high frequency range, when KWTV was licensed. A syndicate including Roy J. Turner, Forrest E. Harper, Luther T. Dulaney, Henry S. Griffing and John T. Griffin and known as the Oklahoma Television Corporation, formed the original firm. Edgar T. Bell, former manager of radio station KTOK, was executive vice-president and general manager. Later the Griffin interests, which had a stock majority in the beginning, acquired stock from the other incorporators. When the KWTV tower was erected it was the tallest man-made structure in the world, at 1,580 feet, being taller than the Empire State Building in New York. Like most records that, too, fell in time.

In 1953 also there were two other television ventures here in the UHF, or ultra high frequency range. They were KLPR-TV with a tower at Britton Road and Lincoln Boulevard and a studio at 128 West Commerce, and KTVQ-TV, in the old Victoria Theater at Northwest Eighteenth and Classen Boulevard. The necessity of converting sets from a VHF to UHF band, before such adaptability was built into receivers, made those two ventures unprofitable. The third VHF station, KOCO-TV, at Northwest Sixty-third Street and Portland, came later after an original beginning in Enid. The 1953 Oklahoma State Fair featured a reunion of the state's Future Farmers of America on the organization's silver anniversary. In August that year the Gold Star Memorial Library on the campus of Oklahoma City University was opened with some 54,000 volumes in its stacks.

January of 1954 saw Fred Jones named chairman of the board of Braniff International Airways, following the death of Thomas E. Braniff. There was recognition of value to the city of the Oklahoma National Stockyards Company as a terminal market in January when a steer, one of a load trucked in by young Jack Haley of Mountain View, was the fifty millionth animal marketed here over forty-four years. Oscar Holderby said that in this time more than $2.5 billion changed hands here in the livestock industry. The last interurban (that to Norman) made its final trip. The old streetcar terminal became a 675 space carport, under John Singletary, while other terminal structures were headquarters of his Globe Life and Accident Insurance Company.

Native Oklahoman Major General Fred S. Borum, retired as commander of the Oklahoma City Air Materiel Area and from the United States Air Force, chose to make his home here. He became an official of Liberty National Bank and Trust Company. Major General William O. Senter, a West Texan, succeeded Borum at Tinker. The Oklahoma Television Authority, an educational outlet, went on the air late in 1954 with its antenna placed on the KWTV tower and equipment supplied by that station and by WKY-TV.

At the 1954 renamed State Fair of Oklahoma, in its new and most modern layout, a ceremony which drew units of the 45th Infantry Division from across the state for the first such assembly off a military reservation, saw Thunderbird colors returned to the division. Colors and standards were retained by the active army in Korea after Oklahomans were rotated home. The army retained the designation in Korea, for esprit purposes, so for a time there were two 45th Infantry Divisions. There was some cause for civic pride out at Will Rogers Field, too, when American Airlines Flight 202 en route from Los Angeles to New York, set a DC-6B down as the one millionth plane to land here.

Civic leaders could add a glow also at learning the city, for the eighth consecutive month, ranked as one of the nation's top ten cities in economic increase indices. For the year of 1954 a construction record was set with $105 million as industrial expansion — the barometer most eagerly watched — showed more than $52 million in outlay. Early in 1955 an Economics Club was organized.

Oklahoma City in 1955 ranked among the nation's top ten cities in the number of earth scientists. It was one of them, Dean A. McGee, who two years earlier headed a Chamber committee to promote additional scientific thinking and education that would stretch beyond known horizons. Later this committee was nucleus of an organization called Frontiers of Science, chartered as a nonprofit foundation September 20, 1955. It sponsored a National Science Fair, and later in emphasizing industrial development based upon the physical sciences, with the Chamber, sponsored a preview of the 1957 Semi-Centennial Exposition at the State Fairgrounds with a 1956 Southwest American Exposition. Frontiers of Science attracted international attention. Its advisors were drawn from leading scientists of this country and Great Britain. The initial organization was expanded quickly to a statewide group with McGee as chairman of the board; E. K. Gaylord as vice-chairman; James E. Webb (then president of Republic Supply Company and later to head the National Aeronautics and Space Administration) as president; Virgil Browne as treasurer and C. Don Ellison as secretary. In a very short meeting $400,000 was subscribed to the foundation to assure its first five years' operation. Doctor Robert MacVicar, dean of the graduate school at Oklahoma State University, was borrowed to be executive director. There were thirty-four trustees on the charter and seven more added later.

Not only was this an idea whose time had come — reaching that milestone on the calendar of vision was expedited. As written in a "Country Boy" column in The Daily Oklahoman on January 10, 1956: "All that Frontiers of Science has is a piece of paper for a state charter, a borrowed office, a lend-leased director, and the faith and credit of men with enough vision to see in it something of value for Oklahoma, even though some of them might not be around to see all fruits of their efforts." Webb took the science foundation story to a White House Conference on business, science and education in 1957.

In November that year President Dwight D. Eisenhower came here to make a major nationally televised and reported address, which praised actions of the Frontiers of Science Foundation and recommended that it be emulated across the nation. Earlier that year Doctor James Harlow, on leave from an associate professorship in education at the University of Chicago, replaced MacVicar as executive director. Frontiers of Science remains a volatile, going organization, sponsoring special days for high school upperclassmen, scholarships, symposiums, seminars, and educational tours. Addressing the Chamber and the Oklahoma City Advertising Club in autumn of 1955. Gaylord, whose life spanned the eras of which he spoke, said prophetically that "within the next twenty-five years man will join his creator in making the (physical) elements he needs. Pioneers subdued the wilderness with rifle, axe and plow. The new pioneers of science will subdue the universe with telescope, microscope, test tube, nuclear reactors and the electronic brain."

Early 1955 saw Oklahoma City awarded location of the National Cowboy Hall of Fame by trustees from the seventeen historical western states forming the governing body of an organization that eventually made reality of one man's dream. He was Chester A. Reynolds, a homesteader in Colorado who left (but retained ownership of) a hard scrabble quarter-section to be a clothing salesman, eventually sales manager, president and board chairman of the H. D. Lee Company of Kansas City. A rodeo buff, the short statured, quiet spoken man in his conservative but obvious city clothes, spent more time around the back side of an arena than in a box seat. Between Chet Reynolds and rodeo cowboys a mutual respect and friendship was developed.

On a visit to the Will Rogers Memorial at Claremore, Reynolds looked with admiration of that excellent statue of Rogers and mused: "Here is a man revered by all the world who always called himself 'a plain ol' Oklahoma cowboy.' This is a magnificent tribute to Rogers. Why not have, somewhere in the west, a tribute to all 'cowboys' who helped develop the American West?" Reynolds found the answer to his own question by traveling thousands of miles at his own expense, talking with business leaders, governors, congressmen and others. Governors of the seventeen western states, as ex-officio members of a board themselves, appointed initially two other persons from their states as members of the board of trustees. At their expense they met in Denver, formed the then uncharted organization, made a public announcement of their plans to have a memorial to builders of the west, and asked that interested cities participate in site nominations. More than 100 responded. The list was reduced to ten. A site selection committee was appointed to inspect them. Supporting Oklahoma City's nomination from the beginning were Stanley Draper and E. K. Gaylord.

Visiting here in March 1955 was a committee headed by Albert K. Mitchell of Albert, New Mexico, with Ray Schnell of Dickinson, North Dakota; A. M. G. "Swede" Swenson of Stamford, Texas, and Fred H. Dressler of Garderville, Nevada. They were due a few surprises. They were shown two potential sites. That on Persimmon Hill on the Northeast Expressway, with its dominant terrain feature, was preferred. They saw also some 400 horsemen riding through downtown streets, in response to enthusiasm the prospect generated. They saw the grand champion steer of the current Oklahoma 4-H and FFA Junior Livestock Show in a hotel lobby. They looked in on a banquet given by Armour and Company for more than 400 young FFA show exhibitors. Impressed, they continued looking in other states, finally deciding on three locations to be recommended to the board: Oklahoma City, Dodge City and Colorado Springs.

The flags of 17 Western states wave daily in front of the Cowboy Hall of Fame.

Reynolds announced findings of the site selection committee and asked those three cities to make a presentation in Denver to the full board. Each city was permitted six representatives in the meeting room, to make a one-hour presentation. Representing Oklahoma were Governor Raymond Gary, former Governor Roy J. Turner, Glenn W. Faris, Ferdie J. Deering, O. C. Brown and Roy P. Stewart. Talks by Gary and Turner and the excellent presentation made by Faris, including movies of traffic by the site, and colored slides of the site itself, were the main arguments. Where representatives of the other two states offered to secure whatever land that trustees desired, if awarded the site, the Oklahomans told them: "This is your site. We have twenty-five acres of city park land with option on the adjoining twelve acres."

In some spirited dialogue the matter of financial support came up. Finally Turner, in effect, guaranteed that Oklahoma would raise more than $500,000 as its initial share. A California trustee, who thought Turner was being goaded into promising increasing figures, at that point said "this has gone far enough — we are here to select a site — not to get money pledges. Most of us know some of the people with whom we are dealing." He called for a vote. Later Fred Hall, then governor of Kansas and a native of Dodge City, declared in a moment of petulance to newsmen outside the meeting room: "Those damned Oklahoma oil men bought it." Unfortunately that went over the wires. Later Schnell and others declared selection was made on site merit alone, including all year availability and transcontinental traffic flow.

Had the "bidding" reached a million dollar figure before Oklahoma City was chosen, folk in our state would have demonstrated later that such a promise was justified, in the shortest, most enthusiastic fund campaign ever held here. Other states did not come in as rapidly. In justification one wonders how much Oklahoma money would have been sent to a distant ate had such a one been given the location. A design contest handled through the American Institute of Architects drew many entries. Two young men from Birmingham, Michigan, were winners. There was some questioning by older trustees at the design. Now it is considered outstanding. A quota system, based upon population, was put on for member states. Aside from Oklahoma, the first states to reach quota were New Mexico and North Dakota, due primarily to interest of their trustees and their personal standing at home. An additional fund drive was made here in 1961. Individual contributions helped.

There was a period of delay following 1959 after excavation and first unit construction was done. A site dedication earlier on November 11, 1955, was most colorful as nearly 2,000 horsemen rode in from the east to cover the triangular shaped field below the hill site. Will Rogers Junior was master of ceremonies. On a very cold January day in 1958 ground breaking ceremonies were held with each state adding a bit of its state's earth. Among celebrities attending were Glenn Ford and Jack Lemmon, whose movie, "Cowboy," had a premier here with proceeds going to the memorial. In early 1961 the first annual Western Heritage Awards program was featured, recognizing outstanding contributions to understanding and appreciation of the West, in print and film media. It drew, and continues to draw here, many outstanding personalities of the entertainment and publishing fields.

Delay in construction ended in July 1964 when funds for completion of the first units were made available through the Oklahoma City Industrial and Cultural Facilities Trust. Now, with the words "Western Heritage Center" added to its original name, course of the institution's progress is constant. Dean Krakel, then director of Gilcrease Museum in Tulsa, had been chosen director. Opened formally in 1965, within two

The Rodeo Hall of-Fame in the southwest wing of the National Cowboy Hall of Fame.

James Earle Fraser's "End of The Trail" was brought from California to Oklahoma City and restored for its final resting place in the National Cowboy Hall of Fame here.

years 640,000-visitors inspected the center, which then featured more than $2 million worth of western art and sculpture, a nostalgic "West of Yesterday" museum and other exhibits. Some of this was acquired by the memorial through purchase, including some of the best Russell and Remington objects, others were donated by helpful supporters. A major acquisition was works and actual studio furnishings of James Earl and Laura Fraser, dominated by the original plaster statue of the "End of the Trail," a gigantic work done originally for a world's fair at San Francisco in 1917. The Hall of Fame secured it from Visalia, California, by offering to restore it (a year's job) and having it cast in bronze, with the coast city getting the bronze for its park. Now the original is housed in the Payne-Kirkpatrick Memorial, (Mrs. David D. Payne with Mr. and Mrs. John E. Kirkpatrick) beside the (Jasper D.) Ackerman Garden. The statue reconstruction was made possible by Mr. and Mrs. Dean A. McGee.

Attendance at the shrine by late 1973 passed the 2,900,000 mark. Reynolds, the founder, did not live to see the center opened but did know

Night view over reflecting pond at the Cowboy Hall of Fame and Western Heritage Center.

that its completion was assured. Featured at the hall is an interesting educational exhibit in a giant national map, in relief, with lighting tracing the major routes of Western expansion. There is a Hall of Great Westerners, with honorees selected by member states and voted upon by trustees; a National Rodeo Hall of Fame whose honorees are named by the Rodeo Cowboys Association; a Hall of Great Western Performers and Charles Schreyvogel Memorial Studio. Other famed artists represented in the hall are Thomas Moran, Henry Farny, William Leigh, Irving Couse, Frank Tenney Johnson, Alfred Jacob Miller, Joseph Sharp, Carl Runguis, Albert Bierstadt, Thomas Hill and Nicolai Fechin. Modern artists also are represented.

24

City, State Half Century

ARCH OF 1955 SAW A GENERAL Motors Training Center opened out on the Northeast Expressway, near Hummell Village, where state mechanics could receive specialized training. The auto age influence was noted downtown, too, when the First National Bank and Trust Company erected a twelve story parking garage and drive-in bank facility. This lasted only until 1972 when it was demolished for a still larger parking structure. A visitor, long absent from a once familiar scene, would look in vain along that block of West Main for Sturms Clothing Store, Pettee Hardware or the original Roach and Veazey Drug Store. All are gone and in the case of the hardware and drug firms, so are other stores that once they had spotted around the city.

Kerr-McGee Industries indicated more of its growth as a producer and marketer of fossil fuels by purchasing Deep Rock, of Tulsa, for $17 million early in 1955. One-way streets made their appearance in May, with traffic bound south on Robinson, Hudson, Dewey, Paseo, Shartel and Brauer. (Some modifications were made later.) North bound movement was on Harvey, Walker and Lee. After a trial some east-west restrictions were dropped. The Order of DeMolay presented the city a bronze bust of Will Rogers, located in the park that bears his name, in June 1955.

Friends of the Zoo made a safari to Africa seeking specimens for Lincoln Park Zoo. A movie made from the musical "Oklahoma!" had a premiere in New York City and staid citizens there had some unexpected entertainment in lobbies of the Astor and Waldorf-Astoria Hotels, and over radio, from the colorfully costumed Surrey Singers of Oklahoma City University. At some appearances, including one in Central Park, the Oklahoma delegation headed by Governor Raymond Gary, also had Gordon McCrae and Shirley Jones who starred in the movie, along with Richard Rodgers and Oscar Hammerstein II, who wrote and composed the show. Producer George Skouras also was around.

Before 1955 faded away C. R. Anthony announced that with purchase of seventy-nine stores of the Woodward chain, there were now 240 Anthony stores dotted across country from the Mississippi River to West Coast, in the company's thirty-third year. Voters approved about one-half of a $40 million public improvement bond issue.

The city's interest in science was demonstrated early in 1956 when an "Atoms for Peace" display, shown only in Geneva up to that time, was put on exhibition here as a forerunner of the semi-centennial year to follow. The National Science Fair in May drew teenagers from thirty-nine states.

With John Dunn as station manager, the Oklahoma Educational Television Authority initiated its "school" classes in science and mathematics. Mistletoe Express, which in 1932 began operations with offices and dock in the converted Boga Ballroom on Northeast Fifth by the rail tracks, early in 1956 began construction of its enlarged plant about a block east. The Chamber staff, in cooperation with representatives of the Oklahoma City Real Estate Board, found it no longer necessary to keep secret the purpose for which options had been taken on an area between Hudson and Harvey, Southwest Sixth and Seventh streets. A new 207,000 square foot Post Office building would sprawl there by 1958.

Appearing on the scene with the new year of 1956 was *Oklahoma Today*, the official state magazine. Trans World Airlines returned to the city after a twenty-two year absence. Originally it was Trans Continental and Western Air, "the Lindbergh Line," named after the noted flier who laid out most of the route. Under auspices of the Jaycees a "Big Brother" movement was inaugurated here in March 1956. Kerr-McGee became the twelfth state firm to be listed on the "big board" of the New York Stock Exchange. W. T. Payne headed a campaign to secure the final $830,000 for completion of Mercy Hospital's $1,725,000 expansion.

Cinerama, the major development in motion picture screening in many years, came to the Warner Theater in May 1956 with a benefit performance that provided seventy-five percent of receipts for the Symphony and the remainder to the Boy Scouts. The Turner Turnpike celebrated its third birthday the end of May with a record that might have silenced any remaining critics of its feasibility: 5,896,000 vehicles had used it; there was $1,768,000 in the bank to start paying off that portion of a $38 million bond issue due two years hence. Liberty National Bank and Trust Company announced that it would erect a sixteen-story parking facility across Couch Drive to the north, topped off by the Petroleum Club. Swinging long steel girders into place for a "catwalk" high in the air, connecting the two structures, provided entertainment for downtowners. The Petroleum Club moved later to the new Liberty Tower.

In May 1956 ground breaking ceremonies for the Baptist Memorial Hospital on Northwest Highway near Grand Boulevard was an event attracting nearly 4,000 persons. Some sixteen years later a planned expansion took place. In July 1956 another educational institution was promised the city area, a year later, when Doctor James O. Baird announced that Central Christian College would be moved from Bartlesville and renamed Oklahoma Christian College. From its original home on the Foster Estate at Bartlesville, the college would expand into a major campus, east of Eastern Avenue on Memorial Road, as its student body and endowments increased.

At long last Lincoln Boulevard, north of the state capitol complex, in 1956 was four-laned to the Northeast Expressway under a $1,074,000 contract to D. E. Steelman. The Chamber and civic leaders previously underwrote some related expense such as utility line removal and right-of-way. In July the then Civil Aeronautics Administration at Will Rogers Field underwent a major expansion. Central Airlines did something a bit different with educational air tours to state cities for youths, aged eight to eighteen, in groups of eight or more. In August a premiere of the Todd-A-O movie version of "Oklahoma!" was held at the State Theater, with $5 tickets as a benefit for the National Cowboy Hall of Fame. OG&E announced plans for a $2 million depot at Southeast Seventy-fourth and High streets. The Fairway King, an electric golf cart made here, by August was buzzing around courses across the nation. Better known to thousands of consumers in national and international shopping centers was a cart invented and first produced here by Sylvan Goldman, who saw need for a space saving "nesting" shopping cart, while operating his Humpty Dumpty and Standard stores.

Labor Day weekend of 1956 here saw a mammoth National Aircraft Show. An added feature was placing soil of three continents around a flag plaza to demonstrate the widespread effect on training facilities at the aeronautics center. Ultimate expansion of Aero Design and Engineering Company at Tulakes Airport was assured by civic underwriting of site costs as the CAA upgraded status of the air field.

Oklahoma's semi-centennial year of 1957 got a noisy and colorful start January 8, with a large downtown parade of bands, Round-up Clubs, Indians and other participants, climaxed by a public bonfire of Christmas trees provided by citizens. In a Chamber report it was said that $131 million was spent or committed the previous year for industrial development here. Of that amount more than $13 million was at the CAA complex. Members of St. Luke's Methodist Church were quite interested in seeing installation of their $93,000 organ with its 5,500 pipes, in the new $1.5 million edifice at Northwest Fifteenth and Robinson. St. Anthony Hospital conducted one of its periodic campaigns for expansion. Early in March it was announced that Western Electric would construct a $35 million plant on West Reno which would employ about 4,000 persons. A pilot plant preceded the major installation with a building in the Willow Springs industrial area.

Naturally the Semi-Centennial Exposition at the fairgrounds, June 14 to July 7, 1957, was a dominant attraction and activity of that year. One feature was participation of eleven nations in the largest trade fair held in the southwest. Getting quite a bit of attention was an exhibit from the Soviet Union, first that country had in the United States since the 1939 New York World's Fair. Exhibits of many kinds from medical to science to automotive, with individuals involved, resulted in a total involvement or representation from twenty-two nations. The United States Postal Department cooperated by issuing an "Arrows to Atoms" commemorative three-cent stamp on opening day. An International Symposium of Science, Industry and Education was also a highlight with leading figures of this and other countries, as speakers. A "Boomtown" reflected some of our more gaudy heritage.

On July 7, 1957, a time capsule was buried at the fairgrounds to be opened in the year 2007, end of the first century after statehood. In November it was announced that Mr. and Mrs. John E. Kirkpatrick were donating $267,000 for a $400,000 Oklahoma Art Center, also at the fairgrounds. Later they provided $400,000 for the Science and Arts Foundation Building nearby. An airport improvement bond issue for $7,497,000 was passed by voters. Annual reports from the Chamber are markers on the road of civic progress. That after 1957 was still another of those "best year ever" accountings, as it was pointed out proudly that almost $181 million was expended or committeed for industrial expansion.

Early in 1958 a new plant for Continental Plastics was indicative of yet another step in man-made products rather than fabrication of natural materials. Security Federal Savings and Loan Association opened its new quarters at Northwest Second and Harvey. A new downtown institution, the Bank of Mid-America, took over the old Baum Building, vacated when Fidelity moved to Park Avenue and Harvey. In August 1960 Mid-America was absorbed by Liberty. Out on the Northwest Highway, near Tulsa Avenue, Wedgewood Village was under construction in February as an amusement park, in competition with the long established Springlake Park of Roy and Marvin Staton's across town. Wedgewood survived a number of years. In March Doctor Jack S. Wilkes became sixth president of Oklahoma City University. Later he would be mayor and still later, until his untimely death, president of Centenary College in Louisiana.

Toward end of the first quarter of 1958, Tinker Field held contracts for a new base hospital and 268 units of permanent housing. The first four phases of the Oklahoma City floodway, to keep the North Canadian under control, were completed by the end of March. In April ground was broken for the Atoka reservoir, a distant but needed adjunct to the city water system, for which funds were provided in a 1955 bond issue. The year 1958 was another "record" for industrial expansion with a figure of $195,015,976.

Not the least construction project announced early in 1959 was that for a new federal building, to be a block long and five stories tall, on Northwest Fourth Street just north of the Post Office and Federal Building on Third Street. It had a maximum price tag of $8,280,000 in

The entrance to Turner Turnpike, state's first turnpike, connecting city with Tulsa.

the congressional authorization and appropriation bill, with a figure of $7,140,000 as a starter. On a joint venture Dow Gumerson and Benham Engineering Company and Affiliates (later Benham, Blair and Affiliates) were the architects. It would contain 262,659 square feet of space. Before year's end an $800,000 research building for the University of Oklahoma Medical Center on Northwest Thirteenth Street would be underway, with a federal grant of $400,000 and matching funds from the legislature. The George Frederickson Field House on the Oklahoma City University campus was dedicated in February, also.

To protect Will Rogers Airport from encroachment and mitigate problems faced by many cities, in March civic leaders underwrote $300,000 to secure 500 acres on the approach patterns, to be repaid later by bond issue funds. Out on Southeast Fifteenth Street a major cross-country truck terminal was put in by Transcon Lines at a million dollar cost. Now called the Federal Aviation Agency, the installation at old Will Rogers Field took over control of the nation's air space. It had a permanent payroll then of 1,875 persons. A helpful $153,000 grant from the parent FAA in Washington aided the city in improving Tulakes Airport, later Wiley Post Airport. After a rather disastrous fire in June, Wilson & Company constructed a new and more modernized plant at the stockyards, which after Armour closed its plant became the only major packer here, although there are a number of independents.

Midyear of 1959 brought the information that Oklahoma City had an evaluation, for tax purposes, of $485 million. This was some $40 million above that of the previous year. Industry conscious folk were pleased to learn that Tinker Field, which had for years attracted the interest and help of many persons, contributed $172 million annually to the area economy. A major shopping area was that of Penn Square, north of the Northwest Expressway and spreading from meandering Deep Fork Creek to Pennsylvania Avenue. This center of seven large buildings was to contain forty-six retail stores and a restaurant, including at the time the largest Montgomery Ward retail store of that national company.

In August Wiley Post Park off South Robinson, adjacent to the now reclaimed area of the floodway, was opened, with its recreational facilities. An Oklahoma Air National Guard building program on the northwest section of Will Rogers Field was underway in September. Many "temporary" World War II buildings were removed. A long awaited and needed structure across the North Canadian was dedicated later in the Agnew Street bridge. October of 1959 saw OG&E making a third enlarement of its Mustang plant, at that time the largest generating plant in its system, and one more step along its continual progress on the energy road. For its achievements in traffic safety, Oklahoma City for 1959 was awarded four certificates in varied classifications by the National Safety Council. This was the only city in the nation to receive that many awards and tied with Grand Rapids, Michigan, for top place among all similar sized cities.

In February 1960 the city saw its first mobile library service. What was termed a $44 million "luxury home and country club project," surfaced with announcement of Quail Creek, a development of a full section included in annexation of 1959. It was bounded by May Avenue, Portland

Avenue, Memorial Road and Northwest 122nd Street. The golf course covered 160 acres. A bit to the south of that, west of May Avenue and between Wilshire Boulevard and Britton Road in the area east of Lake Hefner, another major area development came into being as Lakehurst. It called for 375 homes in the $35,000 and up bracket. Much earlier this had been part of the G. A. Nichols estate, riding academy and related activities.

The U.S. Army Reserve began construction of a half-million dollar armory on West Reno, west of May Avenue, second such facility to that at Lincoln Park. Governor J. Howard Edmondson used a "silver" pick to break ground for two new state office buildings north of the capitol — the Will Rogers and Sequoyah Office Buildings, adjacent to Northeast Twenty-third Street. (Anyone who wonders which building is which should remember that Sequoyah was an Eastern Cherokee and Will Rogers a Western Cherokee (partially) so east or west ancestry identifies the buildings.)

By mid-1960 the Chamber could report a $90 million city growth in six months; that its auxiliary, Oklahoma Industries, had sold its last piece of property in the Willow Springs area (one-time gravel pits, then swimming pools) to Frigiquip Corporation, maker of auto air conditioners, which had 465 dealers in thirty-eight states and six foreign countries; that sixty year old Oklahoma Hardware Company, now under W. E. "Gene" Smith, had grown six-fold to an annual $6 million volume in nine years; that construction was underway on a $2 million Federal Reserve Branch Bank building at Northwest Third and Harvey. Sorey, Hill and Sorey were architects while Builders Construction Company was the contractor.

One of the year's biggest events, though, was a national guessing game. Would Oklahoma City in 1960 attain a population figure of 600,000? Much publicity went out. There were prizes totaling $4,100 in cash, plus merchandise, awaiting lucky guessers who could get closest to census figures for a metropolitan area within thirty miles of the domeless capitol. There were 65,000 entries. To add a bit of flavor official "judges" of the contest were recognized sports figures: Allie Reynolds, the former Yankee pitcher; Charles Coe, national amateur golfing champion; and Tommy McDonald, All-American halfback from the University of Oklahoma and a star of the Philadelphia Eagles. Not the least prize was use of an Aero-Commander airplane for a week, with its crew supplied.

Robert W. Burgess, director of the census, told Senator Robert S. Kerr, and he promptly relayed the information to W. J. Fuchs, chairman of the Chamber contest committee, that the designated area held 534,902 persons. Louis C. Watkins of Maryville, Missouri, was winner of the $1,000 cash prize. By coincidence he also got another $1,000 from Macklanburg-Duncan, which had offered that amount to winner of the guessing game if he was a customer of that firm. A gentleman from New Mexico was second place winner. Natives were represented by Mrs. Jackie W. Adams of Oklahoma City, in third. Not surprising, 1960 was another "record year" in economic growth with a figure of $216,382,243, combining all indices.

Early in 1961 part of the long planned (by civic leaders with Stanley Draper leading) Southwest Seventy-fourth Street Expressway was under construction. It would tie in Interstate 35 to the announced Southwestern

Turnpike, later named for H. E. Bailey, from the city vicinity to a terminus southwest of Waurika, near Red River bridge. This was an eighty-five mile long, controlled access road, requiring $56 million in bonds, among other places connecting the state's largest city with Lawton, soon to be the third largest. In May by gubernatorial and mayoral proclamation, the first week was proclaimed "Fly the Flag Week," and was rather universally observed. Leader in this promotion was Lee Allen Smith of WKY-TV, who later was backed by the Oklahoma City Association of Broadcasters in creating an annual "Stars and Stripes" extravaganza, that has brought nationally known celebrities here for a patriotic program unique in the age of dissent.

In March of 1961 the venerable Huckins Hotel was purchased by R. D. Cravens, who immediately set into action a program of rennovation for that historic hostelry. Orval O. "Sandy" Saunders, one-time farm news director at WKY, then managing director of the American Dairy Association in Chicago, came here as secretary-manager of the State Fair of Oklahoma. During his tenure the fair has, from its profits, added more than $3 million of improvements to the city owned facility. Lone Star Brewing Company, purchasers of Progress Brewery, spent about a million dollars in renovating that plant. In March Lone Star bought the grand champion steer of the Oklahoma 4-H and FFA Junior Livestock Show to herald its presence in the city.

On May 19, 1961, ground was broken for Elm Creek Reservoir, a detention lake which had a dual purpose. It protected the south approach to Tinker Field runways and was terminus of the Atoka pipeline bringing water to the city distribution system. Aero-Commander, later to be a property of the Rockwell interests, rolled out its first turbo-jet executive airplane in May. It would sell for $600,000, as a basic price, and cruise at more than 500 miles an hour. Cato Oil and Grease Company, near the old fairgrounds, had a disastrous fire and rebuilt a new facility to produce products sold over the nation and to other countries. Later it was purchased by Kerr-McGee. In June the FAA placed its aero-medical research here which resulted in an added facility for the FAA Center. Across the city another defense installation came into being with the 32nd Air Division of the U.S. Air Force, coordinated with the Army Air Defense Command, under the North American Air Defense Command.

An illustration of international importance of the FAA Center was provided in mid-1961 by the fact that 327 representatives of fifty countries received training here. Of lasting value to the city and state, although not measurable, was existence and use of a "Host Family" visitation program which permitted foreign visitors to spend some time with a city family. The long term effects are priceless. It was noted in the autumn of 1961 that Oklahoma County, small in area by comparison to most others of the seventy-seven, had more impounded water than any other county, with 11,065 acres of surface water. One of those periodic city bond issues for creation or improvement of municipal facilities was passed to the tune of $39 million.

In September Oklahoma State University opened its Technical Institute here, an adjunct to the Stillwater campus that would make evening courses, in addition to day programs in technical skills below degree level, available to local residents. For $2.7 million in bond funds on right-of-way purchase, the city laid out its share on forty-nine miles of expressway as part of a $60 million new highway development. This was part of a $39.8 million bond issue. Another issue for $47 million would be affirmed in 1962. Growth was keyed to the decade.

Comedian, dancer and serious musician Danny Kaye, helped get 1962 off to a good start in January by appearing with the symphony at a benefit performance. After many years in a downtown hotel the Oklahoma Press Association moved in February to a home of its own on North Lincoln. Announcing additional construction were United Founders Life Insurance Company for a twenty story, circular building near North May and the Northwest Expressway; Kerr-McGee for a similar sized office building in its growing center; Oklahoma Publishing Company for a $2 million, five story structure between the original, ornately trimmed building on North Broadway and the mechanical plant on Northwest Fourth Street. The city was already basking in another "record" year summing up for 1961 with $219,531,092 in capital expenditures. Kerr-McGee early in 1962 announced also that all its research activities would be here in a center near Northwest 150th Street and Portland Avenue.

Preparing for its annual exposition the State Fair of Oklahoma started adding 117,000 feet of new building space, primarily in the livestock area but including housing for a "Children's Barnyard," with mothers and offspring of many animal types. Tinker Field in February 1962 was selected as a site for an automatic switching system for Air Force logistics. The Sheraton-Oklahoma Hotel, the former Biltmore, had a $1.5 million interior "face lifting." Partially in honor of the chain which was to operate the hotel several years, Grand Avenue had its name changed to Sheridan, as the city council in April also renamed Northwest First Street, Park Avenue, and Northwest Second Street, Robert S. Kerr Street. In August Ling-Temco-Vought announced location of an electronics and aerospace plant west of the city. Melpar, another electronics firm, opened a manufacturing facility here on the east side. Cain's Coffee Company built a new $2 million plant on the Broadway Extension, south of Edmond, while Macklanburg-Duncan had a million dollar expansion on North Santa Fe. That firm's payroll increased to 570 persons. The city's development total for 1962 was just under $280 million.

(The former Biltmore Hotel, after being acquired and operated by the Sheraton chain, was sold to Gotham Hotels, Limited, of New York, which closed it in September 1972. In November that year it was sold again to United Funding Corporation of Albuquerque, which opened it February 1, 1973, only to close down on June 2, because of financial troubles. At end of 1973 the hotel remained closed.)

The year 1963 was just starting when Senator Robert S. Kerr died. Services at First Baptist Church drew President John F. Kennedy, Vice-president Lyndon B. Johnson and a host of other dignitaries. Kerr, long time Democratic National Committeeman, first native born Oklahoma governor, developer of a major fuels industry, was called "uncrowned king of the senate" because of his power there.

Near the end of January, Charles L. Jenkins and James Doss announced a $15 million, enclosed shopping mall project, to be built on the original Shepherd homestead on Northwest Twenty-third Street, east of Villa. First called Shepherd Plaza, the name soon was changed to Shepherd Mall. There are seventy retail stores within the project, which encompasses fifty-four acres. The Federal Reserve Branch Bank acquired an addition downtown.

In March 1963 more than 350,000 county residents received Saulk oral vaccine as part of the national drive to eliminate polio. Mid-America Life Insurance Company erected a $1.2 million headquarters on North Lincoln. A drive to obtain $750,000 for support of Mummers Theater was successful. This was matching money for a $1,250,000 grant from the Ford Foundation.

Exploring the concept of a "Tivoli Gardens" similar to that in Copenhagen, for the downtown urban renewal area, the director of that world famed installation was brought here for a talk at the Chamber. A local committee visited Denmark to see the original complex in April 1963. Something new was added to mail addresses as the city received a zip code prefix of 731 on July 1, 1963. Old zone figures were to be added to the prefix. A tennis center on the Oklahoma City University campus emerged bearing the name of Travis Kerr Magana, son of Mr. and Mrs. Cecil Magana and grandson of Mr. and Mrs. Travis Kerr, following a $75,000 contribution. Dan James sold the Skirvin and Skirvin Tower Hotels to the Statler Hotel Corporation in July. A federal grant of $936,000 for improvements at Will Rogers Airport was matched by the Oklahoma City Airport Trust.

In August 1963 a plant for University Loudspeakers was dedicated. This was a subsidiary of Ling-Temco-Vought. Late in September the "world's largest" generating plant was dedicated at Harrah by OG&E. It was a combined cycle gas and steam generating unit, by expanded Horseshoe Lake. That month also saw dedication of the Belle Isle Branch of Oklahoma City Libraries. In October the payroll at Tinker Field was increased to an annual $145 million level. KOCO-TV put up a new transmission tower on Britton Road, east of North Kelley, which it could boast was 250 feet taller than the Empire State Building in New York. KWTV also carried out a major expansion, including a new studio with transistorized telecasting and recording equipment.

As 1963 neared its end the Oklahoma National Stockyards Company could brag that it hosted the "world's largest feeder and stocker cattle market." Virgil and Henry Browne announced that the Oklahoma Coca-Cola Bottling Company would place a 127,000 square foot facility on ten acres across from the fairgrounds on North May. Plant capacity would be 1,800 bottles per minute.

The city's seventy-fifth anniversary came in 1964, basking in afterglow of another "record year" when $317,970,310 was committed for growth. On the anniversary of the "Run" of 1889, instead of a rifle shot there would be a sonic boom, which Stanley Draper insisted was the sound of the future. The State Fair planned improvements on two buildings and erection of a monorail to support a new type of ride over the grounds. Oklahoma Industries, Incorporated, added a third structure to the General

Electric industrial complex in the northwest area. Star Manufacturing Company would build a $1 million plant on a twenty acre site near Interstate 35 and Southeast Eighty-ninth Street. At Northwest Sixth and Hudson, Continental Apartments would rise as the city's first high rise downtown apartment structure. Statisticians decided that the tourist and convention industry was worth $25 million annually to the city and that those dollars turned many times before coming to rest. To dedicate the Fourteen Flags Plaza" at the State Fair, President Lyndon Johnson came to the city, providing some amusement to spectators — and concern to Secret Service agents — when he climbed aboard a saddled horse nearby and put on an exhibition of neck reining. Oklahoma Medical Research Foundation in autumn added a $1 million addition to its facility on Northeast Thirteenth Street. A new building was dedicated at the FAA Center to house national aviation records, for which responsibility was transferred here.

25

Urban Renewal's First Years

IN 1962 A GROUP OF LEADING Oklahoma City businessmen, concerned about the lack of an orderly development program for their community, formed the Urban Action Foundation of Oklahoma City, Incorporated.

Today tall buildings dominating the city's skyline are a testimonial to the vision of those civic leaders. But it is doubtful that even they, despite scope of the goals they set for themselves, foresaw all dramatic results of the urban renewal program they helped launch.

That program, less than a dozen years later, produced more than $200 million in new development.

Oklahoma City's first Urban Renewal Authority was formed by the city council on November 2, 1961, following passage of an enabling act by the state legislature in 1959.

The original OCURA board of commissioners appointed by the council consisted of Granville Tomerlin as chairman; F. D. Moon, vice chairman; C. Kenneth Woodard, secretary-treasurer; Reuben G. Martin and Joe C. Scott, members.

The only member of the original board still serving in 1973 was Moon. Other commissioners by that time were Jim Lookabaugh, chairman; W. M. Harrison, Harvey P. Everest and F. C. Love.

OCURA's modest beginning, in contrast to its extensive operations today, is illustrated by its first annual report published in July 1962. It listed no liabilities, no expenses and no income. Its assets amounted to $8.67 in the form of a corporate seal — paid for by the commissioners.

Eleven years later the authority's twelfth annual report listed assets and liabilities, including funds for operating its three renewal projects, of $94,857,682.

Despite their enforced economizing, however, the first OCURA commissioners were far from idle. Moon estimated they spent more than 1,000 man-hours studying urban renewal laws and procedures, Oklahoma City's housing codes and comprehensive plans and visiting other cities, such as Tulsa and Little Rock, which had renewal activity under way.

By the end of 1962 they were ready to begin planning their first urban renewal program, the University Medical Center project, and an application for planning funds was submitted February 1, 1963.

Meanwhile, in October 1962, the Urban Action Foundation had come into being. Although its immediate concern was downtown redevelopment, its stated purpose was, in part, to "support, promote, devise, plan and initiate . . . a wise and sound program of development and redevelopment, expansion and growth of the urban and metropolitan area of Oklahoma City. . . ."

And the businessmen backed their promises, not only with time and effort, but with cash-ultimately nearly $800,000. Most of this money was for renewal planning or early acquisition of property and was repaid after renewal programs were funded. But a large amount also was donated for travel, equipment, brochures, a documentary movie and other informational aids.

The first president of the Urban Action Foundation was Dean A. McGee. He was succeeded by William Morgan Cain. Other officers included E. K. Gaylord, Donald S. Kennedy and Stanley C. Draper.

Although the community was ultimate beneficiary, it was the fledgling Urban Renewal Authority which received the most immediate help from the foundation. On February 18, 1963, the OCURA Board hired James T. Yeilding, former commissioner of urban renewal in Cleveland, as its first executive director. But no federal funds were available until May of that year, so Urban Action paid the director's salary in the interim.

When federal money was released, Yeilding and a few aides set up offices in the Kerr-McGee Building and began planning the Medical Center project. As both the staff and work load increased, the offices were moved in October 1963 to 22 Park Avenue.

In that same month an application was submitted to the federal government for funds to draw a General Neighborhood Renewal Plan (GNRP) for all of downtown Oklahoma City. But such funds were in short supply, and OCURA faced a prospect of up to a year's delay in beginning planning of a new central business district.

Broadway looking north from Grand in 1937. Nearly all buildings in sight are now gone.

Again the Urban Action Foundation stepped into the breach, urging immediate action on downtown planning and guaranteeing payment of all costs incurred.

With this assurance, OCURA engaged one of the world's leading architectural and urban planning firms, I. M. Pei and Associates, to draw what might prove to be the most far-reaching and innovative plan devised for redevelopment of the central core of a city.

Pei (pronounced "Pay") began work early in 1964, and in December of that year, just one month after federal funds finally were received, he unveiled the dramatic GNRP (or "Pei Plan," as it became known) for revitalizing the city's 528-acre central business district.

The plan immediately captured the imagination of city residents and drew nationwide attention. It won for the city, Chamber of Commerce and Urban Action Foundation, a "Citation for Excellence in Community Architecture" from the American Institute of Architects.

Such awards were not new to Pei's firm. It had received nearly three dozen similar honors for work in cities all over the world. The New York-based company (now I. M. Pei & Partners) designed the terminal buildings at JFK International Airport, FAA air traffic control towers in most major cities, the $250 million Bunker Hill project in Los Angeles, Raffles International Center in Singapore, the planned John F. Kennedy Library in Cambridge, Massachusetts, and scores of other facilities.

But the plan for downtown Oklahoma City, Pei himself reported, was believed to be the first that called for clearing of most of a city's central core and its complete redevelopment with facilities carefully designed — functionally, spatially and esthetically — to support and enhance each other.

The Pei Plan called for five interlocking elements in the downtown area: a business, financial and office district; convention facilities; a garden-type, cultural and recreational center; a retail shopping core and a major residential area.

The proposed gardens reflected the interest in downtown demonstrated by the Urban Action Foundation from its beginning. One of the foundation's first activities was sponsorship of a nationwide competition for the best design of just such a center.

The design was to be based on the concept of Copenhagen's famed Tivoli Gardens, but in keeping with Oklahoma culture and tradition. The contest was climaxed by an elaborate "Scandanavian Ball" honoring Henning Soager, director of Tivoli Gardens.

Elements of the winning entry were incorporated in Pei's proposed cultural and recreational center, which he dubbed the "Oklahoma Tivoli Gardens." (Later the park area officially was renamed Myriad Gardens, but its concept — incorporating cultural, recreational, shopping and entertainment facilities in a unique verdant setting — remains essentially the same.)

After study by the city council and other agencies during the first part of 1965, the Pei Plan was adopted by the council on September 7 of that year.

Pei had recommended the GNRP be carried out in four or five stages, each a separate urban renewal project. With approval by the city

The famous Huckins Hotel at N.W. Main and Broadway, was a victim of Urban Renewal.

Cupolas from Baum Building at N.W. Grand and Robinson were saved from demolition.

of the GNRP, the Urban Renewal Authority in the autumn of 1965 began detailed planning of the first stage, to be known as Project 1-A.

And once more, to avoid delay while federal funds were being sought, the Urban Action Foundation agreed to underwrite cost of the planning. The result was that work was completed in about a year, and the plan for 138-acre Project 1-A was approved by the city council on December 20, 1966. Federal approval followed one year to the day later.

By that time, again thanks to the Urban Action Foundation, buying of property in the project area already had begun. Confident of eventual approval of the plan, the UAF advanced funds late in 1967 for acquisition of the first property in what was to be site of the new Mummers Theatre.

While carrying out the general — and later the more detailed — planning of the downtown renewal program, OCURA in 1963 and 1964 simultaneously was planning the University Medical Center project.

Initial planning for this 240-acre area, south and west of the Medical Center itself, was completed in the spring of 1964, and the plan was submitted to the city council late in June. An uncommonly large number of agencies with varying political jurisdictions were involved in the area. They included the University of Oklahoma, the State Highway Department, Capitol and Medical Center Improvement and Zoning Commissions, the Board of Education and Oklahoma County, in addition to the city.

Reviews of the plan by these agencies required several months, and the application for a federal loan and grant was not submitted until May 1965. It was approved by the Department of Housing and Urban Development (HUD) in October, and field operations in the Medical Center project, the city's first to get under way, began on Valentine's Day, 1966.

By this time planning of the city's third renewal program, the 1,258-acre John F. Kennedy project, was well under way. Bordering the

Medical Center area to the west and extending east to Interstate 35, this project was to be the largest in land area west of the Mississippi River. Its northern boundary is Northeast Twenty-third Street, while on the south it reaches to the MK&T Railroad south of Northeast Fourth Street.

Planning of the project was completed in a near-record six months, with city council endorsement coming in May 1966 and HUD approval following in July. The federal government then held up release of funds, pending clarification and some modification of the plan for relocating families and businesses. The money finally was released in January 1967, and field operations began in March.

Internally, the Urban Renewal Authority itself also experienced changes during this period. Yielding resigned as executive director in October 1966, and this time the Urban Action Foundation offered help of a somewhat different form. It "loaned" OCURA its executive director, Dowell Naylor, to act as special assistant to the Board of Commissioners until a new renewal director could be found.

The post was filled on a permanent basis in January 1967 with appointment of James B. White, then general counsel for the Chamber. A native of Oklahoma City, he was born in a home in what was to be, more than forty years later, within the JFK renewal project area.

In January 1969 OCURA's central office moved from the soon-to-be-razed Twenty-two Park Avenue Building to the Colcord Building at Sheridan and Robinson avenues.

The Medical Center field office, after displacing itself from three other structures due demolition, finally settled in 1973 at the YMCA, 614 Northeast Fourth Street. The Rehabilitation Department opened a field office in April 1968 at 1608 Northeast Twenty-third Street and has remained there since.

By 1967 operations were underway in all three of the city's renewal areas. Work began in the University Medical Center project early in 1966, and JFK and downtown Project 1-A followed within a year.

The original urban renewal plan for the Medical Center project provided about fifty acres for future growth of the Center itself. Scarcely had activity in the area started before the first proposals were raised for expansion of the center to a 200-acre Oklahoma Health Science Center, occupying large portions of both the Medical Center and JFK projects.

The result was that in November 1966 OCURA received funds for replanning the project, and work on the restudy began in January 1967. The new plan provided for buying and clearing, by OCURA and various state agencies, of virtually all land between Northeast Eighth and Northeast Thirteenth streets, from Durland east to Stonewall Avenue.

Even with this proposed expansion early planners greatly underestimated the economic impact of the Medical Center project. The authority's third annual report predicted the renewal program "will result in about $20 million of economic activity in this immediate area and adjacent neighborhoods, including public investment of $10.9 million and private investment of $8.7 million.

By 1973, completed public and private development in the Medical Center project totaled more than $61 million, with another $53 million in construction on the drawing boards. The city's face would change.

Inevitably the change in the project, together with later amendments to the plan, caused delays in the program. Originally scheduled for completion in three years, the project is now due to be closed out sometime in 1974.

The 234-unit Collins Gardens Apartments, sponsored by Avery Chapel AME Church, were constructed in the area in 1967, and by 1973 more than seventy new homes had been completed or were being built in the project. Another eighty homes had been renovated under urban renewal's rehabilitation program of grants and low-interest loans.

In the Health Sciences Center north of Eighth Street, work had been completed on the $13 million addition to University Hospital, a new Basic Sciences Education building, headquarters of the State Department of Public Health, and a central heating and air-conditioning plant to serve the entire center. Construction of the $27 million Presbyterian Hospital was well under way.

Throughout the Medical Center project OCURA has constructed new streets, relocated or replaced water and sewer lines, and carried out other public improvements. Total estimated cost of the program is $38.5 million, of which the federal government has supplied more than $19 million. Remainder of the cost was supplied through non-cash "credits" for work done by the City, University of Oklahoma, State Highway Department and other local agencies.

In the sprawling JFK project to the east of the Medical Center, the emphasis from beginning has been on rehabilitation of existing homes and construction of new residences. By the end of 1973, more than 1,400 home-improvement projects had been completed or were under way, and some 130 new houses had been built. The Oklahoma City Housing Authority also had constructed the 200-unit Marie McGuire Plaza for the elderly at Northeast Twelfth Street and Lottie Avenue.

But in 1973 the federal government ended or sharply curtailed home-rehabilitation loans, and virtually all types of subsidized housing, including public housing. As a result, residential development in the area has almost ceased by end of the year, and prospects for the future were extremely uncertain.

Despite the slowdown, however, OCURA was moving ahead with public improvements throughout the project. The first thirty-eight new houses in the seventy-five-acre JFK Addition, between Northeast Fourth and Seventh streets, were nearing completion; new streets, water lines and other facilities were in place to serve the remainder of 300 homes planned for the addition.

Lottie Avenue was being realigned and rebuilt, and Stonewall Avenue was soon to be widened. Land had been cleared west of Eastern Avenue for a link between Northeast Eighth and Tenth streets to provide an east-west thoroughfare across the project area.

The city had constructed a new fire station at Northeast Twenty-first and Eastern, while land had been cleared for a branch library at Twenty-third and Eastern. A 2½-block area between Kate and Prospect avenues, south of Twentieth Street, had been cleared, originally as the

A photograph of a scale model of one of the plans for Oklahoma City's Urban Renewal.

site for a new elementary school. But the Board of Education shelved plans for the school, pending an acceptable school-integration plan, so the city agreed to develop and maintain the area as a city park.

Net cost of the JFK program by the end of 1973 was approximately $26.9 million, while total federal funds contributed to the project amounted to $28.4 million. The federal share exceeded the net cost primarily because of the large number of relocation and home-rehabilitation grants in the project area. These grants, borne entirely by the federal government, are not counted as part of the project's net cost.

Even before its final approval, success of downtown Project 1-A was virtually assured. Prospective redevelopers were poised at the starting line when the federal government flashed a green light on December 20, 1967. Within six weeks plans had been announced for $65 million in new construction.

Less than six years later, development completed or underway had nearly doubled the initial figure, topping $128 million. On drawing boards were plans for another $135 million in new construction.

Thus Project 1-A alone, the 138-acre first phase of the Pei Plan, was assured by the end of 1973 of producing at least $263 million in new development. Of this amount, $218 million represented private investment.

Pei predicted in 1965 that the entire 528-acre Pei Plan would result in private investment totaling $220 million. Even allowing for subsequent inflation in building costs it is evident that Pei's projections were extremely conservative.

Renewal operations in Project 1-A were expected to take seven years to complete. But after a little more than four years in the field, OCURA had completed more than ninety percent of its work, and only two or three small sites had not been committed for redevelopment.

At the same time, in May 1972, the authority applied for an amendment that would increase the project size by six blocks — to 164 acres — and the federal share of the cost by $34.7 million. The purpose of the change was to permit construction of a four-block retail core, or Galleria, and future expansion of city offices on either side of City Hall. A redeveloper already had been selected for the Galleria, which will occupy the site bounded by Robinson, Sheridan, Hudson and Park avenues.

The application to expand the project was submitted at a time when the federal administration was cutting back on urban renewal expenditures, rather than increasing them. At the same time, however, HUD recognized OCURA's and the city council's contention that momentum must not be lost in rebuilding Oklahoma City's downtown area, and that the Galleria could be key to completion of the entire Pei Plan.

Finally, after more than a year of consultation among city and federal officials and members of the Oklahoma congressional delegation, a compromise was reached. HUD approved a grant of approximately $16 million, and the city council agreed to underwrite the remaining $18.7 million, to be paid out of federal funds received for renewal operations over the succeeding four years. Buying of property in the Galleria site was expected to begin early in 1974.

Approval of the change in the 1-A plan assured the downtown not only of a new $100 million retail core, but of other developments as well. Economic consultants on the Myriad Gardens, for example, predicted that construction of the Galleria immediately to the north would attract private enterprise to the gardens. Investors also were eyeing with renewed interest possible hotel and retail sites near the Myriad-Galleria complex.

The Galleria and the Sheraton Century Center, a full-block hotel and retail complex for which ground was broken late in 1973, will be connected to a pedestrian circulation network constructed by private enterprise.

Other major structures completed in the downtown renewal project include the city's Myriad Convention Center; the thirty-six story Liberty Bank Tower, Thermal Systems' central heating and cooling plant, the thirty-story Kerr-McGee Center, the Fidelity Plaza, Mummers Theatre Building, the fourteen-story First National Center, and parking garages accommodating nearly 3,500 cars.

Long a meeting place for state, regional and some national conventions, Oklahoma City fancies itself as a gathering center. This belief — and doing something about it — reached an apex in 1972 with dedication of Myriad Convention Center.

The result of more than ten years of planning, design and construction, it was Oklahoma City's $23 million response to the need for a mammoth convention and entertainment center.

Looking northwest toward Oklahoma City's downtown over the Myriad Convention Center.

Covering four square blocks, bounded by Santa Fe on the east, Sheridan on the north, Reno on the south and Robinson on the west in the south central business district, Myriad has more than 950,000 square feet of space under roof. There is an array of services and facilities that the embracing name suggests.

By resolution the city council designated Myriad as a memorial to former Mayor Allen Street, who had one of the more harmonious administrations and the longest, at that point, of twelve years.

Within principal areas of the Myriad — a name adopted by the council that emanated from a skull session at the Lowe Runkle Company — are the Great Hall, the Arena, and the Exhibit Hall. There are twenty-four meeting rooms on the upper concourse. More than 30,000 persons could be using the building at the same time.

Design of the Myriad was by the Oklahoma City architectural firm of Bozalis-Dickinson-Roloff. H. A. Lott Construction Company of Houston was prime contractor.

Myriad was financed by two Oklahoma City general obligation bond issues. There was $5 million in 1962, as a start, with an $18 million augmentation in the "Yes 'Em All" bond campaign of 1968, both successful.

Geographically, Myriad is located in the area first claimed by South Oklahoma advocates for lot subdivision on the opening in 1889.

Central and largest element of the Myriad is the Arena, around which are seats for 15,000 spectators. With a total floor area in excess of 30,000 square feet, the Arena can handle any indoor sport from hockey to track meets and circuses.

Stairways, elevators and escalators provide access to the second floor concourse. Sound and lighting systems are versatile. An electronic score and message board can be responsive to activities.

The Exhibit Hall occupies the west wing of Myriad, with 100,000 square feet, all at street level. It is divisable into smaller rooms by electronically operated, movable, sound proof walls.

In the east wing is the Great Hall, a 16,000 square foot ballroom complete with an eighty-by-forty foot stage for dramatic or musical presentations. This hall can accommodate more than 2,000 spectators at a stage presentation, or 1,500 for a sit down dinner. There is a catering concern on the premises, and appropriate press rooms.

Myriad was the first public building in Oklahoma designed with thought of the physically handicapped. Ramps at entrance levels provide access for wheel chairs. Low level water fountains and special lift bars in rest rooms aid this convenience.

Myriad has its own parking space, with sub-surface parking for 1,200 vehicles, with access or departure from two streets. In addition to this, there are some 4,000 additional parking spaces available within reasonable walking distance.

Despite uncertainty of urban renewal financing late in 1973, the city and its Urban Renwal Authority were looking to the future. A $900,000 study nearing completion by end of that year expanded and updated the original GNRP. A consulting team headed by Gruen Associates, Incorporated, Los Angeles, examined in depth economic conditions, physical facilities, transportation needs and resources, land use and other factors in an area ranging from the State Capitol complex on the north to the Canadian River on the south, and from the central business district east to the JFK project.

The consultants' final report, due early in 1974, was expected to recommend changes and improvements around the city's central core in keeping with (and perhaps even as extensive as) all dramatic redevelopment that was already transforming Oklahoma City into the "City of Tomorrow" on land area of its yesterdays.

The Myriad Convention Center is designed for large conventions and major sports events.

26

Born Grown, Filling Out

OKLAHOMA CITY WAS SO BUSILY engaged in growth activities over the years that officials forgot to formalize its status with a seal. In 1965 this was corrected when Mayor George Shirk came up with a plan for a contest. Winner of design competition — and a $500 check — was Larry Anderson, an architectural draftsman. There were four items involved in the design: a plow, a claim stake being driven into the ground, an atom, and a peace pipe with four pendant feathers. The insigne may be seen on city vehicles now in a size large enough to identify its components.

There were some other actions in 1965, too, some of which had portents for the future. The 1965 year saw ground broken for expanded Will Rogers World Airport and inauguration of the first "world" flight, when Trans World Airlines began twice weekly flights from here to Paris and Rome, with intermediate stops at St. Louis, Detroit and Boston. Both the Sheraton-Oklahoma and Skirvin Hotels put in additions that included giant sized ballrooms — a feature lacked previously in handling major convention sit-down dinners for up to 1,500 persons. And — for the first time — in 1965 the city voted a sales tax of one cent per dollar of purchase, after the legislature passed such enabling legislation, the state having retained such taxing power to itself previously.

In some aspects 1965 was a vintage year in Oklahoma City, even if "normal" activities were but progression in business indicators and other indices of the civic scene. For the fifteenth year the Chamber issued its economic growth report and pointed out proudly that 1965 had a 780 percent gain over the first such tabulation. The year saw a growth total of $326,174,339. There were 251,300 persons employed in the city. Manufacturing alone provided 3,200 new jobs in expansion of existing firms and addition of twenty-one new ones. Emphasizing what payrolls mean, the Chamber said that for each 100 industrial jobs created here there would be seventy-four additional ones in retail establishments, services and utilities; 112 more new homes would be needed; 107 more automobiles would be required; there would be a $360,000 increase in retail sales; more taxes; more need for educational and cultural facilities, and for public services necessitating bond issues. And, as if to capsule its own demonstrated activities since 1889, the Chamber made the point that industry seldom locates anywhere by random selection.

If some folk were listening to cash registers jingle as 1966 began, there were others who heard other music and saw dancing to a different set of tunes. Early in January the musical "Hello Dolly" starring Carol Channing, brought to Municipal Auditorium by Mrs. Vinita Cravens, set what was then a national record high in receipts for a week's run. Two extra performances were needed to satisfy ticket demand. Miss Channing declared she was fascinated by Oklahoma City and it was apparent that the feeling was mutual.

There was dedication in January of the Stanley Draper Expressway, primarily a cross-town elevated artery that was a portion of Interstate 40, which marked also culmination of years in planning. In May ground was broken on the Oklahoma City University campus for a $1 million chapel, a multi-function structure named for Bishop W. Angie Smith, and designed by Doctor Pietro Belluschi. Additional recognition for Draper came in May when Elm Creek reservoir was renamed Stanley Draper Lake. In June Will Rogers Airport had the busiest month in its history when 38,885 passengers boarded there and 40,230 deplaned. The C. B. Richardson Children's Zoo was opened in late June at Lincoln Park. July saw the city designated an official port of entry with a customs office that permitted imports to be shipped here from any place in the world without prior off-loading. Outgoing shipments also were affected in the time saving movement. General aviation was aided by construction of a $175,000 hangar at Cimarron Field.

Some national attention was paid to the city in September when Jane Ann Jayroe, a student at Oklahoma City University, was named "Miss America" at Atlantic City. Economic growth in 1966 reached $329,502,047, a $3,327,708 increase over the previous year. Sales of livestock at the terminal market here exceeded $125 million in 1966.

Renovated and remodeled under a $500,000 portion of a bond issue, early in 1967 Municipal Auditorium became Civic Center Music

Penn Square at Northwest Highway and Pennsylvania was the first large shopping center.

Hall, with the Oklahoma City Symphony Orchestra as opening feature. Heard were quite different sounds from those of puffing engines on a railroad switching yard that once covered that area. In February Doctor John F. Olson, successor to Doctor Jack S. Wilkes as president of Oklahoma City University, reported to the OCU Foundation on internal affairs, not quite so visible as the $5 million in construction on five sites then underway. The foundation originated in 1961 with Dean A. McGee and Stanley Draper as principal organizers. Succeeding them in 1967 were Luther T. Dulaney as board chairman and Robert S. Kerr Junior as president. Preservation of portions of the city's most beautiful and historical areas became a matter of civic concern and activity of the Oklahoma City Planning Commission. Later this would develop into a major movement.

In February the Ford Motor Company, which had been active here since assembling cars at its West Main Street plant in 1915 — later a parts depot — put in a sales office and training school at Northwest Thirty-ninth Street and Youngs Boulevard. Later in the year in a related industry, the Fred Jones Manufacturing Company turned out its 300,000th rebuilt Ford engine in thirty years.

In March 1967 new work assignments for the Western Electric plant increased employment to 5,200 and payroll to $38 million. Adding to the cultural and entertainment scene, the Oklahoma City Arts Council planned and conducted a "Festival of the Arts '67" in Civic Center. It progressed to an annual event. American Body and Trailer Company, an activity here since 1926, underwent a major expansion with a plant of 100,000 square feet at a forty acre tract on Morgan Road near Northwest Tenth Street. The site was purchased from Oklahoma Industries, the Chamber's development arm. One product of the company was a "possum belly" livestock semitrailer, with two loading levels for large animals and three for calves or hogs.

Frontiers of Science used as theme of its 1967 symposium for high school seniors, "The Walking Brain: Mechanisms for Survival." This was the eleventh of a series featuring top American scientists in a one day program. Oklahoma City was chosen as site for the National Appaloosa Horse Show. Its success and word of facilities at the fairgrounds here, with cooperative community support, aided also in bringing the National Arabian Horse Show here for repeated visits. Business and professional folk in June backed institution of a "Junior Achievement" program for high school youth for its value in economic education.

In July 1967 General Electric Company, on the fifth anniversary of its first pilot plant here, broke ground for a major plant at West Reno and Morgan Road on a 1,000 acre site. Adding color to those ceremonies was observation, with suitable vehicles and livestock, of the centennial anniversary of the Chisholm Trail which lay nearby, where Texas cattle moved north to railheads following the Civil War. A computer represented modern times. A number of city people in August made a reenactment of travel over the Chisholm Trail from Red River Crossing northward — only they rode in buses instead of on horseback. In July the Statler-Hilton Hotel chain announced plans for a $3 million, seven-story structure in the United Founders area west of North May Avenue by the expressway. Economic growth of the city rose again for 1967 to a $333,722,012 figure. Population of the metropolitan area was said to be 625,700.

Oklahoma Christian College marked beginning of 1968 with construction of two new dormitories, making three in a planned quadrangle arrangement. In January, amid some emotion from the principal that was shared by many who knew of his driving influence, Stanley Draper stepped down as executive vice-president of the Chamber after forty-eight years. Paul Strasbaugh was elevated to that post. Convention bookings for 1968, as the year began, indicated 160,000 persons would attend 234 meetings here. This was an increase over the previous year of 123,000 attending 207 gatherings. OG&E launched its "record year" for construction with $46 million worth programmed in 1968. Major item was a new generating plant at Konawa. The Junior League of Oklahoma City celebrated its fortieth anniversary in February.

Swinging steel balls in March began demolition of downtown buildings for redevelopment, an activity that for several years would feature the civic scene, as old landmarks would fall. In May a Belgian made "Arrows to Atoms" space tower for the State Fair of Oklahoma, complete with outside elevator, arrived and its 350,000 pounds of metal began to be fitted together and erected. In June 1968 Kerr-McGee announced plans to construct the thirty story McGee office tower, to give that firm's complex coverage of a city block, amid expressions of faith in the city's future by Dean A. McGee, chief executive officer. Not far behind this announcement was that of Liberty National Bank and Trust Company, that it would acquire a thirty-five story structure on the near one-block site bounded by Park Avenue and Main, Santa Fe and Broadway. Griffin Enterprises was the developer. Bishop Paul Milhouse succeeded Bishop W. Angie Smith here as Methodist bishop for the Oklahoma-New Mexico area.

Oklahoma Publishing Company in early 1969 said it would construct a five-story parking facility on Northwest Fifth Street, west of the Santa Fe tracks, at a cost of $1 million. Mr. and Mrs. Luther T. Dulaney became major contributors to the National Cowboy Hall of Fame with a donation of $120,000 in art gifts, highlighted by an $85,000 centerpiece in William R. Leigh's "The Leader's Downfall." In 1973 Dulaney would become first Oklahoman to be president of the seventeen state board for the Western shrine.

What had been termed "the Soaring Sixties" by civic leaders came to a fitting end with 1969. For the first time more than one million pounds of cargo was sent from Will Rogers World Airport that year. All business indices were up. The city had an economic index of 195.1 in comparison to a gross national product figure of 184.5. There was a $63 million increase in construction over the previous year, with industrial and commercial building accounting for $34 million of that figure, public and semi-public works $23 million, residential construction $6 million.

In addition to new building activities listed earlier, 1969 saw underway or announced, a spread eastward to Broadway of First National Bank & Trust Company, including a shopping arcade and underground mall connecting more than one million square feet of office areas; a multi-lane enlargement of Santa Fe Avenue (later named E. K. Gaylord Avenue), back of one major new parking facility and connecting another of the Oklahoma City Transportation and Parking Authority. General Electric dedicated its 126,000 square foot facility in June but within a year would transfer that plant to Honeywell.

Other factors in a booming industrial spree in 1969 were location of Dayton Tire and Rubber Company here, near Will Rogers World Airport. The city was chosen as home for corporate headquarters of Wilson & Company and its subsidiaries under native Oklahoman Roy V. Edwards as board chairman. A plant off Interstate 40 near Morgan Road was built for CMI Corporation, which had a fast growth to international prominence as maker of mammoth paving and earth moving equipment. City National Bank and Trust Company expanded, including a later move to the former Liberty Bank Building. A high rise building for Fidelity Bank N.A., to cover most of the block south of Northwest Third Street on the west side of Robinson, was announced.

Other major office shifts, new locations or expansions credited to 1969 included that of the Fleming Company, brokers for IGA Food Stores; a major plant for Haggar Slacks near the airport; facilities for the Food Machinery Corporation; St. Joe Paper Company; Chromalloy-American; Deluxe Check Printers; Diamond Crystal Salt Company; Leggett & Platt; expansions of Honeywell and Westinghouse. The latter would have a major production plant north of Norman, also. During the sixties, $210,291,091 was invested here in new or expanded industrial plants alone.

After leaving the Chamber's top executive staff post earlier, Stanley Draper needed an outlet for his still restless energy and found it assisting in creation of the Oklahoma Heritage Association, as successor to the Oklahoma Memorial Association. Started late in 1927 by Anna B. Korn, the memorial association had as its principal activity inducting business,

The old and new in building styles are combined in the Oklahoma Publishing Co. complex.

The new McGee Tower highlights the Kerr-McGee Center filling a downtown city block.

professional, and leaders of the arts, into the Oklahoma Hall of Fame. By legislative action the association was given responsibility for sponsoring and coordinating "Oklahoma Heritage Week," annually, covering the period in which statehood day on November 16 would appear. Governor David Hall issued official proclamations, also. Hall, elected governor in 1970, was the first native of Oklahoma City to sit in the governor's chair.

One might have thought any previous record could not be topped but 1970 gave every indication of securing attention. Some of this was in

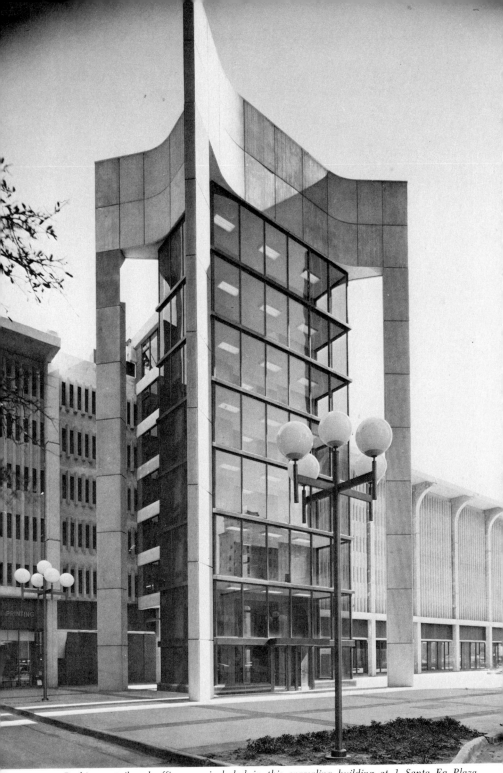

Parking, retail and offices are included in this sprawling building at 1 Santa Fe Plaza.

the downtown area, as much of the 1969 expansion had been, with other activities elsewhere. Early in January, Hertz Corporation said it would locate its national reservation and computer center here for its vehicle renting and leasing service, using space at Lincoln Plaza pending construction out on the Northwest Expressway. Continental Oil Company announced construction of a $6 million plant out southeast to make poly-vinyl plastic. A subsidiary of Oklahoma Natural Gas Company started putting in a $4.8 million thermal heating and cooling plant, near the Santa Fe railroad just northeast of the Myriad, to serve the downtown area. In April, Trammel-Crow Company of Dallas announced start of a 236 acre industrial park near Interstate 40 and South Meridian.

Macklanburg-Duncan celebrated its fiftieth anniversary in 1970, pointing to manufacture of 7,000 items in its product line as compared with the original weatherstrip. Norick Brothers, though, had sixty candles on its birth anniversary cake. From a small shop operated by George and Henry Norick in 1910, one of the largest printers of business forms in the nation grew. Former Mayor James H. Norick, son of Henry, is president of the firm, and the third generation of this family is included among 200 employes. In May the National Foundation Life Insurance Company started its third building at Northwest Highway and Grand Boulevard. Harter Concrete Products Company had its fiftieth anniversary, too.

The Oklahoma Health Center, which had been of major development interest since 1964, by autumn of 1970 seemed assured of growth. There were to be some financial difficulties, not all of them solved in the next three intervening years, but University Hospital and Children's Memorial Hospital were due for renovation and expansion. Presbyterian

The County office building at N.W. Second and Harvey north of the old county building.

Hospital in 1972 would begin construction of its $23 million installation adjacent to the Center on Northeast Thirteenth Street. Near it would be the $2.2 million Dean A. McGee Eye Institute, to be named for the principal donor. Construction was to begin in 1974. Other major donors were Mr. and Mrs. Luther T. Dulaney and Mr. and Mrs. Sylvan Goldman. The Lions Clubs of Oklahoma have a statewide project to raise $350,000 to equip laboratories and other facilities at the Eye Institute. Meanwhile, Mercy Hospital said it would build a high rise, $25.5 million institution in the far northwest portion of the city. Baptist Hospital planned to expand by 600 beds. St. Anthony started a new tower. In Capitol Hill the South Community Hospital was operating as another new service in the city's medical facilities.

As 1970 ended South Oklahoma City Community College would become more of a reality than an idea. The Mummers' new theater opened, rather fittingly, with "A Man for All Seasons." Total employment in the city in December 1970 was 295,600 out of a total work force of 305,700, in contrast to 205,600 and 216,700, respectively, in December 1960. Manufacturing employment alone increased eighty-five percent in the decade by contrast to a national figure of sixteen percent. Citizens revalidated a $76 million issue of general obligation bonds. There was $13.7 million more in building permits issued in 1970, than in any previous year. Reflected was a total of $168 million with permits for 1,670 new residences valued at $32 million, a $6 million increase over 1969. Apartment construction, soon to be a noticeable visual change from the traditional here, called

Looking south toward downtown Oklahoma City over the sprawling State Capitol complex.

for permits on 3,922 units valued at $41 million, at least $10 million above the previous year.

Late January of 1971 saw announcement of a "different" residential development in "The Greens." This was to include a 590 acre block between Portland and Meridian (near new Mercy Hospital) between Northwest 122nd and Memorial Road. Shown in the prospectus was a planned community suitable for 10,000 persons, with a golf course, 500 residential lots in the $50,000 to $100,000 range, with 100 acres reserved for townhouse and apartment living. International trade growth was apparent here when a survey disclosed that 125 local manufacturers shipped a variety of products to other countries. International departments of Liberty, First National and Fidelity banks reported substantial increases over other years in foreign exchange transactions.

In March the census bureau pleased civic leaders by reporting that Oklahoma county, with more than a half-million persons, disclosed a gain of twenty percent in ten years to make it the state's largest. The Oklahoma City metropolitan area now held 640,889 people. Oklahoma State University's Technical Institute in Oklahoma City, in March 1971 dedicated its first building on a new sixty acre campus at 900 North Portland. It had outgrown a former city school building on Northwest Tenth Street. The institute offers technical training at the associate degree level and, in a sense, complements secondary school training given at the Oklahoma City Area Vocational School on South Bryant. The International Visitors Council of the Chamber said that in one year it had contact with 1,286 persons from sixty-nine countries, representing adult visitors, students, military personnel and trainees at the Federal Aviation Center. In May 1971, Oklahoma City University's hopes for a new library were realized in a $1.5 million structure, for which Luther T. Dulaney and Virgil Browne were principal contributors.

In May 1971, U.S. News and World Report cited Oklahoma City as a prime example of "Cities Where Business is Best" in a feature article. The Dayton plant by August was producing 18,000 tires daily. To aid in the city's enrichment an Oklahoma City Cultural Development Foundation (now Allied Arts Foundation) was created in October 1971, with Jack T. Conn as president, with the basic purpose of having a federated fund drive instead of separate campaigns by participating groups. This included the Mummers, Oklahoma Art Center, Oklahoma City Arts Council, Oklahoma Science and Arts Foundation, and the Oklahoma City Symphony. Edward L. Gaylord and J. B. Saunders were co-chairmen of the fund drive.

In November Oklahoma City Federal Savings and Loan (to be renamed Continental), which earlier purchased the Skirvin Tower Hotel, announced that a massive remodeling of that structure would take place. It would be one of but three buildings in the nation, at that time, to be coated with a new exterior facing of double paned glass, coated with a silver alloy that is reflective on the outside, but clear from the inside looking out. R. M. Hollingshead Corporation based in New Jersey, announced that an automotive filter plant it purchased here would be expanded for manufacture of products sold nationally and worldwide. Bank deposits of the city area in 1971 approached $1.6 billion with bank resources of almost $2 billion.

New office and bank buildings are seen in this aerial photo of downtown Oklahoma City.

The annual "Stars and Stripes" show by 1972 was so successful that the National Broadcasting Company picked it up for later telecasts. Two of the principal attractions since the beginning, Bob Hope and Anita Bryant, returned as headliners with athletes, astronauts and other celebrities. Something new was added in 1972 with approval of a hotel and motel room tax to finance promotion of visitors as individuals, or in groups for meetings, conventions and trade shows, to be handled by a joint committee selected by the city council and Chamber. The first federated Allied Arts Fund campaign was held.

Musical comedy star Carol Channing displayed her affection for Oklahoma City by having the world premiere here in 1973 of "Lorelei." Aviation enthusiasm, a factor here since 1910, got a boost when a locally produced Aero-Commander took two world altitude records for piston engined, executive type aircraft away from German built planes. James L. Badgett, president of Schick, Incorporated, flew to 35,450 feet for the first new record, then maintained level flight at 35,000 feet for the second. After twenty-two years Guy Fraser Harrison conducted his final season of the Oklahoma City Symphony.

In May 1972 the city held "A Day of Honor" for local and state Vietnam War veterans at the Myriad, with Jenkin Lloyd Jones of Tulsa as official speaker, although the city's renowned Air Force Colonel Robinson Risner, a former prisoner of war, literally stole the show. To the Oklahoma City Standard Metropolitan Statistical Area (SMSA) was added McClain and Pottawatomie counties (with Oklahoma, Cleveland and Canadian) to indicate a population in excess of 750,000. In a city where decades earlier there were rumors of "underground Chinese tunnels" so plentiful that many persons accepted them as fact, approval was given for a massive $1.3 million downtown pedestrian tunnel, as far north and west as the OG&E Building, and as far south and east as the Myriad, connecting major downtown banks and hotels. Jack T. Conn headed the "syndicate" or joint venture committee from participating firms.

General Motors said an impending "energy crisis" would delay but not deter it from building a major assembly plant here. Investment was estimated in excess of $100 million. The first portion of Interstate Highway 240, a limited access expressway south of Tinker to connect Interstate Highways 35 and 40, was dedicated in late 1973. It was named for the late Lieutenant General Thomas P. Gerrity, former commander of the Oklahoma City Air Materiel Area. A related aviation activity was selection of Will Rogers World Airport as future international headquarters for "The Ninety-Nines," a unique organization limited to 4,300 females who hold active pilot's licenses. The name traces to an original organization of ninety-nine women fliers.

Kerr-McGee announced that it would construct a Robert S. Kerr Memorial Park, north of Couch Drive, west of Broadway, in memory of the firm's founder. It will contain a statue of the former governor and United States senator, a pool and suitable landscaping, and be presented to the city for its park system. Not the least important ground breaking of 1973 came in October at the site of a hotel — retail complex to be known as the Sheraton Century Center, on the block bounded by Broadway and Robinson, Main and Sheridan.

27

Lifeline of Commerce

IT HAS BEEN said that banks are the rivers on which the commerce of a city moves. Oklahoma City has been blessed with good banks, meeting credit needs and always doing more than their part in every civic endeavor. They do compete very strenuously, but when it comes to the welfare of Oklahoma City, they always unite.

It was in a tent on the third lot east of Broadway, on Main Street, that Oklahoma City's first bank opened the afternoon of April 22, 1889. It began accepting deposits while most new residents were still out of breath from the Run. It was called the Oklahoma Bank, but one year later was renamed the First National Bank of Oklahoma City.

Its beginnings were in Albany, in West Texas, three months before Oklahoma Country was opened. The moving spirit was T.M. Richardson, a lumber dealer, who went to Dallas to have stationery, checks, pass books and other necessary bank supplies printed. He bought a safe and some heavy oak desks. Then he chartered a box car and loaded into it the bank equipment and a quantity of lumber. The freight moved on the Santa Fe to the future site of Oklahoma City and was spotted on a siding several days before the opening. More cars of lumber followed.

Richardson staked lots on the northeast corner of Grand and Harvey. However, he was not satisfied with that location, and gave $300 for a lot just east of Broadway on Main Street. A tent was erected on this site.

Later a lot was obtained at the southeast corner of Main and Broadway, and Richardson drew upon his lumber yard for material for a frame building twenty-five by 100 feet in size. Bank fixtures were ordered from Kansas City, and within thirty days the bank was in its first "permanent" home. You have seen replicas on movie sets.

In the early days there were no vaults of armor-plate steel, with 27-ton doors, time locks and automatic alarms, such as The First National has today. In the summer of 1889 when the bank was occupying the little one-story wooden building on the corner of Main and Broadway, it was decided to install some protection against bank robbers. There were no telephones in those days, so battery powered call bells were placed in the W and Drug Store, the Gerson Brothers Clothing Store and the Gerson Drug Store, all just west of the bank. Many push buttons were placed around in the bank, some under counters and some on the floor.

The bank furnished the stores with rifles. It was understood that in case of a hold-up some one would push or step on a button, signaling the stores. The bank closed at four p.m. One day, just after the doors were locked, someone stepped on a push button by accident and in a few seconds the bank was surrounded by riflemen ready to capture the supposed bandits. After several more false alarms, clerks greeted bank robber signals with a similar cry to "wolf" and stuck to their chores of selling pills and neckties. So the elaborate alarm system was abandoned.

Three other banks opened here shortly after the Run. All of them failed. The Merchants Bank was shortest lived. It lasted until 1890. The Citizens Bank (no relation to the present Citizens National Bank) operated under that name for two years, then took up the name Oklahoma National Bank, a name abandoned a year earlier when the Oklahoma Bank became the First National Bank. It liquidated in 1893. The Bank of Oklahoma City was established in 1889, but also liquidated in 1893.

The first real test of Oklahoma City's financiers came with this "panic" of 1893. At that time there were four banks in the city. When the panic was over there were only two, The First National and a newly-established State National, with which the First National was to be merged in 1897. To the credit of the two banks which closed voluntarily when the going became too tough, they paid off dollar for dollar to their depositors later. This was not merely "face saving."

When directors of the First National saw how things were going in the summer of 1893, they brought in several money shipments and the bank's safe bulged with gold, silver and currency. With such an unusual amount on hand officers were apprehensive lest the news leak out and a robbery be staged. It was decided to have the janitor, a Negro named Douglas, sleep in the bank at night. He was instructed to sound an alarm in case anything went wrong.

Farmers State Bank on Grand became the City National Bank and Trust Company.

A few nights later around midnight, an individual whose swigging of red-eye stimulated a desire for excitement, heaved a brick through the bank's plate glass window. The crash startled Douglas from his slumbers. He dived through a jagged hole in the window which the brick had made. His yells of pain and fright soon brought the city's night-watchman who satisfied himself that there was no attempt being made at robbery. Just "one of the boys" having some innocent fun.

When Richardson asked Douglas the next morning why he didn't use the front door key that was in his pocket, instead of jumping through the window, the janitor replied: "Boss, you told me if anything happened to sound an alarm and that's just what I did and lost no time doing it."

The expected run on the city's banks came July 19, 1893. All day long the First National paid off all comers who wanted their money. When closing time came, the bank kept its doors open and continued to pay off in cash. About dark the bank's force was weary and Richardson decided to call a halt. He mounted the front steps of the bank, held up his hand for silence, and told the crowd that he figured twelve hours was a good bank day, even in those times.

"We're going to close up now, folks," Richardson said. "We will be open in the morning and all of you who haven't been waited on today can have your money if you want it. But I want to tell you that there is enough money in our safe to pay off every depositor in full. If any man loses a dollar in this bank, I want to be hanged to that telephone post over there," pointing to a tall pole near at hand.

The next morning the run was over. Many depositors who had withdrawn money the day before brought it back and apologized for their hasty action.

Next to organize was the Bank of Commerce, which started in 1896 and lasted nine years before liquidating.

The first decade of the twentieth century saw the start of several banks, most of which were liquidated or eventually became a part of the State National Bank. Lasting from two to seven years were the Planters and Mechanics Bank, the Livestock Exchange Bank, Columbia Bank and Trust Company, American State Bank of Capitol Hill, First National Bank of Capitol Hill, Oklahoma State Bank, and the Night and Day Bank. Longer lasting was the State Bank of Capitol Hill, which started in 1908, became the Capitol State Bank in 1913, and continued operation until it failed in 1933. This bank, incidentally, was the only Oklahoma City bank to fail during the depression of the 1930s — a much better record than in most cities.

It was during this first decade also that Oklahoma City's other three largest banks got their start. The Farmers State Bank opened in 1903, and in 1930 became the City National Bank. The First State Bank opened in 1908 and is now Fidelity Bank, NA. Although the Liberty National Bank and Trust Company, did not open until after World War I, the old Guaranty State Bank and the Oklahoma Stockyards National Bank, which later joined Liberty, started during that first decade.

In 1897 the First National Bank interests of Messrs. Reynolds, Richardson and Boyle were sold to E. H. Cooke and others. After a merger which followed the bank was known as The State National for twenty-two years. When Hugh M. Johnson bought the Cooke interests in 1919 one of his first acts was to restore the bank's original name, The First National.

On the bank's thirty-eighth birthday, April 22, 1927, came the merger of The First National with The American National, which Frank P. Johnson had built from humble beginnings in 1901 to one of the state's leading financial institutions. For a time then the bank was known as The American-First. Following its taking over the Security National Bank late in 1929 the old name was restored on January 2, 1930, and so it is now — The First National Bank and Trust Company.

The last big merger for the First National Bank and Trust Company was its acquisition of the Tradesman's National Bank, which had been organized in 1911.

The present building on Robinson at Park Avenue was completed and the bank moved December 12, 1931. Prior to "moving day" Lyall Barnhart, Comptroller, worked out a detailed plan for employees and equipment. All items were moved after the bank closed at noon on Saturday. Employees went to work on Sunday to become familiar with their new surroundings before the opening on Monday.

A new building section was added in 1957 and another was completed in 1972. The building, now extending from Robinson to Broadway, gives the First National Center more than 1,000,000 square feet of office space. The bank uses five floors and basement plus space on some other floors.

The bank has grown from its original capital of $50,000 to in excess of $65 million in capital structure in 1974. Deposits December 31, 1973 were $605,170,950 and assets December 31, 1973 were $855,053,453. Present Chairman of the Board is Charles A. Vose. Gerald Marshall is president and Felix Porter is chairman of the executive committee. The bank employs 834 people of whom 126 are officers.

In almost fifty-six years of existence, Liberty National Bank has continued an enviable rate of growth. The bank's total deposits on December 31, 1973, were the largest in Oklahoma, for the fifth consecutive year.

Total resources of $806,996,824 at the end of 1973, were a far cry from the modest beginning on September 3, 1918, in a converted barbershop at the rear of what is now the Oil and Gas Building at Main and Robinson. In 1918 it was the Lee Building and Liberty had a capital stock of $300,000 and a surplus of $30,000. L. T. Sammons was Liberty's first president and Joe Semrod, the current president, is eleventh in the line of succession.

Two years after Liberty opened in the former barbership, the bank moved temporarily to the old Scott-Halliburton Building near Main and Harvey, then returned to remodeled quarters that occupied the entire first floor and basement of the Lee Building. Eventually, the bank occupied all five floors of the building.

In 1950, needing additional space, Liberty purchased the 33-story Apco Tower at Park and Robinson and constructed a 16-story annex to house a Drive-In Bank and provide more office space. The move to those new bank quarters was made March 17, 1952.

First National Bank and Trust Company.

Ground was broken for the present Liberty Tower on the bank's fiftieth birthday, September 3, 1968, and actual construction began in mid-1969.

In the course of Liberty's growth, it acquired three other Oklahoma City banks. The old Guaranty State Bank, then located at Park and Robinson, was merged with Liberty in 1921. C. H. Everest, president of Guaranty and father of Harvey P. Everest, became a Liberty vice president. Guaranty's deposits of $1,250,000 boosted Liberty's deposit total to more than $4 million. In 1926 Liberty purchased the original Oklahoma National Bank, a move that brought an additional $3 million in deposits. In 1960

Liberty National Bank, tallest building in Oklahoma City.

Liberty acquired the Bank of Mid-America.

In Liberty's first four years, deposits went to $5 million and by 1928 to $12 million. They climbed to $20 million in 1938 and by 1943 had more than doubled to $47 million. The 1960 deposit figure of $185 million was the springboard for a 10-year rise to $375 million in 1970.

Total deposits as of December 31, 1973, were $639,090,064, as compared with $303,960,000 recorded at the close of 1967. The loan total had risen from $173,070,000 at the close of 1967 to $361,118,290 at the end of 1973.

Fidelity Bank, N.A.

The six-year period was marked by a number of innovative banking steps, spearheaded by introduction of Liberty Card in the fall of 1966 as the first bank credit card operation in Oklahoma City. Proving a highly suc-

Luncheon and a style show on the plaza of Fidelity Bank, N.A.

cessful bank credit venture, Liberty Card was merged with BankAmericard. In 1970, Liberty introduced Portrait BankAmericard to Oklahoma consumers, providing a unique personal identification feature.

In August of 1971, at the age of fifty-three, Liberty had moved into its third home, the lower nine floors of the 26-story Liberty Tower, the pacesetter for Oklahoma City's sweeping downtown redevelopment. The new quarters were in dramatic contrast to cramped space in which the bank began business September 3, 1918. They are only one block east but a gigantic step in time and fortune from that converted barbershop.

Under W. J. McLean's direction, Liberty National Corporation was formed in 1971 as a one-bank holding company of Liberty National Bank and Trust Company. Later, other subsidiaries organized under

Liberty National Corporation are Liberty Financial Corporation, Liberty Mortgage Company, Liberty Real Estate Company and Mid-America Leasing Corporation.

In the spring of 1974, almost fifty-six years since its founding, Liberty has more than 650 employees.

Roots of the City National Bank and Trust Company are in the Farmer's State Bank, which was established in 1903 on the southwest corner of Grand and Robinson. It had original capitalization of $25,000. H. M. Atkinson was its first president.

In 1909 it became Farmer's National Bank, and at this time had deposits larger than any other state bank. Its board of directors showed the name of a man who would play a major role in the destiny of this bank — Dan W. Hogan. In 1911 Hogan became president, a position which he held forty-four years before moving up to chairman of the board, remaining in this position almost until his one-hundredth birth anniversary.

It was in 1923 that the bank began construction of a new building on the site of its then existing building, at a cost of approximately $125,000. It was next to another new building — the Oklahoma Club, which was destined to be Oklahoma City's leading downtown business club for more than two decades. During construction, the Farmer's National Bank was located in the Colcord Building across the street north. This space recently had been vacated by Fidelity National Bank, which moved across the street east to the Baum Building. In 1930 the bank recognized the urbanization of Oklahoma City when it changed its name from Farmer's to City National Bank & Trust Company.

In 1949 the 46-year-old City National Bank moved a block east and north to the northwest corner of Main and Broadway. It took over the building of the Tradesman's National Bank when that bank merged into the First National. There it erected Oklahoma's tallest sign — 126 feet high.

In 1955 Daniel W. Hogan, Junior, became president, succeeding his father, and the older Hogan was named chairman of the board. Untimely death ended the younger Hogan's career less than three years later and Howard J. Bozarth was elected president.

In 1968 Fred Boston came to the bank as its principal shareholder and board chairman. Two years later he brought in Ben Head, formerly president of May Avenue Bank, to become City National president. In 1971 City National Bank and Trust Company moved from Main and Broadway to the former Liberty National Building at Park and Robinson, as Liberty moved to its new tower in the Santa Fe Plaza. City National's assets at the end of 1973 were $74,193,892.

What is now Fidelity Bank NA (National Association) began in 1908, when seven prominent Oklahoma Cityans formed the First State Bank. The first stockholders' meeting was held April 6, 1908. C. F. Elerick was elected president. Nine days later the bank rented space in the Lee Building, which had been built by Oscar Lee, owner of the Lee, later Huckins Hotel. Monthly rental for lobby and office space was $175.

In 1913, S. P. Berry was elected president to succeed Elerick, and the following year the bank leased quarters in the Colcord Building and moved out of its original location. In 1915, the bank elected Irving H. Wheatcroft as president, succeeding Berry.

Wheatcroft was a British subject who had come to the young state of Oklahoma and invested in the First State Bank. He served as its president and chief executive officer for only four years but during that period, assets of the bank increased from $500,000 to nearly $2 million. Inflation and increase in savings during World War I contributed to this growth. After the war, Wheatcroft was faced with problems in his native England and had to return.

Roy Finnerty became chairman of the board and Fred Finnerty became president. Within a few months, the board voted to convert to a national bank, and to change its name to "The Fidelity National Bank of Oklahoma City."

In early 1923, the Bank moved from the Colcord Building, directly across the street east into the Baum Building. This building, on the northeast corner of Grand and Robinson, had a strikingly decorative exterior. Some of its carved stone was destined to be saved for display in the Santa Fe Plaza and at the Oklahoma Historical Society when the building was demolished for Urban Renewal fifty years later. Upon the move of Fidelity to the Baum Building, its name was changed to The Fidelity Building. The Bank was to remain there more than thirty-four years, longer than at all other locations combined.

John A. Campbell was elected president in 1924 to succeed Finnerty, who died. Campbell served until retirement in 1943 and Royal C. Stuart was elected president. In October, 1948, Royal C. Stuart retired and Charles P. Stuart was named president.

In April, 1956, Fidelity signed a lease agreement for quarters in a new building to be erected on the northeast corner of Harvey and Park Avenue. It was a 17-story building with metal panel siding, named the Fidelity National Building. The bank moved into new quarters in November, 1957. Fidelity sold its former headquarters, including many interior banking facilities, to a group operating the new Bank of Mid-America, which later was acquired by Liberty National. In December, 1959, the bank chose Grady D. Harris Junior as its president. At age thirty-three he was the youngest president of any major bank in the country. In 1964, the bank board elected Jack T. Conn as chairman and chief executive officer. Charles P. Stuart was made honorary chairman of the board. At that time total assets were slightly more than $84 million. While heading the board of Fidelity, Conn served as president of the American Bankers Association, and is the only Oklahoma Cityan ever to serve as ABA president. In that post he stressed community service.

In 1967, Fidelity Bank constructed a drive-in banking facility on the southeast corner of northwest Fourth and Robinson which has won national awards for design and landscaping.

Meanwhile, plans were underway for a new main banking facility in the block bounded by Robert S. Kerr Avenue, Harvey, Northwest Third and Robinson. The new Fidelity Plaza is eighteen stories tall with vertical design featuring masonry columns and glass. It was completed in 1972. The name was changed from Fidelity National Bank and Trust Company to Fidelity Bank, National Association (or NA).

In February, 1973, Fidelity became the first bank in Oklahoma City to have a twenty-four hour, seven day per week, full-service automated teller facility, located at its drive-in area. In December, 1970, assets were $213,028,000 and by the end of 1973 reached $279,439,000.

In 1926 L. D. Lacy, then assistant superintendent of Oklahoma City schools, resigned his position and opened a local office of the Morris Plan Company at 314 North Robinson. The purpose of this new financial institution was to make installment loans to individuals. Most banks at that time restricted lending activities to business firms and did not care to incur the expense of making smaller loans to numerous individuals. The Morris Plan Company also solicited savings accounts from individuals, but was not allowed to accept checking accounts because it was not a commercial bank. It was indicative of change.

By the time of the great depression, this new company had grown to the point that it was able to survive the worldwide financial crisis. The experience of the Morris Plan Company of Oklahoma City and similar companies over the nation proved that consumer credit extended to individuals was a sound concept. Although many people were unemployed and unable to repay their loans, eventual losses from such loans were smaller than those sustained by commercial banks on loans to business firms, in ratio to volume.

As the nation emerged from the depression in the late 1930s, the Morris Plan Company prospered to the point that it sought and obtained a state bank charter in 1941 under the name Central Morris Plan State Bank. This allowed the company to offer checking account services also. The Central Morris Plan State Bank aggressively solicited small checking accounts. By the late 1950's it had grown to the point that it had more checking account customers than any other bank in Oklahoma City (although not nearly as many dollars on deposit as the larger banks). In 1950 the bank moved from its former location at 225 Northwest First to its new building (and its present location) at 304 Park Avenue. This was the first new building to be built in downtown Oklahoma City since the early 1930's.

In 1960 the bank changed its charter from a State Bank to a National Bank and became Central National Bank. Today it serves more than 35,000 depositors and some 10,000 loan customers and has total assets of approximately $70 million.

In 1964, L. D. Lacy became chairman of the board of Central National and devoted most of his time to formation of a new bank in Southwest Oklahoma City, Friendly National Bank, of which he was president and chief executive officer. He was succeeded as president of Central National Bank by his son, Dan Lacy, who continues in that position. L. D. Lacy died in 1972, at age 80.

Economic fluctuations have played a role in Oklahoma City's banking history. The panic of 1893, as has been mentioned, closed two of the four existing banks. March of 1933 was a crucial period for all banks. A bank holiday came during first days of the Roosevelt administration, as a result of a rush of withdrawals throughout the nation. Oklahoma City was not as affected as most other areas. Script, guaranteed by and accepted by merchants, was used briefly for purchases. Most Oklahoma City banks reopened about one week after the "bank holiday" closing. Only the Capital State Bank failed.

During years following World War II money was plentiful and interest rates were low. Rates on savings accounts eventually dropped to one-half of one percent. Banks were not soliciting accounts because they had more money than they could invest profitably. Series "E" government bonds were paying 2.9 percent, which was the highest interest rate available for any high grade securities. Series "G" bonds paid 2.5 percent and had a long maturity period. Some short maturity government securities had yields as low as one-eighth of one percent. At this rate, a person investing one million dollars could expect a yield of only $1,250 annually, or little above $100 per month. The prime interest rate for a borrower was about two percent, and a customer felt abused if he had to pay as much as three percent. There were more funds to be loaned than there were borrowers seeking equivalent dollars.

It was during this period of low interest that the City Council asked for bids on bonds. Bids approximated one and one-fourth percent interest. A special meeting was called to determine whether or not to issue more bonds while interest rates were so low. The concensus was that it would not be necessary because interest rates were not likely to move up. But, conditions did change; interest rates did move up.

At the time of statehood there were eleven banks here. At the end of World War II, there were only eight banks in a much larger city. All were downtown, except the Stockyards Bank in Stockyards City. This bank had been established in 1923. It was a few years after the war that banks began to expand in number, with all new banks located away from downtown. First was Citizens State (now Citizen's National Bank), which has a striking gold-domed structure at Northwest Twenty-third and Western. Next were First State Bank and Trust Company, Northwest National Bank and May Avenue Bank. But this was only the beginning. Today there are twenty-nine banks in the city limits of Oklahoma City and twice that many in the 1974 greater Oklahoma City telephone directory. Shopping center banks no longer are novelties.

What a tremendous growth from one bank in a tent eighty-five years ago! At the end of February, 1974, demand deposits in the standard metropolitan area of Oklahoma City totalled almost $800 million.

Epilogue

RITING, JUSTICE HOLMES ONCE SAID, is the painful process of thought.

He was quite correct, for writing, whether fiction or fact, seldom comes easily — even to professionals. An experienced writer becomes as concerned about lacing informative segments together properly as a homesteader in winter, plaiting personalized bridle reins from strips of a scraped and home cured hide.

Looking backward at the story of Oklahoma City means more than a journey in time. It is a flashback to nostalgia, too, for not only have the city's geographical limits sprawled distantly in almost all directions, internal changes are almost incredible for such a short space of calendar time.

No longer does one take a Sunday carriage drive, or even in a fabric topped touring car, out to Shepherd Lake for a boating outing or picnic. Streetcars no longer run to the turn-around at Belle Isle. In fact you have to live dangerously to get there at all, playing "dodge-em" at Classen Circle, such as kids in bump cars do at Springlake Park. Only now the motor monsters are more lethal.

The first downtown, outdoor swimming pool, installed as part of the Skirvin's Sun Suite, covers space where once the Rock Island passenger depot stood. Animal drawn slips and fresnoes, and men with shovels, later mechanized movers, took thousands of yards of sand and gravel from alluvial beds out on Northwest Thirty-ninth Street, creating small lakes for swimming pools, before industries spread above that reclaimed land.

Southwestern College now stands where Abe Hale's nightclub was on Northwest Tenth Street. Touring big name dance bands no longer play there, or at Billy Gragg's Blossom Heath twenty-nine blocks north. Neither is there a Trianon, Palladium or Springlake Casino to attract the young and light of foot, who would go in early morning to the Kansas City Waffle House — later Bishop's — for a snack, and know they were really living. Food was secondary to social atmosphere.

No longer is there a small but crowded Baxter's Chili Parlor off Broadway, so popular with some persons that Pat Pugh even bought the small sign that hung outside it, to send to Baxter over in Arkansas, when the building was torn down.

Once at old First and Broadway stood a two-story building, built by Charley Colcord in 1909, later housing a barber shop. Behind it on First was a Turf Bar, successor to that earlier infamous one a block south on Battle Row. South of it was a cleaning shop with a "barrel" for strangers in town to use, also facilities for a shower, while one waited for his clothing to be spotted and pressed. Dan James and Leonard Dickerson later had a parking lot there. Now the Liberty Plaza covers it.

There is no Orpheum Theater to visit or a Houdini to see there, puzzling one with his fantastic escape tricks. Long gone is Sherman Billingsley's speakeasy, for he found a better location in New York, that

318

became the Stork Club. The Blue Devils, who first made music on the city's "Deep Deuce" Street (Northeast Second) you knew later as the nucleus of Count Basie's famed orchestra. Jack Teagarten started here before taking his brass, woodwinds and percussion instruments east.

Gone is the "modern" Broadview Hotel that stood at the foot of Broadway, by the street jog on Grand, while lost earlier from above it was a huge electric sign of moving words, perfected by Charles Ittner and other fellows at the University of Oklahoma Engineering School. Depression put into hiding speculative money that might have developed that idea here instead of back east for others.

Where the first few city employes relied upon fines levied under provisional government for their pay, there are some 4,000 city employes now, but at times it appears that the municipality is about as hard pressed for payroll funds.

Pool balls no longer click at the Empire Billiard Parlor, upstairs just east of the Criterion Theater, while that "showplace of the Southwest" also has vanished with urban renewal. Once, for a season, Lyle Talbot headed a repertoire company at the Criterion with a play bill changed weekly. The Myriad's east portion stands on "Hell's Half-Acre" of the turbulent early years, and across Alabaster Row, so-called because of the white figures there.

Gone from downtown are Kerr's, McEwen-Halliburton, Pettee's, Sturm's, May Brothers, Lewinsohn's, Barths, Tom Baugh's and Veazey's. The Golden Pheasant, Joy Boy, and other Chinese restaurants went away. Had anyone dug a bit under the back room of Andy Anderson's lost sporting goods store, next to the equally vanished Commerce Exchange Building, they would have found many pounds of lead. Andy's gun repair shop tested weapons by firing through a hole in the floor for years.

Pawn shops once on Grand, lower Broadway, Robinson and such places, appear to have moved to the "near north side" city areas, several miles away as other businesses vacated buildings in those locations. The "cop shop" no longer is at Maiden Lane and Wall Street.

May Avenue, especially from Northwest Thirtieth on north, is a glaring neon alley. Once it was the perimeter. At Northwest Fiftieth lay a farm where W. G. "Bus" Horton was born. When he batted a homemade baseball around he did not know that one day he would own a minor league team. He views it as a community asset.

At one time the city's Mexican-Americans had a tendency to form an ethnic community by South Walker near the Little Flower Church. Later they drifted northward above Fourth Street. Many Indians seeking some way of life in the city occupied those areas, although as with blacks, the former rather insulated ethnic neighborhoods are breaking up.

Where at statehood in 1907 there were 148 names of individuals or firms listed in a city directory as attorneys, there are but eight names listed now that indicate blood descendants of the same surname. They include Clarence Black, son of Oliver C. Black; Edgar S. Vaught, Junior; Fisher Ames, son of C. M. Ames and a grandson, Perry Ames; Kay Garnett, son of W. K. Garnett; Jack Highley, son of Mont Highley; Mark Meister, son of M. G. Meister; Ross Lillard, son of R. N. Lillard, and George Shirk, son of John H. Shirk.

Where many buildings once familiar stood, in a four block area downtown from Robinson to Hudson, and from Park Avenue to Sheridan, a multi-million Galleria will rise. It, too, will change the ground view, as an increasing number of high rise structures have already affected the city's skyline. Already one has difficulty recalling old scenes.

Many more changes will come. No one can say they will not be for the better. He can remember some of the other times, and scenes, without forgetting that — in Oklahoma City — the only constant is change.

Trackmakers

THE EIGHTY-FIVE YEAR HISTORY of Oklahoma City carries the imprints of many thousands whose tracks have moulded its shape. It is impossible to peer from the present through several generations of recorded and unrecorded history to determine those whose tracks are the deepest. The list below was compiled during reasearch for this book. Those persons listed certainly are trackmakers. No doubt each reader can list many more and, perhaps, would have eliminated some on this list. Most of these men and women were forces for good, but some created their tracks on the bad side. With others the role is debatable.

ABERNATHY, Jack H. — President of Big Chief Drilling Company. Served as president of the American Association of Oilwell Drilling Contractors.

ABERNATHY, Doctor John R. — Minister at Crown Heights Methodist Church. Emcee of Chamber of Commerce Public Forums for more than twenty-five years.

ACKERMAN, Ray — President of Ackerman, Incorporated, Advertising Agency. Commander of Naval Air Reserve forces for Oklahoma City area. For nine years chairman of local National Finals Rodeo committee.

ALEXANDER, Reverend W. H. "Bill" — Pastor of First Christian Church during the 1940s and 1950s.

ALLEN, J. P. — Mayor from 1897 to 1899.

AMERINGER, Oscar — Socialist leader here during the late 1920s and 1930s. Organizer and publisher of the American Guardian.

AMES, Charles B. — Came to Oklahoma as young lawyer in 1889. An incorporator and for a short time president of OG&E. Wrote Democratic Territorial platform of 1900. Later president of the Texas Company. Assistant Attorney General of the United States.

ANDERSON, Carl B. — Oil executive. Prominent in civic, church and political activities.

ANDERSON, J. Steve — Independent oil operator who formed Anderson-Pritchard Oil Company during World War I in partnership with L. H. Pritchard.

ANTHONY, C. R. — Founder of one of the nation's largest chains of dry goods stores, bearing his name and headquartered here.

ANTHONY, W. B. — Private secretary to Governor Haskell; carried the Great Seal of Oklahoma from Guthrie to Oklahoma City during the night, June 11, 1910.

ANTRIM, Doctor Eugene M. — President of Oklahoma City University from 1923 until 1934.

ATKINS, Doctor Charles — Community leader and first black member of city council.

ATKINS, Hannah — First black woman elected to the Oklahoma State Legislature.

ATKINSON, W. P. "Bill" — Developer of Midwest City. Publisher of Oklahoma Journal. Twice candidate for governor.

BAILEY, H. E. — City manager, State Highway Director, developer of state turnpike system.

BAIRD, Doctor James O. — President of Oklahoma Christian College more than twenty years, bringing it from Bartlesville here in 1958.

BAKER, C. G. — '89er and foreman of first jury empaneled in Oklahoma Territory. President of the Oklahoma County Fair during its first sixteen years.

BAKER, John R. — President of Oklahoma National Stockyards Company during late 1920s and the 1930s.

BALL, Ralph — Chairman of Hudgins-Thompson-Ball, architectural-engineering firm designing the largest share of state and city buildings and projects during the 1960s and into 1970s.

BALL, F. Wiley — Longtime civic worker. A director of Civitan International in the late 1920s.

BALYEAT, Doctor Ray M. — Distinguished allergy specialist and founder of a nationally known allergy clinic here.

BARBOUR, C. Wayne — An organizer and president of Allied Materials Company.

BARNARD, Kate — Oklahoma's first commissioner of Charities and Corrections. First woman in the nation to hold such an office in state government.

BARRETT, Major General Charles F. — Long-time adjutant general of Oklahoma, known as "father of the 45th Infantry Division."

BARTON, J. R. — Superintendent of city schools in the 1920s.

BASSETT, Mrs. Mabel — Social worker during the 1920s through 1940s as state commissioner of charities and corrections.

BEALE, Doctor A. J. — Second provisional mayor, who served a troubled term because of land disputes, until federal marshals assumed control.

BEARLY, Fred D. — Lumberman, civic worker and president of Chamber.

BEIDLER, G. A. — First postmaster after the opening.

BEITNAM, Alice — Organized Young Ladies' Seminary in 1889, operating it until public schools opened; a public school principal and a county superintendent.

BELL, Edgar T. — Longtime business manager of Oklahoma Publishing Company, later first manager of KWTV, city's second television station.

BENHAM, David — Senior partner in Benham, Blair and Affiliates, (successor to Benham Engineering Company) following retirement of his father.

BENHAM, Webster L. — Founded Benham Engineering Company in 1909, one of the oldest and largest engineering firms in the Southwest.

BENNETT, Charles L. — Managing editor of *The Daily Oklahoman* and *Oklahoma City Times*; very active in community affairs.

BERRY, William A. — Founder of the juvenile detention home in Oklahoma City. Supreme Court justice in 1960s and 1970s.

BINNS, A. F. — First fire chief when the department was organized in 1892. Longtime civic leader.

BLACKBURN, John A. — '89er and first recorder for the provisional city government.

BLAKE, E. E. — Attorney in the 1920s, who fathered the idea of dams instead of levees for flood control.

BLAKENEY, Ben B. — A leading city oil attorney of the 1930s during major oil discoveries in Oklahoma.

BLAKENEY, R. Q. — Owner and operator of Oklahoma City Packing and Produce Company, beginning in 1908.

BLATT, Rabbi Joseph — Early Jewish leader and head of Temple B'nai Israel.

BLESH, Doctor A. L. — Founder of first clinic, located south of where Huckins Hotel was later.

BLINN, C. J. — Mayor from 1931 to 1933, followed by a long period as county judge.

BOARDMAN, John Rule — Founder, in 1909, of Boardman Company, tank and equipment manufacturer. Active in industrial activity and social service.

BOHANNAN, Luther — Federal judge whose ruling on busing of students for integration and racial balance radically changed Oklahoma City schools from the neighborhood concept.

BOLEN, Hubert L. — State Treasurer. Campaign manager for Henry S. Johnston. Chairman of Oklahoma Tax Commission.

BOND, Reford — Member and chairman of the Oklahoma Corporation Commission from the mid-1930s through most of the 1940s.

BORUM, Fred S. — Air Force officer who played an important role in location of Tinker Air Force Base. Later, as a major general, headed the Oklahoma City Air Material Area.

BOSWORTH, C. M. — Civic worker and national treasurer of the National Association of Cosmopolitan Clubs during the 1920s.

BOSTON, Fred — Attorney, chairman of City National Bank and Trust Company.

BOZARTH, Howard — Banker and civic activist.

BRADFORD, Doctor G. H. — Chancellor of Epworth University, a predecessor to Oklahoma City University.

BRAND, C. Harold — Longtime city realtor who served on the advisory panel of the national Small Business Administration.

BRANIFF, Paul — Started air passenger service from Oklahoma City to Tulsa in 1928, for what eventually became Braniff International Airways.

BRANIFF, Thomas — Insurance, investment firm head; chairman of Braniff Airways.

BREWER, Judge Phil D. — Attorney; superior court judge. Vice president of Oklahoma Historical Society until his death in 1934.

BRISCOE, Powel — Oil and gas producer for more than forty years.

BROCK, Sidney L. — Dry goods store owner. President of Chamber during the 1909-1910 banner year which brought two packing houses and Oklahoma National Stockyards here.

BROOKE, Francis Key — First Episcopal missionary bishop of Oklahoma, serving in the 1890s and early 1900s.

BROWN, Della D. — Widow of John A. Brown. Operated Oklahoma City's largest department store for more than twenty years following husband's death.

BROWN, J. L. — One of city's original leaders in territorial legislation. Headed early fight for State Capitol here as a member of Territorial Council.

BROWN, John A. — Founder and owner of John A. Brown Company.

BROWNE, Virgil — Owner Coca Cola Company. Civic leader spanning five decades.

"BUNKY" — An itinerant printer for the early-day *Gazette* in Oklahoma City, who also wrote caustic comments about the first eight months of Oklahoma City. Real name: Irving Geffs.

BURCHARDT, Bill — Editor of *Oklahoma Today* magazine. Author, past president of the Western Writers of America.

BURFORD, Frank B. — Prominent lawyer and sportsman. International vice-president of Isaac Walton league.

BURFORD, Judge John H. — Receiver in city territorial land office. Later named to Supreme Court; served ten years as chief justice.

BURG, Doctor Clarence — Dean of Music at Oklahoma City University for thirty-four years, during period the school gained international reputation.

BURGE, James C. — Director, Oklahoma Semi-Centennial Exposition, 1957.

BURGESS, John — Operator of "Two Johns" saloon just north of old city hall, one of most notorious early saloons in city.

BURNS, Robert — Prominent lawyer, served as county attorney, and later as lieutenant governor.

BURWELL, Judge Benjamin F. — Prominent early-day Supreme Court justice.

BUTTON, Nelson — City's first four year mayor, 1894-1898.

BUTTRAM, Frank — Oilman, civic leader, philanthropist.

CADE, Cassius M. — Attorney, beginning career around turn of the century, prominent in Republican politics.

CAIN, William Morgan — Organized Cain's Coffee Company in 1920. Civic worker.

CALVERT, Mrs. Maude Richman — Social service leader and author of textbooks.

CAMERON, Doctor Evan Dhu — Baptist minister; territorial superintendent of public instruction; first elected State Superintendent.

CAMPBELL, A. O. — Early contractor, built Skirvin Hotel; chairman of City Park Board and Planning Commission.

CAMPBELL, Wayne — Professor of speech at Oklahoma City University. Leader in dramatic affairs of city, particularly during the 1930s.

CANTON, Brigadier General Frank — First adjutant general of Oklahoma.

CANTRELL, Doctor Roy — Post World War II President of Bethany Nazarene College, serving during its greatest development period.

CAPSHAW, Fred — Member of famous OU football team of 1911, later served six years on the Corporation Commission, two years as chairman.

CARGILL, O. A. — Attorney, rancher and former mayor.

CAREY, C. J. — Head of a Chicago lumber company, then operating thirty-two yards in three states, which moved its general offices here in 1932.

CASADY, the Right Reverend Thomas — Bishop of the Episcopal Diocese of Oklahoma from 1927 to 1953. Casady school is named for him.

CHANEY, Lon Senior — Former worker in Doc and Bill Furniture Company, later a nationally-acclaimed movie actor.

CHOUTEAU, Yvonne — Dancer, descended from fur-trading Chouteaus, who became an international ballerina.

CLARK, B. C. — Founder of Oklahoma's oldest jewelry company, in Purcell, later moving to city. Prominent Methodist layman.

CLARKE, Sidney — '89er and temporary mayor following resignation of William Couch.

CLARK, Will — Chairman of City Park Board prior to World War I, who conceived the idea of Grand Boulevard circling the city with a park in each quadrant.

CLASSEN, Anton H. — Businessman and civic leader of territorial period. Involved in development of city's first public transportation system and Epworth College (later Oklahoma City University).

COBB, Jerri — Test pilot for Aero Commander. First woman in United States to pass tests for astronaut training. Set a national speed record for small two-engine planes.

COE, Charles Robert — Former national amateur champion golfer, who later headed Walker Cup teams in England.

COFFMAN, Sam — Developer of Coffman Monoplanes, Incorporated, which manufactured airplanes here in 1929 and the early 1930s.

COLCORD, Charles F. — First chief of police, pioneer builder, first elected sheriff, U.S. Deputy Marshal. Builder of Colcord Building. Instrumental in building Commerce Exchange Building and Biltmore Hotel.

COLEMAN, William O. — Manager of city airports during the 1950s and 1960s.

CONKLIN, Mrs. Madaline — Superintendent of State Girls School at Tecumseh in the 1920s. Later head of Oklahoma County Home for Girls.

COOKE, Edward H. — Pioneer banker and business leader from the 1890s through World War I. Participated in organization of street railway system.

CONN, Jack T. — Ada banker who came to city as head of Fidelity National Bank and Trust Company.

COTTINGHAM, J. R. — General counsel for Santa Fe Railroad in state from before 1907 into the 1920s; a leader in civic affairs and Republican politics.

COUCH, William L. — Head of the Boomer movement from 1884 through opening of Unassigned Lands; first provisional mayor.

CRAVENS, Robert D. — Real estate and land developer. Owner of Cravens Building (formerly Perrine Building).

CRAVENS, Vinita — City's leading promoter of Broadway stage productions from the mid-World War II years into the 1970s.

CREEKMORE, William — Bootlegger and vice king, beginning about the time of statehood, and continuing until 1917.

CROCKER, Samuel — Native of England who joined the Boomers and edited the *Oklahoma War Chief*. Indicted, but not tried for inciting rebellion. In Oklahoma City he was always espousing unpopular causes.

CULBERTSON, J. J., Junior — City developer following World War I. He and father gave half the site for State Capitol; the land for governor's mansion, Culbertson School and Culbertson Park.

CURNETT, Ada — Oklahoma's only woman United States Marshal, serving during the 1890s.

DALE, Mrs. J. R. — Lecturer and longtime secretary of the Oklahoma State Library Commission.

DAUGHERTY, Fred — Commanding general of the 45th Infantry Division. Federal district judge.

DAVIS, George A. — President of Oklahoma Gas and Electric Company. Adjutant general for state during World War II, unsalaried.

DAWSON, Kaye W. — Developed Dawson Produce Company. Civic leader of the 1920s and 1930s.

DAY, C. C. — Insurance executive and civic leader in the 1930s.

DEAN, Walter C. — Businessman; mayor from 1927 to 1931, first one under city manager form of government.

DeBOLT, A. M. — '89er who opened a lumberyard at Reno and Santa Fe. Built the DeBolt House on Hudson Avenue which rivaled the Overholser House.

DICKERSON, Leonard H. — Businessman and city councilman. Considered one of most powerful persons in city government during late 1940s into 1950s.

DONNELLY, Mike — Mayor 1923-1925, city councilman, county commissioner.

DONOVAN, W. J. — Territorial publisher of the *Press Gazette*, early-day newspaper, claiming to be organ of the Democratic party.

DOUGLAS, Selwyn — A leading territorial and early statehood attorney and early figure in Territorial Oklahoma Masonic bodies.

DOUGLAS, Mrs. Selwyn — Established first high school in 1893. Active in formation of womens' cultural clubs. Obtained Carnegie Library for city.

DRAPER, Stanley C. — Executive vice president of Chamber since shortly after World War I until retirement in late 1960s. A prime mover in city for more than fifty years.

DULANEY, Luther T. — Manufacturer of furniture and distributor of household appliances. One of leading supporters of Oklahoma City University and President of the National Cowboy Hall of Fame; philanthropist.

DUNGEE, Roscoe — Editor of *The Black Dispatch*, and a strong influence in the black community during the 1930s and 1940s.

EARP, Ancel — Insurance firm head, civic worker and World War I adjutant general of Oklahoma.

EDDIE, B. D. — Founder of Superior Feed Mills, then one of largest independent feed mills in the Southwest. Donor of United Appeal Building and the Civic Center '89er statue.

ELLISON, Ralph — City born and educated man, now at New York University, where he has authored *Invisible Man* and other novels.

EMBRY, John — Responsible for securing passage by legislature of separate school laws for whites and Negroes. Later was U.S. District Attorney.

EPPERLY, George I. — Builder most responsible for the development of Del City.

ERNSBERGER, Earl R. — President of Southwestern Light and Power Company when it was headquartered in city during the 1920s and early 1930s.

EVEREST, C. H. — President of the Guaranty Bank when it became Liberty National Bank in 1921.

EVEREST, J. H. — Prominent early-day lawyer, who, in 1900, owned the first automobile in city.

EVEREST, Harvey P. — Founder of Mid-Continent News Company, one of the nation's major magazine distributorships. Later served as president and chairman of Liberty National Bank.

EVERETT, Doctor Mark — Former Dean of the University of Oklahoma Medical School.

FAIN, Winnie Mae — Daughter of sponsor of Wiley Post's record world flying ventures. The famous Post plane, "The Winnie Mae" is now in the Smithsonian Institution.

FARIS, Glenn — Longtime secretary of the Chamber, who upon retirement became unpaid executive of the National Cowboy Hall of Fame; his presentation was largely responsible for its location here.

FIELDS, John — Editor of the *Oklahoma Farmer*; president of the Federal Land Bank at Wichita in the late 1920s.

FINERTY, Fred P. — Early resident of Territorial Oklahoma; president of Fidelity National Bank in the late teens and the 1920s.

FLUKE, Louise — Designer of the Oklahoma State Flag.

FLYNN, Dennis T. — '89er and first postmaster of Guthrie. Second territorial delegate to Congress. A founder of Oklahoma Gas and Electric Company. General counsel for Santa Fe Railroad in Oklahoma.

FLYNN, Streeter B. — Son of Dennis T. Flynn. As an attorney, he played a major role in utility and railroad development.

FRANKLIN, Wirt — Participated in discovery of the Healdton oil field, later active in city field. First president of the Independent Petroleum Association of America. Early proponent of conservation proration.

FRATES, C. L. — Insurance, bond, and development executive.

FRATES, Mex Rodman — Prominent social and civic worker.

FREDERICKSON, George — Vice President and director of Oklahoma Natural Gas Company. President of Chamber immediately after World War I.

FRY, Captain E. G. — Organized in 1920 and directed for twenty-two years city's famous Girls' Kiltie Band.

FULTON, E. L. — First congressman to be elected from Oklahoma City.

GAINER, Ina M. — Columnist for *Oklahoman and Times* and feminine leader identified with the cultural development of city during the 1910s and 1920s.

GAYLORD, E. K. — Publisher of *Daily Oklahoman, Oklahoma City Times,* and *Farmer Stockman.* President of WKY radio and TV along with other business interests. His civic leadership has spanned a century. A Frontiers of Science organizer. Remained active until death at 101 in 1974.

GAYLORD, Edward L. — Executive Vice President of Oklahoma Publishing Company; owner of print and electronic media, transportation, oil interests; supporter of cultural and civic affairs.

GILL, William Junior — Twice city manager, owner of Gill Construction Company.

GLASCOW, M. R. — '89er lawyer and a major spokesman for the Kickapoo faction in opening days.

GOFF, George — Longtime city fire chief from age 28 in 1921. Inventor of several pieces of fire fighting equipment; later sheriff.

GORGAS, Doctor W. C. — Served here in army contingent at time of Run. Later famous as the medical doctor who made the Panama Canal possible through clearing malaria out of Canal Zone.

GOSLIN, Les — A founder of the TG&Y store chain.

GOULD, Charles N. — One of the leading geologists of the world, considered to be the father of oil development in state. Founder of the Oklahoma Geological Survey.

GOULD, Mrs. Charles N. — Leader in city women's activities during the 1920s, giving particular emphasis to beautification of the city.

GOULD, Chester — A native of Pawnee, who drew his first cartoons for the *Daily Oklahoman* and who became creator of the Dick Tracy strip.

GRANT, Whit M. — Mayor 1911 to 1915.

GREEN, Doctor E. G. — First President of Oklahoma City College, later renamed Oklahoma City University.

GRIMES, William "Bill" — Territorial United States Marshal; leader in territorial and early statehood Republican politics.

GUTHRIE, Ledru — First provisional city Attorney and outstanding lawyer following the Run.

GUTHRIE, Will S. — Early civic leader who led the Liberty Bond campaigns of World War I.

HALES, William T. — Merchant, banker, real estate developer after 1890. The Hales Building bears his name. Once called city's largest property owner.

HALL, F. C. — Independent oilman who opened the Chickasha pool and later financed trips and the plane, "Winnie Mae," for Wiley Post's successful world record flights in 1931 and 1933.

HALLEY, John H. — Attorney beginning in 1912. Democratic party leader during the 1930s.

HAMILTON, Joe N. — First executive director of the Oklahoma Society for Crippled Children, serving thirty-one years.

HAMMER, Captain A. B. — Attorney and leader of the Kickapoos following the run. Early church leader.

HAMMONDS, Mrs. O. O. Administrative secretary to Governor Henry S. Johnston, whose alleged influence on him was a dominant factor in bringing about legislative impeachment of the governor.

HARBOUR, J. F. — A founder and partner in the Harbour-Longmire furniture manufacturing and retail company, which in the early 1930s ranked second in size among retail furniture stores in the United States.

HARGETT, James S. — President of General Mills southern division and three term president of Chamber.

HARLOW, Bryce — City native who became a principal speech writer and advisor for Presidents Eisenhower and Nixon.

HARLOW, Doctor James — Former executive vice president of Frontiers of Science Foundation, later a University of Oklahoma administrator, and still later president of the University of West Virginia.

HARLOW, Victor E. — Publisher, printer, civic leader and editor of *Harlow's Weekly*, a commentary on political affairs in Oklahoma.

HARMON, D. A. — Founder, in 1927, Harmon & Mattison Construction Company, which later became Harmon Construction Company.

HARN, W. F. — Gave land, along with the J. J. Culbertsons, for the Oklahoma State Capitol complex.

HARDEN, John J. — Major developer of the 1920s and 1930s, who laid out a number of additions, developed Rose Hill Cemetery and owned Western Paving Company.

HARPER, Forrest E. — President and co-owner of Harper-Turner Oil Company, with Roy J. Turner, major operator in city field.

HARPER, William P. — Attorney beginning immediately after the Run of '89. Oklahoma County Probate Judge at the time of statehood.

HARRELL, Hugh L. — Banker, rancher, civic leader and one time Assistant Secretary of State.

HARRIS, Grady — Civic leader and president of Fidelity Bank, N.A.

HARRIS, V. V. — Financier, industrialist, and philanthropist. His foundation purchased the bell chimes at St. Luke's Methodist Church and helped to finance many other community projects.

HARRISON, Floyd A. — Builder most responsible in the 1950s for development of The Village.

HARRISON, Guy Fraser — Oklahoma City Symphony conductor for more than twenty years,

HARRISON, Walter M. — Managing editor of the *Daily Oklahoman and Times*, who later had his own weekly newspaper and served on the city council. Unsuccessful candidate for mayor.

HARVEY, David A. — First elected delegate to Congress from Oklahoma Territory.

HASKELL, Charles N. — Eastern Oklahoman and a leading delegate to the Constitutional convention; elected first governor of Oklahoma; moved capital from Guthrie to Oklahoma City the night of the location election.

HATFIELD, H. G. — Civic worker of the 1930s and 1940s who served during the late 1930s as president of Kiwanis International.

HAWLEY, Doctor Frederick W. — Pastor of First Presbyterian Church in early 1890s, later overseer of all Presbyterian churches in the area, still later president of Henry Kendall College of Muskogee (now Tulsa University).

HAYES, Judge Samuel W. — Former Chief Justice of state Supreme Court and civic leader. Helped write Oklahoma Constitution as its youngest delegate.

HEAD, Ben T. — President of City National Bank and past commandant of the United States Army Reserve School here.

HEFLIN, Van — One of the nation's leading motion picture actors, born in Walters, reared and educated here.

HEFNER, Robert A. — Mayor 1939-47. Supreme Court justice and oilman. His home is now base of the Oklahoma Heritage Association and Oklahoma Hall of Fame.

HEMPHILL, Ralph T. — State Fair manager for more than twenty years — from 1917 into the 1940s.

HEYMAN, Seymour C. — Clothing merchant and civic leader during city's earliest days; had profound influence on the early public education system and sports in city.

HICKEY, Mrs. J. T. — Choir leader in earliest days of St. Joseph's Catholic Church and a leader in city musical activities.

HIGHLEY, Mont — Early Lawyer who served as chairman of the Park Board and as a member of the Planning Commission.

HIGHTOWER, William E. — President of First National Bank, civic and business leader, chamber president.

HILLS, Lee — Editor of the now defunct Oklahoma News, later executive editor of the Knight publications in Detroit, Chicago and Miami.

HIRSCHFIELD, Norman — Chairman and chief executive officer of ACF-Wrigley Stores.

HOBBS, Hershel — Longtime pastor of First Baptist Church, retiring in 1973. Nationally prominent in religious circles.

HOFFMAN, Roy — Leader of Oklahoma National Guard after Spanish-American War. First National Guard officer in nation to be promoted to a general in World War I. Attorney and civic leader.

HOGAN, Dan W. — Civic leader and banker. Longtime president and chairman of City National Bank and Trust Company. His life spanned more than one hundred years.

HOLLOWAY, William J. — Southern Oklahoma lawyer elected to state Senate then as lieutenant governor. Became governor upon impeachment of Henry S. Johnston.

HUBBELL, Carl — Major league pitcher, created through Oklahoma City baseball, who set a big league record with twenty-four consecutive wins.

HUCKINS, Joseph Junior — Owner of Oklahoma City's first big and thoroughly modern hotel, purchased from Oscar Lee, and enlarged.

HUDSON, Hubert — President of Oklahoma Railway Company who also headed the Oklahoma City-Ada and Atoka Railway.

HUNT, Judge Albert C. — Attorney, a justice of the state Supreme Court, and a leader in the Boy Scout movement of Central Oklahoma.

HUTCHINSON, Doctor Forney — Pastor at St. Luke's Methodist Church from World War I through 1932.

HYDE, Herbert K. — United States District Attorney for the Western Oklahoma District.

JAMES, Guy H. — Major construction contractor from the 1930s into the 1960s, who was serving on the city council at the time of his death.

JAMISON, Homer — Life insurance executive and vice president in the mid-1920s of the National Association of Life Underwriters.

JANEWAY, P. A. — President of Liberty National Bank in the 1920s and early 1930s.

JOHNSON, Edith — *Daily Oklahoman* writer, whose column had wide influence in Oklahoma.

JOHNSON, Frank P. — President of the First National Bank and Trust Company during the 1920s and early 1930s.

JOHNSON, Hugh — Board chairman and President of the First National Bank and Trust Company.

JOHNSTON, John H. — Builder and developer most responsible for the Quail Creek Addition.

JOHNSTON, W. R. — Founder, in the 1920s, of an investment firm bearing his name. It was once the largest organization of its kind in the city.

JONES, Charles G. — Grain mill and real estate operator, railroad builder, twice mayor, and civic leader in city's earliest days. Father of State Fair.

JONES, Fred — Built one of the nation's largest Ford dealerships. Developed a manufacturing company for rebuilding automobile components. Member of the National Defense Advisory Commission during World War II.

JOULLIAN, Edward C. — President of Consolidated Gas Utilities Company, later founder and President of Mustang Fuel Corporation. Particularly prominent in Boy Scout work.

KAVANAUGH, Alfred J. — Major contractor from 1940s into the 1970s.

KEATON, James R. — Pioneer attorney and associate justice of Oklahoma Territorial Supreme Court.

KERR, George G. — Merchant and civic leader, who organized Kerr Dry Goods Company, a leading department store here for more than fifty years.

KERR, Robert S. — Founder of Kerr-McGee Company, later governor of Oklahoma, then elected to U.S. Senate, where he became one of the most powerful members of that body.

KEY, Major General W. S. — Warden, state penitentiary; Works Progress Administrator for Oklahoma. Businessman. Commanded 45th Infantry Division on call to federal service for World War II.

KILPATRICK, John Junior — Civic, cultural and business leader and a member of the Oklahoma Turnpike Authority.

KING, R. R. — Founder and President of American Body and Trailer Company.

KINGKADE, A. Martin — Builder and owner of Kingkade Hotel.

KIRKPATRICK, John E. — Decorated World War II Naval officer and rear admiral in naval reserve; oil man and philanthropist, with major contributions to science and the arts, Oklahoma City Zoo and National Cowboy Hall of Fame.

KLEIN, J. B. — Organized a small steel shop in Oklahoma City in 1909, which grew large, now is Robberson Steel Company.

KNICKERBOCKER, Hubert — Oklahoma Citian who was *New York Evening Post* correspondent in Berlin prior to World War II.

LACKEY, Daniel V. — Mayor 1910-1911.

LACKEY, George — Life insurance agent and vice president during the early 1920s of the National Association of Life Underwriters.

LAIN, Doctor Everett S. — City surgeon of early 1900s, particularly prominent in cancer research.

LATTING, Patience — First woman mayor of Oklahoma City, elected 1971.

LAYTON, Sol A. — Head of the architectural firm that designed more public buildings in early Oklahoma than any other firm. Included were the State Capitol and Central High School.

LEDBETTER, E. R. — Owner of an insurance agency since 1922. An organizer of the Oklahoma City Jaycees.

LEDBETTER, W. A. — Federal marshal, attorney, judge, Constitutional Convention delegate and legal advisor to Governor Haskell.

LEE, Oscar G. — Hotel owner, real estate developer and law enforcement officer, who came here in 1889, later building the Lee Hotel.

LEE, Robert W. — Founder and president of Lee Way Motor Freight Company, one of the nation's large carriers.

LEONARDT, H. E. — Founder of the H. E. Leonhardt Company, operating lumber yards and apartment houses.

LEVY, Harrison — Developer and realtor.

LINCOLN, Miss Louise — Oklahoma Citian who sang in operas in Europe, then joined the Chicago Civic Opera in 1930.

LIPPERT, Walter H. — Founded, in 1920, Lippert Brothers Company, which became a major commercial and industrial contracting company.

LOEWENSTEIN, Morris — '89er (as a child) and early motion picture theater owner and developer.

LONG, Doctor LeRoy — Dean of the University of Oklahoma Medical School from 1915 to 1931.

LONGMIRE, W. M. — Merchant, civic leader. A founder of the Harbour-Longmire furniture manufacturing and retail sales company.

LOONEY, M. A. "Ned" — City attorney who represented three state governors, two United States senators and a Supreme Court justice. Attorney for the Oklahoma Turnpike Authority during the 1950s.

LOVE, John E. "Jack" — Early territorial city councilman who later became chairman of the Oklahoma Corporation Commission.

LOWERY, Doctor Tom — Dean of the University of Oklahoma Medical School, who moved it to its present location shortly after World War I.

LUNN, Harris — President of Boardman Company, fabricators and distributors of industrial equipment.

LUPER, Clara — Black leader in racial demonstrations and civil rights activity here in the 1960s and 1970s.

LYBRAND, Walter A. — Attorney and a member of the Council of the American Bar Association.

MACKLANBURG, Louis A. — Founder of Macklanburg-Duncan Company, one of the nation's largest manufacturers of building supplies.

MacMARTIN, D. W. — Pioneer city lawyer, who frequently represented the underworld in the 1890s.

MADSEN, Chris — Deputy United States Marshal in early territorial days.

MAGEE, Carl — Editor of Oklahoma News who later conceived the idea of the parking meter.

MAGER, Albert — Founder of Mager Mortgage Company. A leader in Boy Scout work on both a local and regional level.

MAKINS, Charles H. — Founder of Makins Sand and Gravel Company and a member of the State Public Welfare Commission in the late 1930s and early 1940s.

MANY, James — Pioneer city builder, civil engineer and contractor.

MARKHAM, Baird H. — Former 45th Infantry Division Commander, director of the American Petroleum Institute.

MARTIN, J. Frank — Mayor from 1935 to 1939.

MARTINEAU, W. R. — Daily Oklahoman city editor, later publisher of the Oklahoma Livestock News, chairman of the Oklahoma City Gridiron Club from its founding until his death.

McALPINE, G. R. — City fire chief during the 1940s and 1950s and past President of the International Association of Fire Chiefs.

McCARTY, J. D. — State representative in the 1940s and 1950s, multiple terms as Speaker of the House.

McCLURE, William J. — Prominent stockman and rancher, conceded to be the first legal settler in future Oklahoma City. He arrived from the east border and his entry was held legal by the courts.

McGEE, Dean A. — An organizer and later head of the huge Kerr-McGee Corporation; business leader from the early 1940s; particularly active in Frontiers of Science but in forefront of all civic and cultural affairs.

McGEE, Tom — Mayor 1933 to 1935.

McLAIN, Lieutenant General Raymond S. — President of American First Title and Trust Company. 45th Division Artillery commander and later a corps commander in World War II. Climaxed military career as comptroller general of army.

McLEAN, William — Chairman and chief executive officer of Liberty National Bank and Trust Company.

McMASTER, Frank — Publisher of city newspapers during the 1890s.

McNEILL, Don — Classen High School graduate who, in 1938, became Oklahoma's first national tennis champion.

McRILL, Albert — Former city manager. Author of book, And Satan Came Also.

MEE, William — President of Security National Bank during the 1920s. Particularly active in industrial and commercial development.

MEERSCHAERT, Right Reverend Theophile — Native of Belgium who was Catholic bishop for Oklahoma from 1905 until his death in 1924. He founded St. Joseph's Orphanage.

MELLON, Thomas P. — Founder of the Mellon Dry Goods Store, one of the leading early stores.

MERSFELDER, Larry C. — Prominent in insurance from the 1920s into the 1960s. Civic worker and author of three published books.

MESSENBAUGH, J. F. — Mayor from 1905 to 1907.

MESTA, Perle — Daughter of hotel developer, W. B. Skirvin, who became best known for her Washington, D.C., parties for the nation's political elite. Minister to Luxembourg under President Truman.

MILLER, Paul — City newsman who became chief executive officer of the Gannett newspaper chain and president of the Associated Press.

MILLS, Clarence — District judge for more than thirty years; supporter of cultural affairs.

MITSCHER, Admiral Marc — Task force leader in the World War II Battle of Midway, who later became commander-in-chief, Pacific.

MITSCHER, O. A. — Prominent in early city government. Mayor 1892-94. Agent to the Osage Indian agency. Father of the admiral.

MONETT, Claude — Attorney and civic leader who played a particularly key leadership role in development and growth of the YMCA.

MONRONEY, A. E. — Founder of the once well known Doc and Bill Furniture Store. Father of former Senator Mike Monroney.

MONRONEY, A. S. "Mike" — Newsman who later served thirty years in the Congress and senate. with particular prominence in aviation and postal areas.

MONTIN, William B. — Head of one of the largest pipeline construction firms in the Southwest, with worldwide operation. President of Chamber.

MOON, F. D. — Principal of Douglass High School and, after retirement, first black to be elected to city School Board. Nationally recognized as an educator.

MOORMAN, Doctor Lewis J. — Physician and founder of first institution in Oklahoma for treatment of tuberculosis.

MORSE, Joe D. — Founder and for twenty-two years President of Home State Life Insurance Company, now merged into American General Life Insurance Company.

MOSIER, Orval O. "Red" — City manager and later executive vice president of American Airlines.

MUELLER, Mrs. Harold — Once "Aunt Susan" of early WKY radio cooking school, who later handled the nation's first network television cooking school, and was food editor of McCall's Magazine. (The former Mrs. Mart Adams.)

MURPHY, R. R. "Pat" — Head of City Park Department for more than a quarter of a century and president in 1953 of the American Association of Park Executives.

MURRAH, Judge Alfred P. — Federal Judge in Oklahoma City, later District Court of Appeals Judge in Denver, still later executive director of the administrative office of the Federal Judicial Center.

NASH, Evans A. — President of Yellow Transit Company and president of Associated Motor Carriers of Oklahoma, who served a long term on the board of the United States Chamber of Commerce.

NICHOLS, Doctor G. A. — Dentist, businessman, builder. Developer of Nichols Hills, exclusive incorporated northern suburb to Oklahoma City.

NINS, E. D. — A telephone pioneer in Oklahoma, later president of Southwestern Bell Telephone Company in St. Louis.

NOBLE, John M. — Founder of a telephone system in the city.

NORICK, James H. — Printing executive. Mayor 1959 to 1963 and 1967 to 1971.

NORTH, Mrs. L. H. — Organizer of the first school here, a tuition school formed in the summer of 1889.

O'NEIL, John E. "Mike" — Wholesale hardware dealer most active in development of parks as chairman of the City Park Board. O'Neil Park is named for him. Headed State Board of Affairs when state capitol was built.

OSBORN, William H. — Secretary to Payne's Oklahoma Colony. Played major role in early Boomer days.

OVERHOLSER, Edward G. — Former mayor (1915-1918) and long-time president-manager of Chamber. Son of Henry Overholser. Lake Overholser is named for Edward.

OVERHOLSER, Henry — One of the principal financiers and promoters in territorial days. Played a leading role in bringing Frisco Railroad to Oklahoma City.

OWEN, J. M. — Former president of the Oklahoma City Federal Savings and Loan Company. Active in civic affairs from the 1890s until his death in 1952.

OWENS, Hugh — Attorney and national Jaycee vice-president, who went to Washington to rise to chairmanship of the Securities and Exchange Commission. Son of J. F. Owens.

PARKER, Deake — Former reporter on the *Oklahoma News* who became editor-in-chief of Scripps-Howard newspapers.

PATRICK, G. W. — First elected mayor of South Oklahoma City, originally intended to be a separate town. Never held office.

PATTERSON, L. E. — Owner of Patterson Streetcar Company system, which was sold to Oklahoma Railway Company prior to World War I Civic gadfly and unsuccessful candidate for mayor.

PATTERSON, Moss — Chairman of Chamber aviation committee; president of Oklahoma Transportation Company; rancher; member State Board of Affairs.

PATTERSON, Orban C. — City's vice king during the 1930s. Convicted in 1940.

PAYNE, David L. — Original head of the Boomer movement until his death in 1884.

PAYNE, Hugh G. — Executive vice president, from its early years until 1963, of the Oklahoma Medical Research Foundation.

PECK, Herbert — County attorney who led one of the early governmental clean-up efforts; a local YMCA leader beginning in the 1920s, later serving as vice president of the YMCA of North America.

PEERY, Dan W. — Early historian and official of the Oklahoma Historical Society.

PENNINGTON, Steve — Major real estate developer during and following the World War II period.

PERRINE, Irving — University of Oklahoma geology professor who formed his own oil company in 1930 and played a major role in oil development of the state.

PERSHING, Reverend J. E. — Congregational minister who, in 1918, was named first Boy Scout executive for city. He was a relative of General Pershing of World War I fame, who in early 1890s was an army recruiter here.

PETERS, Doctor John L. — Former city pastor who conceived and created the World Neighbors organization, with national headquarters here.

PETTEE, William J. — Business and civic leader and founder of the Pettee Hardware Stores, first hardware firm in city.

PORTER, Felix — Executive committee chairman of First National Bank and Trust Company.

PORTER, Reverend Henry Alford — Pastor of First Baptist Church when famous "White Temple" was built at Northwest Third and Broadway. The building later became the Masonic Hall.

PRITCHARD, L. H. — Attorney, a partner with H. Steve Anderson in Anderson-Pritchard Oil Company.

PRUIETT, Moman — One of the best known criminal lawyers of the Southwest.

PUTNAM, Israel M. — Real estate man and philanthropist. Developer of Putnam Heights area.

QUAYLE, Bishop William A. — Methodist Episcopal Bishop, lecturer, and author about the turn of the century.

QUINN, W. A. — Organized U-Save grocery chain which later was purchased by Safeway. Twice city manager.

RAMSEY, W. R. and W. E. — Brothers involved in development of Carter county Oil fields, who later came here to form Ramsey Petroleum Corporation, active in city field.

REECE, Ralph — An organizer and president of Globe Life Insurance Company. He was also an organizer of, and Board Chairman for World Neighbors, worldwide self-help organization.

REYNOLDS, Allie — City man who became one of the top major league pitchers with the Cleveland Indians and New York Yankees. Returned here to become a businessman, with an interest in minor baseball leagues.

RICHARDSON, J. Wiley — Florist, civic leader. First Chairman of the Oklahoma Turnpike Authority.

RICHARDSON, T. M. — President of First National Bank in the 1890s. First treasurer of city's Board of Trade in 1889. Built first multi-story office building (five-story Baltimore Building at northeast corner of Sheridan and Harvey).

RILEY, Doctor Lea A. — A leading city physician of the 1920s.

ROBBERSON, R. W. — Joined the small Klein and Company Iron and Wire Company in 1913 as a roustabout. Developed it into the large Robberson Steel Company.

ROBERTS, Clarence — Editor of the *Farmer-Stockman* magazine until his death in early 1940s.

RODMAN, Roland V. — President, Chairman of Anderson-Pritchard Oil Corporation. Civic leader.

ROGERS, Stanley — Oilman and sheriff of Oklahoma County during 1930s and 1940s.

ROLATER, Doctor Joseph B. — One of earliest leading doctors, who founded the first hospital — the Rolater Hospital — at Northeast Fourth and Stiles (during the 1890s).

ROSE, Oscar — Superintendent of Midwest City Schools. Father of Federal Impact Aid System for education. A junior college is named for him.

RUCKS, Doctor W. W. — Early doctor of the turn of the century, who founded the Oklahoma City Clinic in the early 1900s.

RUNKLE, Lowe — Developer of the largest advertising agency in the state and second in billings in the Southwest.

RUSSELL, Mrs. Angie — Juvenile welfare leader for more than forty years.

RUTH, Charles — Well known municipal gadfly of the 1920s.

RYAN, Doctor J. A. — One of city's first physicians and a leader in the early civic structure.

SANGER, Doctor Winnie Monroney — City's first woman doctor. Women's club leader in 1920s and 1930s.

SAUNDERS, O. O. "Sandy" — Manager of the State Fair of Oklahoma during the 1960s and 1970s.

SCALES, Henry N. — Mayor 1907-1910.

SCHONWALD, Fred — Attorney, independent oil producer, western history buff.

SCOTT, Doctor Angelo C. — Chairman of city's first town meeting. Publisher of city's first newspaper. President of Oklahoma A&M College.

SCOTT, Joe C. — Chief executive of Bankers Service Life Insurance Company and a leader in civic drives. President of state board of agriculture.

SCOTT, S. H. — Dynamic colored attorney and Kickapoo sympathizer in the earliest days. He had strong influence with the Negroes of early city.

SCOTT, W. W. — Business manager of the *Oklahoma City Times*, first city newspaper, formed with his brother, Angelo Scott, shortly after the Run of 1889.

SELLS, Irene Bowers — Society editor for the *Daily Oklahoman* and later the *Oklahoma News.* Her writing was influential in Oklahoma City.

SEWELL, Frank A. — Organizer of a Texhoma and a Clinton bank who later moved here to become president of Liberty National Bank and Trust Company. Father of Mayor Patience Latting.

SHARTEL, John W. — Attorney, real estate developer, and transportation executive. He headed the Metropolitan Railway Company which became Oklahoma Railway Company.

SHEAR, Byron D. — Mayor 1918-1919.

SHEETS, Nan — Organizer during the 1930s, and director for more than twenty years, of the Oklahoma City Art Center.

SHIRK, George H. — Attorney and historian. Mayor 1964 to 1967. President of Oklahoma Historical Society for nineteen years.

SHIRK, John H. — A leading attorney of the 1920s and 1930s. Active in general civic development.

SHIRK, Lucyl — Executive director and builder of Camp Fire Girls organization here. Author of *Oklahoma City — Capital of Soonerland*, published by Oklahoma City Board of Education.

SINGLETARY, R. A. — Crusader for better Oklahoma highways, beginning after World War I. City Chamber representative in Washington.

SINOPOULO, John — Theater owner who developed Delmar Gardens, city's first large amusement park.

SIPES, Jasper — School supply dealer and a founder of the Oklahoma Historical Society, who served many years, both before and after statehood, as its president.

SKIRVIN, W. B. — Developer of the Skirvin and Skirvin Tower Hotels, and oil interests.

SLICK, Tom — Oilman who hit it big as "King of the Wildcatters."

SMALL, Reverend Sam — Evangelist and newspaperman, who founded *The Daily Oklahoman*, failed in the venture, returned to evangelism, later to newspaper work on the *Atlanta Constitution.*

SMITH, W. Angie — Long-time bishop of the Oklahoma-New Mexico conference of the Methodist Church, considered to be one of the most influential individuals in Methodism.
SMITH, Anna Maude — Developer of Anna Maude Cafeteria, recognized as one of the best in the nation. Constant helper in civic enterprises.
SMITH, Doctor C. Q. — President of Oklahoma City University during World War II and during its postwar period of large growth.
SMITH, Gomer — Attorney and political figure of the 1940s and 1950s. Member of Congress and unsuccessful candidate for governor.
SMITH, Lee Allen — WKY-TV official, who headed development of the annual Fourth of July "Stars and Stripes Show," which has brought the city national recognition through network television.
SOHLBERG, George G. — Established in 1904 the Acme Milling Company, first flour mill in city.
SOREY, Lee — Senior partner of Sorey, Hill and Binicker, Architects. Civic worker, particularly active in city's beautification efforts.
SPECK, John K. — Attorney, civic worker and founder of the Halfway House here now named "Speck House."
STAFFORD, Roy — Editor and partner in the *Daily Oklahoman* during early years of the Oklahoma Publishing Company.
STEPHENS, Doctor Waldo — Oil executive, lecturer and civic worker. Internationally active in United Nations affairs.
STERLING, Sheldon — Chamber executive and later city manager.
STEWART, Jimmy — Longtime leader in National Association for the Advancement of Colored People.
STILES, Captain Daniel F. — Commander of a company of soldiers stationed here at time of the Run, and provost marshal of the surrounding area. Later president of the Oklahoma National Bank.
STONE, Grant B. — President of the Chamber at time of statehood.
STRASBAUGH, Paul — Director of the industrial division, later executive vice president of the Chamber.
STREET, Allen — Head of Street and Draper Funeral Home. Early leader in Oklahoma City Boy Scout movement. Mayor 1947-1959.
STUART, Robert T., Senior — Past president of State Chamber of Commerce. President of Mid-Continent Life Insurance Company, which he moved from Muskogee here in 1916.
SULLINS, R. A. — First superintendent of Oklahoma City Schools, with eighteen teachers in the system.
SUTTON, Mrs. Fred — '89er and early-day educator, who formed a subscription school downtown, which later evolved into the city school system.

TAYLOR, General Maxwell D. — Oklahoma Cityan who rose to Army Chief of Staff.
THACH, Thomas — Insurance executive and organizer of the International Host program, which brought about family hosting of thousands of foreign visitors by city residents.
THATCHER, T. C. — Vice President and manager of the Oklahoma City Mill and Elevator Company, largest milling installation in Oklahoma during the 1920s.
THOBURN, J. B. — A foremost early Oklahoma historian.
TILGHMAN, William — One of the best known U.S. marshals of Oklahoma Territory, with Heck Thomas and Chris Madsen, two of "The Three Guardsmen."
THOMAS, General Henry G. — Native of Maine who came to city in the 1890s to purchase and operate the first city waterworks, after operating a grocery.
THOMAS, John D. — Business and civic leader of the early 1900s. After operating a store on Main Street, he built Plaza Court.
TIDNAM, F. H. — Inventor, associate of Thomas Edison, early-day general manager of Oklahoma Gas and Electric Company, and developer of the Tidnam concrete utility poles, manufactured here.
TREAT, Guy B. — Longtime engineer with Oklahoma Railway Company, later became owner and president of Treat Engineering Company.
TROSPER, H. D. — One of city's two original territorial legislators. Trosper Park is named for him.
TUCKER, Morrison G. — Banker and leader in beautification projects in city from the 1950s into the 1970s.

TURNER, M. L. — Territorial treasurer and twice United States Senate candidate. He established the Western National Bank in city.

TURNER, Roy J. — Oilman and cattleman. "Reform" school board president. Governor of Oklahoma who, during his administration, originated the turnpike system in Oklahoma.

URSCHEL, Charles F. — Wealthy city oilman, particularly remembered as the victim of a dramatic kidnapping in 1933.

VanLEUVEN, Mrs. Katherine — Attorney, civic leader, public officer, philanthropist.

VanWINKLE, Lee — Mayor 1899-1901, and 1903-1905.

VAUGHT, Edgar S. — Federal Judge who became senior member of the federal judiciary in Oklahoma. Prominent Methodist layman. President of Lions International.

VIOLET, A. H. — Chairman of the committee which formed the Board of Trade in 1889, which later became Chamber of Commerce.

VLIET, R. M. — Partner in Fox-Vliet wholesale drug firm.

VOSE, C. A. — Longtime head of the First National Bank and Trust Company — from the 1940s into the 1970s.

VOSE, R. A. — President of First National Bank, who was responsible for construction of the present bank building.

VOSS, William B. — Developed Star Manufacturing Company into one of the world leaders in the manufacturing of pre-engineered steel buildings.

WALKER, C. P. — A leader of the Kansas-formed Oklahoma Town Company in 1889. Involved in town political activities.

WALKER, Doctor Delos — A leader of the Oklahoma Town Company. Once Prohibition Party candidate for governor of Kansas. First city school board president. Walker street is named for him.

WALKER, Paul — One-time member of the Oklahoma Corporation Commission who served on the Federal Communications Commission during the 1940s.

WALKER, R. A. — United States Marshal, who brought an end to city's self-government in 1890 on a ruling of the United States Attorney General.

WALLACE, W. R. — Corporate attorney, U.S. district judge, and youngest member of Oklahoma's second legislature.

WALTON, John C. "Jack" — Mayor 1919-1923 and governor of Oklahoma immediately afterwards. Impeached during his first year as governor.

WARR, C. B. — Realtor who created the housing development which became the incorporated town of Warr Acres.

WATTON, Harry C. — Leading portrait photographer here from 1911 until about the time of World War II.

WEAVER, Claude — Oklahoma City postmaster, beginning in 1915 and serving into the late 1920s.

WEAVER, General James B. — '89er, and early leader of Seminole faction of city. He twice ran for president of United States on a minor party ticket.

WEBB, James E. — Imported president of Republic Supply Company in 1950s. An organizer and president of the Frontiers of Science. Later director of the National Aeronautics and Space Administration.

WEBER, Major General Lavern E. — National Guardsman who became adjutant general of Oklahoma in the 1960s, then moved to the Pentagon as director of the Army National Guard. Now Chief of National Guard Bureau.

WEITZENHOFFER, Aaron A. — Founder and president of Davon Oil Company. Best known for his civic and charity work during the period preceding, during, and after World War II.

WELLS, William A. — City architect from 1904 to 1914, who designed the Colcord, Pioneer, and other well known early-day buildings.

WHITE, J. B. — Young Men's Christian Association executive director here for more than twenty-five years, beginning in 1925.

WHITE, James B. — Director of the Oklahoma City Urban Renewal Authority during the downtown redevelopment program of the late 1960s and the early 1970s.

WILEMAN, Ben C. — Builder and residential developer. Active during and following World War II.

WILKES, Doctor Jack — President of Oklahoma City University. Mayor of Oklahoma City 1963 and 1964. President of Centenary College.

WILLARD, Jess — Worked on construction of the dam for Lake Overholser, later defeated Jack Johnson to become world heavyweight boxing champion, until defeated by Jack Dempsey.

WILLIAMS, Carl — Editor of *Oklahoma Farmer Stockman*, named by President Hoover as an original member of the Federal Farm Board.

WILSON, Lyle C. — Former city newsman who rose to vice presidency of United Press International and chief of its Washington Bureau.

WILSON, W. G. "Jerry" — Founder, in 1946, and president of the W&W Steel Company.

WITTEMAN, Anna L. — Superintendent of the Home of Redeeming Love and a leading social worker of the 1930s.

WORKMAN, R. F. — Organizer and owner of one of the Southwest's leading post-World War II real estate firms.

WRIGHT, Muriel H. — Educator, author, Oklahoma historian and secretary and member of the Choctaw Advisory Council.

WYNN, Anne "Big Anne" — 200 pound "madam" of the red light district, who was a political power in city for the first twenty years following the Run.

YOUNG, L. W. — Oil developer and businessman.

YOUNG, Raymond A. — One of the founders, president and chairman of the TG&Y stores, one of the nation's largest variety store chains.

YOUNG, Stanton — Oil and business leader, best known for his civic leadership during the 1960s and 1970s.

ZAHN, Mrs. Fred — Civic worker, Young Women's Christian Association national board member and national "Mother of the Year."

Oklahoma City Mayors

Captain W. L. Couch, 1889.
Doctor A. J. Beale, 1889-90.
W. J. Gault, 1890-92.
O. A. Mitscher, 1892-94.
Nelson Button, 1894-96.
Charles G. Jones, 1896-97; 1901-03.
J. P. Allen, 1897-99.
Lee Van Winkle, 1899-1901; 1903-05.
Doctor J. F. Messenbaugh, 1905-07.
Henry M. Scales, 1907-10.
Daniel V. Lackey, 1910-11.
Whit M. Grant, 1911-15.
Edward Overholser, 1915-18.
Byron D. Shear, 1918-19.

Jack C. Walton, 1919-23.
Mike Donnelly, 1923.
O. A. Cargill, 1923-27.
Walter Dean, 1927-31.
C. J. Blinn, 1931-33.
Tom E. McGee, 1933-35.
J. Frank Martin, 1935-39.
Robert A. Hefner, 1939-47.
Allen Street, 1947-1959.
James H. Norick, 1959-63; 1967-71.
Jack S. Wilkes, 1963-64.
George H. Shirk, 1964-67.
Patience Latting, 1971-.

Presidents, Oklahoma City Chamber of Commerce

Henry Overholser, 1889-91
John H. Burford, 1890
W. J. Gault, 1892-93
O. A. Mitscher, 1892-94
W. W. Storm, 1896, 1897-99
B. M. Dilley, 1898
Anton H. Classen, 1900-01-02
S. C. Heyman, 1903
George G. Sohlberg, 1904
T. D. Turner, 1905
I. M. Holcomb, 1906
H. Y. Thompson, 1907
G. B. Stone, 1908
Sidney L. Brock, 1909-10
O. P. Workman, 1911
Frank J. Wikoff, 1912
S. M. Gloyd, 1913
Charles F. Colcord, 1914
E. K. Gaylord, 1915
E. S. Vaught, 1916-17
J. R. Cottingham, 1917-18
George Frederickson, 1918-19-20
A. W. Boyd, 1920-21
W. J. Pettee, 1921-22
Ed Overholser, 1922-30
John A. Brown, 1931

J. F. Owens, 1932-33-34
G. A. Nichols, 1935
R. J. Benzel, 1936
Virgil Browne, 1937-38
Frank Buttram, 1939
S. W. Hayes, 1940
W. E. Hightower, 1941-42
Fred Jones, 1943
Glenn C. Kiley, 1944-45
J. S. Hargett, 1946-47-48
J. Wiley Richardson, 1949-50
William M. Cain, 1951-52-53
Donald S. Kennedy, 1954
R. J. Spradling, 1955-56
H. B. Groh, 1957-58
Ancel Earp, 1959
Edward L. Gaylord, 1960
John Kilpatrick, Jr., 1961-62
William V. Montin, 1963-64
R. A. Young, 1965-66
Stanton L. Young, 1967-68-69
John R. Parsons, 1970-71
Robert E. Lee, 1972
Norman P. Bagwell, 1973
Edward Cook, 1974

Presidents, National Groups

MANY OKLAHOMA CITYANS HAVE BROUGHT recognition to their hometown through national leadership in business, civic, social, cultural and service organizations. No list is available of all Oklahoma City men and women who have served as presidents of national organizations. Listed below are those whose national leadership was uncovered during research for this book. It is admittedly only a partial list of such presidents.

ABERNATHY, Jack H. — American Association of Oil Well Drilling Contractors.

BASS, B. B. — Mortgage Bankers' Association of America in 1959.

BELFORD, Kenny — 1973, National Association of State Radio Networks.

BLACKSTOCK, Ben — Newspaper Association Managers of North America.

BLUE, Doctor Johnny A. — American Association for Clinical Immunology and Allergy.

BOWMAN, Calvin — National Roofing Contractors Association.

BRANIFF, Thomas E. — National Association of Casualty and Surety Agents.

BRIGGS, Doctor Eugene — Lions International.

BUTTRAM, Frank — Independent Petroleum Association of America.

CONN, Jack T. — American Bankers Association.

COX, Mrs. James Monroe, Midwest City (Marie) — National Association of Indian Women's Organizations.

CROMLEY, Allan W. — National Press Club.

CUNNINGHAM, Morrison B. — American Water Works Association.

CURREATHERS, J. B. — National Retailers Association in 1929.

DONAHUE, Doctor Hayden — Association of Medical Superintendents of Mental Hospitals.

DRAPER, Stanley — American Chamber of Commerce Executives.

DURLAND, Jack — (Chairman) National Coffee Association.

FELLERS, James D. — American Bar Association.

FIELDS, Gus — National Association of Home Builders Executive Officers.

FRANKLIN, Wirt — First thirteen years, Independent Petroleum Association of America.

FROHLICH, Doctor Edward — American Society for Clinical Pharmacology and Therapeutics.

GOLDMAN, S. N. — 1951-2, Super Market Institute. (United States, Canada and Mexico.)

GUM, Eugene P. — State Secretaries of the American Bankers Association.

HILL, Everett Wentworth — Rotary International, 1924.

HARRISON, Walter M. — American Society of Newspaper Editors, 1928.

HATFIELD, H. G. — Kiwanis International.

HAYDEN, O. L. — Order of the Elks in 1928.

HILL, Everett Wentworth — Rotary International, 1924.

HODGE, Doctor Oliver — Council of Chief State School officers.

HOFFMAN, Roy — Two terms, Reserve Officers Association of America.

HOWARD, Doctor Robert Mayburn — American Goiter Association, 1932.

JOULLIAN, Edward C., III — National Natural Gas Processors Association.

KENNEDY, Donald S. — Edison Electric Institute, and the Association of Electric Illuminating Companies.

KEY, W. S. — Wardens' Association of Penal Institutions of the United States.

LACY, Dan — Consumer Bankers Association.

LANDERS, J. B. — Secretaries' Conference, National Association of Builders' Exchange.

LUCADE, T. J. — Co-operative International, 1931.

McALPINE, G. R. — International Association of Fire Chiefs.

McCLAIN, Lawrence — Recreational Dealers of America.

McMULLEN, A. D. — National Retail Credit Association in 1930.

McNICKLE, Major General Melvin F. — Inter-Agency Board of U.S. Civil Service Examiners.

McWILLIAMS, W. J. — Petroleum Equipment Suppliers Association.

MOORE, Preston J. — American Legion.

MURPHY, R. R. "Pat" — American Association of Park Executives.

O'DONOGHUE, Doctor Don — (Founding) American Orthopaedic Society for Sports Medicine.

OSWALT, L. M. — National Lubricating Grease Institute.

OVERMAN, Lyle — American Motor Hotel Association.
OWENS, J. F. — National Electric Light Association, 1931.
PAYNE, William T. — American Association of Oilwell Drilling Contractors.
PORTER, Frank M. — American Petroleum Institute.
RANEY, C. W. "Chuck" — International Welding Supply Association.
ROACH, Tom — National Association of Retail Druggists in 1930.
REED, G. C. — National Oil Mill Superintendents Association in 1930.
REEVES, Ray L. — Master Photo Dealers' and Finishers' Association.
SEWELL, Ralph L. — Sigma Delta Chi, professional journalists fraternity.
SINGER, Harold R. — International Christian Endeavor Field Secretaries Union.
SMITH, Doctor Roger C. — American Association of State Psychology Boards.
SNEED, R. A. — (Commander in chief) United Confederate Veterans.
SQUYRES, Scott — (Comander in chief) Veterans of Foreign Wars.
SWAN, Frank — Bank Marketing Association.
SWAN, Leslie H. — Shrine Recorders' Association of North America.
THOMAS, Tom A. — (Chairman) Precast Systems Clearing House.
TJADEN, Montez — American Women in Radio and Television.
VAUGHT, Edgar S. — Lions International.
WHEAT, Willis J. — National Council for Small Business Management Development.
WHITE, Kenneth R. — National Cemetery Association.
ZAHASKY, Mrs. Mary — American Dietetic Association.

Bibliography

ACKERMAN, Ray — *Tomorrow Belongs to Oklahoma!* Semco Press, Oklahoma City, 1964.
ALEXANDER, Darrel — *History of the Mummer's Theater — 1949-1972.* A doctoral dissertation.
BEALS, Irene Bracht — Necrology, *Chronicles of Oklahoma*, Oklahoma Historical Society, Summer 1972.
BOTTOMS, Byrd Walker — Editor, *Oklahoma, the Beautiful Land* by '89ers, Times-Journal Publishing Company, Oklahoma City, 1943.
BRANDES, Kay K. — *A History of The Theater in Oklahoma City, 1889-1964.* A master's thesis.
BROWN, Andrew Theodore — *Frontier Community: Kansas City to 1870*, Columbia University Press, 1963.
BRYANT, Keith L., Jr. — *Alfalfa Bill Murray*, University of Oklahoma Press, Norman, 1968.
CARGILL, O. A. — *My First Eighty Years*, Banner Book Company, Oklahoma City, 1965.
CHAPMAN, Berlin B. — *Oklahoma City From Public Land to Private Property*, Chronicles of Oklahoma reprint, 1960.
COLCORD, Charles Francis — Autobiography edited by D. K. Higginbotham, privately printed through Oklahoma Historical Society, 1970.
COUCH, Edna M. — Norman, letters to author; tape, Living Legends Library, Oklahoma Christian College, Oklahoma City.
CROY, Homer — *Trigger Marshal: The Story of Chris Madsen*, Duell, Sloan and Pearce, New York, 1958.
CUNNINGHAM, Robert — *Indian Territory*, University of Oklahoma Press, 1957; *Stillwater, Where Oklahoma Began*, Arts and Humanities Council, Stillwater, 1969.
DAVIS, Richard Harding — *The West From a Car Window*, Harper & Brothers, New York, 1892.
EASTMAN, James N., Jr. — *Founding of Tinker Air Force Base*, Chronicles of Oklahoma, autumn 1972.
EVERETT, Mark R. — *Medical Education in Oklahoma*, University of Oklahoma Press, 1972.
FOREMAN, Grant — *A History of Oklahoma*, University of Oklahoma Press, 1942.
GARD, Wayne — *The Chisholm Trail*, University of Oklahoma Press, 1942.
GIBSON, Arrell M. — *A History of Five Centuries*, Harlow, Norman, 1965.
GITTINGER, Roy M. — *Formation of the State of Oklahoma*, University of California Press, Berkeley, 1919.
GOODALL, Leonard E. — *Urban Politics in the Southwest*, Arizona State University, Tempe, 1967. (With Others, paper)
HARRISON, Walter M. — *Out of My Wastebasket*, privately printed 1949.
HURST, Irvin — *The 46th Star*, Semco Press, Oklahoma City, 1957.
KERR, W. F. and GAINER, Ina — *The Story of Oklahoma City*, S. J. Clarke Publishing Company, Chicago, 1922.
LAMAR, Howard R. — *Western Historical Quarterly*, Western History Association, Palo Alto, January 1973.
McREYNOLDS, Edwin C. — *Oklahoma: A History of the Sooner State*, University of Oklahoma Press, 1954.
McRILL, Albert — *And Satan Came Also*, Semco Press, Oklahoma City, 1955.
MORRIS, Lerona Rosamond — *Oklahoma, Yesterday, Tomorrow*, Cooperative Publishing Company, Guthrie, 1930.
NASHERT, Walter — *From Teepees to Towers*, Associated General Contractors, Chicago, 1969.
NELSON, Guy — *Thunderbird: A History of the 45th Infantry Division*, Colorgraphics, Oklahoma City, 1970.
NELSON, Mary Jo — *History in Mortar*, reprint, Oklahoma City Times, July-August, 1972.
RUTH, Kent — *Great Day in the West*, University of Oklahoma Press, 1963.
SAXE, Allan — *Protest and Reform: The Desegregation of Oklahoma City*, doctoral dissertation, University of Oklahoma Library, Norman, 1969.

SCOTT, Angelo — *The Story of Oklahoma City*, Times-Journal Publishing Co., 1938.

SHIRK, George — *Oklahoma Place Names*, University of Oklahoma Press, 1965.

SHIRLEY, Glenn — *Heck Thomas: Frontier Marshal*, Chilton Company, New York, 1962.

STETLER, Gilbert — *The City and Western Expansion: A Western Case Study*, Western Historical Quarterly, April 1973.

STEWART, Ronald Laird — *Influence of the Business Community in Oklahoma City Politics*, Master's thesis, Oklahoma State University, Stillwater, mimeo, 1963.

STEWART, Roy P. — *Oklahoma: A Guide to the Sooner State*, (with others) University of Oklahoma Press 1957: *Country Boy Hornbook*, Colorgraphics, 1968; Selected columns and features, The Daily Oklahoman, 1932-70; Associated Press Yearbook, Oklahoma Section, 1966.

THOBURN, Joseph B. and HOLCOMB, Isaac M. — *A History of Oklahoma*, Doub and Company, San Francisco, 1908.

THOMPSON, Horace — *Municipal Government in Oklahoma City*, mimeo, 1959.

WOODS, Pendleton and BOGGS, Frank — *Myriad of Sports — Profile of Oklahoma City*, Times-Journal Publishing Co., 1971.

INDEX

(This index does not include any of the alphabetical
listings of names following the main text)

344